HOW RABBIS BECAME EXPERTS

How Rabbis Became Experts

SOCIAL CIRCLES AND DONOR NETWORKS IN JEWISH LATE ANTIQUITY

KRISTA N. DALTON

PRINCETON UNIVERSITY PRESS
PRINCETON & OXFORD

Published by Princeton University Press
41 William Street, Princeton, New Jersey 08540
99 Banbury Road, Oxford OX2 6JX

press.princeton.edu

Library of Congress Cataloging-in-Publication Data

Names: Dalton, Krista N., 1989– author.
Title: How rabbis became experts : social circles and donor networks in Jewish late antiquity / Krista N. Dalton.
Description: First edition. | Princeton, New Jersey : Princeton University Press, [2025] | Includes bibliographical references and index.
Identifiers: LCCN 2024040481 (print) | LCCN 2024040482 (ebook) | ISBN 9780691266763 (hardback) | ISBN 9780691266817 (ebook)
Subjects: LCSH: Rabbis—Palestine—Office. | Judaism—History—Talmudic period, 10–425. | BISAC: SOCIAL SCIENCE / Jewish Studies | RELIGION / History
Classification: LCC BM652 .D35 2025 (print) | LCC BM652 (ebook) | DDC 296.09/015—dc23/eng/20240904
LC record available at https://lccn.loc.gov/2024040481
LC ebook record available at https://lccn.loc.gov/2024040482

British Library Cataloging-in-Publication Data is available

Editorial: Fred Appel and James Collier
Production Editorial: Natalie Baan
Jacket Design: Drohan DiSanto
Production: Danielle Amatucci
Publicity: William Pagdatoon
Copyeditor: Rachel F. Van Hart

Jacket Credit: Basket of figs, fresco, 1st century CE. Oplontis. Campania, Italy. © Thaliastock / Mary Evans

This book has been composed in Arno

Printed in the United States of America

10 9 8 7 6 5 4 3 2 1

CONTENTS

ACKNOWLEDGMENTS

THIS PROJECT began with a curiosity about the feelings and relationships formed through gifts. That curiosity has carried me through various iterations of this idea through the years. It is now fitting that I memorialize on the page those whose own gifts of time and friendship made this book possible.

I was fortunate to begin this project at Columbia University where I benefitted from a community of scholars who modeled not just thorough scholarship but generosity of spirit and genuine kindness. Beth Berkowitz offered the greatest gift of the unwavering encouragement of a red pen. She guided me through my doctoral studies and taught me to pursue precision. I am eternally grateful for her boundless enthusiasm and detailed feedback. From Elizabeth Castelli I learned that words matter. She offered a model of how to teach and engage the profession that has shaped my own professional trajectory. Seth Schwartz instilled within me a strong internal voice that informs how I read rabbinic literature. I also had the privilege of studying across the street at the Jewish Theological Seminary (JTS), where I received foundational training from Eliezer Diamond, Richard Kalmin, Marjorie Lehman, and Jonathan Milgrim. Kalmin was instrumental in bringing me to JTS in the first place, which was a transformational place for me as a human and scholar, and for that I owe him an immense debt. It was there that I met Alyssa Gray, who served as an inspiring scholar and mentor, always ready to discuss charity and rabbis. Sarit Kattan Gribetz offered detailed feedback on my dissertation, guidance through the profession, and an invaluable friendship that has made all the difference. I must also thank the estimable Julia Watts Belser for introducing me to the field of rabbinics in the first place, paving the path that made this project possible.

Kenyon College has been a rewarding place to launch my career. I am thankful for the travel support and research grants that Kenyon generously provided me. I thank my colleagues in the Religious Studies department for their support of me and my tenure. I especially thank my colleague

David Maldonado Rivera, who shares my love of all things premodern and is a constant conversation partner. He is generous with his time and humor, and I count myself lucky to share the "late antiquity power corner" with him. I also thank my colleagues Ruth Heindel, Bob Milnikel, and Austin Porter for offering support while I worked on this project. My undergraduate students have offered insightful perspectives and an enthusiasm for learning that makes the work rewarding. I especially thank my advisee Ellie Greenberg for her research assistance with final manuscript preparations. My neighboring Denison University colleague Rebecca Futo Kennedy has been a constant support as we navigate the ups and downs of the Ohio 5.

I also benefitted from presenting my work at conferences of the Association of Jewish Studies, Society of Biblical Literature, Shifting Frontiers, Enoch Seminar, and the Philadelphia Seminar on Christian Origins (PSCO). These venues introduced me to a community of scholars who have provided invaluable professional and research guidance. I owe an immense debt to Gregg Gardner who has been an extraordinary mentor, offering detailed feedback at every stage of my career, inviting me to panels, and modeling a generosity of spirit that I hope to emulate. I would also like to acknowledge Mika Ahuvia, Noah Bickart, Sarah Bond, Erez DeGolan, Natalie Dohrmann, Amit Gvaryahu, Jae Hee Han, Jenny Labendz, Yitz Landes, Hayim Lapin, Lennart Lehmhaus, John Mandsager, Avigail Manekin-Bamberger, Eva Mroczek, Rafael Rachel Neis, Annette Yoshiko Reed, Adele Reinhartz, Michael Rosenberg, Jordan Rosenblum, Shayna Sheinfeld, Michal Bar-Asher Siegal, Moulie Vidas, Miriam-Simma Walfish, Yael Wilfand, Rebecca Wollenberg, and Shlomo Zuckier. From facilitating presentations, responding to my work, sharing panels together, and providing beneficial conversation in the conference halls, I am grateful to have learned from you.

The editorial team at Princeton University Press is extraordinary. Fred Appel has offered unmatched support and enthusiasm, braving tight schedules and literal downpours to steward my writing. I could not have asked for a better editor. Thank you to James Collier and Natalie Baan for their work seeing this book to press, and thank you to Drohan DiSanto, Danielle Amatucci, and William Pagdatoon for their work making the physical book and its circulation possible. I also appreciate the time and thoroughness of the press reviewers whose insightful comments made for a stronger manuscript. What joy it is to receive feedback from such careful readers. This book also owes thanks to my copyeditor, Rachel Van Hart, who did the tedious work of making the production of this book possible with boundless energy.

I have much gratitude for the financial support this project received from Faculty Research Grants at Kenyon College that enabled me to hire a developmental editor, Kali Handelman, as a partner in the writing process. Kali read every early draft and remained a constant conversation companion throughout the toils of writing. I am also the grateful recipient of the Jordan Schnitzer First Book Publication Award, administered by the Association for Jewish Studies, that enabled me to pay for the associated costs of book production.

Parts of this book are based on articles and chapters that I have published elsewhere. I want to thank the *AJS Review*, the *Journal for the Study of Judaism*, and Fortress Press for allowing me to publish reworked portions of the following publications: "Teaching for the Tithe: Donor Expectations and the Matrona's Tithe," *AJS Review* 44, no. 1 (2020): 49–73; "Rabbis as Recipients of Charity and the Logic of Grammarian Piety," *Journal for the Study of Judaism* 53, no. 1 (2021): 94–130; "Torah, Gender, and Rabbinic Expertise," in *Constructions of Gender in Religious Traditions of Late Antiquity*, edited by Shayna Sheinfeld, Juni Hoppe, and Kathy Ehrensperger, Fortress Press, 2024.

There are a community of people that I continually rely upon for feedback, friendship, and fulfilling group chats that have sustained me throughout the publication process. Simcha Gross has been a faithful reader of my writing for over a decade. I am grateful for his candor and companionship. We have collaborated closely on several projects over the years, and I could ask for no better partner with whom to share the vision of expanding ancient Jewish studies. Daniel Picus not only reads my writing, but he feeds me with baked goods. I am grateful for his boundless enthusiasm for rabbis, gardening, and good recipes. Erin Galgay Walsh, my coeditor at *Ancient Jew Review*, is the most faithful of friends. I aspire to match her measure of kindness and wit. This project was also shaped by the global COVID-19 pandemic. In the early days of masks and anxiety, a group of scholars met on Zoom to read poetry to each other. That group included Rebecca Falcasantos, Greg Given, Andrew Jacobs, John Penniman, Sarah Porter, and Carrie Schroeder (among others already acknowledged here), and they have remained a lifeline throughout the writing process.

I am happy to have made a home for myself in Ohio. I want to thank the Dolphin moms, as well as Rabbis Benjy Bar-Lev, Lenette Goldman, and Alex Braver, for the encouragement that I needed to finish this project.

Acknowledgments typically end in thanks to one's family and with good reason. No one writes in a vacuum, and my family played a huge role in seeing this project to the end. Justin, you have borne the brunt of family life in times when I needed to meet a deadline (which were many). You are the one person who has supported me for the entire duration of my career, from undergraduate major, hopeful graduate student, to tenured professor. I cannot measure all the ways this project was supported by you. Ellis, my dissertation baby, you have grown with this project, and Mirah, my pandemic baby, you snuggled in my arms while I balanced a computer on my lap, typing away at various chapters. While my journey with this project has ended, yours is just beginning. I am grateful for the gift of your lives in mine.

HOW RABBIS BECAME EXPERTS

INTRODUCTION

The Construction of Expertise in Tales of Rabbis and Donors

THIS BOOK tells the story of how rabbinic Torah scholars became religious experts within the Jewish communities of Roman Palestine from the second through fifth centuries CE.[1] This period saw the organization of a small group of literate Jewish men who devoted their lives to the interpretation and teaching of their sacred ancestral texts. They devised their own methods of reading attuned to vocabulary and grammar and created chains of interpretation spanning generations now canonized in rabbinic literature.[2] Students attached themselves to the orbits of these charismatic teachers and sought to emulate their speech and behaviors.[3] Yet this mastery of words and habit did not make

1. The word Torah (lit. "law" or "instruction") has two interrelated meanings. First, it refers to the first five books of the Bible (the Pentateuch) that were known to ancient Jews as a collection called *Torat Moshe*, the Law of Moses. Second, the rabbis used the concept of Torah expansively to refer both to the entire canonical Hebrew Bible (the written Torah) and to their growing body of teachings (the oral Torah). In this sense, the rabbis thought of Torah as a broad universe of interpretive possibility. I use the word "Torah" typically to refer to the broad rabbinic sense of the word and will specify *Torah Moshe* when describing the first five books of the canonical Bible.

2. For an overview of the organization of rabbis in antiquity, see Hezser, *Social Structure of the Rabbinic Movement*; S. Schwartz, *Ancient Jews from Alexander to Muhammad*, Miller, *Sages and Commoners in Late Antique 'Ereẓ Israel*; and Lapin, *Rabbis as Romans*. For an overview of distinctive rabbinic methods of textual interpretation, see Porton, *Understanding Rabbinic Midrash*; Jaffee, *Torah in the Mouth*; Rosen-Zvi, *Between Mishnah and Midrash*.

3. Rubenstein, "Social and Institutional Settings," 59; Sivertsev, *Households, Sects and the Origins of Rabbinic Judaism*, 9–12; P. Alexander, "The Rabbis and Their Rivals," 57–62; and Hezser, "Rabbis and the Image of the Intellectual" on early rabbinic disciple circles where students were mentored in close proximity to their rabbi. See Hezser, *Social Structure of the Rabbinic Movement*, 332–52, for a survey of the relationship between named rabbis and their students.

these men automatic experts. Expertise is a social phenomenon, something people do in relational contexts rather than something people possess. Rabbinic expertise was thereby shaped by interactions in the streets. Rabbis socialized and noshed with neighbors. Friends of rabbis called upon them for advice or legal favors. In exchange for their expert judgments and instruction, rabbis received social invitations, donations, communal appointments, and recognition of value. I argue that it was these everyday interactions of mutual exchange just as much as their time in the study house that cultivated rabbinic expertise.

This periodization is not to suggest that this was the first flourishing of Torah study. Schools and scholars had populated not only Judaea but also Egypt, Asia Minor, and other diasporic places that Jews called home.[4] We could speak of authors, such as Philo or Ben Sira, or the communities of Qumran and Alexandria, whose texts survive and attest to ongoing care. Ancient Jewish sages were animated by the stories, language, and intertextual potential of the Hebrew Bible.[5] The men we call "rabbis," a term initially used interchangeably with "sages" (חכמים) to denote teachers deeply entrenched in a preexisting world of textual knowledge, would eventually signify a new form of expertise entirely.[6] Roman annexation of Judaea in 63 BCE followed by the long aftermath of the destruction of Jerusalem and its Temple in 70 CE changed the stakes of Jewish study. Jewish intelligentsia, who had comprised the leadership of Judaea, were forced to flee to the north, making new homes in Galilean cities such as Tiberias, Sepphoris, and Lydda.[7] With the Temple reduced to rubble, many fundamental aspects of Torah that relied on a central Temple complex were no longer operative.[8] The basic set of assumptions that grounded Torah knowledge transformed

---

Other scholars describe the centrality of disciple circles as a primary form of rabbinic education: see Lieberman, *Hellenism in Jewish Palestine*, 83–99; Jaffee, *Torah in the Mouth*, 65–83 and 126–52; and Tropper, *Wisdom, Politics, and Historiography*. On the institution of the study house or *beit midrash*, see Lapin, "Jewish and Christian Academies"; Mandel, "Concerning the Public Role of the Early Beit Midrash"; Marks, "Who Studied at the Beit Midrash?"

4. For examples of Torah engagement in the diaspora, see Niehoff, *Jewish Exegesis*; Rajak, *Translation and Survival*; Shemesh, *Halakhah in the Making*; Gruen, *Diaspora*.

5. Kugel, "Thinking About Scripture."

6. See Hezser's argument in *Social Structure of the Rabbinic Movement*, which posits that the title "rabbi" was used unofficially before and after 70 CE, only later to become the primary title of those associated with the rabbinic movement.

7. Rozenfeld, *Torah Centers and Rabbinic Activity*, 115–202.

8. For scholarship engaging the ways rabbis engaged with defunct Torah laws and Temple institutions, see Cohn, *Memory of the Temple*; Shemesh, *Halakhah in the Making*; Balberg, *Purity, Body, and Self in Early Rabbinic Literature*; and Balberg, *Fractured Tablets*.

under these overwhelming constraints.[9] Consequently, new questions emerged surrounding ritual practice and observance. A distinct domain of knowledge developed that expanded the sense of Torah to encompass new rabbinic teaching as a result of these questions.

Rabbinic men rose to prominence in a period when Torah expertise stood at a critical juncture. The Torah's vision of Jewish piety rested upon the notion that if Jews would be faithful to its precepts, God would bless the land and make them prosper in return.[10] This promise of divine favor was brutally upended when the Romans wrested Jewish autonomy from the region. This loss of autonomy was not just a theological problem but one that brought tangible institutional destabilization. Human representatives of this promise (i.e., priests) were unmoored from their institutional base. Unlike other peoples across the ancient Mediterranean, the Jews had only one national priesthood on which to rely.[11] The loss of both Temple and palace meant the loss of the political, economic, and social jurisdiction that went with them. Priests could no longer offer a surety of how things were supposed to work. Resentment and suspicion surely arose among some Jews.[12] As the author of 2 Baruch wrote with the Temple's loss heavy on the mind,

> Moreover, you priests, take you the keys of the sanctuary,
> And cast them into the height of heaven,

9. With the dismantling of the Temple precinct, the boundaries of what Torah knowledge was and could be necessarily shifted. I do not contend that the rabbis represented a fundamentally different form of ancient Jewish biblical interpretation or were the first to claim Torah expertise, but I do suggest that the foundation for their study was distinctive. The what of their interpretation may not have changed, but the why and how were impacted by a sequence of events related to Roman imperialism. Here I rely on Berthelot's thinking about the term "impact" in *Jews and Their Roman Rivals*, 25–26.

10. See Deut. 28 and Lev. 26 for the covenantal promise of reward for obedience, as well as the general affirmation of the covenant statutes in Exod. 15:26, 18:20; Lev. 18:4–5, 18:26, 20:8, 20:22, 26:3, and 26:15; Deut. 4:1, 4:5–6, 6:17–24, 8:11, 11:13, 11:22, 11:32, and 26:16.

11. Himmelfarb, *Between Temple and Torah*, 105. See Gross, "Hopeful Rebels and Anxious Romans," for the argument that Jewish interconnectivity was "centered on the temple in Jerusalem" (489).

12. The theme of criticizing priests during periods of imperial conquest is well documented throughout the Bible's prophetic literature. According to Tiemeyer, the prophets viewed the Babylonian destruction of Jerusalem in 586 BCE not solely as a consequence of the populace's sin but also as a result of the priests' neglect of their sacred responsibilities as custodians of Israel's cult (*Priestly Rites and Prophetic Rage*, especially 207–17). I make the assumption that a similar dynamic between some Jews and their priests occurred following Roman conquest.

And give them to the LORD and say:
"Guard Your house Yourself,
For lo! we are found false stewards." (2 Bar. 10:18)[13]

The priestly experts who guarded the house of the Jewish God are depicted here in the posture of confession. They admit to their obvious failure for which this author condemns them. Whether it is fair to castigate the priesthood for the devastation wrought by the hands of the Romans or not, in this author's mind, the captain goes down with the ship.

One of the traditional assumptions that has largely been called into question is the idea that the rabbis simply took up the Jewish leadership mantle vacated by the priesthood.[14] This was surely not the case. For one, the institution of priestly authority rested upon centuries of habit across the ancient Mediterranean and was constitutionally affirmed for Jews in the Torah.[15] The status of priests was further bolstered by their hereditary claim to their position as ritual specialists. They belonged to a tribe designated as intermediaries between the Jewish God and people, performing the routine offerings and sacrifices that ensured the maintenance of their covenant relationship.[16] Even if Jews outside Jerusalem did not regularly frequent the Temple, tithes and other gifts were sent from afar to support their work.[17] Elite priestly families had

---

Though certainly not every Jew would have felt the same feeling about the Temple's destruction, the destruction of the Second Temple came at a much later point in the development of Torah both as an idea and collection of scrolls. It is reasonable to think that a dissonance would emerge with the Temple's absence. I speak in broad terms here to capture the fundamental ideological tensions that could shift how traditional experts were perceived.

13. Translation from Becker, "2 Baruch," 1574.

14. See Büchler, *Political and Social Leaders*, 69–71; Alon, *Jews in Their Land*, 27, 100–103; Urbach, "Talmudic Sage" and *The Sages, Their Concepts, and Beliefs*; Graetz, *Geschichte der Juden*, 1–8; Dinur, *Yisra'el ba-Golah*, 5–7; Jaffee, *Torah in the Mouth*, 66. Goodblatt, *Monarchic Principle*, 232–76 assumes the persistence of the Sanhedrin. For examples of recent interventions to complicate the transition from priests to rabbis, see Schäfer, "Rabbis and Priests," 155–72; P. Alexander, "The Rabbis and Their Rivals"; Z. Weiss, "Were Priests Communal Leaders in Late Antique Palestine?," 91–111; Hidary, "Rhetoric of Rabbinic Authority." However, even in these more recent publications, there is a latent assumption that the rabbis are the obvious successors, albeit if not as seamless in their transition.

15. Lev. 8–10. See S. Schwartz, *Imperialism and Jewish Society*, 2 and 63–64 for the significance of the Torah as a national law code.

16. Exod. 32:26–29; Num. 3; Deut. 18.

17. Exod. 30:11–16; Neh. 10:32–34. Cf. Philo, *Her.*; 186, *Spec. Leg.* 77–78, 291, 312; Josephus, *Ant.* 14.110–113; Cicero, *Pro Flac.* 67. In addition to the expected annual tithe, Josephus describes gifts sent from the diaspora: Josephus, *B.J.* 4.567, 5.5, 5.201–205; *Ant.* 18.82, 20.51–53.

long comprised the political leadership of Judaea, pacifying imperial rulers so as to facilitate the continuation of the Temple cult.[18] To suggest that rabbis just took up the role of ritual and legal experts because they asserted expertise in Torah is not a simple claim.

In fact, evidence suggests that for some time, few Jews were compelled to arrange their lives according to rabbinic guidance. Rabbinic texts express repeated discontent with persons they describe as *amei haaretz*, or ordinary Jews who did not heed their advice.[19] In one early source, rabbis are advised to avoid the assemblies of such ignorant men.[20] Other sources indicate friction between rabbis and non-rabbinic Jews, with accounts of some sages being robbed,[21] mistreated,[22] or ridiculed.[23] Archaeological evidence in addition to critical reading of rabbinic sources reveals that rabbis did not run synagogues, nor did they hold automatic standing as teachers or judges in their local communities.[24] Once thought to be universal, rabbinic influence in this period is now understood to be primarily aspirational.[25]

New sources of expertise also competed for the attention of Jews within the province. Roman imperial expansion established new forms of local administration, introduced a distinct and imposing legal environment, expanded points of cultural interaction, and shaped the very roads that marked the countryside. Already under the client-king Herod (37–4 BCE), Judaea had physically transformed with a newly constructed harbor, palaces, and temples dedicated to the Roman emperor Caesar Augustus.[26] Herod even

18. For a survey see Schäfer, *The History of the Jews in Antiquity*, 13–64.

19. The most comprehensive book on the subject to date is Oppenheimer's *The 'Am Ha-Aretz*, which argued that the *am haaretz* represented two categories of people: those who neglected their tithes and purity status and those who were largely ignorant of Torah. Furstenberg by contrast argues convincingly that there was no literal group at all but rather the term functioned as a discursive legal category marking the non-rabbinic Jew in rabbinic thought ("Am Ha-Aretz in Tannaitic Literature").

20. M. Avot 3:10.

21. Y. Terumot 8:10, 46b.

22. Y. Ta'anit 3:4, 66c.

23. Y. Berakhot 2, 5c.

24. Levine, *Ancient Synagogue*, 174–209. Alon, "Those Appointed for Money." Even as Alon assumed rabbinic supremacy, he identified the open competition between rabbis and upper-class non-rabbinic elites.

25. S. Schwartz, *Imperialism and Jewish Society* is largely credited with advancing this position.

26. Mazor, "Imperial Cult in the Decapolis," 355.

went as far as to call for the celebration of festivals and games honoring his political patron.[27] Following the Temple's destruction, the province continued to populate temples and altars devoted to the imperial cult, bearing with them the notion that the peace and happiness of the empire depended upon divine benevolence through the hand of the emperor.[28]

This period also saw the circulation of ritual specialists who did not derive their authority from priesthoods or kings.[29] Instead, they trafficked in promises and charisma. Some hawked amulets and incantations, others were miracle workers whose abilities extended to bringing life-sustaining rain and bodily healing.[30] The presence of self-authorized ritual specialists, or "freelance experts" as Heidi Wendt has termed them, rose in prominence during the first centuries of the common era.[31] The nascent community of Christ followers who moved in such circles, and would later come to dominate the Roman imperial scene, added an additional voice to the din.

This was a time period when claims of expertise were heterogeneous and uncertain, the competition between experts intense, and the mechanisms of gatekeeping and adjudicating competing claims were weak.[32] Nowhere is this dynamic more illuminated than in the Babatha archive. Found in a Judean desert cave in Wadi Hever in 1961, these thirty-five legal documents—largely

27. These acts allegedly prompted a group led by sages named Judas son of Hezekiah and Matthias son of Margalothus to remove a golden eagle that Herod had mounted above the entrance to the Temple's inner sanctum, for which Herod later had them executed. Josephus, *B.J.* 1.648–55.

28. Rüpke, *From Jupiter to Christ*, 8.

29. Wendt, *At the Temple Gates*; Frankfurter, "The Great, the Little"; Stowers, "Religion of Plant and Animal Offerings."

30. Frankfurter, "Dynamics of Ritual Expertise," 159. Much work has been done analyzing the role of amulet and incantation bowl makers, magicians, and rainmakers, other ritual specialists in late antiquity, which has been conveniently collected in the volumes *Magic and Ritual in the Ancient World* (Brill, 2002) and *Guide to the Study of Ancient Magic* (Brill, 2019). See the recent work of Manekin-Bamberger about the legal specialization of incantation bowl makers (*Seder Mezikin*). Rabbinic texts refer to some rabbis with mystical power or who operated as rain makers, but these sources also position rabbis in competition with these other ritual specialists. On bringing rain, see M. Ta'anit 3:8; Y. Ta'anit 3:4, 66c; Lev. Rab. 10:4. On competition, see Levinson, "Enchanting Rabbis"; Y. Sanhedrin 7:19, 25d; and Y. Hagigah 2:2, 77d.

31. Wendt, *At the Temple Gates*, 6.

32. I draw from Eyal's *The Crisis of Expertise*, which contends that there are cycles when the public can no longer identify who their primary experts are or what universally shared values expert judgments should depend upon.

bills of sale and marriage contracts—provide a window into the life of an ordinary Judean woman and her family in the first century CE.[33] While the owners of these documents used Aramaic scribes and, in some places, used similar clauses both prescribed and proscribed in rabbinic law, in other contracts they swore "by the genius (*tyche*) of the Lord Caesar" and employed Greek scribes.[34] No mention of a Jewish court appears, but the authors registered their contracts with local Roman officials. Babatha's *ketubah*, or marriage contract, was written in Aramaic and contained the promise that she would be a wife "according to the law of Moses and the Jews."[35] In her stepdaughter's marriage contract, by contrast, the groom promised to feed and clothe her "in accordance with Greek custom."[36] Examining the ways these documents do and do not align with rabbinic law offers a window into the fluidity of legal habits and choices available to Jews in antiquity. These documents represent, in the words of Hannah Cotton, "the raw material of which life is made on which the rabbis wished to put their own stamp."[37] There were a range of ritual and legal experts available to Jews, of which rabbis were but one.

For all these reasons the rabbis did not easily or immediately achieve widespread recognition as Jewish ritual and legal experts. Yet, despite the overwhelming evidence to the contrary, there remains a persistent perception that the rabbis were the natural experts to fill an institutional gap left by Roman conquest.[38] Their skill in Hebrew at a time when most Jews spoke Greek, their extensive knowledge of the textual contents of the Hebrew Bible, and their commitment to Jewish piety renders them obvious candidates. Their qualifications are further reinforced by the hindsight of readers who know that rabbinic Judaism would become the normative frame for many Jews into the modern era. Even if scholars recognize that ordinary Jews likely did not orient

33. On the significance of the Babatha archive, see Yadin, "Legal Interactions in the Archive of Babatha"; Esler, *Babatha's Orchard*; Czajkowski, *Localized Law*; Greenfield and Cotton, "Babatha's Property and the Law of Succession"; Ilan, "Witnesses in the Judaean Desert Documents." This point is repeated in Dalton, "Testimony of Ancient Books," 55 to complicate the simplistic binary between lived and textual religion.

34. P. Yadin 24; cf. P. Yadin 11 and 16.

35. P. Yadin 10.

36. P. Yadin 18.

37. Cotton, "Rabbis and the Documents," 190.

38. Urbach, for example, reasoned that the early rabbis derived authority from "their intellectual standing" ("Talmudic Sage," 119). This line of reasoning assumes that intellectual learning and knowledge assure one standing as an expert.

their lives as the rabbis would have wished, what has shifted is only the assumption that these ordinary Jews simply did not listen to their natural experts.[39]

Recent insights in expertise studies emphasizes that one does not become an expert through the acquisition of specialized knowledge alone. Such an understanding construes expertise as a primarily cognitive endeavor, taking for granted that acquisition of knowledge equates to an objective state of competence that merits respect.[40] Expertise in this view is considered a possession of individuals who have trained and acquired mastery at a high degree. Because rabbis possessed knowledge of Torah and skills in its interpretation, their expertise is assumed as a fact.

Instead, social theorists claim that this portrait of expertise neglects the ways expertise is a relational phenomenon.[41] Expertise is a dynamic produced through interaction between would-be-experts representing what they know and others perceiving, accepting, and/or rejecting their judgments. This is not to say that possession of "real" knowledge is not an important part of the equation, but it is only one piece of the puzzle.[42] Relationships of trust form when non-experts, or those without claim or access to a domain of knowledge, choose to believe in the reliability, value, and skill of those deemed expert with said domain, which requires effective persuasion and verified performance on the part of the expert that influences broader social perception of their value.[43] This dynamic thereby influences how would-be-experts convey specialist knowledge and uphold their credibility. Expertise is therefore not tied to a cognitive understanding of possessing "truth," but to the wide array of relationships that authorize and reinforce the function of expertise.[44]

It is with this in mind that I bring new scrutiny to the expertise of rabbis in late antiquity. The rabbis of Roman Palestine were not de facto experts within

39. See, for example, Morton Smith's critique of Goodenough's argument for the self-conscious marginality of the rabbis in light of ancient Jewish iconography, by contending that ordinary Jews were largely apathetic or ignorant of rabbinic teaching ("Goodenough's Jewish Symbols in Retrospect").

40. See, for example, Coady, *What to Believe Now*; Goldman, *Social Epistemology*; Fricker, "Testimony and Epistemic Autonomy."

41. See the work of Turner, *Politics of Expertise*; Collins and Evans, *Rethinking Expertise*; Goldman, "Experts: Which Ones Should You Trust?"; Agnew, Ford, Hayes, "Expertise in Context." They each approach the issue of social relation differently, which will be discussed later in this introduction.

42. Here I draw from Carr's "Enactments of Expertise," 10, 18.

43. On the significance of trust to expertise, see Watson, *Expertise*, 11–26.

44. On expertise as conceptual function, see Quast, "Expertise," 18–26.

Jewish communities but rather men who joined localized disciple circles, possessing a measure of social flexibility that afforded the time to study. Their status as experts was not the product of an expertise vacuum created upon the dissolution of the Jerusalem priesthood. Nor did their skills as Torah scholars necessarily mandate that other Jews should obey them. Their expertise was instead dependent upon their ability to persuade others that their mobilization of Jewish cultural resources was beneficial to them. This persuasion was enacted through everyday interactions that played an essential role in the growing perception that rabbinic knowledge was valuable.

A relational approach to rabbinic expertise assesses the objects and people that made the enactment of their expertise possible.[45] The possibilities for examination are wide ranging and not easily distilled into one arena, but for the sake of scope, this project looks to the explicit and implicit support to be gained through patronage and its related forms. Connections with wealthy friends and acquaintances were crucial. The rabbinic texts this book examines depict instances where merchants, householders, civic administrators, or relatives shared a measure of disposable wealth and other resources with rabbis.[46] Not only was patronage a tangible potential product of these relationships, but gifts of hospitality, including food, banquets, and housing, direct donations in the form of tithes and charity, and even communal appointments and other favors signaled gestures of support. These friendships also facilitated social occasions for rabbis to perform as experts in public view, whether engaged in rhetorical exposition at a dinner party or summoned to offer legal advice on a matter of business. Assistance like this not only provided tangible backing but served as a public vote of confidence that telegraphed to others the value of rabbinic expertise.

These relationships also imposed their own set of constraints. At the same time that rabbinic texts recognize valuable tangible support, they also express heightened anxiety about the way such relationships could intrude into the rabbinic domain with expectations of favors or personal instruction.[47] This project examines the sticky situation of funding expertise. Not only did

45. On expertise as enactment, see Carr, "Enactments of Expertise."

46. On aspects of supporting Torah scholars, see Labovitz, "Scholarly Life"; Dalton, "Rabbis as Recipients of Charity"; Kalmin, "Relationships between Rabbis and Non-Rabbis"; Marks, "Follow that Crown."

47. On reciprocity as a dynamic of social relationships, see the work of Komter, "Gifts and Social Relations"; Kolm, *Reciprocity*; Godbout and Caillé, *The World of the Gift*; Gouldner, "Norm of Reciprocity." These build upon the earlier anthropological studies of Mauss, *The Gift*; and Malinowski, *Argonauts of the Western Pacific*.

these reciprocal expectations threaten the credibility of the rabbinic expert, who might be accused of trading objectivity for profit, but they inverted the power relations inherent to expertise itself. Experts wield epistemic authority because expertise constructs a distinction between those who know and those who do not know. Experts do not merely regurgitate an internal cache of facts that provides automatic authority, but, as E. Summerson Carr argues, expertise is an "intensively citational institutional action," producing and organizing what counts as knowledge and who has claims to it.[48] The authority of expertise stems from this power to communicate the boundaries of an authoritative domain of knowledge that will be understood as such, which insists upon a measure of autonomy and insularity on the part of those who contribute to the domain. While this dynamic is inherently unstable, donors upend the table with expectations that intrude upon the constructed specialist domain. This project examines stories attuned to this pressure and illuminates the interpretive arguments aimed to mask the power of these relationships, defend rabbinic autonomy, and assert credibility as impartial judges and ritual specialists. At stake was not only the perception of rabbis as experts but the virtue of the Torah itself.

This book is an examination of rabbinic knowledge as a domain of expertise constructed through relationships of mutual obligation sustained through expectations of exchange. These relationships brought benefit and risk. They strengthened ties between rabbis and wealthy people that provided avenues for wielding expert influence and receiving donations that authorized and reinforced the status of rabbis as Jewish experts. They also brought tension from potential encroachment upon rabbinic ideals, intrusion into an expert domain, and unwanted demands. Expertise studies draws attention to the relational processes that made rabbinic expertise possible while also making legible the tensions that it generated. It is precisely these stories of tense encounters that allow us to see how rabbinic expertise was socially constructed, performed, and defended rather than self-evident. If expertise is a "relation" or "interaction" between experts and "consumers," then transactions of social exchange between rabbis and their wealthy friends are meaningful nodes for understanding how rabbis became experts.[49]

48. Carr, "Enactments of Expertise," 19. For similar arguments in the context of modern science, see Latour, *We Have Never Been Modern*, and *Science in Action*.

49. Turner, "Circles or Regresses?," 26.

Expertise as Social Enactment

Expertise is one of those concepts so pervasive in ordinary language that we use it all the time without questioning what it means. In its most basic sense expertise describes knowledge attained through specialized skill that warrants our trust.[50] Yet were we to probe the scope of this concept, we'd encounter a range of situations that unsettles neat definition. How does someone become an expert? How do others recognize that someone is an expert? Is someone an expert because they are better than someone else at a certain skill? Do they have more experience or education? Must someone be certified through institutional mechanisms, such as receiving a PhD or passing the Bar Exam, or can expertise emerge through personal experience, such as intimate knowledge about one's body? How do we reconcile when experts fail or when competing experts bid for our trust? What does it mean when ordinary people feel that they know more than the experts? These questions demonstrate that expertise in fact refers to a range of different aspects describing how and who we know to trust in society.[51]

Despite the conceptual relationship between them, expertise is not synonymous with knowledge. Knowledge refers to all the things learned through education and experience. The study of these distinctions and the different classifications of knowledge and means of acquisition comprise an entire field of philosophical study. In epistemology, a distinction is often made between knowledge of how to do something (ability) and knowledge of facts (propositions), a distinction characterized in Gilbert Ryle's *The Concept of Mind* (1949) as "knowing how and knowing that."[52] For example, I know how to swim and ride a bike. At the same time, I could not verbalize exactly how I know those things other than to demonstrate with my body by plunging into the water or pumping my legs. Propositional knowledge, by contrast, describes things known to be true that can be articulated through a statement, such as two plus two equals four, or the fact that New York is a city. Michael Polanyi characterized this difference as one between explicit, easily verbalized knowledge and tacit knowledge, the kind of knowledge that cannot be

50. Ericsson and Towne, "Expertise."

51. "Trust" is another term that is used in a myriad of ways. McKnight and Chervany suggest a "typology of trust" that maps the related concepts and dispositions invoked by the senses of trust. "What Is Trust," 829–30.

52. Ryle, *Concept of Mind* and "Knowing How and Knowing That," 212–25.

easily expressed.[53] While explicit knowledge could be studied by reading books and manuals, tacit knowledge could only be acquired through personal experience.

Expertise is related to these broader questions of how knowledge is constituted and learned. Where knowledge encompasses skills, experiences, beliefs, and capacities learned in forms both abstract and practical, expertise generally refers to an active mastery of a domain of such knowledge. But where does expertise derive from? A growing interdisciplinary subfield of psychologists, philosophers, and social scientists are divided in their approaches to answering this question. The ongoing debate centers on whether expertise is something cognitively possessed or whether it is something socially attributed or constructed. Scholars who follow the cognitive or "truth-based" view focus on the individual's journey to becoming an expert and their performance in that role. They aim to understand the roles of both the conscious and subconscious mind in the expert's experience. In other words, what is the magic cognitive sauce and true beliefs that they possess? Scholars of the social or "performance-based" view are more focused upon what expertise implies—what does it describe, how is it authenticated, what authority does it produce, what social roles emerge, and who trusts in it? They analyze the external processes of evaluating experts and how society interacts with them. The disagreement between these two positions stems from the question of whether expertise objectively exists in and of itself or whether it is a product of human interaction. This book is situated within the social perspective, but it is useful to identify the stakes of the debate so as to see how the rabbinic material contributes as an important case study to this broader interdisciplinary conversation.

From the cognitive position, expertise is something experts possess because of the unique capacities of their minds. Cognitive science has typically centered the self and consciousness within the brain, analyzing how the self is organized as a cognizing unit within the body's fleshy regions. The self in these terms is a wholistic entity that engages with the external world through chemically induced emotional behaviors. Oxytocin prompts feelings of trust; adrenaline stimulates mechanisms of defense. Viewing expertise in cognitive terms means that expertise is a product of these internal processes. As psychologists Merim Bilalić and Guillermo Campitelli surmise, "Expertise is a prime example of how various cognitive processes, such as memory, attention, and perception,

53. Polanyi, *Personal Knowledge*.

come together to enable a truly magnificent performance."[54] Their research charts how experts show functional and structural changes within the brain that enable their superior act. Other scholars have studied the excellent memory of experts and the effects of deliberative practice upon the cognitive mechanisms of the brain.[55] These studies attempt to prove that experts are really the best at what they do because of their unique cognitive capabilities.

Expertise in this view is argued to be objectively "true" because an individual possesses real mastery over a domain of knowledge whether their expertise is recognized or affirmed by anyone else. An expert in chess is still a master even if they only play in Washington Square Park on Thursdays.[56] Whether expertise is configured around "knowing how" to do something well or "knowing" the "truths" of a domain, experts must possess something real that distinguishes them from non-experts. Another version of this perspective emphasizes the "truth" inherent to real expertise. Alvin Goldman has called this a "truth-linked" approach because he argues experts have greater truth-possession and error-avoidance.[57] Similarly, David Coady argues that an expert possesses "a greater store of accurate information" than most people.[58] By grounding the epistemic authority of expertise in the mind, the objectivity of expertise is affirmed. The neurons firing in the brain produce the capabilities and logical operators that enable an expert's ability to know at a level of mastery, shaping the likelihood that they will be objectively correct in their expert judgments. Experts can be trusted, therefore, because their expertise is a real possession.

The problem with this cognitive and "truth-linked" account of expertise is that people we would otherwise consider experts do not apply under this criterion. The history of science is filled with superseded theories espoused by experts of the past that are no longer believed to be true. Humorism, the idea that illness could be attributed to an imbalance of the body's humors, dominated the field of medicine until the advent of germ theory in the mid-nineteenth century.[59] Under a "truth-linked" approach, premodern scholars of medicine would not be considered experts because they did not know the

54. Bilalić and Campitelli, "Studies of the Activation and Structural Changes of the Brain Associated with Expertise," 233.

55. On memory, see Ericsson, "Superior Working Memory in Experts"; on the effects of deliberative practice, see Ericsson, "Differential Influence of Experience."

56. Gobot and Charness, "Expertise in Chess."

57. Goldman, "Expertise."

58. Coady, *What to Believe Now*, 28

59. Hippocrates, *Hippocrates, Volume IV*. Bhikha and Glynn, "Theory of Humours Revisited."

"truths" of their domain.[60] Fortunately, it is not the case that every expert who expounded humorism in premodern medicine lacked the cognitive ability to generate accurate information. Certain technological advances enabled medical and scientific experts to build upon and eventually set aside erroneous scientific beliefs. This diminished veritism suggests that experts do not simply possess more accurate or true information than ordinary people.

A further challenge to the cognitive or "truth-linked" accounts is that they do not sufficiently describe what experts do. Experts do not just know things in their mind, but they do things with what they know in a skilled, intuitive manner not easily expressed in propositional form. The recent interest in studying expertise arose in part from research in artificial intelligence technology that confirmed the significance of intuitive tacit knowledge. The field of cybernetics devoted itself to understanding the arrangements of communication within biological and social systems.[61] It drew attention to embodied causality, or the feedback loops between cognition, bodies, and external environments that guide expert action.[62] Take the example of a helmsman steering a ship, from whom cybernetics derives its name.[63] In the midst of stormy seas, without stable landmarks or a clear view of the celestial sky, the helmsman steers the ship by interpreting the meaning of the wind and currents and the sensations of his body with his own reasoning and experience in quick instinctual movements. The knowledge of what to do is a balance between the laws of sailing that he carries in his mind, his body's perception of the real-time environment, and his intuitive reaction all channeling through a continuous loop.

Researchers interested in simulating human intelligence in machines sought to replicate this information pathway through knowledge engineering. Their attempt was largely a failure. While computers could do hard things, like master chess or prove mathematical theorems, they could not replicate the instinctual problem-solving capabilities of human experts. This failure was famously termed "Moravec's paradox," because Hans Moravec, along with other researchers, found that it was difficult for robotics to achieve even the

60. It could be argued that the truth condition only refers to the possession of more true beliefs than most people at a given time, but that does not resolve the problem that supposedly expert assumptions were false.

61. The earliest published instance of the term "cybernetics" is Norbert Wiener's *Cybernetics*.

62. Wiener, *Cybernetics*. For a survey of early cybernetics, see Hayles, *How We Became Posthuman*.

63. Gage, "The Boat/Helmsman."

basic instinctual intelligence of children.[64] Machines could not stand in for formal models of human cognition because some aspects of knowledge are not easily expressed in reducible form. Expertise could not be simply distilled into a repertory of cognitive rules that could be programmed into a machine because expertise is not produced through the interiorizing of knowledge systems.[65] The large failure of artificial intelligence to replicate the instinctual behavior and reasoning of experts prompted scholars to look beyond strict cognitive explanations of expertise.

A number of social constructionist approaches have shifted focus from the individual expert's possessed knowledge to various external factors that influence the signification of expertise. One social factor is reputation. Neil Agnew, Kenneth Ford, and Patrick Hayes advocate that the minimum criterion of expertise is "to have at least one reasonably large group of people . . . who consider that you are an expert."[66] They propose that expert status and authority are not intrinsic but are bestowed by others who acknowledge the individual as an expert. Ben L. Martin similarly states that "expertness is an ascribed quality, a badge, which cannot be manufactured and affected by an expert himself, but rather can only be received from another, a client."[67] This perspective emphasizes the contingency of expertise that relies on social attribution to come into being. However, if expertise is *only* a reputation, then is expertise real? Some researchers fear the reputational approach produces a world of charlatans, where snake oil salesmen masquerade as experts through an acquired reputation while in reality pawning tricks.[68] While approaches focusing only on reputation overlook the role of skill in establishing a lasting reputation, epistemologizing expertise does not resolve the problem. Non-experts, by definition, cannot assess an expert's credibility based on the affirmation of objective truth because they are not experts. Instead, the value of the reputational approach is the attention shown to how experts gain credibility through socially informed processes of validation. Reputation is not

64. Moravec, *Mind Children*, 15.

65. Neil M. Agnew, Kenneth M. Ford, and Patrick J. Hayes argue, "Expertise is not synonymous with knowledge. Expertise, unlike knowledge, does not reside in the individual, but rather emerges from a dynamic interaction between the individual and his physical / cultural domain." "Expertise in Context," 67.

66. Agnew, Ford, and Hayes, "Expertise in Context."

67. Martin, "Experts in Policy Processes," 159.

68. See the critique in Watson, *Expertise*, 144–64.

inherently less real because it is a product of social relations; reputation is earned because of real performance deemed to be credible and valuable.

Harry Collins and Robert Evans alternatively shifted focus from externally ascribed reputation to the internal processes of socialization within an expert group. They contend that to become an expert in a domain of knowledge is "a matter of becoming embedded in the social life of the domain, acquiring what is to a large extent, tacit knowledge, so as to internalise the associated concepts and skilful actions to the point of fluency."[69] Spearheading a new interdisciplinary field called Studies of Expertise and Experience (SEE), their research assesses the "interactional expertise," or the jargon, demeanor, and intuition acquired through social interaction with a specialist group.[70] Collins and Evans stress that expertise extends beyond merely acquiring propositional knowledge or a reputation. What it means to be expert is shaped by the interactions of those working with a domain of knowledge.[71] However, an exclusive focus on the socialization of a specialist group fails to assess the ongoing external processes of public recognition, social persuasion, and institutional compulsion that naturalize a sense of who a community's experts are and the various ways non-experts engage with (or reject) them. Reputation and socialization are important facets of expertise, but each alone fails to capture the full scope of a relational approach.

Stephen Turner, by contrast, contends that "experts are not just knowers. They are people making claims within a social relationship."[72] These claims encompass internal and external relationships and wield real power. They distinguish between types of people (i.e., those who know and those who do not know) and draw boundaries around the domain of knowledge experts claim to control. Experts also claim the means to make that knowledge legible. Their

69. H. Collins, "Studies of Expertise and Experience," 68.

70. This tacit knowledge cannot be easily learned through verbal explication but must be absorbed through observation and interaction. As they argue, "socialization not embodiment is what underpins expertise." Collins and Evans, "A Sociological/Philosophical Perspective on Expertise," 28.

71. Collins and Evans ultimately aim to identify *real* expertise in a contemporary moment when science and its related professions are being called into question. However, they are perhaps too cautious about overemphasizing social construction, which they fear could compromise the objectivity of expertise. They maintain the epistemological truth of a specialist group's domain of knowledge with which the right exclusion criteria could distinguish real experts from imposters ("A Sociological/Philosophical Perspective on Expertise").

72. Turner, "Circles or Regresses?," 26.

knowledge constructs objects that provide occasions for the performance of their expertise. Joseph Dumit, for example, asserts that "expert objects" such as brain scans create opportunities for expert medical interpretation.[73] Non-experts choose to trust these claims, not because they themselves can evaluate what is true, but because they believe in the credibility of the expert. They attribute expertise to those claiming expertise, which is its own type of claim. Institutions and funding emerge to support both the attribution and specialist claim of expertise. "Expertise" is therefore the word we use to describe a range of social configurations, claims, and tools that enable the possibility of enacting the ongoing distinction between experts and non-experts.

The rabbis of late antique Roman Palestine are a particularly useful case to consider when thinking about the relational components of enacting expertise. They appear in our sources just as a new domain of knowledge was being produced through the socialization of like-minded men forming the rabbinic specialist group. The Torah, both as textual entity and broader imaginal world of stories, characters, and values, served as a shared cultural object between these men and other Jews. Rabbis made claims about what constituted rabbinic knowledge and used those claims to construct their own objects for expert performance. Rather than brain scans, we might think of more relevant premodern cases, such as a farmer's field or the fluid discharges of a body, which are framed as objects requiring rabbinic diagnosis.[74] These claims distinguished who was a true Torah expert, someone affiliated with the rabbinic specialist group with the capacity to diagnose objects of their knowledge, and who was not. They developed a unique jargon, methods of argumentation, and a repertoire of teachings that reinforced this distinction and generated the rabbinic "interactional" expertise identified by Collins and Evans.

However, practical skill and interactional intuition alone did not empower rabbis as experts. Rabbinic expertise was demonstrated in social interaction, expressed through verbal jargon, tied to the cultural object of the Torah, perceived by a public, and enabled by strategic allies who contributed recognition, trust, and donations to support their expert claims. These processes enabled rabbinic expertise to be enacted, thereby producing the very knowledge they professed to be experts in. This network or "assemblage" of relations resists

73. Dumit, *Picturing Personhood*.

74. Fonrobert, *Menstrual Purity*, 114: "The rabbis, equipped with the science that they themselves created, are now the judges to tell a woman whether she is menstruating, whether she is a *zavah* or whether she has merely an internal wound."

locating expertise within an individual or reputation and instead assesses all the capacities and contexts required to make an expert performance possible.[75] The rabbis represent an interesting case where we can chart the production of a new domain of knowledge and its social and material outgrowth through communities of people.

There is a further critical need for an analysis of the relational processes of expertise within premodern sources because expertise studies is dominated by a preoccupation with modernity.[76] According to Gil Eyal, discussion of expertise accelerated in the twentieth century, as legal questions arose about the official roles of experts, especially in courtrooms and policymaking.[77] People began questioning what deference should be paid to experts, whose testimony should be treated as "expert," and what influence experts should wield in politics.[78]

This focus has led some researchers to assume that expertise is a byproduct of the rise of modern science, dismissing the premodern and employing versions of an old evolutionary teleology that views scientific achievement as the pinnacle of human civilization.[79] Modern professions and scientific experts are viewed as the apex of an evolutionary trajectory from the primitive knowledge leaders of the past. Take for example this description of the professionalization of modern experts within the *longue durée* of history:

> From a historical point of view we can see various predecessors of modern experts. For instance, we can conceive of priests or shamans as an extreme, undifferentiated version of "experts" in premodern societies, encompassing

75. This approach relies heavily on Foucault and his influence in actor-network theory (*Archaeology of Knowledge*), especially the work of Latour (*Science in Action*).

76. Scholars of the ancient world have begun to demonstrate that professionalization did in fact occur prior to the advent of science. See the recent edited volume, Verboven and Laes, *Work, Labour, and Professions in the Roman World*.

77. Eyal comes to this figure based on Google Books Ngram data. Eyal, "Expertise," 2–3.

78. Latour, *Science in Action*. Scientists represented a new kind of professional expert in so-called democratic societies, whose authority of knowledge of scientific facts posed a threat to those processes. Some argued that the scientific facts should supersede the consent of the governed via their chosen policy makers. Much of expertise studies scholarship is preoccupied with responding to the particular problems posed by scientists as experts in modern democracies. See the recent discussion in Turner, "Balancing Expert Power."

79. This teleology is as old as the disciplines of anthropology and religious studies, as exemplified in Frazer, *Golden Bough*. In recent scholarship of expertise, see Winegard, Winegard, and Geary, "The Evolution of Expertise," which replicates this evolutionary model.

> the roles of counsel, physician, and medium. In the rising empires of antiquity we see the growing importance of scholar-officials—experts with literacy skills—such as the Chinese mandarins often charged with extended official duties in astronomy, architecture or bureaucracy. In medieval times merchants and artisans (bakers, shoemakers carpenters, etc.) formed trade guilds that controlled quality standards, prices, and the rules for apprenticeship thereby organizing the work and markets for craftsmanship in European cities. The historical view shows two trends: differentiation and (self)-organization. Guilds were self-organized and can be considered the predecessors of today's professions. (Mieg and Evetts, "Professionalism, Science, and Expert Roles" 127)

Here Harald Mieg and Julia Evetts chart an evolutionary path from the "undifferentiated" priests of the past to scholars of antiquity to the medieval guilds of Europe that they claim were the precursors to modern experts. These premodern figures are different, they argue, because they do not possess the "collegial organization" or the truth of scientific systems of knowledge that mark the modern professions as distinct.[80]

This teleology of the primitive past to scientific discovery is wrong. Priests served as both ritual experts and textual scholars, rather than being replaced by them, and continue to persist to the present day. Nor did scholars only emerge in the waning days of antiquity or always hold the same authority as civic officials. Medieval guilds were not the first to organize communities of skilled people; many took their cues from the ancient Roman collegia. This model insists upon an artificial teleology that disassociates geographic contexts and equates every iteration of priest, scholar, and guild through thousands of years of history as signifying the same thing. The key revelation is not an ontological difference between past experts but rather how science has become the accepted basis of "truth." As Bruno Latour and others have insisted, one of the fictions of the Enlightenment is that everything in the premodern world is religious and superstitious while modernity is defined by the secular truth of science.[81] But modern experts do not actually have greater organization or stronger claims of truth. They are grounded in a scientific knowledge system rather than other systems of knowledge, and modernity has decided that science is "true" where other systems of knowledge are false.

80. Mieg and Evetts, "Professionalism, Science, and Expert Roles," 129.

81. Latour, *We Have Never Been Modern*.

The above teleology presents modern professions as unique "epistemic communities, that is, groups or networks of experts who share knowledge and beliefs that are in general linked to values and interest."[82] The rabbis of Roman Palestine throw such assumptions of modernity's particularity out the window. Rabbis developed "theories about our world" and shared "terminology, a set of assumptions, and paradigmatic cases" about the world.[83] Rabbinic texts reflect distinct jargon and methods of interpretation that seek not only to interpret Torah but to apply its meaning to both theoretical and everyday practice. Just as the medical profession is "tied to the value of health" or the legal profession is "tied to the value of justice," rabbis were tied to the value of Torah. They sought "social recognition and influence" just like any profession in modernity because they believed that their interpretations of Torah held social value.[84] The rabbis are not the first nor the only specialist group in the premodern world that confounds a simplistic teleology of expertise, but this project argues that they offer a significant case for examining the dynamics of authority, knowledge, and persuasion animating the enactment of expertise.

Expertise and Patronage

This project focuses on the social relationships that enabled rabbinic transmission and performance of knowledge during the first few centuries of the common era. Rabbinic texts from this period provide important glimpses into the relationships between rabbis and their clients. Rabbis dined with the wealthy and met in the homes of their well-connected friends. These interactions fostered relationships built on trust and mutual obligation, which were crucial to the authorization of rabbinic knowledge. However, these relationships also invoked expectations of reciprocity. While they provided a mutual support system, where each party could rely on the other for help and resources, they also intruded upon the autonomy of the rabbinic expert. This book surveys rabbinic texts that showcase these points of contact and the efforts made by rabbis to distinguish these relationships from patronage.

Stephen Turner documents how expertise and patronage are closely intertwined in modern science, contending that "scientists solve the problem that any possessor of embodied knowledge faces: how to convert one's knowledge

82. Mieg and Evetts, "Professionalism, Science, and Expert Roles," 132.

83. Mieg and Evetts, 132.

84. Mieg and Evetts, 132.

into money."[85] This conversion takes a variety of forms: from large-scale employment, such as research or teaching salaries or offering judgments in a paid advisory capacity, to endowed fellowships, grants, or corporate-funded research aimed at producing a particular (ideally marketable) product. Turner's interest goes beyond the general observation that funding facilitates the production of knowledge. He considers the processes by which experts are compelled to transmit their knowledge to non-expert clients, participating in an exchange of knowledge for resources. He claims that scientists are constrained by the wishes of their employers and donors, as they often must use the resources they receive toward their funder's desired ends. Experts therefore cannot exist in epistemic isolation because of the constraints of these relationships of mutual obligation. As Turner dryly states, "The practice of patronage is a response to the fact that the distribution of wealth and the distribution of knowledge and knowledge-generating talent are misaligned."[86]

The production of rabbinic knowledge did not have access to modern infrastructure like higher education, research labs, and government agencies. However, rabbinic sources indicate that the basic reciprocal dynamic of funding expertise identified by Turner is present in these premodern sources. Early rabbinic texts depict rabbis meeting in each other's homes or in the homes of friends and using those occasions to debate a matter of Torah or the application of a law. Those meetings did not occur in a vacuum. Someone paid for dinner, owned the home, and offered hospitality out of their largesse. Houses or rooms of study (*batei midrash*) were built by private donors, such as in Dibbura and Sepphoris or by the Silani family in Tiberias.[87] Students in rabbinic disciple circles needed funds to clothe and feed themselves while devoting their days to study. Stories of wives and parents supporting their Torah scholar kin in extraordinary ways highlight the considerable financial and material challenges such scholars faced. Hillel's wife, for instance, is said to have sold the very braids upon her head to support his study.[88] Bible teachers were employed with communal funds and rabbinic judges charged a fee for their time.

85. Turner, "Scientists as Agents," 376.

86. Turner, *Politics of Expertise*, 2.

87. On the Dibbura synagogue inscription, as well as distinguishing epigraphical rabbis from their literary counterparts, see Miller, "'This Is the Beit Midrash'" and Fine, "'Epigraphical' Study Houses." For a textual description of a house of study in Sepphoris, see Y. Pe'ah 7:4, 20b. See also discussion in Lapin, "Jewish and Christian Academies," 511. For Tiberias, see Y. Horayot 3:7, 48a.

88. Y. Shabbat 6.1, 7d. On this story and its parallels, see Marks, "Follow That Crown."

Rabbis may not have published articles or conducted conferences, but their teachings were eventually collected into anthologies—edited volumes as it were—that demanded scribal technology and tools.

Rabbinic literature is less forthcoming about the costs associated with their work, but Christian counterparts wrote letters and kept ledgers that have survived and detail the many ways their patrons supported their scholastic work. Jerome, for example, was supported financially by widows and received books, which were gift commodities at the time, from wealthy friends to assist his scholarship. Their funds contributed to the material production of texts, such as buying papyrus or parchment, to the building of personal libraries, and even to the hiring of stenographers to take dictation and assistants to read over his drafts. Jerome writes with envy that a friend supplied Origen, the famed ascetic scholar from an earlier century (185–253 CE), with "parchment, money, and copyists," which allowed him to produce "innumerable books."[89] Megan Hale Williams has argued that the austerity of ascetic life was necessarily shattered by the infrastructures of scholarly expertise, which required unencumbered time, libraries, workplaces, tools of the trade, and the means of textual production and dissemination. Scholars in late antiquity could not work in isolation, yet with funding came a loss of control. Jerome complains about patrons who commissioned translations when he wished to work on other things. Other patrons took his writings and circulated them in ways that he found distasteful.[90] Williams writes that "in general, Jerome's readers knew what they wanted him to write, and it was not what he had planned for."[91]

Turner details similar demands upon scientists who are beholden to the interests of their funders. These demands may threaten the scientists' autonomy in terms of control over scientific standards and choice of knowledge production methods.[92] Donors, including patrons, employers, and one-time gift givers, provide the financial support that enables knowledge production. Funding also grants authorization to the experts themselves, validating their work and expanding their reputation within their field. Scientific projects that are awarded federal grants, for example, are viewed as passing a bar of viability

89. Jerome, *Epist.* 43.1. All references to Jerome's letters adapted from Jerome and F. A. Wright, *Select Letters of St. Jerome* (Cambridge, MA: Harvard University Press, 1975).

90. On Jerome's tense relationship with his elite networks, see Williams, *The Monk and the Book*, 233–60.

91. Williams, *The Monk and the Book*, 247.

92. Turner, "Scientists as Agents," 381.

and importance. Yet with benefit also comes threat. Clients can expect privileges or oversight in exchange for their investment. They might want to be involved in the production of knowledge, solicit special favors, or lay claim to the expert's time. Whether showing up in a lab, demanding research updates, or even holding a congressional oversight hearing, the clients of experts can invoke the power of being a donor at any time.

While Turner is thinking about modernity, his insights shed light on an important dynamic that I argue was present between rabbis and their clients. In stories about rabbis engaging with donors, employers, or potential clients, there are similar dynamics of benefit and risk. These stories describe conflict, gendered insults, and contests of superiority between rabbis and their acquaintances. These stories typically resolve with the rabbi in a position of expert authority, as we might expect from texts authored from the rabbis' perspective, but they also preserve tensions that suggest similar scenarios in real life were fraught. They offer cases of how expertise and patronage were intertwined in the ancient past. Although this entanglement manifested in distinct ways in rabbinic relationships, it resembles the tensions that plague the production of expertise today.

There are three key concepts that I use to formulate the intersections of knowledge production and patronal support of expertise within rabbinic literature. The first is specialist groups. I define a specialist group as an epistemic community of experts and professionals with a shared set of beliefs, values, and skills in a particular domain of knowledge. The rabbis formed a new epistemic community that used distinct hermeneutical methods, the boundaries of which demarcated members of their specialist group from non-specialists. These boundaries were both formal, such as education requirements and lineage of instruction, and informal, such as shared experiences or contacts. The shared beliefs and values of the rabbinic epistemic community served as a foundation for rabbinic work and constructed an ideological boundary designating rabbis as the spokespeople of Torah.

The second concept is friendship. Friendship, as Elizabeth Telfer defines it, encompasses a broad spectrum of interpersonal relationships comprising reciprocal services, mutual contact, and joint pursuits.[93] These are intricate relationships that disrupt clean boundaries and norms. While in some contexts "friendship" conjures notions of intimacy and social proximity, this project uses the term expansively to consider the broader network of relationships that include acquaintances, family, and rightful friends because each level of

93. Telfer, "Friendship."

intimacy shares the tugs of mutual obligation. Such relationships were invaluable to the cultivation of rabbinic expertise, even as they complicated the ideals of rabbinic autonomy and expert authority. Michael Satlow and Eliezer Diamond have both rightfully framed the ideal of devotion to Torah study as an ascetic ideology that forsakes worldly preoccupations for higher-order concerns.[94] This impulse, Satlow contends, understood Torah study to be "an activity of the elite" because it assumed that most Jews could not engage in the total mastery of the rabbinic curriculum.[95] I argue that this ascetic impulse is a fundamental product of drawing boundaries of specialist groups but did not represent a totalizing insularity. Rabbis could not exist in epistemic isolation. They had friends, family members, and other acquaintances who both validated the rabbinic specialist group and through their interactions directly shaped the rabbinic domain of knowledge.

The final concept that I use is donor systems. By donor systems I refer in the broadest terms to social relationships that make possible the production of expertise, which allows me to collect a range of rabbinic texts that are seldom treated together. I survey texts where charity, tithes, patronage, benefaction, communal funds, food gifts, hospitality, and even dinner parties supported rabbinic work. While scholars have analyzed the fundamental differences between these types of gifts, emphasizing distinction can have the adverse effect of siloing textual evidence. I want to illuminate the way these types of gifts are conceptually related, which contributed to the similar ways rabbis imagined their engagement with them. Marcel Mauss contended that "the terms commonly used—present and gift—are not themselves exact,"[96] and Mark Osteen frames the difficulty well: "The Question of the gift is thus a question of categories, and we fail to account for them adequately if our classification remains rigid."[97] The benefit of casting a wide net is that I can group the limited sources that we have from rabbinic literature together so as to assess their shared links. While hospitality and charity are different types of transactions, for example, they share conceptual logic in the rabbinic material.

My aim is to think expansively about the social relationships that influenced and supported rabbinic expertise through expectations of mutual

94. Satlow, "'And On the Earth You Shall Sleep,'"; and Diamond, *Holy Men and Hunger Artists.*

95. Satlow, "'And On the Earth You Shall Sleep,'" 220.

96. Mauss, *The Gift*, 124.

97. Osteen, *Question of the Gift*, 23.

obligation. This means looking at texts that explicitly describe gifts of goods and money but also stories where acquaintances and friendships were forged with the theoretical potential for future gifts.[98] It will invariably frustrate some readers that I employ the category of donors to discuss certain examples where no explicit gift exchange is stated in the text, but I do this intentionally. Informal interactions were not only occasions where rabbis performed their expertise, but they helped forge friendships of varying stripes. Friendship imposes expectations of reciprocity that often manifest in later, tangible support. By including these kinds of interactions within our scope, we can better assess the microtransactions that contribute to tangible exchange.

For example, I once met a neighbor at a mutual friend's barbecue. We followed each other on social media, made plans to meet up, and had dinner together over several months. Eventually, she asked if I would consider donating to a local campaign she was running. Although the candidate was not from my district and I did not know him well, I felt compelled by our casual acquaintance to contribute. Analyzing my donation to that campaign might lead to assumptions about my political party and investment in local politics. However, such analyses would fall short if they did not account for the social interactions that led to the donation in the first place. I would not have donated if she had not asked. Nor was she forming a friendship with me in a long game attempt to fundraise. These soft expectations of reciprocity are rooted in the social norms we develop through our social interactions with others. They are not always explicitly stated, but they influence our behavior and the choices we make. My neighbor's request for a donation was not a formal agreement or contract, but rather a natural extension of our growing acquaintanceship and shared interests.

When rabbinic experts received gifts of hospitality, goods, or social favors, these did not come without strings attached. Gift exchange ties individuals together through shared obligation to balance their social debts to each other. Theories of this inherent gift reciprocity begin with Marcel Mauss's seminal work, "Essai sur le don."[99] A French sociologist at the turn of the twentieth century and nephew of Émile Durkheim, Mauss was preoccupied with

98. See Van Berkel, *Economics of Friendship*.

99. For commentaries on Mauss's work, see Lévi-Strauss, *Introduction to the Work of Marcel Mauss*; Sahlins, *Stone Age Economics*, 149–83; Firth, *Symbols*, 368–402; Parry, "The Gift, the Indian Gift and the 'Indian Gift,'" 453–73; Bourdieu, *Logic of Practice*, 98–111; Derrida, *Given Time*; Weiner, *Inalienable Possessions*; Carrier, *Gifts and Commodities*.

understanding the social relationships generated through gifts. In these essays, Mauss contends that gifts are never free, but activate an entire social system comprised of "religious, legal, moral, and economic" expectations, which inherently place constraints upon it. Fundamental to the gift is a system of exchange, Mauss insisted, requiring that each gift be reciprocated. Some gifts are returned in kind, others must exceed the gift's value, and still others will fail to ever fully reciprocate the initial gift. Society is built, Mauss argued, upon these transfers of gifts. Givers and the recipients of gifts enter a continual relationship of masked obligatory actions encoded with social meaning. As Mark Osteen contends, "Gifts at once express freedom and create binding obligations, and may be motivated by generosity or calculation, or both."[100]

Recent scholarship has drawn attention to the ways Jewish giving interacted with institutions of patronage and benefaction.[101] Patronage is a formal system of gifts sustained by reciprocal exchange.[102] These relationships took a variety of forms, including between landowners and tenants, wealthy elites and scholars, and even between the emperor and the citizen body. Donations could take the form of individual personal gifts and favors, or come in the form of benefaction (*euergetism*), which expected civic leaders to personally finance the building of monuments, city centers, and festivals in exchange for their social position.[103] As a "patron of public life," the benefactor was repaid for their efforts through civic honors and memorialization through inscriptions.[104]

The rabbis had reason to be uneasy with formal patronage and benefaction. Seth Schwartz has argued that the rabbis inherited an ideal of "corporate

100. Osteen, *Question of the Gift*, 14.

101. S. Schwartz, *Were the Jews a Mediterranean Society?*; Gardner, *Origins of Organized Charity*; Gardner and Wealth, *Poverty, and Charity*; Gray, *Charity in Rabbinic Judaism*; Wilfand, *Poverty, Charity, and the Image of the Poor*; Sorek, *Remembered for Good*; Marks, "Who Studied at the Beit Midrash?"

102. Saller, *Personal Patronage* argues that these relationships are inherently asymmetrical because the donor—who is often of a superior social position—controls the purse strings and so holds power over the recipient of their attentions. The recipient is perpetually in the donor's debt. However, we should be careful to not assume a flat asymmetry that might distract from more overlapping cases with less hierarchical differences.

103. Andre Boulanger coined the term in *Aelius Aristide et la sophistique dans la province d'Asie au IIe siècle de notre ère*. "Euergetism" is itself a neologism derived from the epigraphic habit of honoring civic donations from *euergetai* or benefactors.

104. Veyne conceived of benefaction as a canopy upheld by three "themes": voluntary patronage, political trade, and memorialization. *Bread and Circuses*.

solidarity" from the Torah that resisted relationships of social dependency.[105] The association of patronage with imperial "Romanness" in addition to the imposition of social debt may have sat uneasily in rabbinic thinking. This book contributes to this examination of patronage but from a different vantage point. Unease could be provoked from the expectations that coincide with the funding of expertise. Donors to rabbis expected the same reciprocal favors as patrons in other settings. But I argue that rabbis would not have wanted their donors to become their patrons because it usurped their expert autonomy. In addition, by linking Torah expertise with the exploitative mechanisms of patronage and employment, it might devalue Torah itself. This project surveys the arguments that rabbinic literature produces to negotiate the constraints of patronage as a way to retain the tangible benefits of donors while distancing rabbinic experts from a position of social debt.

Rabbis may have resisted the logic of Roman patronage and constraints of reciprocity in some contexts, but their expert domain could not ignore the benefits of donors. Scholarly expertise required donor buy-in because it both sustained knowledge-producing work and authenticated their claims of expertise. Rabbis who formed friendships with wealthy neighbors would have become accustomed to the expectations of reciprocity. They therefore developed interpretive strategies to reframe these gifts, either by invoking religious categories like tithes or charity, or by reconfiguring the power of the donor relationship to assert the religious and symbolic legitimacy of supporting Torah scholars. Gifts for rabbis were therefore framed as a public good rather than selfish private funds by introducing God as a meaningful entity into the socioeconomic relationship.

Rabbinic expertise was continually enacted and challenged through social interactions. These interactions provided opportunities for rabbis to make expert pronouncements, offer advice, and provide interpretation both within their expert group and outside of it. Through such occasions, rabbinic expertise itself was shaped, as rabbis were compelled to transmit their knowledge to non-experts in a convincing form. The relationships between rabbis and their wealthy friends therefore provide a useful window into these dynamics. These relationships imposed explicit expectations of reciprocity and required the rabbinic expert to persuade and defend their claims to people who wielded power over them. By doing so, these acquaintances pierced the veil of epistemic isolation that often characterizes expert groups. Expertise is a delicate

105. S. Schwartz, *Were the Jews a Mediterranean Society?*, 18.

balance between autonomy and client needs, and it requires ongoing effort and adaptation to maintain.

Methodology and Rabbinic Texts

I have primarily focused on rabbinic sources from the Roman province of Syria Palaestina that were largely composed prior to the fifth century CE. My interest is in the rabbis living in Roman Galilee who produced these sources within a specific imperialized place. These men initially referred to themselves by somewhat generic terms like *hakhamim* (sages) or *zeqenim* (elders), but we now know they were becoming a new class of Torah experts that emerged as a legible group in the second century CE.[106] They saw themselves as an extension of the *Torat Moshe*, the ancestral collection of Jewish law and legend, and cultivated a distinct expertise in the nitty gritty components of an increasingly atomized biblical text. They produced a particular form of piety that I call "grammarian piety," which meant they viewed the granular linguistic components of the Hebrew Bible as both an intellectual and spiritual avenue awaiting rabbinic generative hermeneutics.[107] Their thinking fashioned a particular landscape of Jewish culture—transcendent in the sense that they linked their novel traditions to the biblical and Second Temple past and yet also contingent upon the concerns of their day.

Their earliest textual material is called *tannaitic* after the first generations of rabbis, the *tannaim,* or reciters, who authored it.[108] Their most important textual corpus is the Mishnah. Codified around 200 CE, this anthology collects rabbinic teachings composed in a distinct Hebrew describing how laws in the Torah might be applied in their post-Temple context. This collection became the foundation for rabbinic thinking. The Tosefta, a related companion collection, serves a similar purpose and covers many of the same topics as the Mishnah, but it also contains different material and teachings authored after the Mishnah was collected. The next group of texts are called *amoraic* because they were composed by the rabbinic *amoraim,* literally "those who speak." This group took the Mishnah and used it as a textual anchor to think

106. Hezser, *Social Structure of the Rabbinic Movement*; S. Schwartz, *Imperialism and Jewish Society*; Lapin, *Rabbis as Romans*.

107. For more on grammarian piety, see Dalton, "Rabbis as Recipients of Charity."

108. On the meaning of *tannay* in the Palestinian Talmud and the role of the sages themselves as reciters, see Vidas, "What Is a Tannay?"

with. The resulting tractates of the Palestinian Talmud (and later Babylonian Talmud) are formally commentaries upon the Mishnah, but they are best viewed as anthologies of commentary, original teachings, stories, and folklore, including quotations from both the Tosefta and other non-Mishnaic teachings called *baraitot*, inspired by the content in the Mishnah. Scholars largely agree that this Talmudic collection was redacted sometime in the fifth century CE, while the only full extant manuscript (Leiden Or. 4720) dates to the thirteenth century.[109] Other commentaries and teachings from both the tannaim and amoraim are collected in midrashic form, meaning a prooftext from the Torah served as the textual anchor rather than the Mishnah. These texts similarly contain legal commentary, folklore, stories, as well as different versions of passages that appear in the Talmud.

The sources that comprise these volumes of rabbinic literature are difficult to date. While we think we know more or less when the collections received their near final form, it is difficult to pin down individual events, rabbis, or passages therein. All rabbinic texts are comprised of layers of material dating to different rabbinic generations, signaled by differences in language and composition structure. These anthologies span hundreds of years, collating the thoughts of generations of teachers and students with attributions to individual rabbis resting upon precarious historical ground. This means that when a source in the Talmud attributes a saying to an earlier tannaitic rabbi, for example, the historicity of that attribution is suspect, especially when one saying might be attributed to different rabbis in different sources.[110] Other times rabbis who were not contemporaneous with each other may show up in the same scene. While time travel makes for compelling rhetorical effect, it does not allow us to do concrete historical work. Thus, one cannot swiftly carve out historical proof from the page.

I read these texts first as redacted versions, parsing the argumentation, interpretive techniques, and composition of the passage at hand. Then I consider carefully what kind of realities are being depicted and theorize what the implications might be. I am making a general historical argument about the kinds of exchanges rabbis likely had with their clients in the second through fifth centuries CE based upon anecdotal stories in rabbinic literature. While these stories cannot be unproblematically taken at face value, I operate under the

109. See Mayer, *Editio Princeps*, for the manuscript and book history of the Palestinian Talmud.

110. Neusner, "Why We Cannot Assume the Reliability of Attributions."

general assumption that they provide and assume real social patterns. People ate with each other, gave each other gifts (in various forms), and sought favors from friends in late antiquity. I therefore read these anecdotal stories for glimpses of the social transactions encoded, even when the text serves a different interpretive and/or legal purpose. I assume that while those individual accounts may be fabrications themselves, they represent plausible types of social interactions understood by the authors.

What this means in practice is that I may have a text that depicts Rabbi Gamaliel and a wealthy Jewish merchant at a banquet when there may in fact have never been such an occasion. Or there may have been such a banquet but it was Rabbi Yoḥanan not Rabbi Gamaliel in attendance, or the wealthy merchant may have not in fact been a merchant. The banquet could be loosely informed by historical circumstances or not at all! The text does not relay historical events and figures with reliability. I do not, however, believe that should stop us from historicizing the text. We can ask what the representation of Rabbi Gamaliel and a wealthy Jewish merchant might tell us about similar banquets and similar social relationships. We can consider intentions, anxieties, and aspirations in the discernible choices made in the composition and redaction of the text. This historicizing does not leave us with hard evidence, neither does it leave us with nothing.

The other issue to consider when using rabbinic sources is whether one is making a synchronic or diachronic argument. This book spans those texts traditionally identified as tannaitic (Mishnah, Tosefta, Halakhic Midrashim) with those identified as amoraic (Talmud and Hermeneutical Midrash). There are meaningful differences between the two periods, and amoraic literature often includes details and practices that are absent from tannaitic literature. When useful, I identify trends or differences between these sets, but I prefer not to argue from absence. There is a tendency to view rabbinic literature through an evolutionary model where earlier strata are deemed underdeveloped.[111] But just because an early rabbinic source does not describe something, such as fundraising, for example, does not mean we can say with confidence that rabbis of that period never received donations. Absence can occur because such practices were foreign or because the genre or the focus of the redactors led to its omission.

This raises a methodological problem since the assessment of rabbinic expertise rests between the redacted textual tradition and the living people who interacted with rabbis, both of whom we know very little. This requires an element of

111. See the critique of this method in Strassfeld, *Trans Talmud*, 28.

imagination to fill in the gaps and reconstruct theoretical scenarios about when rabbis met with other people and forged relationships of mutual exchange. When possible, I make reference to contemporaneous contexts and sources to compare how other related agents within the ancient Mediterranean interacted with their clients. In order to understand certain dynamics and settings within these stories, I make comparison to customs, habits, and logics shared by Jews and their neighbors in this period in order to illuminate subtleties not explicitly stated within the text but that could very much be informing their meaning. This means looking at patterns of Roman architecture and dining habits, comparing donor habits between Jews and Christians, and considering other points of cultural reference. I do so with the belief that such comparison can help us theorize the kinds of relationships in which rabbis would have been engaging and their significance given the limitations of our source material.

I also at times move freely between tannaitic and amoraic texts in pursuit of thematic threads. The benefit of this approach is that I can meaningfully describe different theoretical aspects of expertise across the rabbinic corpus that demonstrate relation with each other. Identifying donor relationships in rabbinic literature is complicated by the fact that the rabbis themselves often thwarted associations with systems of patronage. While textually veiled, however, rabbinic texts retain glimpses of rabbinic donor relationships that help us theorize what such relationships might have looked like in practice within an ancient Mediterranean context. Sifting through the limited anecdotal evidence available allows the theoretical aspects of rabbinic expertise to come to the fore. The downfall is that one cannot make precise historical arguments that account for the different phases of rabbinic textual development. Part of my goal is to pull out the social dynamics of supporting expertise that would have mattered at any point to a legible group of rabbinic specialists. There are drawbacks to this approach—this is not a thorough study of every relevant textual reference nor a concrete portrait of rabbinic institutionalization or all instances of Jewish donations—but the book offers a thematic look at key aspects of expertise that employs imagination and theory to consider the possibilities behind the textual material.

Overview of the Book

The first chapter introduces the rabbis of Roman Palestine in the years following the Jewish revolts and provides a survey of their socialization as an expert group. Literate Jewish men participated in a shared social life and in so doing internalized the behaviors, ways of thinking, and conceptual language of the emerging rabbinic domain of knowledge. They did not become "rabbis" overnight. Instead, their association with likeminded men constructed a distinct expertise that emerged around a new domain of knowledge. They developed a real set of skills, methods, and techniques that organized rabbinic knowledge into anthologized texts. These texts drew boundaries around knowledge of Torah through a linguistic repertoire of jargon that only specialized rabbinic experts could be taught. By knowing such jargon, they signaled to members within and outside the expert group that they belonged. Their expertise then required rabbis to use their skills in practical forms for clients because expertise is legitimated by an audience. I ultimately show that the rabbis shared a core piety with their Jewish clients that provided meaningful social recognition. In turn, this recognition legitimized the expert roles that rabbis sought to both create and fill.

After considering the formation of a rabbinic domain of expertise, the second chapter introduces the rabbinic cultivation of valuable friendships by focusing on one particular space: the dinner table. Dinner parties in the ancient Mediterranean were a means of sharing wealth and protection with one's friends. Yet these arrangements did not just linger over dinner. They formalized a network of guest-friendship that could be called upon to offer other services, such as donations, gifts, protection, or recommendations for civic positions, all of which made such relationships barely distinguishable from patronage. This chapter analyzes a series of anecdotal texts depicting rabbis at the dinner table or invited into the homes of wealthy Jews where rabbis performed their expertise in Torah. Whether grilling a guest on their Torah knowledge or examining their host's tithed foodstuff, I argue that they flexed their expertise in Torah in order to both solicit interest in their work and temper the associations of patronage at play. The dinner table proved an important place of socialization both within the rabbinic domain of expertise and external to it.

The next two chapters consider tangible donations from clients in the form of tithes and charity. Chapter three weaves together rarely analyzed accounts of rabbis receiving tithes and argues that these gifts should be understood as patronage-adjacent donations. Setting aside a tithe of the harvest in order to finance the services of temple personnel and royal administrators was common throughout the ancient Near East and functioned as a kind of obligatory tax necessary for the maintenance of cultic centers. However, following the Temple's destruction, members of wealthy priestly families joined with burgeoning rabbinic study circles, coming to embody the dual identities of priest and rabbi. Their relationship to the now-defunct Temple system was in question, specifically whether they were entitled to benefit from tithes. This chapter examines textual depictions of people giving tithes to priestly descendent rabbis and shows how Talmudic texts reframed the tithes for priests as donations for rabbinic expertise. I further argue that the logic of patronage inherent to these relationships was intentionally masked by the naming of the gift as a tithe within the text. When seen through the lens of donor networks, these texts portray a different kind of rabbi: one not at odds with the priestly establishment but benefiting from its patronage networks.

Chapter four examines the tension between financial support and rabbinic expertise, highlighting how rabbinic thought negotiated the conflict between receiving funding and maintaining expert epistemic autonomy. It highlights the challenges that emerge when funding both shapes and limits the kind of knowledge production possible, while also providing the recognition that justifies that production in the first place. I analyze the suspicion of unjust profit, potential accusations of corruption and bribery, and the direct encroachment upon expert autonomy that funding could facilitate. Even as the Torah was worth all the riches in the world, and by extension rabbis as its experts should be entitled to communal support, the risk of negative perceptions, invasive donors, and loss of credibility made some wary. The chapter assesses how rabbis reframed their funding under the umbrella of charity, deploying divine investment logic to deflect reciprocal expectations and attract even greater tangible investment. This reframing allowed rabbis to present themselves as conduits for donors' divine investments, thereby preventing them from being seen as indebted to their donors. If God would reward the donor for their divine investment, then the rabbi was off the hook.

The concluding chapter reflects upon how the social production of expertise relies heavily on public recognition and validation, often legitimated through financial support. This support not only enables the expert status but also emphasizes the credibility of their domain. At the same time, these relationships of mutual obligation entangle the expert in social relationships that intrude upon their autonomy. While one might assume that experts hold all the power because they possess knowledge that others do not, the expert is placed in the position of needing to persuade donors, clients, employers, and peers, thereby exchanging their autonomy for social and material recognition. Despite potential aversions to patronage, rabbinic experts engaged in financial relationships and developed rationales to balance the tension between resisting profit and acknowledging the social value of their intellectual worth.

This exploration into rabbis and their social circles aims to show that while recognition of rabbinic expertise did not necessarily translate into immediate and widespread rabbinic-influenced behavior among the Jewish population in Roman Galilee, everyday social interactions were vital sites where this rabbinic knowledge could be absorbed by those who came into contact with rabbis, eventually producing the sense of what it meant to belong to the rabbinic orbit. The effect of these physical interactions was to produce a specialized grammarian-inspired discourse that distinguished a legible group of experts and offered value to non-experts. In this way, ordinary Jews played an important role in the establishment of rabbis as religious experts, directly shaping the domain of knowledge from which they were technically excluded.

1

Socialization and Piety of Rabbinic Expertise

RABBI YEHOSHUA once traveled to visit the famed Rabbi Yoḥanan ben Zakkai at Beror Hayil.[1] Yoḥanan was an early rabbinic sage who legend says played a pivotal role in the transformation of Galilee into a new spiritual center following the destruction of Jerusalem.[2] Eager to speak with his former teacher, Yehoshua greeted Yoḥanan from the street as townspeople observed the joyous reunion. These bystanders, perhaps simply eager to share with their neighbors, or, as rabbinic authors would have us believe, to honor the esteemed sages, brought them figs.[3] The Tosefta recounts that this unexpected gift prompted a halakhic conundrum. Those traveling with Rabbi Yehoshua asked him, "Must we tithe these figs?"

This brief anecdote about two important rabbinic figures appears within a larger legal discussion about the permissibility of traveling donkey-drivers and merchants to eat untithed produce. Rabbi Yehoshua's travels present a case that is useful for the rabbinic authors to think with. "If we are going to spend the night, we are required to tithe," he instructs his companions. From here the anonymous redactors begin an extended discussion, probing the lengths and limits of this rule. We learn nothing more about Yehoshua's stay—the

1. T. Ma'sserot 2:1. For conjecture regarding the name of this location, see Kaminka, "R' Yohanan Ben Zakkai," 73, which relies upon Krauss's essay "Die Römischen Besatzungen in Palästina."

2. See M. Avot 2:8, which states that R. Yoḥanan learned from Hillel and Shammai. Most of his legend is preserved in much later collections. B. Gittin 56b; Lam. Rab. 1:5; *Avot de-Rabbi Natan* 4. He is said to have presided over a just court. Sifre Deut. 144; B. Sanhedrin 32b.

3. Y. Berakhot 2, 5c reports that figs were picked daily so that they would be harvested as soon as they ripened.

conversations that must have gone late into the night as these men reclined to dine, the reluctance Yehoshua might have felt when the time came for him to leave his elder teacher and return home. Those details rarely make it into rabbinic stories. But this brief glimpse into the ordinary moments of gift and friendship illuminate how rabbinic expertise was enacted through everyday social relationships. The travel companions do not learn this directive seated within a study house or poring over a scroll, but while standing dust-covered and weary from their travels, as the alluring scent of figs waft from the baskets of the gazing bystanders.

This story illustrates a recurring textual motif. Rabbinic literature recounts the travels of rabbis to each other's homes, their gatherings with friends, occasions of passing one another on the street, or meeting in a local bathhouse. Whenever rabbinic texts bother to share these windows into everyday life, they are typically accompanied by a rabbinic ruling or debate that allegedly arose from these situations. This makes sense because the purpose of rabbinic literature is to record rabbinic knowledge rather than offer detailed biographies of these men.[4] Everyday anecdotes punctuate an impressive array of teachings that span generations. Yet while not the primary textual focus, I propose these everyday encounters offer a unique perspective on the relational dynamics that were crucial to the development of rabbinic expertise. The specific encounters recorded in these texts may not have occurred exactly as described, or at all, but they reveal the spontaneous, circumstantial, and unprompted scenarios rooted in everyday life that sparked the fount of rabbinic thought.

This chapter explores the development of a legible group of rabbinic experts through a process of socialization. It underscores expertise as a relational process, an insight drawn from expertise studies, which evaluates the things that people do to enact expertise rather than the knowledge that they possess. The Sifre Devarim, a rabbinic book of midrash on Deuteronomy, resonates with this perspective: "If one merely learned Torah, he has fulfilled one commandment; if he learned and observed what he has learned, he has fulfilled two commandments; if he learned, observed, and performed, there is no one better."[5] This dictum hints at the way Torah expertise encompasses something people do. Taking such doing seriously as a theoretical frame illuminates

4. On the difficulties of deriving rabbinic biographies from Talmudic source material, see Neusner, *Development of a Legend* and *Eliezer ben Hyrcanus*; Green, "What's in a Name?"

5. Sifre Deut. 48:13.

how rabbis became intimate with a distinct way of knowing and learned to communicate that familiarity to those in their social vicinity.[6]

I draw from the work of sociologists Harry Collins and Robert Evans, who argue that an important and underexamined aspect of expertise is social immersion in a specialized community.[7] This immersion enables individuals to gain knowledge, skills, and firsthand experience, as well as to internalize the norms and expectations of a specialist group. Collins and Evans call this affective knowledge "interactional expertise" because it is a kind of expertise learned through social interaction.[8] The expert internalizes the tacit knowledge and intuition that informs *how* they contribute expertise. They learn the jargon, mannerisms, etiquette, and bodily demeanor that signifies their legibility as experts. This kind of expertise is not acquired through the mastery of propositional knowledge but from socialization with other people.[9] Where Collins and Evans aim to intervene in the philosophical debates about language and computers, I intend to examine how socialization played an important role in the formation of a distinctively rabbinic interactional expertise that went beyond mere knowledge acquisition.

I begin by situating the emergence of rabbis within a period of Roman provincialization. These men made their homes in Roman Galilee and formed friendships with others who shared their commitment to keeping Torah traditions alive in a landscape where competition between would-be experts was high and claims to authority weak.[10] Certain questions were particularly salient in this period: who qualifies as a Jewish religious expert and why? What should be the relationship between Jewish experts, civic authorities, and the

6. H. Collins, *Tacit and Explicit Knowledge*, 133. Neusner in "The Phenomenon of the Rabbi in Late Antiquity" argued that "sainthood was achieved through study of Torah and imitation of the master" (8), which hinted at the important role of imitation in the formation of the rabbinic subject. Fraade, *From Tradition to Commentary* discusses the role of commentary in the formation of a collective self-understanding of a distinct class of sages.

7. Collins and Evans, "A Sociological/Philosophical Perspective," 26.

8. Collins and Evans, *Rethinking Expertise*, 24. Collins and Evans, "A Sociological/Philosophical Perspective," 24.

9. This is different from saying that Torah knowledge was also meant to be practiced, an important point that Hezser makes in "Rabbis and the Image of the Intellectual," 173. Where Hezser emphasizes that ancient rabbis acquired both intellectual and physical mastery of rabbinic instruction, I am making a different point about expertise outside of intellectual knowledge possession.

10. Eyal argues that once the number of contenders for expertise increases and claims are weakened, a crisis of expertise ensues. Eyal, "Expertise," 1, and *Crisis of Expertise*.

imperial state? What are the implications of specific interpretations and applications of Torah? Who is accountable for these outcomes? Torah scholars already conversant with pietistic movements that marked the turn of the century responded to the impact of Roman provincialization by shaping an emergent domain of rabbinic knowledge that revolutionized Jewish approaches to these questions.

I then examine the interactional expertise that developed within the rabbinic domain. Domains of knowledge represent fields or scopes of practice that require affiliation with a specialized group for access.[11] For instance, medicine encompasses various fields that focus on specific applications, questions, and regulatory aims, requiring specialized training and credentialization before medical experts can practice within them. Likewise, rabbinic expertise in Torah offered fields of unique specialty requiring apprenticeship.[12] This apprenticeship involved not just transmitting the knowledge of Torah and rabbinic teachings but also socializing students into a way of knowing that distinguished them as experts. This way of knowing I call "grammarian piety" because it was animated by specialist grammarian-inspired methods, concerned with atomizing and excerpting texts in order to produce novel knowledge about Torah and its application. This scrutiny of texts was not just a textual exercise but it was a means of exercising devotion. The rabbis saw Torah study as the supreme act of piety, and one that they were uniquely positioned to pursue.[13] They possessed specialized skills to work with Jewish texts so as to produce new interpretive meaning that then authorized their work. The effect of this process was to produce a form of piety that only members of their specialized group were authorized to attain but whose application could theoretically benefit all.

The formation of a specialized group did not mean that only rabbis had access to Torah knowledge. In fact, any Jew could theoretically access Torah, and rabbinic literature occasionally mentions such individuals expressing their own exegetical opinions or serving as children's teachers, judges, and scribes.[14]

11. Watson, *Expertise*, xix.

12. Lapin has relatedly argued that the rabbis emerged as "champions of a 'discursive practice,'" which was "a specialized way of speaking about certain topics (discourse) that is closely tied to the appropriation or manipulation of power on the level of government, institution, and through a specialized way of controlling behavior, the body itself." *Early Rabbinic Civil Law*, 33.

13. Satlow, "'And on the Earth You Shall Sleep.'"

14. The biblical notion of a "kingdom of priests" (Exod. 19:6) suggests that all people of Israel have a claim to the covenant. See Himmelfarb, "'A Kingdom of Priests.'" Novick explains how

What the rabbinic domain introduced was a distinct form of access: a particular form of expertise and hermeneutics (grammarian), forms of behavior (piety), and an emergent community (interaction). Together these parts constructed the boundary of rabbinic expertise that distinguished those who knew Torah in a "rabbinic way" from those who did not. While there is a tendency in modern scholarship to view the rabbinic domain as elitist, I contend that the perceived insularity depicted within these sources was a fundamental part of the constructed boundaries of expertise projected in rabbinic literature.[15] This does not mean that gender, wealth, and power were not social factors in gatekeeping who had access to the specialist group. Rather, I aim to demonstrate that what is frequently criticized as elitism is then subsequently invoked in scholarship to claim that rabbis showed little concern for other Jews, except when they sought to exercise communal authority.[16] This line of thinking tends to isolate rabbis from their communities rather than recognizing the social construction for what it truly is.

I conclude the chapter by situating rabbinic expertise alongside others who shared an investment in Torah. The synagogue, for example, already existed as a sacred institution with communal Torah reading, homiletic sermons, and habits of prayer, to say nothing of ornamental religious art and architecture.[17] Evidence for charitable activities associated with the synagogue speak to a community investment in behaviors and spaces meaningful for Jewish piety.[18] In one Talmudic text, rabbinic expertise is framed as part of this larger setting, linking the synagogue with rabbinic houses of study (*betei midrash*): "Rabbi Jeremiah in the name of Rabbi Abbahu: 'Seek the LORD where He is to be found' (Isa. 55:6).

---

the notion of covenant served as an important frame for maintaining the integrity of collective entities, such as the people of Israel, within rabbinic legal frameworks. Novick, "Covenant and Community." See Hezser, *Social Structure of the Rabbinic Movement*, 467–89 for an overview of potential rabbinic competitors.

15. For example, Schofer, *Making of a Sage*, 22.

16. The framing of rabbis as seeking authority appears even when the conclusion is that such attempts were largely unsuccessful. See Goodman, *State and Society in Roman Galilee*, 93–111; S. J. Cohen, "Place of the Rabbi in Jewish Society," 164.

17. Fine, *This Holy Place*; Levine, *Ancient Synagogue*; Kasher, "Synagogues"; Runesson, *Origins of the Synagogue*, 192–93. On the diachronic development of rabbis in synagogues, see Millar, "Inscriptions, Synagogues and Rabbis"; Levine, "Synagogue Art"; P. Alexander, "Rabbis and Their Rivals." Y. Megillah 3:1, 738 claims there were 480 synagogues in Jerusalem during the reign of Vespasian. On this source see Meyers and Fine, "Ancient Synagogues," 9.

18. On synagogues and hospitality, see Gardner, *Origins*, 104–3. For inscriptions that speak to charity, see Satlow, "'Fruit,'" 257.

Where is He to be found? In synagogues and houses of study. 'Call on Him when He is close' (Isa. 55:6). Where is He close? In synagogues and houses of study."[19] To be sure, the relationship between rabbis and the synagogue was not always easy and underwent diachronic development as rabbis began to take greater interest in roles as homilists or communal stewards.[20] But the distance between the rabbinic pietistic group and the synagogue was not vast; as Stuart Miller argues, it is likely that synagogue officials and those in attendance "would have been considerably closer" to the rabbinic class.[21] Rabbinic expertise was integrated within an already existing landscape of Jewish piety.

While foundational textual knowledge was crucial to the rabbinic domain, rabbinic expertise emerged through ongoing engagement with other stakeholders of Torah, both rabbinic and otherwise.[22] The nature of articulating a specialist epistemic community meant there would be a difference in how rabbis and non-rabbinic Jews interacted with Torah. Experts are by definition expert because they have access to a knowledge domain that others do not.[23] Even though the piety of rabbinic grammarians was exclusive, distinguishing them as a specialist group, it shared a kinship with the piety of other Jews. Those who cared about Torah would not have readily ignored rabbinic figures, even if this recognition did not necessarily translate into widespread and immediate adherence to rabbinic teaching. We may be skeptical of the realia behind the Tosefta's townspeople who shared their figs with Rabbis Yehoshua and Yoḥanan ben Zakkai, attributing the anecdote to rabbinic wishful thinking. But the rabbis had more in common with their Jewish neighbors than

19. Y. Berakhot 5:1, 37b. See also Y. Megillah 3:4, 74a. Fine, "'Their Faces Shine'."

20. On the diachronic development of rabbinic influence in synagogues, see P. Alexander, "Rabbis and their Rivals," 65–66; Millar, "Inscriptions, Synagogues and Rabbis"; Z. Weiss, "Actors and Theaters, Rabbis and Synagogues." On rabbinic and synagogue liturgy, see Langer, "Rabbis, Nonrabbis, and Synagogues." On the pagan imagery in some synagogues that might conflict with the rabbinic ethos, see Miller, "'Epigraphical' Rabbis, Helios, and Psalm 19." Porton contends that rabbinic homilists emerged much later ("The Rabbinic Sermon").

21. Miller, *Sages and Commoners*, 218.

22. The assumption that rabbinic expertise was dependent upon their possession of Jewish knowledge traditions is persistent through scholarship. Urbach, for example, argued that "the force" of a rabbi's authority "derived first and foremost from his knowledge of the Torah" ("Talmudic Sage," 121). More recently, Hezser suggested that rabbis fit within a pattern of ancient intellectuals who possess "traditional knowledge" and expand upon it with creative production ("Rabbis and the Image," 173). The explanatory focus remains upon expertise defined as the knowledge rabbis possessed and used, rather than upon relational dynamics.

23. Watson, *Expertise*.

not.[24] This chapter explores how the enactment of rabbinic expertise drew boundaries while at the same time drawing upon an affective commitment to the shared cultural object of Torah.

The Impact of Imperialism upon Jewish Piety

The rabbis emerged in the wake of several cataclysms. A series of revolts, the first resulting in the destruction of the Temple in 70 CE and the final ending with the displacement of Jews from Judaea in 135 CE, had crushed hope of restoring Jewish autonomy in the region.[25] The Roman suppression of Jewish unrest had major demographic ramifications. Josephus and Tacitus report massive casualties during the First Jewish Revolt (66–73 CE), with some modern scholars speculating that up to one-third of the Jewish population died or were taken captive during the conflicts.[26] Even if these reports are exaggerated, archaeological evidence confirms significant destruction and devastation.[27] Josephus reports that roughly 97,000 people were taken captive.[28] Others likely fled. Half a century later, during the Bar Kokhba Revolt (132–135 CE), there were again massive casualties while much of the remaining Jewish population was evicted from the district of Judaea.[29] Writing of the aftermath, Cassius Dio relates that "practically all of Judaea was made desolate."[30] The land became

24. For an overview of the centrality of Torah to many Jews in the Second Temple period, see J. Collins, *Invention of Judaism*. For specific locales, see Ilan, "Torah of the Jews of Ancient Rome"; Himmelfarb, "Torah between Athens and Jerusalem"; Altmann, "Significance of the Divine Torah."

25. On the finality of these revolts and the costs of provincialization, see S. Schwartz, "Impact of the Jewish Rebellions," 234–52.

26. Josephus, *J.W.* 6.430; Tacitus, *Hist.* 5.8–12. Schäfer, *History of the Jews*, 131.

27. See Berlin and Overman, *First Jewish Revolt*, for analysis of how archaeological evidence corroborates and complicates Josephus's narrative of casualties and destruction. For example, see the evidence from Yodefat in Avshalom-Gorni and Getzov, "Phoenicians and Jews," 74; and Aviam, "Yodefat/Jotapata," 133.

28. Josephus, *J.W.* 6.4220–1, 9.3. I agree with Schwartz's argument that Josephus's count of 97,000 captives is likely more accurate than not because captives were viewed as a commodity to be counted. S. Schwartz, "Impact of the Jewish Rebellions," 144. On resettlement after revolt, see Zissu, "Rural Settlement," and R. Adler, "Archaeology of Purity," 63–65 on *mikvaot* (ritual baths) in Judaea. On the reported evictions of Jewish inhabitants, see Eusebius, *HE*, 4:6. See Mor, *The Second Jewish Revolt*, 328 for caution about these numbers.

29. Cassius Dio estimates, though likely exaggerated, 580,000 (*Roman History*, 69.14).

30. Cassius Dio, 69.14.1–2.

the property of the empire, and Jewish farmers became tenant laborers with heavy rent.[31]

The physical landscape was also radically altered. Roman bathhouses, markets, stadiums, and pagan temples were constructed, even in predominately Jewish cities. In Jerusalem the emperor Hadrian constructed the new city of Aelia Capitolina (*Aelius*, his family name, and *Capitolina* for the Capitoline triad of Jupiter, Juno, and Minerva) from the war-torn ruins.[32] He turned the city into a typical Roman town, even raising a temple to Jupiter upon the ash of the former temple mount.[33] Widespread constructions of roads were carved into the countryside, creating a grid of imperial military traffic.[34] Cities adopted Roman municipal coinage, displaying the bronzed image of the emperor rather than the typical Jewish iconography of pomegranates, *lulavim* and *etrogim*, and date palms.[35]

These changes were introduced into a landscape already heavily marked with signs emphasizing Roman command. Roman gods had taken their place on monumental coinage and statues ever since the arrival of Roman imperialism in Judaea (63 BCE). When the Roman statesman Gabinius refounded Beth Shean (Scythopolis) as a Roman city in 57 BCE, for example, newly minted coins displayed the visage of the city's so-called founding triad, Dionysus, Zeus, and Tyche.[36] The agora's eastern temple, constructed later in the first century CE, was dedicated to the goddess Demeter and her daughter Persephone.[37] With the imperial cult came the Roman calendar and public festivals celebrating key moments of Rome's history that infused the temporal landscape with the ideology of a collective Roman past.[38] This posed a direct challenge to

31. Josephus, *J.W.* 7.216–17. See Safrai, *Economy of Roman Palestine*, 358–69, for the structure and production of private farming systems.

32. The dating for exactly when this reconstruction began is debated, but Cassius Dio links it to Hadrian's 130 CE grand tour of the eastern part of the Roman Empire. On the Roman character of the new city, see Eck, "Die Colonia Aelia Capitolina," 129–39.

33. Cassius Dio, *Roman History* 69.12.

34. Isaac, *Limits of Empire*, 107–12; Isaac and Roll, "Legio II Traiana," 201–3; See Oppenheimer, "Jewish Community," 62–63; Pucci Ben Zeev, "New Insights."

35. S. Schwartz, "Impact of the Jewish Rebellion," 249. On Jewish iconography, see Goodman, "Coinage and Identity," 163–66; Hendin, "Current Viewpoints."

36. Mazor, "Imperial Cult in the Decapolis," 357. On the Jewish inhabitants of the city, see 2 Macc. 12:30 and Josephus, *B.J.* 2.466–76, 7.365. On the city's history, see Avi-Yonah, "Scythopolis," 123–34.

37. Mazor, "Imperial Cult in the Decapolis," 357.

38. On the rabbinic resistance to Roman calendars, see Gribetz, *Time and Difference*.

certain forms of local Jewish custom, only amplified by the brutality of imperial conquest. An early rabbinic source remarks that in Beth Shean non-Jews would adorn their shops on such holidays while Jews kept their shops bare.[39] While this rabbinic anecdote valorizes pious Jews resisting Roman cultural encroachment, the daily life for Jews in Beth Shean was certainly less neat.

To add insult to injury, Jews who continued to observe their ancestral customs had to pay two denarii per year as a replacement for the two-shekel Temple tax formerly disbursed to the Jerusalem Temple complex.[40] Perhaps as penalty for the role certain priestly families played during the First Jewish Revolt, the Romans saw fit to not only permanently decimate the central religious precinct of the Jews but to enact a tax penalty. This was a severe departure from the typical Roman practice of preserving the sacred sites that they inherited when conquering new provincial populations or, in the case of revolt, allowing the city to rebuild damaged temples and shrines.[41] In antiquity gods and men routinely interacted. The houses of those gods were respected for both their symbolic and economic function. Regular temple festivals and crowds engaging in acts of pious commerce contributed to a sense of cohesive cultural rhythm, facilitating exchange of animals, goods, prayers, and taxes on a routine calendar cycle.[42] Their proper cultic maintenance ensured divine support, even for imperial conquerors. One of the alleged transgressions that brought about the siege of Jerusalem recounted in later rabbinic storytelling was the cessation of sacrifices conducted in the emperor's honor.[43] Not only did Romans upend cult and commerce in the region, but the destruction devastated the house of the Jewish God.

39. M. Avodah Zarah 1:4.

40. Josephus, *J.W.* 7.218, and Cassius Dio, *Roman History* 66.7.2. This tax was paid until at least the mid-third century CE. Goodman, *Judaism in the Roman World*, 29. Josephus recounts the Roman perception that the Temple's priests had grown rich from offerings and used their wealth to mount the revolt. Evidence suggests that Emperor Domitian later extended this tax to include new groups of people and enforced it severely. Suetonius, *Dom.* 12.2. Gambash argues that the Romans largely associated the Judaean revolts with the Temple and priesthood because of the notable involvement of priestly families (*Rome and Provincial Resistance*, 158–61).

41. Gambash, *Rome and Provincial Resistance*, 162; Gross, "Hopeful Rebels and Anxious Romans," 500–501; Woolf, "Provincial Revolts in the Early Roman Empire."

42. For studies of the role of temples across the Roman empire, see Padilla Peralta, *Divine Institutions*. For participation in imperial cult as a sign of romanization, see Price, *Rituals and Power*, 78–100.

43. Lam. Rabbah 4:3; B. Gittin 56a.

Beyond the obvious displacement of human bodies and destruction of the Temple and homes, the remaking of the land and its surrounding districts into an independent Roman province had profound effects upon Jewish life in the region. No longer a minor district, leadership of the province was reorganized with a governor of first praetorian and then consular rank who brought with him a standing legion, transforming Jerusalem into a military colony.[44] The region's name was changed to Syria-Palaestina, and it joined the predominantly Jewish districts of Judaea, Samaria, Galilee, and Peraea into a larger provincial territory spanning Anatolia. More than imperial administrative reshuffling, Hannah Cotton describes the change as "suppressing the Jewish identity of the province."[45]

The area had been formerly recognized as an independent polity, both by Rome and by every prior imperial state for at least five centuries, when the Persians first established the province of Yehud in 539 BCE. But full annexation brought an end to the central Jewish political and cultic institutions affiliated with the state. The Torah of Moses and its priests and courts were no longer formally recognized by imperial authorities.[46] Instead, Roman courts could now oversee the adjudication of legal disputes, and Jews registered contracts and bills of sale with local civic authorities.[47] The priestly families who derived their status from the Temple's jurisdiction lost all authorizing claims to their class at the same time political power was wrested from the Judean leadership.

44. Schäfer, *History of the Jews*, 135; Cotton, "Impact of the Roman Army"; Eck, *Rom und die Provinz Iudaea/Syria Palaestina*. The exact date for the consularis shift is not known, but Isaac and Roll suggest that a second legion is already attested in 120 CE ("Legio II Traiana," 131–32). See also Avi-Yonah, "When Did Judea Become a Consular Province?"

45. Cotton, "Some Aspects of the Roman Administration," 81. Geiger goes so far as to theorize that the Greek-speaking inhabitants of Palestine petitioned the name change ("The Bar-Kokhba Revolt").

46. See Berthelot, *Jews and Their Roman Rivals*, 257–339 for the competition between Torah and Roman law. Berthelot argues that the imposition of Roman law was one of the factors that made this period, compared with earlier imperial periods, significantly different for Jews.

47. On the influence of Roman law within provincial territories, see Czajkowski and Eckhardt, "Law, Status and Agency"; and Czajkowski, *Localized Law*, on the evidence of the Babatha archive. Czajkowski argues that the Judean population was distinctly slow to adopt Roman legal options, in part due to the all-encompassing nature of Torah as a legal system ("Law and Romanization in Judaea"). On the challenges of Roman law for Jews, see Goodman, *State and Society*, 155–71; J. Collins, "Law in the Late Second Temple Period"; and Berthelot, *Jews and Their Roman Rivals*, 257–339.

Rome treated the Jewish population with uncharacteristic brutality, intent on memorializing their utter defeat through celebratory coins and monuments.[48] Provincialization picked up with swift, crushing speed, but the Jews were not easily granted entrance. Gil Gambash argues that Jews were treated "as foreign enemies of the empire" in the immediate years after revolt.[49] Some Jews rallied around ideas of resistance, conjuring apocalyptic notions of messianism and eschatological victory over Rome, but those efforts were quashed in total.[50] For the majority of Jews in the region, survival was more palatable than resistance. The Jews in Sepphoris, for example, refused to join the revolts entirely, and renamed themselves first *Eirenopolis* ("city of peace") and then *Diocaesarea* ("God of Caesar"), likely in a bid to reassure the Romans of their compliance.[51] Jews adjusted to imperial constraints and went about their lives, even if alienation and resentment lingered, because what else could they do? The total triumph of Rome meant that whatever Jewish life was, or had been, would be perpetually inflected by the imperial norm going forward.

The long first century of the Common Era (approximately 63 BCE to 135 CE) represented the confluence of several vectors that introduced precarity for Jews living in Roman Palestine.[52] It was not just the destruction of the Temple alone, or the reorganization of the province, or any one revolt or charismatic personality, but a convergence of all of these things and more that led to a protracted moment of change. The rabbis appear within our sources

48. Gambash argues that these acts of commemoration treat the Jews as barbarians and foreigners newly conquered, when in reality they were an already annexed part of the empire (*Rome and Provincial Resistance*, 154–57, 162). Relatedly, Gross has argued that both rebels and Romans understood that the stakes were high ("Hopeful Rebels and Anxious Romans"). See also Millar, *Rome, The Greek World, and the East*, 102.

49. Gambash, *Rome and Provincial Resistance*, 144.

50. Pucci Ben Zeev, *Diaspora Judaism in Turmoil*, 128–42; Applebaum, *Jews and Greeks*, 242–60. On the book of Revelation as resistance to Rome, see Emanuel, *Humor, Resistance, and Jewish Cultural Persistence*.

51. S. Schwartz, *Ancient Jews*, 81–82, and "Impact of the Jewish Rebellions," 252. On the unique status of Sepphoris, see Miller, "Intercity Relations in Roman Palestine"; and Meyers, "Sepphoris."

52. Eyal likens a crisis of expertise to a vortex supplied with energy from several different engines whose interaction and mutual amplification locks each other into a self-sustaining circular movement. Any of these engines alone could not cause an extended crisis, but their confluence generates the spark of social uncertainty. Eyal, "Response to Riccardo Emilio Chesta's 'What Is Critical?'"

toward the end of this distinct period, raising the question of how to make sense of their rise in light of Roman imperialism.[53]

First, what impact did these changes have upon Jewish practice and belief?[54] Where some scholars see the Temple's destruction as absolute "shattering" of a Jewish religious system, others see a moment of "radical hope" where Jews could recall former loss and look toward a future of restoration.[55] The disruption of the priesthood and Temple cult could signal the "death" of pre-70 CE Jewish identity, a "deep crisis of faith," or represent a momentary sad event that Jews could withstand.[56] Whether orienting around 70 CE as a "watershed" moment or a hard transition between Second- and post-Temple Judaism, these perspectives share the assumption that Judaism is a *something* that could be shattered, salvaged, or maintained. Yet herein lies the problem. Judaism is not like a vase, whose shards might litter the floor in the hands of a clumsy child, or whose cracks the masters of kintsugi might mend, or whose visage requires devoted polishing to shine. Judaism is not an object, but rather a term describing patterns of thought and behavior linked to a network of associations shared by communities of people who varied in their understandings of what made them Jews.[57] These patterns follow certain recurring routines, but they also converge in meaningful ways, whether as a result of traumatic national events or because people are complex.

53. See Rosen-Zvi's "Rabbis and Romanization" review of Hayim Lapin's *Rabbis as Romans* for the stakes of this question.

54. For a survey, see Klawans, "Imagining Judaism after 70 CE." See this recent edited volume for a range of perspectives, Schwartz and Weiss, *Was 70 CE a Watershed in Jewish History?*

55. S. Schwartz, *Imperialism and Jewish Society*, 175; and Neusner, *First Century Judaism in Crisis*; contra: Klawans, *Josephus and the Theologies of Ancient Judaism*; and Najman, *Losing the Temple*.

56. Schremer, *Brothers Estranged*, 29.

57. Here I draw from Taves, *Religious Experience Reconsidered*, to shift from assumptions of religious experience as a fixed and stable thing to instead consider how people attribute meaning toward their thoughts and behaviors. This also reframes religion as a category that can be useful for our study of the ancient world, even as recent scholars have insisted that the term "religion" is shaped by modernity (Nongbri, *Before Religion*; Barton and Boyarin, *Imagine No Religion*). Yet just because a word is absent from a given language does not render the concept void of utility. We can define our terms with awareness of the distance between modern formulations of ideas and our ancient sources while still deploying the category because it helps establish a reference point. In the case of Jews, if there is no religion in antiquity, then there can be no Jewish religion, which severs ancient Jews from a range of pietistic expression whose patterns are legible as religious.

When the Romans prevailed following the Great Revolt, the Jerusalem cult with its institutions of temple and priesthood ceased to exist as an organizing principle. This means that much of the application of Torah as understood at the time was no longer operative. No more pilgrimage festivals, collection of tithes, or sacrificial atonement.[58] Temple priests no longer made functional sense if there was no cultic ground for them to stand upon. When the Romans disintegrated Judaean society, those Jewish leaders at the helm were displaced. The authority of their office within the district was disrupted by the imposition of Roman bureaucracy. Not only that, but the sheer loss of numbers due to death, enslavement, and displacement on such a large scale irrevocably changed the demography of the Jewish public. The landscape of Jewish life would have been profoundly impacted by the totality of these changes in ways that we cannot neatly parse but should in no way discount.

At the same time, Roman imperialism also coincided with a period of intense pietistic affiliation. The decades leading up to the First Jewish Revolt are commonly referred to as the era of "sectarian Judaism" due to the prevalence of formal groups of literate men, such as Pharisees and Sadducees, who championed a range of holiness projects driven by different modes of piety.[59] The Sadducees were mostly comprised of high-priestly families whose focus was on the Temple and its priesthood.[60] The Pharisees were Torah scholars and members of priestly families—as most scribes were—who promoted the inclusion of laypeople in Temple and purity ritual.[61] The Pharisees were not antagonistic to the priesthood, but instead defended their claim as stewards of extra-priestly practices, and according to Josephus were widely acclaimed throughout the populace.[62] Though both groups were eventually marginalized due to the strategic efforts of the client king Herod to diminish their influence,

58. On atonement, see Klawans, *Purity, Sacrifice, and the Temple.*

59. For a survey of archaeological evidence of the holiness projects in the first century BCE, see Y. Adler, *Origins of Judaism.*

60. Regev, "Flourishing Before the Crisis," 53–54; Magness, "Sectarianism before and after 70 CE."

61. Regev, "Flourishing Before the Crisis," 55–57. Josephus, *Ant.* 18.1:2–4. See also Josephus, *J.W.* 2.119–66 and *Ant.* 13.171–73, 18.12–20.

62. Josephus, *Ant.* 18.1:2–4. Fraade, "'They Shall Teach Your Statues to Jacob.'" Sussman argued that their lenient rulings invited wider participation in Jewish ritual purity ("History of Halakha and the Dead Sea Scrolls," 196). Noam has expanded upon Sussman's observations by focusing on corpse impurity as an area of particular leniency in both Pharisaic and later rabbinic teachings (*From Qumran to the Rabbinic Revolution*).

at the height of their prestige, members of these groups held significant power within Jerusalem at a time of rising interest in Jewish holiness projects.[63]

First-century Jerusalem was known as "the most famous of the cities of the East," according to Pliny the Elder,[64] in part because Herod was renovating and expanding the Temple complex, as well as his palaces. With these renovations came an influx of economic prosperity and pietistic affiliation.[65] Different groups participated in their own holiness projects that capitalized upon the broader interest in Jewish piety and its focal point: the Temple. The New Testament records clashes between the Pharisees and Sadducees, as well as with Jesus and the followers of his own pietistic movement over Torah debates.[66] The Essenes, another reported sect of highly introversionist tendencies, rejected Jerusalem Temple society altogether in favor of their close-knit communities.[67] While these groups advocated different interpretive positions, they shared what Seth Schwartz has identified as an "ideological core."[68] Torah and Temple animated their concerns.[69] Even the Essenes who were not authorized by the Jerusalem authorities based their identity on their rejection of that institution and championed their own version of a priesthood.[70]

The rabbis came into self-consciousness amid immense national trauma but also intense pietistic affiliation. They were a small professional class of

63. S. Schwartz, *Imperialism and Jewish Society*, 45. They were part of the legal establishment of Judaea under the Hasmonean dynasty. See S. Schwartz, *Ancient Jews*, 66–70; Regev, "Hasmoneans' Self-Image"; Sanders, *Judaism*, 497–708. See Sanders, *Judaism*, for an overview of these groups. For the significance of purity in the Second Temple period, see Furstenberg, *Purity and Identity in Ancient Judaism*.

64. Pliny, *Nat. Hist.* 5:70.

65. S. Schwartz, *Imperialism and Jewish Society*, 45–48.

66. Matt. 5:20, 9, and 23; Luke 11–12. It should be noted that much of these texts were authored after the destruction of Jerusalem in 70 CE. On their differences, see Regev, "The Sadducees, The Pharisees, and the Sacred." On Jesus as part of intra-Jewish interpretive debates, see Furstenberg, "Jesus against the Laws of the Pharisees" and "Defilement Penetrating the Body."

67. Vermes and Goodman, *Essenes according to the Classical Sources*. On the relationship of the Essenes to Qumran, see Atkinson and Magness, "Josephus's Essenes and the Qumran Community."

68. S. Schwartz contends that "the three main sects are evidence not simply of Judaism's diversity but also of the power of its ideological mainstream" (*Imperialism and Jewish Society*, 49).

69. S. Schwartz, 74.

70. See, for example the Community Rule scroll and Hempel, "Interpretive Authority" on the role of priests therein. For a survey, see Fabry, "Priests at Qumran"; and Goodman, "Qumran Sectarians."

men, composed, at least in part, of a remnant of Judaean intelligentsia (priests, scribes, and Pharisees) who largely fled to Galilee following the destruction and restructuring of the province under Rome.[71] They were conversant with the religious learning and social status that various Jewish groups had achieved under the height of Judaean pietistic fervor. How these men came to associate with each other as "rabbis"—that is, as authoritative post-Temple scholars of ancestral Jewish traditions who shared distinct hermeneutical methods—is not entirely known. Their own myth of origins recounted several centuries later describes a convening of sages at the city of Yavneh.[72] Through an alleged agreement between Rabbi Yoḥanan and the Roman emperor Vespasian, these men met intent upon saving the Torah from obsolescence following the Temple's destruction.[73] It is more likely, however, that the things they already had in common facilitated their connection.[74] These were men who possessed technical skills that did not arise in a vacuum. They were participants in already existing Jewish holiness projects.

What began as loose social connections between men of similar rank, literacy, and ideological investment began to cohere into a group of some kind, though its precise early contours remain elusive. They became largely known to us as "the rabbis" through the production of texts that comprise the canon of rabbinic literature, but throughout the first through fifth centuries CE during that textual formation, these men were hardly a monolithic group. Catherine Hezser has offered the most convincing assessment to date, arguing that informal networks formed between circles of individual sages and their

71. Classical scholarship argued that the rabbis were the heirs to the Pharisees because the Pharisees disappeared and the rabbis appeared in our sources around the time of the destruction of Roman Judaea. This view has been largely complicated, in part because the rabbis never identify themselves as former Pharisees (compare to the apostle Paul in Phil. 3 and Acts 22:2–5). For more, see Neusner, *Rabbinic Traditions about the Pharisees*; Reed, "When Did Rabbis Become Pharisees?"; Furstenberg, "'We Rail Against You, Pharisees,'" 283–311; Schremer, "Sages in Palestinian Jewish Society," 553–81.

72. See S. J. Cohen, "Significance of Yavneh"; Shemesh, *Halakhah in the Making*; Hezser, "Uncertain Symbol."

73. T. Eduyyot 1:1; B. Gittin 56a–b.

74. Noam has convincingly demonstrated that early rabbinic legislation shared methods and principles with earlier texts found at Qumran. Noam, "Emergence of Rabbinic Culture," and *From Qumran to the Rabbinic Revolution*. See also the work of Shemesh, *Halakhah in the Making*, who advocates a developmental model of halakhah; J. Baumgarten, "Tannaitic Halakhah and Qumran"; and Halivni, "Early Period of Halakhic Midrash."

students.[75] These rabbinic networks were neither centralized nor unified, leading some scholars to move away from referring to these men as a singular "movement." Stuart Miller, for example, has recently insisted that the term implies "an organizational level and institutionalization that does not quite fit what is being described here."[76]

Despite the decentralization of rabbinic Torah scholars and relatively minimal institutional infrastructure, I maintain that the intentional gatherings of rabbinic men in this period produced a discernibly new expertise. Anthropologist E. Summerson Carr argues that to be socialized as an expert involves "establishing a deliberate stance in relation to a set of culturally valued or valuable objects" that forms an "expert register" or a way of speaking that is recognized as "a special kind of knowledge."[77] These men met intentionally to discuss and debate the application of Torah and from this socialization emerged not only distinctive methods of textual interpretation but an "expert register," or the jargon, mannerisms, and behaviors that marked inclusion within an emerging specialist group.[78] They learned to think and act in accordance with a specific way of knowing that set them apart from non-rabbinic Jews who might be functioning in related legal and ritual roles but who lacked facility with this specialist discourse.[79]

The emergence of this deliberate rabbinic posture has been attributed to various factors: whether as a result of the Temple's destruction, internal Jewish debates, the expansion of universal Roman citizenship in 212 CE, or driven by the immersion of a Roman legal landscape with which to inspire rabbinic legislation.[80] I do not aim to resolve this particular debate as it is likely no one factor can carry all explanatory power. Rather, I aim to trace the consequence of this deliberate rabbinic posture. Students of rabbinic teachers learned not just to interpret and engage Torah-centered teachings but also absorbed how to frame their knowledge as rabbinically expert. In other words, rabbinic students learned not just *what* to say when representing objects of Torah knowledge but *how* to say it as well.[81]

75. Hezser, *Social Structure of the Rabbinic Movement*, 492.

76. Miller, *Sages and Commoners*, 447n.2.

77. Carr, "Enactments of Expertise, 20.

78. Jaffee, *Torah in the Mouth*; Schofer, *Making of a Sage*. For initial numbers, see Levine, *Rabbinic Class*, 66–69; and Lapin's analysis in *Rabbis as Romans*, 64–67.

79. See Furstenberg, "Rabbinic Movement," 25.

80. On this latter and newer intervention, see Furstenberg, "Rabbinic Movement," and the critical responses by Czajkowski, "Need for Rabbinic *Nomikoi*"; Rosen-Zvi, "Rabbis as *Nomikoi*?"; and Dohrmann, "Roman Civil Jurisdiction."

81. Carr, "Enactment of Expertise," 21.

This legibility of how was undoubtedly shaped by the imperial restructuring of the province. Rabbis could not count on former claims of expert authority, such as priestly lineage, which many of the early rabbis in fact held, nor could they easily insert themselves into imposing Roman structures of legal expertise.[82] Ishay Rosen-Zvi convincingly argues that the rabbis articulated "an alternative empire" that rooted rabbinic legislation in everyday life in order to propose an alternative text to Rome.[83] This meant that while rabbinic literature might have rejected much of the Roman political system and imagined their parallel Torah-centered universe, they were responsive to how Jews might live Torah-oriented lives within its landscape.[84] An emerging specialist domain can claim expertise, but its spokespeople must still nurture buy-in. Rabbis sought to cultivate trust that their way of knowing was valuable amid a landscape of increased competition and a moment when central core values were challenged.

Rabbinic literature portrays its experts as pious stewards. Even in the absence of the Temple, they upheld the sanctity of the Torah. They neither completely disregarded the old Temple system nor perceived themselves as instigators of a new religious endeavor. On the contrary, they invested effort in remembering the Jewish past and situated their teachings as if seamlessly fitting within a counterfactual continuum.[85] The earliest rabbis especially envisioned the former Temple, legislated sacrificial rituals and tithes, and even discussed its maintenance and design after it had lost its basis in reality.[86] This was itself a political statement of Jewish resilience. To insist that life must go on as usual even when it is no longer functionally possible is a deliberate act.

82. Hezser, *Social Structure of the Rabbinic Movement*, 70–71. Hidary, "Rhetoric of Rabbinic Authority," 16; Dohrmann, "*Ad Similitudinem Arbitrorum*." Cf. Furstenberg, "Rabbinic Movement" to Rosen-Zvi, "Rabbis As *Nomikoi*?"; Dohrmann, "Roman Civil Jurisdiction, *Nezkikin*, and Rabbinic Professionalization"; and Czajkowski, "Need for Rabbinic *Nomikoi*."

83. Rosen-Zvi, "Rabbis and Romanization," especially 241–44. See the related argument in Halbertal, "History of Halakhah." Other scholars have demonstrated the ways rabbinic literature might reflect aspects of Roman law, which need not be displaced by Rosen-Zvi's insights. See Lapin, *Rabbis as Romans*; Bertholet, *Jews and Their Roman Rivals*; Dohrmann, "Boundaries of the Law."

84. Berkowitz, *Execution and Invention*; Dohrmann, "Manumission and Transformation"; and Rosen-Zvi, *Is the Mishnah a Roman Composition?*

85. See Cohn, "Affect and Ritual in the Mishnah" on the significance of Temple ritual to the rabbis.

86. See S. J. Cohen, "Rabbi in Second-Century Jewish Society," 922–90; and Rosen-Zvi, *Mishnaic Sotah Ritual*, 239–54. On the Temple in rabbinic thought, see Cohn, *Memory of the Temple*; Schumer, *Memory of the Temple*.

Jewish cultural survival was not self-evident in this period. Rabbis advocated that Torah, as a cultural object shared between Jews, could persist through interpretation and study. Writing about the deliberate stance of rabbinic midrash, for example, Rosen-Zvi writes, "The promises written in the Torah bec[a]me a tool for survival in the bleak present."[87] Rabbinic literature animates with both a total fixation upon Torah and artificial indifference to Roman imperialism that rings sharply against the realities of the province.[88]

Much of rabbinic literature would be arguably new and innovative, but it was entrenched in the assumption that rabbis were dealing with culturally significant objects, the value of which were self-evident to other Jews. As Rabbi Hananiah ben Akashia stated, "The Holy Blessed One, desired to make Israel worthy, therefore He gave them much Torah and many commandments."[89] This statement can be read as aspirational, attempting to coerce other Jews into a rabbinic pietistic movement, but it can also be read as a meaningful declaration that all Jews share in a cultural object that persisted. Of course, Jews in this period would have different senses of what that meant, but the rabbis were not the only ones who shared pietistic affiliations or a connection to Torah. Kimberley Czajkowski, for example, argues that the Judean population was distinctly slow to adopt Roman legal options, in part due to the all-encompassing nature of Torah as a legal system.[90] The failure to acknowledge the Roman legal apparatus as legitimate marked the silent political stance of the rabbinic authors. Early rabbis not only built their internal measures of expertise but linked the value of their knowledge to a persistent Jewish piety amid a landscape of loss.

Socialization of Grammarian Piety and Rabbinic Interactional Expertise

The earliest rabbis called themselves "sages" (*hakhamim*) and viewed themselves as part of a lineage of Torah scholars stretching back to Moses at Mount Sinai.[91] They cited stories and events from their ancestral past and expounded

87. Rosen-Zvi, "To See the Voices," 205.

88. Schwartz, *Were the Jews a Mediterranean Society*, 110–29.

89. M. Makkot 3:16.

90. Czajkowski, "Law and Romanization in Judaea."

91. M. Avot 1. See the nuancing of this common reading of Avot by Schremer, "Avot Reconsidered," which draws attention to a minority stream of rabbinic thought that was more cautious about so seamlessly linking rabbinic teachings with Sinai.

upon ritual and law that assumed the existence of a Temple complex.[92] Yet mastery of their growing body of teaching represented a new domain of knowledge. By the end of the second century, the earliest rabbis, or tannaim (circa first through third centuries), had produced a body of literature unlike any contemporaneous writing and without precedent in earlier Jewish literary texts.[93] The Mishnah, an anthology of tannaitic teachings compiled around 200 CE, was composed entirely in Hebrew at a time when Aramaic and Greek were both more common and Greek was recognized as a prestige language of erudition in the Roman Near East.[94] Its contents envisioned a Jewishness driven by halakhah, best defined as the rabbinic perception of the totality of Jewish laws and traditions. Observance of halakhah meant modeling behavior around a set of precepts that the rabbis argued expanded the true meaning of *mitzvot* (biblical commandments).[95] Later generations of rabbis, the amoraim, (circa fourth through sixth centuries), used the Mishnah as the basis for their own teachings, later collected in the Palestinian (fifth century) and Babylonian (sixth century) Talmuds.[96]

The Mishnah was the most comprehensive Jewish legal system from the period and its composition indicated that a specialist group had emerged within Roman Palestine.[97] By the third century rabbis had formed study circles in Galilean cities, such as Tiberias, Lydda, and Sepphoris, which eventually boasted houses of study (*batei midrash*) for rabbinic teachers and their students.[98] These places were apparently attractive centers, perhaps in part

92. Gafni, *Jews and Judaism*, 42–75.

93. As Seth Schwartz explains, the Mishnah is the first Jewish document "to posit the absolute centrality of halakhah" ("Impact of the Jewish Rebellions," 250). Moshe Halbertal argues, the "transformation of existing commandments" into a "dense field of instructions" and new obligations is a completely unique phenomenon to the rabbis ("Mishnah and Halakhah," 234).

94. On the significance of this linguistic difference, see Millar, "Transformations," 150.

95. Halbertal, "Mishnah and Halakhah," 233–34.

96. On the formation and redaction of the Talmuds, see Halvini, *Formation of the Babylonian Talmud*; Vidas, *Tradition and the Formation of the Talmud*; Stemberger, "Dating Rabbinic Traditions"; Milikowsky, "On the Formation and Transmission." For theories regarding the Tosefta's relationship to the Mishnah, see Hauptman, "Tosefta as a Commentary on an Early Mishnah"; and Friedman, "Mishnah and Tosefta."

97. Lapin, "Rabbis of History and Historiography," 11. See also Tropper, "State of Mishnah Studies"; and Azzan-Yadin, "Halakhic Midrashim and the Mishnah." On the progressive urbanization of rabbis, see Lapin, *Rabbis as Romans*, 68.

98. Rubenstein, "Social and Institutional Settings," 59; Lieberman, *Hellenism in Jewish Palestine*, 83–99; Jaffee, *Torah in the Mouth*, 65–83, 126–52; Tropper, *Wisdom, Politics, and Historiography*,

because large gatherings of rabbis were actually few and far between. Urban demographics offered easier access to other like-minded men.[99] If not near a rabbinic study house, sages and their colleagues met in the homes of generous friends or in inns.[100] These gatherings were occasions of study and debate enjoyed over food and wine. The Mishnah represents a snapshot of these conversations, even as it presents itself as synthesized halakhah whose form suppresses the social character of its scholastic context.[101]

The significance of the Mishnah extends beyond its actual content, which does not encapsulate all rabbinic perspectives on halakhah.[102] Instead, it signaled the enculturation of a specialist group.[103] Social interactions between rabbinic men provided far more than opportunities to learn what others knew about Torah. They facilitated the socialization of *how* to know in a rabbinic way.[104] Much of the idiosyncrasies of the Mishnah, which begins as if in mid-conversation and continues by stitching together terse legal units, conveys that there is more going on behind the scenes of its production. Barry Wimpfheimer argues that the form of the Mishnah "teaches its readers to read," commanding the reader to "think through the abstract conceptualizations that stand behind its concrete cases" in order to "understand the conceptual direction the Mishnah wants them to take."[105] Wimpfheimer draws our attention to the way the Mishnah not just anthologizes rabbinic thought but initiates

157–88; Sivertsev, *Households, Sects*, 9. On the institution of the beit midrash, see Lapin, "Jewish and Christian Academies"; Mandel, "Concerning the Public Role of the Early Beit Midrash"; Marks, "Who Studied at the Beit Midrash?"; Fogel, "The Orders of Discourse in the House of Study (Beit Midrash)."

99. Lapin, "Rabbis and Cities."

100. This is discussed in chapter 2.

101. Rosen-Zvi, "Introduction to the Mishnah," 1. See the discussion in Wimpfheimer, "Mishnah's Reader."

102. See the arguments in Yadin-Israel's *Scripture as Logos* and *Scripture and Tradition* that posit diverse positions within early tannaitic legal midrash. For the resonance with earlier Jewish legal thinking, see Noam, "The Emergence of Rabbinic Culture" and *From Qumran to the Rabbinic Revolution*; Shemesh, *Halakhah in the Making*; J. Baumgarten, "Tannaitic Halakhah and Qumran"; Halivni, "Early Period of Halakhic Midrash." See Rosen-Zvi, *Between Mishna and Midrash* for an introduction to the logic and interpretive goals of tannaitic literature.

103. Such enculturation Collins and Evans contend necessary for expertise (*Rethinking Expertise*, 30).

104. This point is illustrated by the comparative case of Mertz's examination of how to "think like a lawyer." Mertz, "Recontextualization as Socialization," and *Language of Law School*.

105. Wimpfheimer, "Mishnah's Reader," 366–67.

the reader into a way of thinking like a rabbi. Rosen-Zvi relatedly argues that both the Mishnah and Midrashic collections contain conscious rhetorical "gestures" that serve to mark the differences in opinion and orientation that animated the study house, whereby the "the rhetoric is thus the message."[106] This invitation is embedded within the text's structure, creating a unique affective response aimed at encouraging participation in its expert logic.[107]

A distinct way of knowing like a rabbi signaled the formation of an emergent community with its own legible behavior and methods of expertise. Those therein understood the capacities of Torah as a knowledge system dependent upon the rabbinic interpretive repertoire. I call this way of knowing "grammarian piety" because this expertise was at once technical and reverential. Rabbinic literature conveys a deep belief that traditional texts held a matrix of meaning anchored to textual linguistic units that awaited rabbinic interpretive skill. This technical skill required a close, atomistic, grammatically sensitive view of not just the written Torah but eventually of the Mishnah, Tosefta, and other rabbinic sources comprising rabbinic oral law, or received rabbinic traditions. "So you should accumulate the words of the Torah as general rules, and you should break them into smaller units and set them forth as 'drops of dew,'" Sifre Deuteronomy proclaims, referring to the study of oral law at the heart of the rabbinic specialist group.[108]

A fixation with atomized texts was not unique to the rabbis. Grammarian scholars throughout the late ancient Mediterranean defined themselves through their mastery and facility with extracted texts.[109] They cultivated grammarian expertise by dissecting writings into linguistic units that could be studied, excerpted, and rearranged. This process was not merely a linguistic exercise. As C. Mike Chin has argued for late ancient Christians, otherwise ordinary grammatical work could become "a forum for the articulation of religious difference, as philology is taken to mark religious identity."[110] Rabbis defined themselves through their grammarian-inspired techniques and

106. Rosen-Zvi, "Rhetorical Self in Tannaitic Halakha," 362.

107. Fraade, *From Tradition to Commentary*; Jaffee, *Torah in the Mouth*; E. Alexander, *Transmitting Mishnah*.

108. Sifre Deut. 306. On the metaphors of rain and dew, see Fraade, *From Tradition to Commentary*, 96–7.

109. See Chin, *Grammar*; Kaster, *Guardians of Language*; and Macrae, *Legible Religion*, on the roles of grammar and textualization in late antiquity.

110. Chin, *Grammar*, 99.

infused a distinct religious sensibility to their work. Grammarian expertise in the rabbinic domain of Torah meant mastering holiness.[111]

The key to this way of knowing was identifying textual units that could anchor the layering of rabbinic ideas. Rabbinic expertise was an intensively citational action that animated its own expert evidence through mastery of linguistic anchors. To illustrate this point, let us trace a single mishnah concerning the agricultural allocations for the poor through the Mishnah and Palestinian Talmud's tractate Pe'ah:

> One who does not allow the poor to gather, or one who allows one but not another, or one who helps one of them [to gather] behold he is a robber of the poor. Concerning him it is said: "Do not remove the boundary of the rising ones (*olim*)." (M. Pe'ah 5:6)[112]

מי שאינו מניח את העניים ללקט, או שהוא מניח את אחד ואת אחד לא, או שהוא מסיע את אחד מהן, הרי זה גוזל את העניים. על זה נאמר: אל תסג גבול עולים.

In order to understand this mishnah, the rabbinic expert would need to understand not just the biblical sense of the commandment but the rabbinic interpretive layering provided here. The commandment of *pe'ah* derives from the biblical instruction that farmers should leave the corner of their fields and the gleanings that fall upon the ground for the poor to gather.[113] This mishnah understands the content of the biblical law, and elaborates upon this general principle with the assertion that the poor should have uninhibited access to their food.[114] It then adds a popular saying, which resembles a biblical proverb, and asserts the rights of "the rising ones," a reference to the evocative image of poor gleaners ascending to glean.[115]

111. See the work of Wollenberg, *Closed Book*, and Picus, "Words of the Righteous," to see how notions of holiness informed the rabbinic relationship with the materiality of Torah.

112. See also M. Pe'ah 7:3.

113. Lev. 19:9–10, 23:22.

114. Deut. 24:19. See Brooks, *Support for the Poor*, 96–97 for this passage in full and Tosefta parallels.

115. This quote in the Mishnah shares a similar formulation to that of both Prov. 22:28 and 23:10 in the Masoretic biblical text: "Do not remove an ancient/eternal boundary" / אל תסג גבול עולם. The Mishnah shares the imperative against removal of a boundary, but this mishnah's version vocalizes the letters עולם as עולים "rising ones," the plural noun from the root עלה "to ascend" rather than the adjective עולם "ancient/eternal." Naomi Cohen has written on this difference, arguing that the saying as represented in the Mishnah represents not the Masoretic biblical text but rather a popular proverb circulating independently. N. Cohen, "Al Taseg." Notably, when the Leiden

The Talmud responds to this mishnah, not by examining the plain textual issue of theft of agricultural allocations for the poor or returning to the biblical rule, but by pursuing a grammarian investigation of the term "*olim,*" or "rising ones":

> R. Yirmeyah and R. Yosef—one said these are the ones rising from Egypt; the other said these are the ones who lost their property. A blind man is called plenty of light. R. Yitzchak said: "you shall bring the homeless poor into your house" (Isa 58:7). R. Avin said: if you do this, I will credit it to you as if you had presented first fruits in the Temple. It says here, "you shall bring," and it says there, "The choicest of the first fruits of your soil you shall bring into the house of the Lord your God" (Exod. 23:19).

> רב ירמיה ורב יוסף. חד אמ׳. אילו עולי מצרים. וחרנה אמ׳. אילו שירדו מנכסיהן. לסמיא צווחין סגיא נהוריא. אמ׳ ר׳ יצחק. "ועניים מרודים תביא בית." אמ׳ ר׳ אבין. אם עשית כן מעלה אני עליך כ(י)[א]לו הבאת ביכורים לבית המקדש. נאמ׳ כאן "תביא". ונאמ׳ להלן "ראשית בכורי אדמתך תביא בית יי׳ אלהיך" וגו׳.[116]

Rabbi Yirmeyah and Rabbi Yosef take us out of the context of gleaners and propose other euphemistic senses of the "rising ones," either those who "rise" from Egypt or those who "descend" and lose their property. Rabbi Yirmeyah interprets the literal sense of the term but with reference to a physical ascent from Egypt, evoking the biblical account of the enslavement of the Israelites. In this case, the identity of the poor could actually be anyone who is an Israelite descendant who was once "raised" from the precarity of slavery. Rabbi Yosef flips the word's literal meaning. Just as "a blind man may be called plenty of light," so too those who lose their property, thereby "descending," may be called "rising." Rabbi Yosef has in mind "the formerly wealthy poor," or those who have encountered loss.[117]

Following the paired teachings of Rabbi Yirmeyah and Rabbi Yosef, Rabbi Yitzchak quotes from Isaiah 58:7, and Rabbi Avin offers a teaching based on a shared root association with a different biblical verse. The relationship of this

Talmud manuscript quotes this mishnah as the basis for its own discussion, it vocalizes the quotation as it appears in the Masoretic biblical text, using עולם "ancient/eternal" rather than the Mishnah's עולים "rising ones." Likely, a redactor identified the text as a "quotation from Proverbs" and "fixed" its vocalization. Regardless of the vocalization in the Leiden manuscript, the rabbinic interpretation in the passage is inspired by the earlier vocalization of עולים or "rising ones."

116. Y. Pe'ah 5:6, 19a; Sussmann, ed., col. 100.

117. Gray, "Formerly Wealthy Poor."

biblical passage to the Mishnaic context is not explained as in Rabbi Yirmeyah and Rabbi Yosef's interpretations, though it is conceptually linked to the Mishnah's insistence on the obligation of a householder. Just as a householder should not disrupt the ability of the poor to glean, a householder is obligated in Isaiah 58:7 to "bring the poor into his house," perhaps understood in this context as extending the protection and oversight of his household.[118]

Amid this web of hermeneutic sense that weaves wordplay with logic, grammarian exercise illuminates a new interpretation from Isaiah 58:7b. Rabbi Avin explains that God will credit those who bring the poor into their home as if they were bringing first fruits to the temple. First fruits (*bikkurim*) are described in the books of Exodus and Deuteronomy as a tithe of the agricultural produce.[119] The farmer was to take the tithe to God's dwelling place (understood as the Jerusalem Temple) and recite a liturgical script.[120] Then the householder, his family, and all the Levites and foreigners who resided with them were to partake in a festive meal.[121] However, after the Romans destroyed the Temple in 70 CE and barred Jews from Jerusalem after 135 CE, pilgrimage festivals were no longer viable.[122] Rabbi Avin suggests an alternative possibility for the fulfillment of the first fruits commandment.

How does Rabbi Avin know about this alternative? Grammarian expertise identifies a parallel linguistic unit, the verb תביא or "you shall bring," in a different biblical verse:

118. On the householder's role in redistributive agriculture, see Gardner, "Pursuing Justice," 54–56.

119. Exod. 23:19 and 34:26. Exodus also describes a separate festival of first fruits in 34:22. The rabbis understand first fruits in light of the seven kinds of produce described in Deut. 8:8 (M. Bikkurim 1:3).

120. Deuteronomy assumes the presence of a centralized temple complex by accommodating householders who might have far to travel. Those unable to transport their goods are allowed to convert them to money so that their tithes might be carried more easily (Deut. 14:24–26). These first fruits were to be shared with one's household (Deut. 14:26) and shared with "the Levite and the foreigner" (Deut. 26:11).

121. Every third year—that is every third and sixth year of the sabbatical cycle—farmers were to give the full tithe to both the Levites and the poor, specifically to foreigners, widows, and orphans. Deuteronomy 14 does not include the Levite and foreigner in the yearly first fruits tithe (Deut. 14:28–29).

122. M. Bikkurim 2:3 describes the differences between *terumah*, second tithe, and first fruits in the rabbinic post-Temple perception. Both terumah and second tithe apply to produce before and after the Temple, while first fruits only applied to produce prior to the Jerusalem Temple's destruction. See also M. Ḥullin 10:1.

Isaiah 58:7b: And homeless poor **you shall bring** into your house.
ועניים מרודים **תביא** בית

Exodus 23:19: The choicest of the first fruits of your ground **you shall bring** into the house of the Lord your God.

ראשית בכורי אדמתך **תביא** בית יהוה אלהיך.

The hook of a shared verbal form (*gezerah shavah*) creates a striking substitutionary parallel. Homeless poor are equated with first fruits; the householder's home is equated with the Jerusalem Temple. It is important to observe how categorical boundaries are intentionally blurred by juxtaposing these verses. An agricultural tithe is certainly not the same type of transaction as the extension of one's house/household to the homeless poor; rather, the two are conceptually linked and bound by a shared verbal form, contributing to a broader discourse of charitable acts serving as an accommodation for defunct Temple-bound commandments.[123] Here the household domain is paralleled with God's cultic domain, and the shared linguistic unit endows the former with some of the latter's function.

This example demonstrates the grammarian fixation that comprises much of Talmudic and midrashic collections. This is not to say that every instance of rabbinic thought incorporates the grafting of linguistic units into its argumentation. While the literal sense of grammarian work is a large part of the rabbinic corpus, rabbinic knowing also encompassed techniques of memory (and forgetting), logical argumentation, and the ability to define the objects of their expertise.[124] By using the term "grammarian," I aim to signal both technical linguistic jointure and the distinctive posture of rabbinic thinking within a textual ecosystem. Rabbis did not simply read the Bible and explicate its meaning.[125] Rabbinic scholars devised an entire intellectual pietistic program. The rabbinic specialist culture emerged organically as literate men participated in this pietistic project, focusing at times on granular textual details with which to elaborate an extensive social praxis. They learned how to define the objects of their expertise and represent them using a precise hermeneutic only accessible to those socialized into the specialist community.

Much attention has been placed upon the knowledge transmission process of rabbinic disciple relationships, notably Martin Jaffee's *Torah in the Mouth*, that

123. On rabbinic innovations with charity, see Gardner *Origins of Organized Charity* and *Wealth, Poverty, and Charity*.

124. On the strategy of forgetting, see Balberg, *Fractured Tablets*.

125. On rabbinic ambivalence for a written biblical text, see Wollenberg, *Closed Book*.

need not be rehearsed here.[126] Rabbis learned from their teachers how to contribute their own knowledge in proper time and in a recognizably rabbinic way. As Gary Porton relays, "The rabbis' main goal was to study Torah and to train other rabbis."[127] This aligns with the observations of Harry Collins and Robert Evans, who contend that expertise arises from immersion in a specialist culture that results in the accumulation of both contributory and interactional expertise.[128] Contributory expertise is gained through practice, whereby students learn how to contribute knowledge to the domain of expertise. This would correlate with the rabbinic grammarian praxis and memorization of received traditions. Rabbinic students would study both the words of their teachers and the way their teacher formed their arguments in order to learn how to contribute themselves. The more students remembered the words of their teacher, the more trustworthy it was deemed.[129] Those who went on to contribute their own expertise in practice were ranked by their facility and skill, as illustrated in Mishnah and Palestinian Talmud Sanhedrin, which describes students appointed to rabbinic courts for the purposes of calendar intercalculation.[130]

The other type of expertise Collins and Evans identify is interactional, which reflects a kind of linguistic socialization that produces embodied knowledge.[131] This interactional expertise not only fosters a certain way of knowing but a "third kind of knowledge" between formal propositional knowledge and embodied skill.[132] Relatedly, E. Summerson Carr offers a further examination of the processes of expert socialization, whereby novices must master a linguistic register of technical terms and jargon, an intonation of speech, as well as embodied verbal signs such as facial expressions and gestures, and a specific way of speaking that signals a special kind of skill.[133] This kind of interactional expertise attained through close socialization is at once powerful and yet ephemeral; as Collins and Evans argue, it "can be lost if time is spent away from

126. Jaffee, *Torah in the Mouth*. For theories of oral transmission, see Finkelstein, "Transmission of the Early Rabbinic Traditions"; and E. Alexander, *Transmitting Mishnah*.

127. Porton, "Rabbinic Midrash," 154.

128. Collins and Evans, *Rethinking Expertise*, 24. Collins and Evans, "Sociological/Philosophical Perspective," 24.

129. M. Eruvin 2:6.

130. M. Sanhedrin 3–4 and Y. Sanhedrin 1:2, 19a.

131. Collins and Evans, *Rethinking Expertise*, 28.

132. Collins, "Interactional Expertise as a Third Kind of Knowledge."

133. Carr, "Enactments of Expertise," 20.

the group."[134] Rabbis observed the cadence and rhythm of Torah study, the public reasoning and physical posture of proficient teachers, the facial countenance and gestures of animated speech, as well as the myriad other expressions that produced rabbinic specialist culture. These embodied interactions provided a model for observation, internalization, and imitation that ritually transformed these men into rabbinic experts.

The explanatory power of interactional expertise lies in its ability to take socialization, especially through informal and casual avenues, as a fundamental component of forming a specialist group. Hanging out together provides a fertile ground for drawing the contours of a specialist group. One of the major debates in the field is when we can speak of rabbis as "rabbis," that is, as a legible group, movement, or network that was distinct from the sources of Jewish expertise that came before. While scholars have rightfully pushed the formal institutionalization of rabbis further toward the early medieval period, that does not mean we should eschew speaking of rabbis as a legible specialist group earlier in late antiquity. Rabbinic literature attests to the socialization processes already happening at local levels that produced the rabbinic way of knowing.

Interactional expertise draws our attention to a different form of rabbinic transmission, which involved learning how to know in a rabbinic way through embodied experiences. Jaffee's study of early rabbinic oral-performative tradition observed that "ad hoc decisions of Sages" could become binding practice.[135] This insight noted that at times rabbinic halakhah derives from bodily action rather than traditional transmission of knowledge. Students of individual rabbis observed the cadence and rhythm of their teacher's Torah study, the public reasoning and physical posture of proficient teachers, the facial countenance and gestures of animated speech, as well as the myriad other expressions that produced rabbinic specialist culture. These embodied interactions provided a model for observation, internalization, and imitation that ritually transformed these men into rabbinic experts.

We have limited evidence for what daily interactions might have looked like, nor can we experience the house of study as Moses famously does in later rabbinic storytelling.[136] But there are instances, particularly in the Tosefta,

134. Collins and Evans, *Rethinking Expertise*, 3–4.

135. Jaffee, *Torah in the Mouth*, 77.

136. See B. Menahot 29b for Moses in the beit midrash of R. Akiva. The Tosefta, more than any other tannaitic corpus, quite often includes these kinds of personal anecdotes when discussing a legal teaching. This difference could reflect the way the Tosefta is more rhetorical and the

where the observation of bodily habits became rabbinic knowledge itself. These provide a sense of how rabbinic men observed each other, creating a process whereby interactional experiences generated knowledge that could later be orally transmitted. One place where rabbinic literature describes active observation of rabbinic behavior is prayer.

For example, in Tosefta tractate Berakhot, we learn how Rabbi Akiva, an early rabbinic sage, used to pray:

> R. Judah said, "When R. Akiva would pray with the congregation, he would shorten [his prayer] on account of them. And when he would pray by himself, one could leave him in one corner and find him [later] in another corner on account of his bowing and prostration" (T. Berakhot 3:5).

> אמ׳ ר׳ יהודה כשהיה ר׳ עקיבא מתפלל עם הצבור היה מקצר בפני כולם. וכשהוא מתפלל בינו לבין עצמו ,אדם מניחו בזוית זו ומוצאו בזוית אחרת מפני הכרעות והשתחואות.[137]

This anecdote appears in a passage discussing the intention of those who recite *shmoneh esrei* or a series of eighteen benedictions meant to be prayed quietly. While his teachings are recorded throughout rabbinic literature, here we have knowledge derived upon witnessing his bodily habits. Amidst a crowded gathering, he recited the words quickly in order to avoid holding up the rest of the people waiting for him to finish. When he prayed alone, he allowed himself to become fully engaged with the words, both emotionally and physically. What is remembered is not just the physical and auditory difference in R. Akiva's prayer but an illustration of spiritual intimacy that might serve as a model for others in their personal recitation.

Such insights into how Rabbi Akiva prayed could only be obtained through close proximity to both the public and private aspects of his life. We learn from another passage that Rabbi Meir witnessed an inaudible recitation of the Shema when sitting before Rabbi Akiva, even though "the sages say one should recite the *shema* out loud."[138] Others took note of Akiva's habits and let them shape their own behavior. This embodied transmission of rabbinic posture was incorporated into the domain of rabbinic knowledge, introducing the category of inaudible recitation.

Mishnah more functional. See Novick, *What Is Good*, 115. On the oral transmission of teaching, see Jaffee, *Torah in the Mouth*, 65–83.

137. Ed. Lieberman, 12. See also M. Berakhot 4:3 and B. Berakhot 31a.

138. T. Berakhot 2:13.

Further in the chapter, another anecdote derived from physical observation is included to explain when an abbreviated version of *shmoneh esrei* might be warranted:

> *One who is walking in a place of danger* and of bandits *recites a brief prayer* [M. Berakhot 4:4]. What is this brief prayer?
>
> R: Eliezer says, "May your will be done in the heavens above, and provide comfort to those who fear you and do what is good in your eyes. Blessed be the One that hears prayer."
>
> R: Yose says, "Hear the prayer of your people Israel and fulfill their requests quickly. Blessed be the One that hears prayer."
>
> R: Elazar Bar Tzadok says, "Hear the voice of the cry of your people Israel and fulfill their requests quickly. Blessed be the One that hears prayer."
>
> Others say, "Your people has many needs, but they are short minded. May it be your will Hashem our God that You may provide for each one all of his needs and to each creature so that they should not want. Blessed be the One that hears prayer."
>
> R: Elazar bar Tzadok says, "My father *used to pray an abbreviated prayer on Shabbat nights*: 'And from your love Hashem our God that you love Your people Israel, and from Your compassion, our King, that you had on the children of Your covenant, you have provided for us, Hashem our God, this great and holy Seventh day, with love.' And over the cup [of Kiddush] he says, "Who has sanctified the day of Shabbat" and he does not conclude [the blessing] (T. Berakhot 3:7).

היה מהלך במקום סכנה ולסטין מתפלל תפלה קצרה. אי זה הוא תפלה קצרה? ר׳ ליעזר או׳, יעשה רצונך בשמים ממעל, ותן נחת רוח ליריאיך והטוב בעיניך עשה. ברוך שומע תפלה. ר׳ יוסה או׳, שמע לתפלת עמך ישראל ועשה מהרה בקשתן. ברוך שומע תפלה. [ר׳ אלעזר בר׳ צדוק אומ׳, שמע קול צעקת עמך ישר׳ ועשה מהרה בקשתם. ב׳ שומע תפילה]. אחרים או׳, צרכי עמך מרובים ודעתן קצרה. יהי רצון מלפניך ה׳ אלהינו שתתן לכל אחד ואחד צרכיו ולכל גויה וגויה די מחסורה. ברוך שומע תפלה. אמ׳ ר׳ לעזר בר׳ צדוק אבא היה מתפלל תפלה קצרה בלילי שבתות. ומאהבתך ה׳ אליהנו שאהבת את ישראל עמך. ומחמלתך מלכנו שחמלת על בני בריתך, נתת לנו ה׳.אלינו את יום השביעי הגדול והקדוש הזה באהבה. על .הכוס הוא או׳, אשר קדש את יום השבת ואינו חותם.[139]

Amid a string of abbreviated prayers offered for one to recite in different contexts, we learn about the habits of a rabbinic home. Rabbi Elazar bar Tzadok, likely

139. T. Berakhot 3:7, ed. Lieberman, 13.

from childhood, witnessed his father truncate his prayer because of Shabbat. The text provides no other detail, no further description to set the scene of what young Elazar felt as he watched his father recite, but this observation is offered as a valid teaching derived from observing a sage's actions. It is added to a passage related to prayers truncated by occasions of danger because it provides a related example of truncation. In so doing, the bodily habits of a sage open up a realm of possibility of when prayers might be abbreviated in less dire circumstances.

In a related example, the Talmud states that Rabbi Yonah would whisper his silent prayers while in synagogue but would pray them aloud while at home so that the members of his household could also learn.[140] This example of prayer transmission emphasizes routine household habits that reveal how Rabbi Yonah hoped to socialize his household into rabbinic practice. Notably, this exposure to rabbinic prayer knowledge is open to all members of the household regardless of gender. We might imagine his daughter skipping down the hall while mumbling to herself, "Baruch atah, Adonai, Ha'El HaKadosh (Blessed are you, Adonai, the holy God)" in clumsy time with her father. While transmission of words is certainly at hand, there is a further interactional depth to the experience. A posture of piety was cultivated through emulation and observation. In the same passage, his son Rabbi Mana insists, "the people in my father's house learned prayer from him," by which he means both the content of rabbinic prayer and the culture of rabbinic prayer.

Observation of rabbinic fathers provided a significant source of rabbinic interactional expertise.[141] Early rabbinic circles comprised several households whose fathers compelled their family in halakhic directions.[142] These households served as "role models of piety," as Alexei Sivertsev has argued, that served to reinforce the perception of rabbinic expertise through visual observation.[143] In Mishnah tractate Pe'ah, for example, Rabban Gamaliel remarked, "we had this custom in the house of my father" concerning the types of pe'ah given for certain trees.[144] In a different discussion concerning whether a block

140. Y. Berakhot 4:1, 29b.

141. See the recent dissertation of Walfish, "Parents and Sages as Agents of Culture" for analysis of this dynamic in the Babylonian Talmud.

142. Sivertsev, *Households, Sects, and the Origins of Rabbinic Judaism*, 194; Sivertsev, *Private Households and Public Politics*, 117–83. See also Neusner, *Judaism*, 250–56, and *Economics of the Mishnah*, 50–71; and Lapin, *Early Rabbinic Civil Law*, 119–241.

143. Sivertsev, *Households, Sects, and the Origins of Rabbinic Judaism*, 215.

144. M. Pe'ah 2:4. See also Sifre Deut. 2:4. See Sivertsev, *Households, Sects, and the Origins of Rabbinic Judaism*, 222–31 for more ancestral traditions of Rabban Gamaliel. Also, Kanter, *Rabban Gamaliel*, 25–26.

of wood not originally intended to serve as a seat can contract impurity, Rabbi Eleazar bar Tzadok again cites the precedent of his father's house: "Two blocks were in the house of my father, one unclean, and the other clean. I said to father, 'On what account is this unclean, and the other clean?' He said to me, 'This one which is hollowed out is unclean, and the other which is not hollowed out is clean. 'And on it sat Haggai the prophet.'"[145] The memory of learning how his own father determined the halakhic distinction is invoked to provide proof for the law. Not only was his father's ruling deemed permissible, but even more so through the legendary detail that the prophet Haggai directed his own behavior accordingly. Rabbinic experts learned by example how to correctly identify the object of rabbinic knowledge and diagnose the proper response.

Carr insists that the semiotic study of expertise must take account of visual signs as much if not more than verbal signs.[146] Visual observation of rabbinic teachers happened routinely, but it could also have major halakhic consequences. In Tosefta tractate Demai, a collection of teachings concerning produce suspected of not being tithed properly, we learn how one rabbi's actions set a new halakhic precedent over the learned opinion of his colleagues:

> R. Simeon says, "[There are] three decrees with respect to *dema'i*." It so happened that our rabbis entered Samaritan towns along the road. They [Samaritans] brought vegetables before them. R. Akiva hastened to tithe them as certainly untithed produce. R. Gamaliel said to him, "How did your heart compel you to transgress the words of your colleagues, or who gave you permission to tithe?" R. Akiva said to him, "Have I established a law in Israel? I have only tithed my own vegetables." R. Gamaliel said to him, "Know that you have established a law in Israel by tithing your own vegetables." And when R. Gamaliel came among them, he declared their grain and their pulse to be *dema'i*, and the rest of their produce to be certainly untithed (T. Demai 5:24).[147]

ר׳ שמע׳ או׳ שלש גזירות בדמאי. מעשה שנכנסו רבותינו לעיירות של כותים שעל יד הדרך. הביאו לפניהם ירק, קפץ ר׳ עקיבא ועישרן ודאי. אמ׳ לו רבן גמליאל היאך מלאך ליבך לעבור על דברי חביריך, או מי נתן לך רשות לעשר. א׳ לו וכי הלכה קבעתי בישראל? א׳ לו ירק שלי עישרתי. א׳ לו תדע שקבעתה הלכה בישראל שעישרתה ירק שלך. וכשבא רבן גמליאל ביניהם עשה תבואה וקיטנית שלהן דמאי, ושאר כל פירותיהם וודאי. וכשחזר רבן שמעון בן גמל׳ ביניהם ראה שנתקלקלו ועשו כל פירותיהן ודאי.[148]

145. T. Kelim 2:2–3.

146. Carr, "Enactments of Expertise," 27.

147. Cf. T. Demai 1:11.

148. T. Demai 5:24, ed. Lieberman, 93.

Samaritans represented a category of suspicious people because they were known for not fully observing Torah laws.[149] Elsewhere in the Tosefta we learn that the position toward Samaritans had softened to some degree. Jews may derive benefit from their fruit and unleavened bread, and dishes prepared by Samaritans were generally considered okay to consume.[150] But Akiva applies a more stringent rule for his own interactions with Samaritans, echoing a teaching in Mishnah Beitzah 2:6 that permits sages to choose more stringent behavior.[151] However, Rabbi Gamaliel is troubled by the potential standard set by Akiva's actions. Tzvi Novick describes this concern as a worry for the "contagious" character of personal stringency.[152] Because Rabbi Akiva has a reputation as a great sage, others might seek to mirror his behavior and thus shift the halakhic line toward a more stringent position.

The power of Akiva's visual cues demonstrates the significance of social observation in the formation of expertise. Others learned how to conduct themselves not just from the verbal words of sages but from the visual signs of the expert's bodily habits. Expertise depends on relationships of trust with others who perceive the expert as doing the "right" thing. Peers and students relied upon the example of rabbinic experts to enact their expertise in their everyday behavior, that is, "If Akiva feels he must tithe, then we must tithe." Rabbi Gamaliel is attentive to this dynamic and ultimately chooses against his own judgment to treat Akiva's actions as a halakhic precedent because it affirms a more important point—the confirmation of Akiva as a rabbinic expert. Rather than invalidate Akiva's behavior, he supports the perception of his expertise.

The worry about setting halakhic precedent through the behavior of rabbinic experts also appears in Tosefta Berakhot in the context of prayer.[153] Rabbi Ishmael and Rabbi Eleazar ben Azariah are said to have chosen opposite postures for prayer, with Rabbi Ishmael choosing to recline and Rabbi Eleazar ben Azariah choosing to remain upright. When the time for the Shema appeared, Rabbi Ishmael arose, while Rabbi Eleazar ben Azariah chose to recline. They discuss their different habits, informed by different views of Beit Hillel

149. Elizur, "Ha-Kutim be-divrei ha-Tannaim (Samaritans in Tannaitic Literature)," 393–414; Friedheim, "Some Notes about the Samaritans," 194–95. For recent trends in scholarship, see Chalmers, "Samaritans, Biblical Studies, and Ancient Judaism."

150. T. Demai 4:27.

151. See the parallel in M. Eduyyot 3:10 and the discussion in Novick, *What Is Good*, 130.

152. Novick, *What Is Good*, 131.

153. T. Berakhot 1:4. See Jaffee, *Torah in the Mouth*, 78.

and Beit Shammai,[154] but then the text supplies an additional explanation. They purposefully chose different postures so that "the students should not witness" them both recline and establish the law accordingly.

Perhaps the most famous rabbinic habit that endures today is Hillel's sandwich. The Tosefta recounts that Hillel the elder would make a sandwich with matzah, roast lamb, and bitter herbs during the Passover seder.[155] The Palestinian Talmud notes that other rabbis disagreed with Hillel's interpretation of Numbers 9:11 ("They shall eat it on matzot and bitter herbs"), for fear that the Torah's obligation to consume matzah and the rabbinic obligation to consume bitter herbs would nullify each other for the purposes of observing mitzvot.[156] The later Babylonian Talmud explains that while the law was not settled in Hillel's favor, the sandwich was inserted into the seder meal not to fulfill the blessing of eating matzah and bitter herbs, but rather "in remembrance of the Temple, in the manner of Hillel."[157]

This is not to say that everything rabbis did was unquestionably valid. Rabbinic literature also preserves observations about what *not* to do. Rabban Simeon ben Gamaliel reported in Tosefta Shevi'it: "In Acre I once saw Simeon b. Kahana drinking wine with the status of a heave-offering." Heave-offerings, we learn, could not be imported from another country into the land of Israel.[158] When Simeon b. Kahana admitted that the wine came from Cilicia, Rabban Simeon ben Gamaliel recounts that he was made to drink the wine on a boat so as not to import the wine. In a different scenario from tractate Ma'aser Sheni, Rabbi Yehudah ben Gadish reports that his father's employees used to sell brine in Jerusalem for consecrated *ma'aser sheni,* or second tithe money, which would ordinarily not be allowed for purchase since brine contains only water and salt.[159] His rabbinic interlocutors dismiss his family's example, saying, "Who said this?" They venture that fish may have been sold with the brine, thus rendering the sale valid and dismissing Rabbi Yehudah ben Gadish's example as credible for the domain of rabbinic knowledge.

Peppered throughout technical discussions are glimpses of the power and fear of visual observation. In one case, the entire town of Beth Shean was permitted

154. M. Berakhot 1:3.

155. T. Pesaḥim 2:2.

156. Y. Hallah 1:16, 2b. See also, B. Pesaḥim 115a and B. Zevahim 79a.

157. B. Pesaḥim 115a.

158. T. Shevi'it 5:2; M. Shevi'it 6:6.

159. T. Ma'aser Sheni 1:14. See also M. Ma'aser Sheni 1:5.

to harvest during the Sabbatical year for commercial use because of the actions of one rabbi, Rabbi Meir.[160] Joshua ben Zeruz, the son of Rabbi Meir's father-in-law, reported that he saw Rabbi Meir buy vegetables from a garden during the sabbatical year. "He permitted all of it!" Joshua emphatically insisted, to which Rabbi Zeira dryly retorted, "This implies that nobody should act in public." Rabbi Zeira went on to try and explain Rabbi Meir's actions away, "this was a particular case," but at the end of the day the people of Beth Shean were permitted, and not only Beth Shean but also Caesarea, Bet Guvrin, and Kefar Zemah.

Visual observation and embodied socialization played an important role in the development of rabbinic expertise. Rabbinic scholars were not only studying Torah but also each other. The behaviors and habits of distinguished sages could set the example for how rabbinic experts ought to think and act and informed their understanding of rabbinic law. To become a rabbinic expert required socialization within a community of specialists so that the way of knowing how to discern the proper objects of rabbinic knowledge could be learned through repeated embodied interactions. In this way, rabbis learned both head knowledge, such as the words of written Torah and the oral interpretations of their teachers, as well as interactional knowledge, or the behaviors, habits, and discursive signs of other sages. The formation of the latter, far more than the former, served to distinguish those who had access to this way of knowing from those who did not.

Socialization could also serve to validate those within the rabbinic specialist group. Rabbis relied on each other to recognize that their expertise was valid, thereby affirming their ability to define objects of rabbinic knowledge.[161] This dynamic is illustrated in tractate Pe'ah regarding tithe quantities from a field planted with two kinds of wheat:

> It happened that Rabbi Shimon of Mitzpah planted his field [with two different kinds of wheat] and came before Rabban Gamaliel. They both went up to the Chamber of Hewn Stone and asked [about the law]. Nahum the scribe said: I have a tradition from Rabbi Meyasha, who received it from Abba, who received it from the pairs [of sages], who received it from the prophets, a halakhah of Moses from Sinai, that one who plants his field with two species of wheat, if he uses one threshing-floor, he gives only one pe'ah, but if two threshing-floors, he gives two pe'ahs. (M. Pe'ah 2:6)

160. Y. Demai 2:1, 22c.

161. Carr, "Enactments of Expertise," 22; Cetina, *Epistemic Cultures*, 135.

מעשה שזרע רבי שמעון איש המצפה לפני רבן גמליאל, ועלו ללשכת הגזית ושאלו. אמר נחום הלבלר, מקבל אני מרבי מיאשא, שקבל מאבא, שקבל מן הזוגות, שקבלו מן הנביאים, הלכה למשה מסיני, בזורע את שדהו שני מיני חטין, אם עשאן גרן אחת, נותן פאה אחת. שתי גרנות, נותן שתי פאות.[162]

The proceeding mishnah concerns how many portions of pe'ah are obligated depending on the different seeds planted in the same plot. While ordinarily pe'ah must be allotted per different type of seed, we learn that when a farmer plants his field with two kinds of wheat, he only brings the portions of pe'ah for the number of threshing floors used—one threshing floor, one portion of pe'ah—representing a middle case for the rule. Farmers who plant two different kinds of wheat, likely as a way to ensure disease resistance for their crop, will therefore not suffer an undue tax burden. Only in the case of an abundant harvest would they be obligated to designate multiple pe'ah portions.

The technical halakhic question introduces an occasion for the performance of uncertainty. Rabbi Shimon sowed his seed with different strains of wheat and wondered what he should do. He sought out Rabban Gamaliel, the famed early Jewish patriarch known for his expertise in agricultural allotments, having previously ruled against farmers giving excess tithes.[163] While Rabban Gamaliel provides a model of proper deference to the transmitters of Temple traditions, he also strategically performs uncertainty. Carr relays that expertise can be produced through such a performance, where experts carefully calibrate their verbal and bodily conduct in order to achieve a favorable outcome. This is exemplified by Matoesian's study of a medical trial witness, who outperforms a prosecuting attorney through gestures, "dramatic shakes of the head," and the feigning of doubt.[164] Rabban Gamaliel's uncertainty serves to initiate a textual sequence that in turn elevates rabbinic expertise with divine authority. As Carr claims, people emerge as expert "not in unmediated relationships to culturally valued objects," in this case the allocation of tithes, but rather through "the discursive processes of representing them."[165] Although Rabban Gamaliel could have invoked his own knowledge, the text imagines the physical process of the great patriarch presenting himself before Nahum the scribe

162. Kaufmann, *Toldot ha-emunah ha-yisre'elit*, 45.

163. M. Avot 1:16. The pair of sages refers to pairs of sages who led the Sanhedrin in the Second Temple period as listed in Mishnah tractate Avot 1 and Hagigah 2:2.

164. Carr, "Enactments of Expertise," 23, citing Matoesian, "Role Conflict as an Interactional Resource."

165. Carr, "Enactments of Expertise," 23.

in order to hear the transmission of knowledge that derives from Moses himself. This physical recitation serves to assert the authority and antiquity of a rabbinic law by providing proof of its divine origin, which in turn authenticates rabbinic expertise.[166]

My emphasis upon socialization should not detract from the essential role propositional knowledge transmission played in rabbinic apprenticeship. Students were initiated into this domain of rabbinic knowledge ideally from an early age. In one tradition, children are instructed to begin learning Torah at the age of five, Mishnah at the age of ten, and Talmud at the age of fifteen.[167] Ideal rabbinic students memorized the Torah and the Mishnah, as well as the teachings of their individual teachers, through careful oral recitation.[168] To know Torah to its fullest extent was not just to know that Deuteronomy 6:7 instructs Jews to recite the Shema "when you lie down and when you get up" but to also know that Rabbi Eliezer taught that evening recitation could extend until the first watch, while other rabbis thought until midnight, and Rabban Gamaliel insisted until dawn.[169] The Sifre even provides an ideal quota for weekly and monthly study.[170]

However, if we only assess the content and form of propositional knowledge transmission, we risk reinforcing a notion of expertise that views it as a property that elite individuals possess rather than a dynamic organized by collaborative and institutional social relations. To be sure, rabbinic literature portrays itself as precisely a treasured and exclusive possession of rabbinic initiates. But expertise lies not in the possession of knowledge but in the operative claim. The transmission of rabbinic knowledge was significant because the process helped bolster the reputation of teachers and authorized students as experts, thereby enacting the expertise that was claimed.

This point is illustrated well in one Talmudic passage describing a group of respected tannaitic sages who allegedly gathered before the elderly sage Rabbi Dosa ben Harkinas shortly after the destruction of the Temple.[171] Upon seeing

166. The Mishnah on occasion uses this formula of linking rabbinic traditions back to Moses as a means of authenticating rabbinic teachings. See, for example, M. Yadayim 4:3.

167. M. Avot 5:21.

168. On the importance of orality to rabbinic learning, see Jaffee, *Oral Tradition*; Hauptman, *Rereading the Mishnah*; E. Alexander, *Transmitting Mishnah*; and Kiperwasser, "From Oral Discourse to Written Documents." On the remarkable similarity with Greco-Roman philosophical schools, see Goldin, *Studies in Midrash*, 57–76; and S. J. Cohen, "Patriarchs and Scholarchs."

169. M. Berakhot 1:1.

170. Sifre Deut. 48:3, 48:10.

171. Y. Yevamot 1:6, 3a.

the venerable men, Rabbi Dosa praised their remarkable mastery of Torah by highlighting relevant biblical prooftexts. To Rabbi Yehoshua he cited Isaiah 28:9: "To whom will he teach knowledge, and to whom will he explain the message? *Those who are weaned from milk, those taken from the breast.*" We learn that Rabbi Yehoshua's mother used to take his crib to the local synagogue so that he could listen to the words of Torah. Upon seeing Rabbi Akiva, Rabbi Dosa declared, "Lion cubs will be poor and hungry, *but those who seek the Lord will not lack any good thing*" (Ps. 34:11). This verse referred to Rabbi Akiva's humble background that did not prevent him from rising in the ranks of rabbinic experts.[172] To Rabbi Eleazar ben Azariah he declared, "I was a youth but now I am old (*zakanti*)" (Ps. 37:25), a reference to the fact that according to another Talmudic tradition Rabbi Eleazar ben Azariah had been granted entrance to the yeshiva at the age of 16.[173] Supposedly upon his arrival, all the hair upon his head turned white, signaling his immediate elder (*zaken*) status as a great sage.

The effect of this passage is to praise skilled rabbis by conveying how their Torah expertise was with them at an early age. It communicates a naturalized assumption that rabbinic experts are expert because of their mastery of Torah knowledge. But while the text assumes expertise is a cognitive possession, it also undercuts its own point. Rabbi Dosa ben Harkinas attributes the status of expert to these men and assigns biblical proof to their legendary origins. Those proofs serve to authenticate their status as experts. While the text assumes their expertise with a descriptive prooftext, the prooftext actually serves to authenticate that which it claims to describe. The passage emphasizes that the three rabbinic figures were immersed in a community of Torah—whether through a crib in the synagogue or early entrance to the yeshiva—and from that social immersion they became rabbinic masters.

One of the peculiarities of rabbinic study circles was the mandate that students attribute traditions to their teachers. The Palestinian Talmud insists, "any

172. On R. Akiva's youth and poverty, see Yadin, "Rabbi Akiva's Youth."

173. Y. Berakhot 4:1, 33a. The text goes on and attributes Eleazar ben Azariah's rise to fame because he was a direct descendent of Ezra. This sheds light on R. Dosa ben Harkinas's chosen prooftext, which speaks to this privileged background: "I was a youth but now I am old, *yet I have not seen the righteous forsaken or their children begging bread*" (Ps. 37:25). It also pulls back the curtain to reveal the social circumstances that led to this rabbi's fame. A kinship network is revealed that would have been comprised of not just his wealthy father's household but also the political and business relationships that supported that wealth. R. Eleazar is a member of an elite class and an elite lineage, which consoles the jealous R. Akiva. For, in fact, R. Eleazar does not possess more expert skills than R. Akiva; he possesses the prestige of wealth.

teaching of Torah that is not attached to the authority of a named source is not a valid teaching of Torah."[174] Elsewhere we learn that Rabbi Yochanan required that his students remember his name and complained when his student Rabbi Eleazar neglected to honor him with attributions.[175] The Talmud even imagines that King David himself wished to be such a sage whose words were remembered in the study house.[176]

This habitual model reflects itself in a repetitive citational formula in rabbinic literature: "Rabbi X in the name of Rabbi Y." For example, "Rabbi Shimon [taught] in the name of Rabbi Yehoshua ben Levi, 'Once the king bows down deeply he does not get up until he finishes his entire prayer.'"[177] While scholars do not recognize these attributions as historically reliable, they have rightly drawn attention to the deferential systems of honor at work. Students were instructed not just in their teacher's knowledge but in their position within a social hierarchy. Elsewhere rabbinic students are even discouraged from contributing their own expertise in front of their former teachers due to the potential dishonor it might generate.[178]

Carr argues that expertise is made manifest through power relations that "are both repressive and productive" in order to reproduce a social hierarchy expressed by "disciplined social actors."[179] Attribution made students into docile bodies, compelled by the intersection of knowledge and power enacted through the ritual of citation.[180] Rabbinic students not only sought to memorize the teacher's words but to embody the very habits of their teachers by observing their daily habits and emulating their religious practice in the home, synagogue, and market; in the course of their travels; and even as they ate meals.[181] They appear to have performed menial tasks in exchange for the

174. Y. Shabbat 19:1, 17a.

175. Y. Berakhot 2:1, 4b; and Y. Sheqalim 2:5, 11a. See the analysis of this story in Picus, "Words of the Righteous," 37–38.

176. Y. Berakhot 2:1, 4b.

177. Y. Berakhot 1:5, 10a. Scholars are skeptical that these attributions can be understood as direct historical references. Neusner, "Evaluating the Attributions"; D. Kraemer, "On the Reliability of Attributions"; S. Stern, "Attribution and Authorship"; Kalmin, *Sages, Stories, Authors, and Editors*, 1–13; Hayes, *Between the Babylonian and Palestinian Talmuds*, 9–16.

178. Lev. Rab. 20:6; and B. Berakhot 31b.

179. Carr, "Enactments of Expertise," 18.

180. Foucault has greatly influenced the study of expertise. *Discipline and Punish*.

181. Rubenstein, "Social and Institutional Settings," 59; Levine, *Rabbinic Class*, 60; Jaffee, *Torah in the Mouth*, 530, 541.

instruction of their teachers: working on their estates, assisting them with dress, and even washing their sandals.[182] The process of becoming a rabbinic expert was therefore social but also asymmetrical.[183] Citation served as its own form of discipline that authenticated the expertise of students through the submission to those perceived as more expert than themselves.[184]

In one Talmudic discussion about monuments for the dead, Rabban Simeon ben Gamliel even elevates this citational practice into its own tangible memorial: "One does not build mausoleums for the just; their words are their remembrance."[185] The just here could refer to any righteous person, but in the context of the rabbinic specialist group, it hits especially close to home. Daniel Picus argues that this passage demonstrates that "teaching with correct attribution does more than simply venerate the memory of the dead . . . it literally brings them back from it, creating a situation in which a teacher's authority is heightened and likened to the authority of their own teacher."[186] Building upon Picus's insights, I argue that the citational practice facilitated not just the transmission of knowledge or the support of hierarchies of honor but it produced the naturalness of the rabbinic specialist group.[187] The expertise of the speaking rabbi is reinforced through the authority of the citational rabbi invoked as an authority, and the citational power in turn reinforced the perception of expertise for the whole rabbinic specialist group writ large.

The rabbis became legible as a specialist group through transmission of knowledge and the interactional observations attained through socialization. Their developing texts wove biblical and rabbinic traditions together, constructing a base of rabbinic authorities whose teachings would become foundational for later rabbinic thinkers. They also developed a cultural repertoire that made rabbinic sages legible to each other. In the process, an exclusive boundary was constructed—not necessarily due to mere elitism—but because such a boundary is inherent to the demarcation of expertise. Those experts who know in a rabbinic way have access to a citational repertoire that by definition non-experts do not. The challenge for the rabbis, like any specialist group, was

182. T. Shabbat 12:12; T. Ḥullin 2:24; T. Nega'im 8:2. Also see Y. Shabbat 3:1, 5c). See the list of tasks in *Pesikta de-Rav Kahana* 11:8 (p. 184).

183. Carr, "Enactments of Expertise," 19.

184. Jaffee, *Torah in the Mouth*, 150; Picus, "Words of the Righteous," 52. On honor in rabbinic circles, see S. Schwartz, *Were The Jews a Mediterranean Society?*

185. Y. Sheqalim 2:5, 74a. Cf. Gen. Rab. 82:11.

186. Picus, "Words of the Righteous," 44.

187. Bourdieu, *Language and Symbolic Power*.

persuading those without the skills of their domain that their knowledge was valuable. The key to this persuasion would come through social relationships with other Jews who shared a value of Jewish piety.

Piety and Persuasion in Rabbinic Social Circles

Rabbinic expertise was intended for limited clusters of like-minded people who embraced a rigorous lifestyle of study. And yet, no expert exists in isolation. Rabbinic men were forming intimate connections with each other within a social context filled with other people. Wives, children, and other household members, friendly merchants and other householders, slaves, neighbors, and other people encountered in day-to-day activities came into contact with rabbinic men. While these other people lacked the training to contribute knowledge, that is, the full ability to do rabbinic work, they could acquire interactional expertise or "social fluency" through the same methods of observation that rabbis learned from each other.[188] Stuart Miller observes that rabbinic households served as "nodal points" for the dissemination of rabbinic thinking about purity, tithing, festivals, life cycle events, and other halakhic matters.[189] Members of these households altered their behavior in ways that echoed rabbinic habit, which were then observed by others that they came into contact with. Collins and Evans emphasize that this interactional expertise is a kind of third knowledge that anyone who spends time in social interaction can acquire, not just those credentialed or authorized by a specialist group.[190]

There is an ordinary subtlety with which these pietistic behaviors could spread.[191] In one Talmudic case, Rabbi Immi was teaching a group the rabbinic rules of *kilayim*, or how to avoid forbidden mixtures between certain plants and animals.[192] Someone in the audience turned to his neighbor and informed him, "you are wearing *kilayim*!" The flush of shame and shock that must have flooded the neighbor aroused Rabbi Immi to action. "Strip yourself of your garment and give it to him," he commanded. This case appears in the textual

188. Collins and Evans, *Rethinking Expertise*, 90.

189. Miller, *Sages and Commoners*, 462. For a closer examination of rabbinic households, see Sivertsev, *Households, Sects, and the Origins of Rabbinic Judaism*.

190. Collins and Evans, *Rethinking Expertise*, 70.

191. Hasan-Rokem, *Tales of the Neighborhood*.

192. Y. Kil'ayim 9:1, 41a. These laws are based on the Torah's prohibitions against mixed species in Lev. 19:19 and Deut. 22:9–11.

record in order to illustrate the words of Rabbi Zeira: "The dignity of the public is important enough to temporarily override a prohibition."

The Talmud neglects to dish on the details of this spectacle. The tension that filled the space as the man humiliated his neighbor must have rippled through the friend groups for weeks. There may have been some turned away from such zeal, others skeptical of those in attendance at all. But there were likely others who would be inspired by Rabbi Immi's defense. The fact that there was a crowd at all implies that there were some Jews who might want advice on how to understand the Torah's prohibition, "Do not wear a garment made with two different materials."[193] Rabbi Immi knew that rabbinic expertise advised that "not one thread should touch his flesh," but he sat amid those with suspect garments and shared his knowledge tailored to the social setting. Witnesses likely whispered about the event, "Did you hear what he did? Did you hear what Rabbi Immi made him do? He took the whole garment off! No, I don't think he got it back." As gossip mills exposed the interpersonal slight, they would have served to disseminate a rabbinic idea and potentially praise the valor of the rabbinic expert who defended it.

Rabbinic literature is very aware that rabbinic households had neighbors. Time and again references to how a neighbor plants or what a neighbor owns or what a neighbor sells punctuate rabbinic halakhic thinking. "If his field grew wheat but his neighbor's field grew another species, he can go ahead and sow some of that same species on his adjoining space," Mishnah Kil'ayim 2:7 advises, admitting that the neighbor's actions would make it so that one could not tell that the rabbinic field contained mixed species. Where rabbinic literature offers guidance for insiders on how to modify halakhic observance when in contact with others, those others would have also observed rabbinic behavior. "So you planted only wheat in that plot? What were you thinking? Will that help with the harvest?" a neighboring farmer might inquire. "You know, I'm hoping for a good year. Rabbi Shimon suggested planting only one species there." These kinds of hypothetical scenarios do not survive in the written record, but they are an important interactional aspect of how social behavior spreads.

There has been a recent turn in scholarship to decenter the rabbis from narratives about Jewish antiquity. This is with good reason. In her study of the Mediterranean diaspora, Ross Kraemer writes that narratives about Jewish history assume a measure of homogenization, so that "all Jewish history in antiquity is the history of a unified, linked, singular, fundamentally rabbinic

193. Lev. 19:19.

'Jewish community.'"[194] This insight underscores the diversity of Jewish populations spread across the ancient Mediterranean and beyond, who might not have been in contact with the sages of Roman Palestine or Sasanian Persia. This reiterates the point made earlier in this chapter: Judaism is not a single entity but an umbrella category covering a variety of practices and beliefs sharing enough similarities to warrant the classification. Mika Ahuvia relatedly claims that "the majority of Jews in Late Antiquity were likely unaware of the sages and their endeavors."[195] The scholarly consensus understands that the rabbinic orbit was small and limited and exerted no institutional control over Jewish communities.[196] Ancient Jews were not rabbinic. By prioritizing rabbinic sources, other ancient Jewish practices, beliefs, and experiences have been marginalized.

Rabbinic texts themselves reinforce this sharp difference when expressing frustration with non-rabbinic Jews who seem uncertain of proper rabbinic observance or who ignore rabbinic advice. For instance, Lydda (or Lod) is identified as a place where people were ignorant of Torah.[197] In one Mishnaic passage we learn of an occasion when Rabbi Tarfon ruled that a sale was fraudulent when the merchandise was up-charged by one-third of its real value, instead of one-sixth as other sages taught. The merchants of the city were content with Rabbi Tarfon's ruling because it meant they could charge more for their merchandise. However, Rabbi Tarfon also ruled that buyers had a longer period of time to retract the sale. The merchants became upset and rejected both of his rulings, insisting, "Let Rabbi Tarfon leave us as we were."[198] A different story from the Palestinian Talmud describes a butcher in Sepphoris who sold unkosher meat. Upon his death, Rabbi Ḥaninah refused him a proper burial.[199]

In other cases, rabbis dismissed attempts at Jewish observance that they encountered. We learn in Mishnah Makhshirin that the people of Maḥoz would moisten their wheat with sand, a general practice to minimize the dust generated from storage, but one that made the wheat susceptible to impurity according to rabbinic law. The sages criticized them, saying, "if you have always

194. Kraemer, *Mediterranean Diaspora*, 28–29.

195. Ahuvia, "Jewish Towns and Neighborhoods," 34. Kraemer, *Mediterranean Diaspora*.

196. Goodman, and Alexander, *Rabbinic Texts*; S. Schwartz, *Imperialism and Jewish Society*; Lapin, *Rabbis as Romans*.

197. Y. Pe'ah 8:9, 21b; and Y. Sanhedrin 1:2, 18c–d. However, a different tradition in Y. Ta'anit 3:4, 66c states the opposite and instead targets Sepphoris for neglect of Torah.

198. M. Bava Metzi'a 4:3.

199. Y. Avodah Zarah 2:3, 41a.

acted in this manner, you have never prepared food in purity!"[200] The text assumes that the people of Maḥoz had intended to observe the purity laws of the Torah but were unaware of the potential threat of their actions. In another account "the people of Jericho" did not know how to properly leave pe'ah when growing vegetables, even when they would properly pile grain in preparation for the omer (or first grains).[201] Sometimes practices differed because rabbinic advice differed. "Who allowed you to [drink, buy, do] this?" certain rabbis ask when encountering Jews who act in a way contrary to their professional opinion.[202] These types of anecdotes attest to the diversity of Jewish and rabbinic practice and the ways it could diverge from rabbinic ideals.[203]

However, the trend in scholarship to minimize the influence of rabbinic Jews has also siloed the rabbis in ways that reproduce older narratives of rabbinic insularity. It has become commonplace for scholars to presume that the religious identity of ancient Jews was quite different from that of the rabbis.[204] This impression is not without some validity. Archeological discoveries in cemeteries[205] or synagogues,[206] of new caches of documents[207] or of artifacts such as incantation bowls[208] and amulets[209] attest to a multivocal Jewish life beyond that depicted in rabbinic texts. This insight was initially revelatory to the field. Earlier generations of scholars assumed that the rabbis had immediate and major influence in Jewish society.[210] Part of this expectation was

200. M. Makhshirin 3:4.

201. See M. Pesaḥim 4:8; T. Pesaḥim 3:19–20. Cf. Shamma Friedman, *Tosefta Atiqta*, 380–404.

202. For example, Y. Avodah Zarah 4:11, 44b (also Y. Avodah Zarah 2:4, 41c); and Y. Nedarim 2:5, 50a.

203. For a full survey, see Hezser, *Social Structure of the Rabbinic Movement*, 353–404.

204. See, for example, Goodenough, *Jewish Symbols*, 184–98.

205. K. Stern, *Writing on the Wall*.

206. See, for example, Boustan and Britt, "Historical Scenes in Mosaics." Magness, "'Foundation Deposit,'" and "Helios and the Zodiac Cycle."

207. See, for example, Cotton, "Rabbis and the Documents" and Esler, *Babatha's Orchard*.

208. See, for example, Neusner, "Rabbis and Community," 445; and Schiffman, "Forty-Two Letter Divine Name." Schiffman argues that "these incantations and the attendant magical practices could not have had the approval of the rabbinic authorities" (97). For a refutation of this view, see Gross and Manekin-Bamberger, "Babylonian Jewish Society."

209. Bohak, "Jewish Amulets, Magic Bowls, and Manuals."

210. See Büchler, *Political and Social Leaders*; Alon, *Jews in Their Land*; Urbach, *Sages*; Finkelstein, "Some Examples of the Maccabean Halaka." C.f., Urbach, "Class-Status and Leadership," 60, 64.

informed by the later medieval academies with dynastic rabbinic authorities. Scholarship built on the idea of the rabbi as the sole arbiter of ancient Jewish religion could no longer claim that rabbinic texts attested to the lived religious experiences of Jews. A shift to read rabbinic literature not as the historical record but as rhetorically inflected aspirations introduced a "discursive turn" to the field. Attempts to unearth the "lived religion" of ordinary Jews further yielded a timely corrective to a narrative of ancient Jewish history written from the sole vantage of rabbinic men.[211] Scholars of antiquity seeking to move beyond the scope of gods and doctrine have sought to examine the ordinary, largely illiterate, people on the margins of the canon. In doing so the theological and institutional portrait of the ancient world derived from texts has been questioned, complicated, and enriched by the evidence afforded from analysis of the everyday lives of ancient people.

At the same time, Adiel Schremer has argued convincingly that scholars who are quick to demonstrate that ancient Jews were not rabbinic have a strange conception of observance, where: "'observance' is a virtue demanding totality. *Any* sort of failure to follow the law completely is automatically deemed a *severe crime*."[212] In this framework, Torah is conceived of as "a crystallized state of being or knowing" to be either accepted or dismissed.[213] But in reality, people have misaligned beliefs and actions all the time.

Gil Eyal calls this dissonance a "pushmi-pullyu" effect, or the two-headed process of reliance and rejection inherent to expertise. At the same time that there is reliance upon a domain of knowledge, there are occasions of skepticism of its spokespeople.[214] Eyal is thinking of modern debates about vaccination, where those advocating against vaccination are deemed "anti-science" because of their behaviors. But those same non-expert skeptics accept "science" in other parts of their lives, such as driving cars without understanding how the mechanical components work or ingesting Tylenol for migraines without knowing precisely what it contains or what its range of effects may be. Scientists are not granted epistemic authority by virtue of the truth of their specialized knowledge alone or through their membership in a specialist group, but by their ability to persuade others of their credibility and value as its spokespeople. In this way, expertise is not a descriptive label but rather a

211. Lewis, "Ordinary Religion"; and Rüpke, "Lived Ancient Religion."

212. Schremer, "Religious Orientation of Non-Rabbis," 325, emphasis original.

213. Carr, "Enactments of Expertise," 19.

214. Eyal, *Crisis of Expertise.*

set of social claims whose enactment sheds light on the tenuous links of trust that support it.

Certainly many ancient Jews did not observe the totality of rabbinic halakhah, but that does not mean they lived lives completely foreign to the orientation of rabbinic piety. Their actions can ignore or directly contradict that of rabbinic experts in their midst, but that does not mean they reject the domain of Torah knowledge that links them together.

There is a frustrating absence of evidence to attest to the likely varied Jewish responses to the period of intense national trauma at the hands of the Romans, but what we can observe is that Jewish customs persisted. The Roman historian Tacitus, writing in the early second century CE, describes the characteristics of the Jewish people with derision but also with remarkable legibility:

> These rites, whatever their origin, can be defended by their antiquity; their other customs are sinister and abominable, and owe their persistence to their depravity. For the worst (*pessimus*) among other peoples, renouncing their ancestral religions, always kept sending tribute and contributing [to Jerusalem], thereby increasing the wealth of the Jews. Further, the Jews are extremely loyal toward one another, and always ready to show compassion, but they regard other people with the hatred of enemies. They sit apart at meals and they sleep apart, and although as a nation they are prone to lust, they abstain from intercourse with foreign women; yet among themselves nothing is unlawful. They adopted circumcision of the genitalia so that they could be recognized by their difference. Those who are converted to their ways follow the same practice, and the earliest lesson they receive is to despise the gods, to disown their country, and to regard their parents, children, and brothers as of little account. (Tacitus *Hist.* 5.5.1–2)

We must read against the hostile tone, but even so, his account contains standard tropes of Jewish practice. Circumcision, cultic festivals, and nods toward Jewish communal solidarity persist. Gifts toward the Jerusalem Temple complex attest to the significance of its institutions in the mind of Tacitus, who also admits that converts may be attracted toward Jewish practices. Even though most Jews across the diaspora were largely integrated into non-Jewish society, Tacitus reacts to a legible Jewish self-consciousness.[215]

215. See the collection of essays by Kraabel in Overman and MacLennan, *Diaspora Jews and Judaism*; Trebilco, *Jewish Communities in Asia Minor*, 173–83; Rajak, "Jews and Christians as

A foundational component of Jewish self-consciousness was the Torah: not simply its laws but what it signified as a cultural unit. When writing about the epistemic authority of scientists today, Stephen Turner explains that scientists do not operate as individuals but as the corporate voice of "science":

> The cognitive authority of scientists in relation to the public is, so to speak, corporate. Scientists possess their authority when they speak as representatives of science. And the public judgments of science are of science as a corporate phenomenon, of scientists speaking as scientists. (Turner, *Politics of Expertise*, 23)

Here Turner describes the epistemic authority constituted through the collective scientific voice. The individual scientist exists as an expert because they tap into the authority of the broader scientific community. This authority is legitimized by the public's perception that the scientific community maintains high standards of competence, and that the resulting advancements in science are beneficial to society. At its core, the public participates in this corporate phenomenon with a shared sense of Science as a significant domain of knowledge.

Turner's formulation can help illuminate the relationship between Torah, the rabbis, and the Jewish public. Rabbis were a loose association of individual learned men who taught as "representatives" of Torah. Their expertise lay not simply in their cognitive knowledge of texts but in the "corporate phenomenon" of Torah that empowered rabbis to speak as the spokespeople of Torah. Other Jews who cared about Torah as a cultural object might not have ordered their behavior according to the words of a local rabbi, but it is conceivable that they would have cared about those who claimed to be spokespeople of Torah. This also does not mean that rabbis would have received automatic status as experts. As Eyal and Turner point out, the public offers judgments upon representatives of a domain of knowledge, which means rabbis were always in a position of persuasion. Rabbis had to work to validate their role as experts by cultivating their perception as experts in the eyes of other Jews. They set themselves up as judges and teachers while deploying the saturated symbols of Torah and the Second Temple past in order to solicit investment in their expertise. This investment could take the form of patronage, gifts of food, or tithes, as well as the cultural capital gained from the acknowledgment that their rabbinic ideas were valuable to those outside the rabbinic specialist group.

Groups," 247–62. On the integration of Jews within the diaspora, see Feldman, *Jew and* Gentile; and Gruen, *Diaspora*, and *Heritage and Hellenism*.

Rabbinic literature certainly assumes some people valued them. In one Talmudic passage, Rabbi Yohanan saw a man leaving Sepphoris and inquired about what was happening in the city. The man informed him that one of the great rabbis had died, and everyone was busy attending to him. Rabbi Yohanan assumed it was his teacher, Rabbi Ḥaninah, and so he gathered his best Shabbat clothes and tore them in mourning.[216] Later in the same passage we learn of another event in Sepphoris. On one occasion, Rabbi Ḥiyya bar Abba saw everyone running and inquired as to where they were all going. He was told, "Rabbi Yochanan is preaching in Rabbi Benaiah's study house and everybody is running to hear him."[217] These anecdotes appear in a legal discussion about the habits of certain rabbis who tore their garments upon hearing of the death of their illustrious teachers, but they also assume that other people would care about their own words and deaths.

Gifts of food also appear with frequency. For example, people brought Rabbi Eleazar ben Rabbi Shimon cabbage of extraordinary sweetness[218]; another person brought a sack of leeks to Rabbi Yitzchak bar Tevelai[219]; and Rabbi Yose was sent a large citron from Sepphoris.[220] Once Rabbi Abbahu, Rabbi Yose ben Ḥaninah, and Rabbi Simeon ben Lakish passed by the orchard of Doron, when a sharecropper brought them a peach so large that they and their donkeys ate from it with some leftover.[221] Catherine Hezser argues that the sheer number of anecdotal depictions of food gifts suggests that donations of this sort did happen.[222] While gifts of food often appear in tractates dealing with agricultural tithes, they could also take the form of invited dinners. In one account, Rabbi Shmuel ben Natan describes the mouthwatering meal of eggs that tasted as buttery and savory as sweetbreads (lit. פִּינְקְרֵסִין, likely derived from the Greek πάγκρεας) that he was served near the springs of Geder.[223] Hospitality, discussed at length in the following chapter, went hand in hand with gifts of food as ways for clients to honor the legal and ritual expertise rabbis could provide.

216. Y. Bava Metzi'a 2:11, 8d; parallel in Y. Horayot 3:4, 48b.

217. See the parallel in Y. Horayot 3:4 that includes the missing detail that R. Ḥaninah was leaning on R. Ḥiyya bar Abba.

218. Y. Pe'ah 7:3, 20b.

219. Y. Demai 2:1, 22d.

220. T. Demai 4:14.

221. Y. Pe'ah 7:4, 20a and in B. Ketubbot 112a.

222. Hezser, *Social Structure of the Rabbinic Movement*, 355.

223. Y. Shabbat 3:1, 5d, with a parallel in Y. Terumot 2:1, 12a.

Furthermore, the rabbinic orbit grew because sons were sent to study with individual sages. This choice signals an important element of buy-in to rabbinic expertise. If a wealthy householder sent their son to apprentice with a rabbi, that would communicate an exchange of significant social capital—both for authenticating the rabbi's own expertise and for interpersonal rewards of supporting sages. Students were expected to attend to their teachers in a servile capacity, with accounts of students performing a range of personal services, such as caring for their teacher when ill,[224] working on their property,[225] or helping them dress and wash.[226] In exchange, the student could expect personal Torah instruction and, as one source insists, "acquire life in the world to come."[227] This offer of eternal life, and all that it signified about Torah as a shared Jewish cultural object, was apparently persuasive to some because sons continued to appear before the feet of rabbinic experts.

Rabbinic texts also assume that some people did seek their expertise. For example, in the Tosefta we learn that a certain old man in Ardascus would weigh his basket when it was full and then weigh it again when it was empty so as to ascertain the precise weight, and Rabbi Meir would praise him.[228] On one occasion the tenant of Rabbi Ba ben Mina took pigeons he found on a palm tree to the Babylonian sage Rav for advice.[229] According to another story, the daughter of Rabbi Ḥiyya the Elder lent Rav money. She came and asked her father in which type of metal (silver or gold) she should receive her money back.[230] Similarly, Rabbi Yochanan's relative asked his advice about the price of oil.[231] In yet another text, Segabion, the head of the synagogue at Achzib, purchased a vineyard in its fourth year from a gentile in Syria. Then he came and asked Rabban Gamaliel whether the produce was liable to the restrictions on fourth-year yields. He replied, "'Wait until we can dwell upon the law.'"[232]

Ancient Jews lived within their ancestral land and outside it, navigated unique imperial constraints as well as the ordinary limits of being a person in antiquity trying to eat and survive, interacted with religious experts of various

224. T. Shabbat 12:12.

225. Y. Shevi'it 6:4.

226. T. Megillah 8:2; Y. Shabbat 3:1, 5c; *Pesikta de-Rav Kahana* 11:8 (p. 184); Lev. Rab. 2:4.

227. *Mekhilta d' Rabbi Ishmael*, Amalek 4.

228. T. Terumot 3:4.

229. Y. Bava Metzi'a 1:4, 7d–8a.

230. Y. Bava Metzi'a 4:1, 9c.

231. Y. Bava Metzi'a 4:2, 9d.

232. T. Terumot 2:13.

stripes, and cultivated piety in a variety of forms. But if we take seriously the notion that many Jews found value in their ancestral traditions, thought of God as a real agent in the world, and felt inclined toward pious practices to whatever degree, then that requires us to acknowledge that the rabbis were not so unlike their Jewish neighbors. Some ancient Jews regarded individual rabbis with respect. They valued their opinions—even if they did not fully implement them—and sought out their teaching. They eventually attended sermons that rabbis delivered in their synagogues or homes.[233] They also recognized rabbinic expertise in a variety of forms, such as sending sons to them for study and offering gifts of food, and in other ways such as hospitality, tithes, and charity, as later chapters will address. These kinds of social interactions were a means of legitimizing the expert roles that rabbis sought to both create and fill.

Recent work on incantation bowls in Sasanian Persia has shown that while Babylonian rabbinic texts are wary of non-rabbinic ritual expertise, some incantation bowls name influential rabbis as authoritative figures. Avigail Manekin-Bamberger and Simcha Gross insist that the makers of these bowls assumed that "rabbis were personages that could be touted as notable neighbors and respected ancestors; were thought to possess power over legal deeds, courts, and bans; and whose stories served as powerful precedent for the client's own quandary."[234] There are ordinary human contradictions that cannot be resolved here. First, that incantation bowls could be a less desirable route to managing demons than holier methods—Babylonian Talmud Eruvin 54a extols the sick to study Torah for their health care rather than seek out an amulet. Second, rabbis did not oversee the incantation bowl trade. One could imagine rabbis looking down on ritual expert competition. But the presence of named rabbis on these bowls attests to a more multivocal ancient Jewish landscape where ordinary Jews and rabbis mingled.

Nor does the insular, elite character of specialist expertise mean that rabbis only looked inward. Their specialist group believed that their expertise in Torah brought benefit for the world. "Be of the disciples of Aaron, loving peace and pursuing peace, loving people and drawing them close to the Torah," Mishnah Avot extols.[235] Rabbinic literature assumes that their expertise

233. Though the evidence for widespread rabbinic homilies is much later. See Porton, "Rabbinic Midrash."

234. Gross and Manekin-Bamberger, "Babylonian Jewish Society," 28.

235. M. Avot 1:12.

should be valued, but this does not need to read as a simplistic bid for power and authority even if that could be an effect. Rather, the Torah was a shared cultural object of value to some Jews. The rabbis may have initiated a new type of Jewish piety that depended upon their unique grammarian skill, but they did so with the conceptual tools that they already possessed, which stemmed from a broader Jewish piety that animated other people.

Recognizing that piety played a significant role in the development of rabbinic expertise changes our understanding of the relationship between rabbis and their communities. While it may be true that few Jews modeled their full behavior after rabbinic guidance, it does not mean that rabbis were disconnected from the religious lives of everyday Jews. Rabbis argued that they were spokespeople of Torah and used its cultural significance to persuade those who already valued the Torah as a conceptual entity of significance. This helped to establish them as experts and to gain recognition among their social circles.

Conclusion

Rabbinic specialists emerged over the course of a long century of turmoil, upheaval, and social change. Jews were forced to reexamine who was credible as a Jewish religious expert and what their relationship with their communities should be. At the same time, other aspects of Jewish life persisted, and support for Jewish ritual expertise increased. The rabbis represented one strand of broader increased reliance upon Torah as a meaningful cultural object. The rabbis are no anomaly. Their emergence during a period of imperial upheaval attested to the broad need for Torah expertise. While they were not uncritically accepted as the only religious experts, there were some who valued and trusted them because of a broader public reliance upon Torah.

All claims to expertise rest precariously on thin webs of trust, and this period put immense strain on that trust. If God no longer had a symbolic home, where did he dwell? If sacrifices could no longer be performed, how would Jews handle matters of sin and impurity? If priestly experts have lost their authorizing claim, what purpose for them remained? Not only had priestly expertise failed, but new types of knowledge emerged. Provincialization introduced different sources of authority: Roman courts to settle disputes, Roman contracts to facilitate purchase and sale, Roman authorities to oversee the comings and goings of the province. An entirely new imperial infrastructure was installed in the land that for the first time did not center the ancestral traditions of the Jews.

Within this setting a group of Torah scholars fashioned an entirely new domain of knowledge. Those initiated into this way of knowing adopted the posture of grammarian piety, using painstaking scrutiny of linguistic forms as gateways to new knowledge about Torah. This grammarian piety contributed to the sense of the rabbi as a unique kind of expert in late antiquity. That expertise, however, could not be constituted solely by the acquisition of knowledge or skills. A student could master rabbinic hermeneutics and learn every meaning of Torah, but knowledge in and of itself does not produce expertise. There is a naturalness to the assumption that the rabbi is a Torah expert, which the lens of expertise theory unsettles. Socialization played an essential role in teaching rabbinic men how to be rabbinic experts, including their mannerisms, logic of thought, and specialized jargon that conveyed that their knowledge was trustworthy, and their social interactions with others disseminated a certain cultural fluency.

Rabbis constructed the apparatus of their hermeneutical knowledge and used it to persuade others to their claim. In the process, a perception of expertise grew among rabbinic study groups and within their limited networks. This process was tenuous and with no guarantee of what we now know would become the normative frame for many Jews into the modern era. No individual rabbi or even gathering of rabbis devised a large-scale takeover of Jewish life, nor is it apparent that they would have even wanted to. Instead, the contingent, coincidental, and capacious nature of social interactions began a long process of persuasion until *rabbinic* expertise, not just Torah expertise, became valuable to enough people to warrant notice.

The following chapters of this book delve deeper into rabbinic socialization both within and beyond the specialist group, starting with the unique setting of the dinner table. This book argues that rabbinic expertise was not a result of mastering specialized interpretive skills. Instead, it was a dynamic produced through social interactions. While rabbinic literature portrays rabbis as divinely authorized experts due to their specialized Torah knowledge, it also reveals moments of vulnerability when rabbis are challenged to enact their expertise to others. Therefore, the "expertise" of rabbis refers to the social processes that established, normalized, and spread an emerging rabbinic knowledge domain. By shifting the perception of expertise from a possession of knowledge to a framework produced through social interaction, the contingent production of rabbinic expertise is animated within the ancient sources.

2

Dinner Parties, Friendship, and Rewards for Hosting Rabbis

NO SETTING provides a more ready occasion for the enactment of expertise than the dinner party.[1] When people dine together, they create a self-contained community suspended in time. Each participant attends both to personal nourishment and to the social bonds of those gathered.[2] These are spaces for self-presentation, where demeanor, attire, and conversation are carefully crafted for the communal setting. They are also scripted affairs with implicit rules that must be performed delicately so as not to upset the interpersonal balance. Offending a host can have repercussions that spill over from the dinner table.[3] For would-be experts, these settings are a prime opportunity to cultivate social recognition and leave an impression through rhetorical skill on those in attendance. Dinner parties provide a place for fostering a sense of community and therefore make an ideal setting for networking, demonstrating expertise, and building social capital.

The rabbis were no strangers to the cultural power of dining. Tannaitic and amoraic texts both describe rabbis receiving and extending invitations to be guests in others' homes. Hospitality and banquet culture were also crucial social institutions in the ancient Roman world.[4] Wealthy individuals were

1. For the broader phenomenon of banquets in antiquity and the performance of expertise, see Klotz and Oikonomopoulou, *Philosopher's Banquet*; König, *Saints and Symposiasts*.

2. See the edited collection, Chou, Kerner, and Warmind, *Commensality: From Everyday Food to Feast*.

3. Nadeau, "Table Manners." For an example in rabbinic literature, see the scenario sketched in *Derekh Eretz Rabbah* 9.

4. Dunbabin, *Roman Banquet*; D. Smith, "Greco-Roman Banquet"; Donahue, *Roman Community at Table*; Stephenson, "Dining as Spectacle"; Faas, *Around the Roman Table*. See also the

expected to share their largesse by feeding and entertaining friends and clients, making daily dining with members of their social circles "part of the normal routine of life."[5] These dinners were both localized events of conviviality and nodes within a larger web of social expectations.[6] Friendship forged over food created a social circle with common values and goals, supported through the exchange of gifts and favors. Familial bonds and personal associations were nourished as much as the body. Rabbis participated in these habits of hospitality, and their stories envision these occasions as unique opportunities to perform as Torah experts and form vital alliances. They interjected their Torah knowledge into dinner conversations, debated matters of ritual and hermeneutic ambiguity with those gathered, and even created halakhah from their dining habits. In the process, they formed beneficial relationships with wealthy families who could support their work as Torah scholars.

This chapter examines stories of rabbis at banquets and gathering in the homes of others as places where recognition of rabbinic expertise could be cultivated. Whether grilling a guest's Torah comprehension during dinner or inviting a host into discussion, the rabbis in these stories performed expertise strategically for the social occasion. The benefit was twofold: participants were socialized into the rabbinic domain while at the same time rabbis formed partnerships with wealthy families who could provide tangible support in the form of hospitality, word-of-mouth praise, and donations.

I begin by examining how rabbinic meals shared in the culture of dining in Roman Galilee. Ancient Roman banquets were a display of social power and status. They were used to reinforce social hierarchies and demonstrate wealth and influence. The extravagance of the food, drink, and entertainment served at these banquets was a way for the host to show off their resources and impress their guests.[7] I demonstrate that not only did rabbis attend and host such

---

sourcebook, Donahue, *Food and Drink in Antiquity*. On the rise of more hierarchical dining, see Luley, "Colonialism, Dining, and Changing Strategies of Power," 750–80. On the decline of dining as a site of networking, see Dannell, "Samian Cups and their Uses," 161; and Allison, "Naming Tablewares," 192.

5. Garnsey, *Food and Society*, 136.

6. As Neil Coffee contends, "the Roman tradition of hospitality gave rise to the custom of hosting and attending dinner parties" (*Gift and Gain*, 155). On the social role of meals in the ancient world, see Nielsen and Nielsen, *Meals in a Social Context*; Marks and Taussig, *Meals in Early Judaism*.

7. Bergquist, "Sympotic Space"; D'Arms, "Control, Companionship, and Clientela," and "Roman Convivium."

meals, but they harnessed the social power of these banquets by elevating Torah and their role as Torah experts. The rabbinic dinner table introduced sequenced benedictions, acknowledging that the food and drink ultimately belonged to God, and they emphasized that those with whom they dined were offered unique access to Jewish piety.[8] Participants were socialized into a culture of banqueting that honored those with Torah knowledge, encouraging the elite to value Torah experts as useful friends. Just as powerful as any sermon or lecture—if not more—these meals were opportunities to cultivate support for the rabbinic domain.

At the same time, the friendships formed in these settings were intertwined with "webs of social obligations."[9] Reciprocal obligations, particularly between those of more elite status, formed the foundation of powerful economic, political, and social networks in the ancient Mediterranean.[10] Hosts and guests understood they owed each other invitations, gifts, and favors as part of their social bond, even as these expectations could resemble patronage.[11] Patronage was a system of asymmetrical relationships forming an extended, and often long-term, system of transactions exchanged between two parties.[12] This formal exchange relationship implied social subservience and dependency that no friend wanted to feel. Hospitality was therefore a type of gift exchange that required sleight of hand to mask feelings of inferiority or debt.[13] By accepting and extending invitations of hospitality, rabbis knowingly took part in a cultural institution that both imposed reciprocal commitments and expected them to be polite about it.

These expectations could pose a challenge for rabbis. Not only did the prospect of reciprocity inflict pressure upon ideals of Jewish solidarity that resisted

8. On rabbinic dining practices, see Rosenblum, *Food and Identity*, *Rabbinic Drinking*, and "Jewish Meals in Antiquity"; R. Weiss, *Meal Tests*.

9. Verboven, "Friendship among Romans," 414.

10. Nicols, *Civic Patronage in the Roman Empire*. See the collection of essays in Satlow, *Gift in Antiquity* that apply Mauss's theories of gift exchange to the ancient world.

11. Saller, *Personal Patronage*, 13. On the relationship between friendship and patronage, see Verboven, "Friendship among Romans," 412–14. Wolf, "Kinship, Friendship, and Patron-Client Relations."

12. Saller defined a patronage relationship with three defining features: reciprocal exchange, long-term relationships, and asymmetrical status between the patron and client (*Personal Patronage*, 1–3).

13. For recent theories of hospitality as gift exchange, see Warde, Paddock, and Whillans, "Domestic Hospitality"; Lynch, et al., "Theorizing Hospitality"; Agier, *Stranger as My Guest*.

feelings of social debt between Jews, as recent scholarship has explored, but they put rabbis in a difficult position as experts.[14] The reputation of rabbinic expertise depended on recognition that their knowledge was valuable, no better signaled than through invitations of hospitality that cemented their position within valuable social networks. However, these occasions embroiled rabbis in relationships that expected certain access to their expertise. As this chapter will demonstrate, householders might expect a rabbi they invited over for dinner to rule in their favor later. They might expect a rabbi to attend other social events in order to capitalize on their association with a Torah scholar. They might summon him to teach on demand. Moreover, the expected exchanges of honor and gifts that came with hospitality placed rabbinic experts in positions of social debt to their clients rather than as autonomous Torah experts. Rabbinic experts could not isolate themselves within their specialist group. Instead, social relationships encroached upon their expertise and left their mark.

In order to resist such encroachment, rabbinic texts reframed hospitality toward rabbis as an extension of charity. The personal investment logic of charity—that giving to the poor would benefit the giver with divine reward—provided a template to work with.[15] Hosting rabbis could bring rewards to the host, so that rabbis were the one ultimately doing the favor when receiving hospitality. In this way, these sources assert that the wealthy should invite a rabbi for dinner, while making it clear that this does not buy them exclusive rabbinic access. Instead, the host should count themselves lucky to receive immediate return on their investment through their interactions with Torah scholars in their home. I contend that rabbinic literature fashions social acquaintances with rabbis as dependent upon recognition of their Torah expertise so as to mask the social expectations invoked by hospitality. Rabbis hoped to benefit from the social capital and tangible support that socializing offered, but it also required careful negotiation.

The dinner table was an important part of cultivating rabbinic expertise. Those in attendance were invited into the realm of rabbinic knowledge, learning the etiquette of the rabbinic table and acquiring an acquaintance with the kind of piety that rabbis articulated around the table. These real-time occasions of dining and hanging out in someone's home contributed to the

14. For recent scholarship on Jewish solidarity and economic relationships, see S. Schwartz, *Were the Jews a Mediterranean Society*; Sorek, *Remembered for Good*; Wilfand, *Poverty, Charity, and the Image of the Poor*.

15. Gardner, *Wealth, Poverty, and Charity*, 117.

subsequent development of rabbinic law and paved the way for the growing perception of rabbis as religious experts. By reframing hospitality with religious rhetoric and rewards, rabbis could benefit from their friendships while also creating a new avenue of Jewish piety that (ideally) resisted undesirable reciprocal expectations.

Rabbinic Banquet Culture

The Roman dinner party, or convivium, was at its core an occasion for diners to recline upon couches and partake in a combination of mixed wine, food, and conversation with friends.[16] Sometimes these banquets were public affairs designed to entreat favor for politicians or as sponsored feasts and religious festivals for the public (known as *epulua* or *convivia publica*).[17] Other times private dinners between patrons and clients, aspiring recruits to the governing class, or among social peers wielded links of friendship around the dinner table.[18] These events were therefore never fully private. They were public in the sense that prominent members of society used the convivium habit to cultivate social relationships of significance. It was by such means that the important leaders of their city became members of table communities whose conviviality maintained the structures of public life.[19]

Wealthy householders signified their rank by reclining at these meals and designed their homes to facilitate the practice. One of the most important and elaborately decorated rooms in the Roman-style aristocratic house was the banquet hall, called triclinium for the three couches arranged around a central table in a U (or extended U plus T) pattern.[20] Elaborate mosaics, many still surviving today, marked the center floor. Recent attention has been paid

16. See Murray, "Convivium," for an overview of the evolution of the convivium as a social institution. On the archaeology of the convivium space, see Hudson, "Changing Places."

17. On the Roman sponsored community feast, see Donahue, *Roman Community at Table*.

18. See, for example, Pliny the Younger, *Ep.* 6.19.1, where candidates running for office are given a convivium. Garnsey, *Food and Society*, 137; Dunbabin, "Convivial Spaces"; Stein-Hölkeskamp, "Class and Power," 85; Konstan, *Friendship in the Classical World*, 122. On the various (and at times interchangeable) terms for Roman dinners, see Donahue, "Roman Dining," 255–60.

19. D. Smith, *From Symposium to Eucharist*, 146.

20. Garnsey, *Food and Society*, 136. Often a T pattern adjoined the U pattern as extended seating. However, by the fourth and fifth centuries, the triclinium gave way to the *stibadium*, which featured a semicircular couch. See Dunbabin, "Triclinium and Stibadium," 121–48; Hudson, "Changing Places,"; Polci, "Transformation of the Roman *Domus*."

to the architecture and décor of this space, particularly by Katherine Dunbabin and John D'Arms.[21] Their work concludes that the room layout and elaborate ornamentation were intentional social tools. They were meant to spark conversation among the guests while at the same time reinforcing the status of the host. By investing time and resources into the construction of a dynamic meeting space, householders of this period set a tone for their socializing. As Dunbabin insists, the persistence of these designated dining rooms suggests that "there can be little doubt that the owners of these houses see this as their most important social activity."[22]

Rabbinic literature makes repeated reference to a *traklin* dining room, likely derived from the Latin.[23] Archaeological evidence attests that at least some Galilean and Syrian houses adopted or imitated these Roman architectural features.[24] The magnificent House of Dionysus in Sepphoris (200 CE), for example, has a fifteen-paneled mosaic floor shaped in the U plus T pattern depicting scenes of the god of feasting.[25] In the lower part of the city, the House of Orpheus contains two triclinia, one larger and more grandly decorated, suggesting it was used to host important guests. Zeev Weiss, writing about the surviving houses of the wealthy in both Sepphoris and Tiberias, contends that the setting and decoration of these triclinia validated the room as "a focal point of the house."[26] The décor strategically embedded the social importance of reclining to dine and hosting friends within the physical structures of the Galilean home. The rabbis of this period would have been reclining in similar homes or were at least familiar with their architectural intent.[27]

Rabbinic literature describes convivium-styled banquets for both ordinary meals as well as for the celebration of Jewish festivals and Shabbat.[28] Most

21. Dunbabin, "Convivial Spaces," *Roman Banquet*; D'Arms, "Performing Culture."

22. Dunbabin, "Triclinium and Stibadium," 128.

23. See, for example, M. Eruvin 6:6; M. Bava Batra 5:4; T. Shabbat 16:18; T. Pesaḥim 10:1; B. Bava Metzi'a 5:3; Y. Rosh Hashanah 4:2, 59b. For analysis of the archaeological evidence, see Hirschfeld, *Palestinian Dwelling*.

24. Meyers, "Aspects of Everyday Life in Roman Palestine," 194. For the presence of the triclinium in rabbinic literature, see Hirschfeld, *Palestinian Dwelling*, 21–107, 260–61; S. Schwartz, "No Dialogue at the Symposium?," 208; Golar, "Domestic Architecture," 56.

25. Z. Weiss, "Houses of the Wealthy," 318.

26. Z. Weiss, "Houses of the Wealthy," 324.

27. T. Berakhot 5:5. See Klein, "Torah in Triclinia," 335; Baruch, "Adapted Roman Rituals"; S. Schwartz, "No Dialogue at the Symposium?," 207–16; Keddie, "Triclinium Trialectics."

28. On this point, see S. Schwartz, "No Dialogue at the Symposium?," 208–9.

famously, the Mishnah incorporates the convivium model into the Passover seder, requiring even the poorest of participants to recline upon couches and drink mixed wine during dinner in order to symbolize the Israelite freedom from slavery.[29] The Tosefta includes detailed instructions for reclining, washing, and drinking wine at a rabbinic banquet meal, emphasizing the expected attention to order and status:

> What is the order of reclining? When there are only two couches, the greatest reclines at the head of the first, the one second to him below him. When there are three couches, the greatest reclines at the head of the middle one, the one second to him reclines above him and the third below him, and so on [according to seniority]. What is the order of handwashing? If there are less than five guests, they begin with the greatest; if five or more, with the least. What is the order of the mixing of the cups [of wine]? During the meal, they begin with the greatest; after the meal they begin with the leader of the benediction. If he wished to show honor to his teacher or to one greater than he [and have the servants pour his wine first], he is permitted to do so. (T. Berakhot 5:5–7)

> כיצד סדר הסב? בזמן שהן שתי מטות, גדול מסב בראשה של ראשונה שני לו למטה מימנו. בזמן שהן שלש מטות, גדול מסב בראשה של אמצעית שני לו למעלה ממנו, שלישי לו למטה ממנו. כך היו מסדירין והולכין. סדר נטילת ידים כיצד? עד חמשה מתחילין מן הגדול, מחמשה ואילך מתחילין מן הקטן. סדר מזיגת הכוס כיצד? בתוך המזון מתחילין מן הגדול, לאחר המזון מתחילין מן המברך. רצה לחלוק כבוד לרבו או למי שגדול ממנו, הרשות בידו.[30]

Wine accompanies the food and is dispensed throughout according to the different stages of the meal. Attention is paid to the social status of the guests and the order of their reclining, which reflects the broader social signification of order and placement within the physical space. Spatial hierarchies were built into the convivium meal itself as banquet halls arranged in the triclinium (and later *stibadium*) style facilitated careful seating arrangements ordered by social status.[31] Someone had to recline upon the central couch, and that someone was often the guest with the most clout. Guests experienced the feast alert to their place in the social hierarchy.[32] Different ranks of food could be served as

29. M. Pesaḥim 10:1. See Bokser, *Origins of the Seder*; Rosenblum, *Food and Identity*, 63–68, 128–30, 162–70.

30. Ed. Lieberman, 26.

31. Stein-Hölkeskamp, "Class and Power."

32. D'Arms, "Performing Culture," 313.

an "intentional tool" for further distinguishing the status differences between guests, thereby affirming the social relations between guest and host.[33] Here competition coexisted with convivial solidarity so that these banquets walked the edge of social unity and hierarchical divisions of power. The convivium required a balancing act between rank and camaraderie, which the Tosefta echoes with its own careful arrangement.

The convivium was based on the Greek and Etruscan symposium, an exclusively male and aristocratic occasion for drinking and entertainment following dinner that was likely inherited from the ancient Assyrians.[34] While some might think that rabbinic banquets imitated their conquerors or "Judaized" the Greco-Roman dinner table, the reclined banquet was a ubiquitous institution stretching back to the kings of the Near East.[35] In fact, one of the earliest textual depictions of such a banquet anywhere appears in the biblical condemnation voiced by Amos, the eighth-century BCE Israelite prophet:

> 4 Alas for those who lie on beds of ivory,
> and lounge on their couches,
> and eat lambs from the flock,
> and calves from the stall;
> 5 who sing idle songs to the sound of the harp,
> and like David improvise on instruments of music;
> 6 who drink wine from bowls,
> and anoint themselves with the finest oils,
> but are not grieved over the ruin of Joseph!
> 7 Therefore they shall now be the first to go into exile,
> and the revelry of the loungers shall pass away. (Amos 6:4–7, NRSV)

The prophet denounced the luxurious banqueting of the ruling elite in Samaria who lounged upon couches while ignoring the matters of their city.[36] The emphasis upon reclining and the order of events marks these banquets as

33. Hudson, "Changing Places," 114.

34. Garnsey, *Food and Society*, 129; Dunbabin, *Roman Banquet*, 14.

35. On the antiquity of the reclined banquet, see Dentzer, "Aux origines de l'iconographie du banquet couché"; Reade, "Symposion in Ancient Mesopotamia"; Matthäus, "The Greek Symposion," 256–60. On the influence upon rabbinic meals, see Stein, "Influence of Symposia Literature"; and Rosenblum, *Food and Identity*, 101 and 169.

36. For commentary on the meal in this passage, see Eidevall, *Amos*, 173–74. Amos warns of the ensuing divine judgment brought by a hostile army, understood by scholars as the Assyrian invasion in 733 BCE (Amos 3:11, 6:14).

symposium-styled affairs. The participants partook in entertainment and excessive drinking signaled by the chosen vessel of bowls (*mizrāq*) rather than ordinary cups (*kôs*) following their meal of fine meats. Ornate couches bedecked with carved ivory decorations, which archaeological evidence confirms as a commodity for this period, attest to the extravagance of the event.[37]

The Roman convivium inherited the symposium's reclined banquet setting but emphasized the meal itself.[38] Drinking coincided with dinner rather than followed, and the meal set the stage for the evening's conversation. Rabbinic banquets more closely resemble the convivium model by emphasizing the sequence of the meal, but these habits should be considered part of a broader phenomenon of reclined dining. Reclining to dine, ritualized wine drinking, and a sequenced dinner were broadly understood features of banquet meals in the ancient world. It likely would not have occurred to the rabbis to conduct a banquet meal in any other way.[39]

Besides the elaborate architecture and décor that enhanced these meals, the convivium was a powerful social spectacle in itself. Cicero, for example, insisted that the difference between the Roman and Greek customs could be observed in the banquet's very name:

> For our fathers did well in calling the reclining of friends at feasts a *convivium* (lit. living together), because it implies a communion of life, which is a better designation than that of the Greeks, who call it sometimes a "drinking together" (*symposium*) and sometimes an "eating together," (*sundeipnon*) thereby apparently exalting what is of least value in these associations above that which gives them their greatest charm (*Sen.* 13:45; ca. 44 BCE).[40]

In this passage Cicero romanticizes the social bonds formed at Roman banquets, portraying them as opportunities for communal living beyond mere consumption of food and drink. These events fostered a sense of community,

37. According to Philip King, "Samaria yielded over 500 ivory fragments, dating to either the ninth or the eighth century B.C.E.," *Amos, Hosea, Micah*, 143.

38. On the differences between the symposium and convivium, see Murray, *Sympotica*; D'Arms, "Control, Companionship, and Clientela," 327–48. Garnsey is less convinced that there were substantive differences in the Greek and Roman contexts (*Food and Society*, 136–37).

39. See S. Schwartz, "No Dialogue at the Symposium?," 208 for analysis of how common these elements would have been in the rabbinic thinking of the Passover seder. On the practice of reclined dining and hypothetical rabbinic wealth, see Wilfand, "Was There Really 'an Arrogance of Wealth'?," 24–29. Cf. Gardner, "Who is Rich?"

40. See also Cicero, *Ad Fam.* 9.24.3.

facilitating social belonging that persisted beyond the meal. Despite Cicero's efforts to distinguish the Roman convivium from the Greek symposium, the two shared more in common than not. The dining room served as "a private theater," providing an intimate setting for conversation and entertainment.[41] As John D'Arms explains, the host of the convivium functioned as "spectacle-maker," whose larger purpose was to strengthen his own social influence within a hierarchical society.[42] The host served as maestro of the reclined banquet, orchestrating a meticulously planned event to please his guests, reinforce social ties, and enhance his own social standing.

The ideal rabbinic banquet is similarly attuned to the power and spectacle of speech at the convivium, harnessing the setting to amplify Jewish piety. First, the rabbinic table featured ritualized benedictions to punctuate the meal.[43] This in itself was not unusual for the convivium setting. The Romans had a sense of divine responsibility for their guests and often invoked *dii hospitales* (hospitality gods) or even *Jupiter Hospitalis* in their texts and material tokens (tesserae) to honor these gods invoked at the feast.[44] Earlier Jewish texts show that it was already customary to offer prayers to the Jewish God in conjunction with meals.[45] The rabbis expanded upon these dinner habits and codified benedictions into Jewish law. They took the words of Deuteronomy to heart—"eat your fill and bless the Lord your God"—and elaborated their content, when such blessings were needed throughout the course of a meal, who was obligated to recite them, and the circumstances that might pose a challenge to the fulfillment of this divine command.[46]

These benedictions served to punctuate the elements of the meal. Mishnah Berakhot describes blessings for the type of food being eaten, such as "fruit of the vine," "fruit of the tree," or "fruit of the ground."[47] These ritual words brought attention to the specific types of foods being consumed and to the Jewish God

41. Rossiter, "Convivium and Villa," 203.

42. D'Arms, "Performing Culture," 313; and Klein, "Torah in Triclinia," 332.

43. Kraemer, *Jewish Eating and Identity*, 73–86; Rosenblum, *Food and Identity*, 98–101; Bokser, "Ma'al and Blessings over Food." On rabbinic attention to the poor's ability to eat special meals, see Gardner, "Let Them Eat Fish."

44. Nicols, "Hospitality Among the Romans," 425. For example, see Tacitus, *Ann.* 15.52 and Cicero, *Verr.* 4.22. See the collection of tesserae in Chamorro, "Ius Hospitii y Ius Civitatis."

45. Deut. 8:10; Jubilees 22:6–9; Josephus, *J.W.* 2, 8:5; Weinfeld, "Grace after Meals in Qumran."

46. Deut. 8:10. On who was allowed to recite food blessings, see M. Berakhot 7:1.

47. M. Berakhot 6. See Kraemer, *Jewish Eating and Identity*, 73–86.

as their creator. The conclusion of the communal meal was marked by a special benediction over a cup of wine, known as *birkat hamazon*.[48] The Mishnah explains that if people reclined to eat (Berakhot 6:6) or three men "ate as one" (Berakhot 7:1), it constituted a communal meal requiring the need to designate someone to recite the benediction. The communal recitation added an additional layer of social cues to the convivium. The participants would be clear that they were partaking in a meal observed by the *Jewish* God rather than Jupiter.

While recitation of rabbinic benedictions helped facilitate a distinctly Jewish table community, at the same time it showcased the rabbinic expertise required to know how to conduct such a table. The creation of table liturgies served to sacralize Jewish domestic space, so as Laura Lieber explains, "the domestic table" could become "a humble but no less holy altar."[49] The table as altar was portable and ubiquitous in a way the Jerusalem Temple was not, but it still required liturgical expertise to unlock its full potential. Those who knew the proper rabbinic benedictions were afforded table honors, which the Palestinian Talmud adds by expanding upon the Tosefta's initial attention to order of reclining: "R. Abba in the name of Rav teaches: 'those who are reclining are forbidden to taste anything until he who blessed tastes first.'"[50] The text promises that those who learned proper benedictions would be treated as if they were the highest-ranking person in attendance. Rabbinic banquets did not resist social expectations of rank and honor but rather capitalized upon them by eschewing typical markers of status in favor of those with proximity to the rabbinic specialist group.

The rabbinic table therefore served to initiate those gathered into a way of knowing that required rabbinic expertise to guide the meal. This expertise introduced the second component of Jewish piety to the dinner table: Torah table talk.[51] By the end of the second and first centuries BCE, Roman

48. No standardized text for the blessing appears in rabbinic literature, but general themes are referenced. M. Berakhot. 7:3; T. Berakhot 3:9, 6:1; Y. Berakhot 1:8, 3d, and 7:1, 11a; B. Berakhot 48a–49b. Louis Finkelstein theorized that in its initial form the benediction was a single sentence: "*Baruch atah Adonai eloheinu Melech haolam hazan et haolam kulo b'tov b'hesed uvrachamim*"; "Blessed are You, Lord our God, King of the Universe, who nourishes the whole world in goodness, mercy, and compassion" ("Birkat Ha-Mazon", 227). On the *birkat hamazon* in rabbinic literature, see Marks, "In the Place of Libation."

49. Lieber, "Jewish Prayer, Liturgy, and Ritual," 488.

50. Y. Berakhot 6:1, 10a.

51. For the use of the term "Torah table talk" in the rabbinic context, see Rosenblum, *Food and Identity*, 98. Rosenblum contends that such practices allowed Jews to "secure their Jewish identity" through the atmosphere of dining with Torah discussions (*Food and Identity*, 101).

sympotic literature began to emphasize the role of scholarly conversation during the convivium meal.[52] These literary banquet scenes featured extended conversations throughout the meal, using aspects of the dinner to inspire each stage of the discourse. Guests at such meals were expected to demonstrate their rhetorical skills as part of the evening's entertainment, their words serving as a performance for all in attendance. The rabbinic table similarly emphasized rigorous articulation and interpretation of Torah as a unique and important part of dining with rabbis.[53]

Mishnah Avot goes so far as to equate the words spoken by rabbis dining together with the cultic sacrifices of the former Jerusalem Temple:

> If three have eaten at one table and have spoken over it words of Torah, it is as if they have eaten from the table of God [lit. *makom*], as it is written (Ezek. 41:22), "And he told me: This is the table that stands before the Lord." (M. Avot 3:3).

The table depicted here portrays at least three sages sharing a communal meal and discussing Torah.[54] The central table is likened to the altar, as per the prooftext from Ezekiel where the divine messenger relays to Ezekiel the dimensions of a wooden altar in a visionary temple. This passage belongs to an exhortatory chapter praising the expertise of rabbinic sages. It is noteworthy that only the rabbinic expert can facilitate this connection to God. Although the text is phrased generally, its audience is those sages within the rabbinic orbit who have learned how to talk about Torah in terms recognized by the rabbinic specialist group. Later in the chapter, the text insists that the divine presence dwells with those occupied in rabbinic Torah study: "R. Halafta of Kefar Hanania said: when ten sit together and occupy themselves with Torah, the Shechinah abides among them, as it is said: 'God stands in the congregation of God' (Psalms 82:1)."[55] Although anyone could share Torah at the dinner table in theory, the understood subject is the rabbinic sage and his students who have expertise from their interactions within the rabbinic specialist group. They are portrayed as nurturing an expertise in Torah that

52. Garnsey, *Food and Society*, 131. See also König, *Saints and Symposiasts*, 15.

53. For the dynamics of women participation in such meal discussions, see Lehman, "Who Gets a Voice at the Table?"

54. Rosenblum argues that to partake in a meal with an unlearned sage would be tantamount to idolatry (*Food and Identity*, 101).

55. M. Avot 3:6.

saturates every aspect of their life so that their very dining habits are infused with piety.

Banquets were a ritual activity of consumption charged with symbolic media. Rabbis participated in the expected habits of feasting, but their texts imagine that they did so in terms that showcased Torah and by extension their expertise. Their eating was not ordinary but was infused with a specialized knowledge, not only of the proper benedictions but of how to prepare food, which ingredients were valid for mixing together, and how to cook said food.[56] This knowledge transformed their tables into a sacred space that their specialist group served as steward.

A pair of stories from the midrashic collection Genesis Rabbah illustrate how rabbinic expertise elevates the gathering. The first contends that the very food at the rabbinic Shabbat meal is superior to ordinary Roman banquets.

> Our Rabbi made a feast for Antoninus on the Shabbat. They brought before him prepared foods that were cold. He ate from them and found them very tasty. He [Rabbi] made a feast for him [Antoninus] on a weekday and brought before him steaming foods. He [Antoninus] said to him [Rabbi] those [the cold food on Shabbat] tasted better to me than these [warm foods]. He [Rabbi] explained that the warm weekday food was missing a single spice. He [Antoninus] said to him, and is there anything in the king's treasury that is lacking? He [Rabbi] said that the food was missing Shabbat. Do you have Shabbat? (Gen. Rab. 11:4)
>
> רבנו עשה סעודה לאנטונינוס בשבת. הביא לפניו תבשילין צונן. אכל מהם וערב לו, עשה לו סעודה בחול הביא לפניו תבשילים רותחין. אמר לו אותן ערבו לי יותר מאלה. אמר לו תבל אחד הן חסירין. אמר לו וכי הקילרין שלמלך חסר כלום אתמהא. אמר ליה שבת הן חסירין, אית לך שבת אתמהא?[57]

Dialogues between Antoninus and Rabbi Yehudah ha-Nasi, the fifth-generation tanna and Jewish patriarch, appear throughout rabbinic literature.[58] While modern scholars debate the identity of Antoninus, which could refer to any number of Antonines who were former Roman emperors or governors, such as Antoninus Pius, Marcus Aurelius, Caracalla, or the Severan

56. On the history and reception of rabbinic ideas about kosher eating, see D. Kraemer, *Jewish Eating and Identity*.

57. Gen. Rab. 11:4 (ed. Theodor-Albeck, 90).

58. Gen. Rab. 67:6; Y. Megillah 1:11, 15a; B. Avodah Zarah 10a–b; and B. Sanhedrin 91a–b. See Naiweld, "There Is Only One Other" for analysis of the Bavli's Sanehdrin dialogue.

Elagabalus (Marcus Aurelius Antoninus Augustus), the specific identity is not critical to the passage's point.[59] It could even be a way of decontextualizing the persona of the emperor as an imperial archetype. Antoninus is amazed at the delectable taste of the cold Shabbat foods—served cold in accordance with rabbinic prohibitions against lighting fire on the Sabbath—compared to everyday food and seeks to find out the secret to their preparation. The rabbi explains that the special element is Shabbat itself, and no other spice or ingredient in the king's vast pantry could match its deliciousness.

The story is undeniably a fantasy. Sarit Kattan Gribetz argues that the passage functions as a counterpolemic to Christian sources that describe Jewish food as unappealing due to Sabbath cooking restrictions.[60] That a Roman, even more so a high-ranking Roman, would be impressed by Jewish foodways speaks to a rabbinic attempt to elevate Jewish piety in the eyes of others. But even more than a show of Jewish pride, the story also celebrates the proficiency of the rabbis. They are the ones who know how to observe the biblical commandment "Six days you shall labor and do all your work. But the seventh day is a sabbath to the Lord your God; you shall not do any work" (Exod. 20:9–10). The Mishnah proposes thirty-nine categories of "work" (*melakha*), including all labors related to the growing, harvesting, and preparation of food.[61] This expertise distinguishes the food at Rabbi Yehudah's table and is what Antoninus craves. The power dynamics of the meal hinge on the claim that Rabbi Yehudah possesses the greatest wealth because his household possesses the correct knowledge to prepare Shabbat food. This argument is particularly persuasive for non-rabbinic Jews who might be enticed by the admiration of an imperial guest—if even he who has access to all the luxurious food in the world appreciates the rabbinic foodways, how much more so should Jews who share an ancestral relationship to the Torah?

The way rabbinic knowledge of Shabbat is featured in this story speaks to the social power of the convivium table. If the convivium is indeed a place where those present can share a "communion of life," as Cicero suggests, then this was a crucial setting for introducing others to the world of rabbinic culture. In fact, dining may have been one of the primary ways in which the values and practices of rabbinic Judaism spread throughout their communities. If one

59. For more on Antoninus, see Meir, "The Historical Contribution of the Legends of the Sages"; Newmyer, "Antoninus and Rabbi on the Soul"; and S. J. Cohen, "Conversion of Antoninus."

60. On this passage, see Gribetz, "Between Narrative and Polemic," 42.

61. M. Shabbat 7:2.

tastes of the food at a rabbinic prepared table, those foodways may be taken back to one's household. Or if one attended a banquet with a rabbi who offered a particular benediction, others may seek to emulate him in their own home. "Where did you learn to recite in that way?" a neighbor might inquire. To which the response could be, "I heard Rabbi Yehoshua recite like this when I went for Shabbat dinner." To which the neighbor might exclaim, "Oh, tell me what food he served!" Accounts of rabbis attending banquets show the significance of the banquet table as a platform for enhancing the perception of rabbis as experts.

Later in the same chapter from Genesis Rabbah we learn of another banquet hosted by a pious Jew where Torah is the focus despite the lavish convivium context:

> Once R. Ḥiyya b. Abba was invited to a banquet hosted by a man in Laodicea. They brought before him a huge table that was loaded with every kind of produce that was created during the six days of creation. And in the center of the table, a child was sitting, reciting "The earth is the Lord's and all that is in it, the world, and those who dwell in it" (Ps. 24:1). Why? So that the owner would not grow conceited. I said to him, "My son, how did you merit all of this wealth?" "I was a butcher," he replied, "and whenever I saw a good animal, I set it aside for Shabbat." (Gen. Rab. 11:4)
>
> אמר רבי חייא בר אבא פעם אחת זימנני אדם בלודקיא. והביא לפנינו טרפיזין[62] טעון בי"ו מוטות, ובו מכל מה שנברא בששת ימי בראשית. ותינוק אחד יושב באמצעיתו. והיה מכריז ואומר: "לי"י הארץ ומלואה תבל ויושבי בה" (תהילים כד א). למה? שלא תגבה דעתו שלבעל הבית עליו. אמרתי לו בני מאיכן זכיתה לכל הכבוד הזה? אמר לי, טבח הייתי, וכל בהמה שהייתי רואה טובה הייתי מפרישה לשבת.[63]

This passage reads like a scene from a Charles Dickens novel. The host is a wealthy householder, attested by the table loaded with varieties of food of which many were likely obtained through import. One can imagine in a Dickens-like fashion a table of roasted meats soaking in their juices, figs and olives adorning platters, foreign spices cloying the air. The display of food signifies the host's status and his generosity to his friends. The significance of banquet food in forging social relationships is elsewhere described in the Tosefta by comparing the perspectives of a good and bad guest. The good guest praises the labor and value of the host's effort, declaring, "May my host

62. Related to the Greek τραπέζιον or small table.
63. Gen. Rab. 11:4 (ed. Theodor-Albeck, 91.)

be remembered for good. How many kinds of wine did he bring before us! How many kinds of cuts [of meat] did he bring before us! How many kinds of cakes did he bring before us! And he prepared all this just for me."[64] These lavish culinary offerings would serve to impress the guests and reinforce the host's social status. And yet in the center of it all, a small child sat reminding all in attendance that such bounty belongs to God.

We learn that the householder merited this wealth because he was once a butcher who would set aside the best animals for the Shabbat feast. Catherine Hezser notes that his actions are not necessarily evidence of rabbinic influence but rather the host's own "idiosyncratic" personal piety.[65] Such a reading suggests that the host may not have been directly connected to the rabbinic cohort but was pious enough to value inviting a Torah scholar to dinner. This story appears in a chapter devoted to the power of God's blessing of Shabbat, as described in Genesis 2:3, as well as the non-rabbinic Jews and non-Jews who benefit from this blessing. This particular passage is used as evidence that Jews living outside the land of Israel—in this case, the wealthy city of Laodicea in Syria—would be rewarded with wealth for their observance of Shabbat and other festivals.[66] The emphasis upon merit and reward reframes Rabbi Ḥiyya's attendance at such a banquet. He was not seeking favor or benefit from association with a wealthy householder but dining with a real mensch. The presence of a rabbi served as its own reward for the host's personal piety and would require no reciprocation to the host.

The invitation to attend this banquet represents the type of invitation that rabbis might receive from wealthy Jews who valued their expertise or sought to benefit from their attendance at their banquets. While the host may or may not be rabbinically observant, the text explains why he is a worthy rabbinic dining companion. He simultaneously signals his wealth and status, as expected at the convivium meal, while reminding his guests that God is the ultimate benefactor for the meal. Rather than becoming indebted to the host, the guests are assured that the host is only a conduit for divine favor sharing his bounty with friends. The food itself is a creation of God, and the man's wealth is dependent on divine reward for his righteous deeds. The rabbinic guests are still participating in a banquet interlaced with status and honor, but it is one also infused with the values of Torah. The wealthy host will not expect

64. T. Berakhot 6:2.

65. Hezser, "Interaction Between Rabbis and Non-Rabbinic Jews," 152.

66. Rev. 3:17 notes the wealth of the city. See parallel in B. Shabbat 119a.

further reciprocal favors from his rabbinic guest apart from his presence at the event because his largesse belongs to God.

Rabbis ate in spaces where the luxurious décor, foodstuff, entertainment, and eating vessels signified wealth, and the spectacle of the occasion cultivated relationships among the elite. Yet when they describe these meals, they emphasize Torah as the central priority. Seth Schwartz argues that rabbis were supremely anxious about the exchange of status and dialogue at the convivium table.[67] He contends that the rabbis imagined "an alternative social system" that closely resembled the Roman banquet, but where "the currency whose exchange generates and sustains the system is not wealth and social clout, but Torah."[68] Part of the strategy of elevating Torah, I argue, was a response to their positionality as Torah experts. The spectacle of elite self-representation was not absent from rabbinic banquets, but their storytelling actively wrote a social script dependent upon recognition of the primacy of Torah. The result of such a rhetorical move was multifaceted. The banquet table became a place for the performance of Jewish piety, while at the same time those who were experts in Torah were elevated in status. This shift would disentangle ordinary expectations of reciprocity and thereby rearrange the optics of power and hierarchy.

While knowledge of Jewish foodways, Shabbat customs, and religious observance are mainstays of modern Judaism, in rabbinic literature they represent rabbinic proposals for how to engage Torah in the lives of everyday Jews. Rabbinic texts emphasize that the invocation of Torah and the presence of Torah scholars are the best ways to conduct a Jewish meal. Therefore, dining required someone in the rabbinic orbit—either a rabbi, a family member of rabbi, or someone who had attended a meal with a rabbi—to give guidance on how to conduct the meal. In this way, rabbinic banquets harnessed the cultural power of the convivium in order to elevate Torah study as the supreme feature of the night. Convivium participants who expected lavish food and entertainment were encouraged to view Torah in that light. This did not mean setting aside the cultural expectations of signifying wealth with bountiful feasts. Rather, it meant including Torah experts who could elevate the evening. In the process, rabbinic authors argued for their own status as Torah experts by emphasizing the unique access to Jewish piety they offered as dining companions. Their tables transported those in attendance to the halls of the former Jerusalem Temple, many of whom would never have had access to its holiest corridors. Their benedictions stressed the Jewish God over any other god.

67. S. Schwartz, "No Dialogue at the Symposium?," 194.

68. S. Schwartz, 215.

Halakhah at the Dinner Table

Rabbinic banquets were not only pious spaces for elevating Torah but also places for performing and cultivating rabbinic expertise. Banquets featuring rabbis as guests and hosts were formative settings for developing their own sense of "groupness." Feelings of friendship between men with shared ideological investments formed and contributed to the sense of themselves as rabbinic experts. Although this does not imply that rabbis were a strong institution at this point, their friendships laid the groundwork for an association built on a mix of knowledge of Torah and invitations of hospitality. Those who regularly dined together were socialized into the rabbinic domain and acquired awareness of how rabbis perceived the world. Their dining practices distinguished their group from outsiders who did not know or did not participate in rabbinic norms.

Imagine an individual sage and other Torah enthusiasts—either rabbis like himself or householders with an appreciation for his expertise—are connected through an invitation to attend a convivium meal. The ensuing conversation over dinner and mixed wine would be sprinkled with debate over interpretations of mitzvot (divine commandments), explanations of particular biblical stories, and questions over potential textual meaning. The individual sage would be pressed to perform his expertise by contributing his own elucidations and opinions, which would be tested by his companions. He might cite his teacher or his teacher's teacher in order to give weight to his words. Over the course of the meal the sense of solidarity between these men would emerge. They would have a sense of each other's expertise and an awareness that their conversation contributed to the construction of a base of knowledge considered as Torah. This dinner would not be a one-off occasion, but rather diners would know that this cycle would repeat in coming weeks with other invitations to dine. Social relationships would be reinforced that would manifest outside of these Torah conversations and spill into everyday life.

We have glimpses of this convivium habit in rabbinic literature, featuring both banquets among rabbis and with non-rabbis. Banquets between rabbis are often worthy of textual memorialization because they provide the setting for a particular rabbinic law determined by rigorous debate. In one Tosefta passage, Rabbi Akiva and Rabban Gamaliel were seated at a meal in Jericho among the elders of the town when Rabbi Akiva quarreled with Rabban Gamaliel about the number of required blessings after a meal.[69] The quarrelling

69. T. Berakhot 4:15.

between these two appears to happen routinely during their travels. Another text mentions that they entered a Samaritan town and quarreled about whether to tithe the vegetables brought to them by Samaritans.[70] Similarly, another text states that Rabbi Akiva and Rabban Gamaliel again quarreled while seated at a meal with elders in Rome.[71] This repeated emphasis of leading rabbinic sages debating over dinner suggests that such meals happened routinely. They played an essential role in the development of rabbinic knowledge and socialized participants into the emerging habits of a specialist group.

The fact that rabbinic debate is a central feature of these meals reflects an important aspect of convivium culture. Banquets were a stage for self-representation. Dining etiquette, gestures, visual presentation, and one's bearing in such gatherings played a significant role in cementing social standing. Failure to perform appropriately, such as interrupting at dinner, spitting or clearing one's throat, or lagging behind conversation, would face immediate judgment from those gathered.[72] The ritual symbolism of these feasts was constituted through a semiotic relationship of self-performance.[73] Torah scholars were not immune to the dynamics of status infused into their table study. Consider this rabbinic debate at a banquet, as illustrated in the Tosefta:

> It happened that Rabban Shimon ben Gamaliel and R. Yehudah and R. Yose were reclining in Akko and Shabbat began [lit. the holiness of the day came upon them]. Rabban Shimon ben Gamaliel said to R. Yose berabbi, "If you wish, we can stop on account of Shabbat." He [Yose] said to him: "Every day you value my opinion over that of Yehudah, and now you value Yehudah's opinion over mine? 'Does he mean, cried the king, to assault the queen in my own palace?' (Esther 7:8)' " He [Shimon] said to him: "Then let us not stop, lest the law be established permanently [lit. for generations]." They said: "They did not move from there until the law was established according to [the opinion of] R. Yose." (T. Berakhot 5:2)

מעשה ברבן שמעון בן גמליאל ור׳ יהודה ור׳ יוסה שהיו מסובין בעכו וקדש עליהם היום. אמ׳ לו רבן שמעון בן גמליאל לר׳ יוסי ברבי, רצונך נפסיק לשבת. אמר לו בכל יום אתה מחבב דברי בפני יהודה, ועכשיו אתה מחבב דברי יהודה בפני: (אסתר ז

70. T. Demai 5:24.

71. T. Beitzah 2:12.

72. Dunbabin and Slater, "Roman Dining," 461. See also Donahue, "Roman Dining."

73. M. Douglas, "Fundamental Issues in Food Problems" and Elias, "Civilizing Process."

הגם לכבוש את המלכה עמי בבית. אמ׳ לו אם כן לא נפסיק, שמא תקבע הלכה לדורות. אמרו לא זזו משם עד שקבעו הלכה כר׳ יוסי.[74]

When the time for Shabbat arrived during the course of a banquet, these rabbis debated whether to pause the meal and acknowledge the temporal transition with prayers or to wait until they finished eating.[75] Two different rabbis in attendance had conflicting opinions. Rabbi Yose did not want to interrupt the meal, while Rabbi Yehudah thought otherwise. The dinner party did not proceed until they "fixed" the halakhah according to Rabbi Yose, who said to wait until after the meal. The meal's temporal challenge became the subject of the dinner conversation, offering the attending rabbis an opportunity to perform their expertise and defend their position.

The setting for this rabbinic ruling is fascinating. The text imagines a rabbinic debate during dinner with no reference to the householder who owns the space. We can presume they are eating at a householder's home since Akko, like Jericho and Rome, is a named location that rabbis frequented as houseguests.[76] Also, none of the named rabbis are said to have lived in those locales.[77] Wealthy householders sympathetic to or eager to appear associated with rabbinic expertise opened their homes, shops, and banquet halls to rabbinic gatherings. While we could imagine all sorts of reasons for these invitations—kinship networks, friends of friends, business acquaintances—what is memorialized in rabbinic texts is the way these connections facilitated the conversations of rabbis and subsequent development of rabbinic law. The texts take it for granted that rabbinic social networks supplied housing and a convivium meal.

The main crisis of this particular dinner conversation stems from a clash of expertise. Rabbi Yose is the presumed host of the convivium meal, and we can assume that if the rabbis gathered for a feast that would coincide with the arrival of Shabbat, they were fully aware of the debate to ensue. Rabban Shimon ben Gamaliel, a third-generation tannaitic sage who succeeded his father as patriarch, awkwardly interrupts the meal to ask Rabbi Yose whether or not

74. Ed. Lieberman, 25–26; and Y. Pesachim 10:1, 37b. See Lieberman, *Tosefta Ki-Fshutah*, Zer. part 1, 72–74.

75. On the *birkat hazimmun* (blessings) for meals, see Heinemann, "Birkath Ha-Zimmun and Havurah-Meals."

76. Also, R. Yehudah's opinion is preserved in the following passage regarding the actions guests should take while dining and drinking with a householder (בעל בבית). T. Berakhot 5:3.

77. R. Yose is most associated with Sepphoris (B. Sanhedrin 32b), while Rabban Simeon ben Gamaliel and R. Yehudah are most associated with Usha (B. Rosh Hashanah 31b).

they might pause for prayers according to Rabbi Yehudah's contrary opinion. This test of Rabbi Yose's expertise at the convivium table was a moment of public shame. As John D'Arms writes of the convivium's social dynamics, "being subjected to the ridicule of a host or another powerful man was perhaps the most common source of embarrassment for guests of lower rank."[78] Given Rabban Shimon's status and the religious and political leadership that he represented, his hesitation to follow Rabbi Yose's opinion carried authorizing weight.

Rabbi Yose is enraged by this shaming request and accuses Rabban Shimon of waffling in his support. Why attend a convivium hosted by Rabbi Yose if you're going to question the rules of his table? Yet Rabbi Yose does not argue for the merits of his opinion. Instead, his tactic of persuasion is to perform his expertise through the invocation of a biblical proof text from a similar banquet setting. He cites the story of Esther, in which a Jewish queen married to the Persian king Ahasuerus thwarted Haman, the king's evil advisor, and his attempts to destroy the Jewish people. During a private banquet, Esther reveals Haman's treachery to the king, and Haman begs for his life by throwing himself on Esther's couch.[79] The king accuses Haman of seeking to assault his wife and orders his execution. Using this proof text, Yose accuses Rabban Shimon of waging a similar assault on his honor that violated the social terms of their banquet.

Rabban Shimon is compelled by Rabbi Yose's logic but also chastened for his shaming tactics. Gil Klein rightfully argues that Rabban Shimon changes his position not because of a religious belief in Shabbat observance but because of "the etiquette of honor at the banquet."[80] Rabban Shimon is accused of violating the social etiquette of the dinner table, which causes him to side with Rabbi Yose and ensure that his opinion becomes legal precedent. It is possible to take this point a step further. Rabban Shimon is not only aware of the codes of honor that supported the convivium as a Roman social institution but he is also shamed by Rabbi Yose's Torah expertise. Rabbi Yose's choice of prooftext outdoes all other claims. Rabbi Yose is the king whose halakhic expertise, the queen, is assaulted by Rabban Shimon, who plays the role of the villainous Haman. The biblical prooftext implies that Rabban Shimon's dismissal of Rabbi Yose's halakhic opinion is equivalent to sexual violence and the destruction of the Jews. Though perhaps

78. D'Arms, "Performing Culture," 313.

79. Esther 7. The rabbis understand the verb נפל/ fallen as imminent sexual assault, while the Septuagint insists that Haman was groveling. See B. Sanhedrin 105a.

80. Klein, "Torah in Triclinia," 339. Klein disagrees with Seth Schwartz's claim that the rabbis tried to subvert Roman codes of honor at the convivium, suggesting that this passage proves that when dining with each other, rabbis would follow standard convivium rules.

a bit dramatic, Rabbi Yose's deft display of Torah knowledge shames Rabban Shimon on both social and ideological levels.

Michael Dietler suggests that the setting of an intimate dinner party contains both lines of solidarity and competition and is therefore euphemized "in a symbolic practice that encourages collective misrecognition of the self-interested nature of the process."[81] Rabbis did not shy away from the intimacy of the banquet table; it infused their own specialist group with simultaneous strains of solidarity and competition. Sometimes this tension is flattened by the nature of our texts, but the ripples of debate are preserved. In a different passage, Rabbi Tarfon, Rabbi Akiva, and Rabbi Yose the Galilean are said to have reclined to dine at Beit Aris, near Lod.[82] A question was raised before them: Which is greater—study of Torah or deeds of Torah? Rabbi Tarfon and Rabbi Akiva took opposing sides, and one can imagine the heat in the room rising. Everyone else at the table replied, "Study is greater, since study leads to deeds," siding with Rabbi Akiva. The passage continues listing yet more opinions and biblical prooftexts that reinforce Akiva's position. Rabbi Tarfon must have sat crestfallen, perhaps fighting back alternating rage and dismay, as the rabbinic majority supported Akiva. The intimate dynamics of these affairs touched on an array of feelings that served both to forge solidarity and friendships while also reinforce hierarchy and status. The banquet table was a way of demonstrating rabbinic interpretive skill and receiving recognition for expertise, while at the same time it could spell disaster for some.

The pressure to demonstrate expertise was not limited to dinner with other rabbis but also extended to banquets with non-rabbinic acquaintances, albeit with a different tone. In these settings, rabbis showcased their knowledge to wealthy elites with whom they hoped to cultivate social relationships and solicit support for their rabbinic endeavors. This dynamic is illustrated in a story about Rabbi Yannai hosting a wealthy man at his own banquet:

> It happened that R. Yannai was walking along the road and met a lavishly dressed person, and said to him: "Would my master wish to dine with us?" The man replied: "If it pleases you." He [Yannai] brought him to his house [and fed him and gave him something to drink]. He [Yannai] examined him in Bible and found him wanting, in Mishnah and found him wanting, in Talmud and found him wanting, in Aggadah and found him wanting. He

81. Dietler, "Theorizing the Feast," 73.

82. Sifre Deut 41:3.

then said to him: "Recite the blessing [over the food]." He [the guest] replied: "Let Yannai bless in his own home." Whereupon he [Yannai] said: "Can you repeat what I say?" The man replied, "Yes." He [Yannai] said, "Say, a dog has eaten Yannai's bread." He [the guest] arose]and grabbed him] saying: "What is this? My inheritance is in your possession, which you are withholding from me!" He [Yannai] replied: ["And what is your inheritance that I have?" He said: One time I was passing by a school and I heard the voices of children reciting,] children recite, 'The Torah that Moses commanded us is the inheritance of the Congregation of Jacob' (Deut. 33:4). It is not written 'of the congregation of Yannai,' but rather 'of the congregation of Jacob.'" When they had appeased one another, Yannai asked: "By what right did you merit eating at my table?" The man replied: "I never heard nor repeated an evil report, nor have I ever seen two people fighting without making peace between them." He [Yannai] said to him: "You have such *derech eretz*, and I called you a dog!" (Lev. Rab. 9:3)

מעשה בר׳ יניי שהיה מהלך בדרך פגע בו אדם אחד שהיה משופע ביותר. אמר לו משגח ר׳ לאיתקבלא גבן. אמר לו מה דהני לך. הכניסו לתוך ביתו [האכילו והשקהו].[83] בדקו במקרא ולא מצאו, במשנה ולא מצאו, בתלמוד ולא מצאו, באגדה ולא מצאו. אמר ליה בריך. אמר ליה יברך יניי בבייתיה. אמר ליה אית בך אמר מה דאנא אמר לך. אמר ליה אין. אמר ליה אומר ״אכל כלבא פסתיא דיניי.״ קם צריה [תפסיה].[84] אמר ליה מה ירתותי גבך דאת מוני לי. אמר ליה דמינוקייה. [ומה ירתותך גבי, אמר ליה חד זמן הוינא עבר קמי בית ספרא, ושמעית קלהון דמניקיא אמרין][85] (דברים לג, ד): תורה צוה לנו משה מורשה קהלת יעקב. מורשה קהלת ינאי אין כתיב כאן אלא קהלת יעקב. מן דאיתפיסין דין לדין אמר ליה למה זכית למיכל על פתורי? אמר ליה מן יומיי לא שמעית מילא בישא וחיזרתי למריה, ולא חמית תרין דמיתכתשין דין עם דין ולא יהבית שלמא ביניהון. אמר ליה כל הדא דרך ארץ גבך וקריתך כלבא.[86]

Rabbi Yannai was a first-generation amora in the early third century CE residing in Upper Galilee. Rabbinic legend suggests that he was extremely wealthy, stating that he founded a school in Akhbarah and possessed an extensive estate

83. Included in *Sefer Rabbot* Constantinople 1512 manuscript, most likely to qualify what it meant to invite someone to their home.

84. Included in *Sefer Rabbot* Constantinople 1512, Munich 117, London 169, and Oxford, Bodleian Opp. Add. fol. 51 manuscripts as a description of rising in anger.

85. Included in *Sefer Rabbot* Constantinople 1512 manuscript as an explanatory statement.

86. M. Margulies, *Midrash Wayyikra Rabbah*, 177–79, with some variation.

his own students would manage.[87] In this account, Rabbi Yannai happens upon a rich man "lavishly dressed," acting as a signifier of the man's wealth and status. Rabbi Yanni seizes upon the opportunity to invite him into his home.[88] The narrative suggests that while a stranger, the man's association with a particular class of wealthy elites made him a worthy dining companion and potential expansion of Rabbi Yannai's social network.

The rich man's lackluster response to Rabbi Yannai's invitation suggests initially that the rich man is the one doing Rabbi Yannai a favor. However, soon the tables turn with Rabbi Yannai's intense probing. He examines the guest's knowledge of Torah and of different types of rabbinic literature and feigns disgust with his guest's ignorance. This probing of knowledge during a guest-host relationship appears elsewhere in rabbinic texts. In Tosefta Ma'aser Sheni 3:18, for example, a group of rabbis enter a householder's house, presumably for a meal, and immediately worry that his produce has been improperly tithed—though one would think that if the status of the produce was in question, the rabbis would have inquired before arriving! But the story unfolds in such a way that the rabbis display their expertise in dubiously tithed foodstuffs in the middle of the social gathering, with the host parading the rabbis off to another room to show them his chest of golden dinars as evidence of his first fruits tithe.[89]

A similar situation is happening here at Rabbi Yannai's table. Yet, why would Rabbi Yannai expect a non-rabbi to be knowledgeable about the breadth of rabbinic teaching in the first place? I suggest that Rabbi Yannai does not expect his guest to possess such knowledge; rather, the story unfolds in such a way as to expose his guest's ignorance so as to demonstrate his own expertise. The Hellenistic Jewish scribe Ben Sira (second century BCE) offers a useful lens through which to understand Rabbi Yannai's examination.[90] Ben Sira warns that during formal banquets a host might test the sage's wisdom, writing, "Do not try to treat him as an equal, or trust his lengthy conversations; for he will test you by prolonged talk, and while he smiles he will be examining

87. Y. Eruvin 8:4, 24a describes *beit Yannai*, and Y. Shevi'it 8:6, 23b suggests that R. Yannai had an extensive estate that his own students worked and shared in the profits from. B. Bava Batra 14a states that he planted four hundred vineyards.

88. See Upson-Saia, Daniel-Hughes, and Batten, *Dressing Judeans and Christians in Antiquity* for the dynamics of class and dress.

89. Also in *Avot de-Rabbi Nathan* A 6, and *Avot de-Rabbi Nathan* B 11. Cf. T. Shabbat 2:5, T. Sotah 13:3, T. Pesachim 10:12.

90. On social etiquette in Ben Sira, see D. Smith, *From Symposium to Eucharist*; and S. Schwartz, "No Dialogue at the Symposium?"

you" (Sirach 13:11). As an occasion for aristocratic self-representation, Rabbi Yannai's probing demonstrates the breadth of his specialized knowledge so as to impress his wealthy guest. Whether this is a smart tactic is unclear, but the textual conceit assumes that Rabbi Yannai's demonstration would encourage the wealthy guest to admit that he needed Rabbi Yannai's expertise, perhaps even prompting him to provide tangible support.

Following his extensive probing, Rabbi Yannai instructs his guest to give the benediction over the meal. This invitation was a formal request from the host as a sign of honor. In another rabbinic account, a king invited Rabbi Shimon to lead the benediction over a meal and Rabbi Shimon sarcastically refused as a sign of disrespect.[91] It is unclear whether we are to understand the guest's refusal here as an insult to Rabbi Yannai or as a sign that he in fact did not know how to recite the proper benediction, but in either case Rabbi Yannai calls the man a dog in response to his refusal.[92] Cristiana Franco explains that such an insult places the recipient at the bottom of the scale of honor, writing, "It is an intimidation and a demand for subordination. It is a claim to treat the insulted person as one would a dog, toward which superiority is taken for granted and exercised in constant commands and regular calls for subjection."[93] Rabbi Yannai's use of such an insult is a direct attempt to assert superiority over his wealthy guest in conjunction with his displays of Torah expertise. At stake for Rabbi Yannai was the recognition of his expertise, that while the wealthy guest may be landed, or socially connected, or of a higher rank, his "proper" posture toward the rabbi should be one of deference to an expert. The guest should be honored to eat at Rabbi Yannai's table. Instead, throughout the textual sequence the guest fails to be impressed by Rabbi Yannai, requiring the tactic of shame on Rabbi Yannai's part to elicit the desired social relationship.

But the wealthy guest does not take the insult lying down. The guest claims his own authority of Torah—he accesses Torah as a timeless Israelite inheritance, regardless of whether he can actually recite biblical texts, rabbinic teachings, or even the dinner benediction. This assertion of a different kind of expertise aligns with the category of ubiquitous expertise, as defined

91. See M. Berakhot 7.1 and Gen. Rab. 91:3. Susan Marks argues that these blessings were part of the culture of "table talk" similar to the libation rituals in Roman homes ("In the Place of Libation," 82).

92. For a survey of cultural perceptions of dogs in rabbinic literature, see J. Schwartz, "Dogs in Jewish Society," 273.

93. Franco, *Shameless*, 77.

by Harry Collins and Robert Evans. Ubiquitous expertise is the knowledge that people possess that identifies them as part of a social group and which they acquire through social immersion within that group.[94] This type of expertise comprises folk custom, popular understanding, as well as primary source knowledge. This latter category resonates with the guest's knowledge of the biblical passage claiming that the Torah is the inheritance of every member of the tribe. He essentially asks whether rabbinic experts are needed, as all Israel has access to Torah by divine right.

The rabbinic authors recount this exchange to affirm a boundary between rabbinic experts and other Jews. They echo Collins and Evan's claim that "the ubiquitous expertise of ordinary people should not be confused with the expertise of technical specialists."[95] The social dynamics encoded in the story could be imagined like this: Rabbi Yannai hoped to form a personal alliance with a wealthy Jew and initiated their friendship with an invitation to dinner. Over the course of the meal, the wealthy Jew failed to be wooed by Torah table talk. Perhaps when Yannai brought up a passage of Torah, the wealthy Jew brought up the New York Mets. Or when Yannai shared his thoughts about a teaching from a great rabbinic sage, the wealthy Jew asked him to pass the bread. Whatever the conversation entailed, the text assumes that the wealthy guest could not participate in the learned conversation of the rabbinic table and might not have been very impressed by the rabbi's expert prowess.

The text is not troubled by the guest's failure to keep up. In fact, the rest of the passage insists on the boundary between the rabbinic expert and the ordinary non-specialist Jew, taking pains to explain why we know that the two are different. The wealthy man provides the answer for their difference by citing genealogical claims over specialized knowledge, and the passage resolves—perhaps redacted too neatly—by the wealthy man displaying facility in *derech eretz*, that is, proper Jewish conduct. While specialized Torah knowledge remained an exclusive rabbinic ideal, the participation of the Jewish public in the more general ethics of Jewish piety was the more practical rabbinic goal. This principle is articulated in Mishnah Avot "the sages declared, 'If there is no *derech eretz* there is no Torah, and if there is no Torah there is no *derech eretz*" (3:17). Another way we might understand that passage is that if there is no non-expert buy-in and tangible support, there are no experts. A synergetic relationship is

94. Collins and Evans, *Rethinking Expertise*, 13.

95. Collins and Evans, *Rethinking Expertise*, 16.

struck between Rabbi Yannai and the wealthy guest. Rabbi Yannai's authority is reaffirmed while the wealthy guest's own status is recognized and validated by Rabbi Yannai's expert pronouncement of his valuable *derech eretz*.

Rabbi Yannai claims authority in Torah based on rabbinic expertise. His knowledge throughout the examination of the guest marks him as an expert. But the wealthy elite does not appear impressed, and instead claims his own expertise in Torah based on the timeless claim of Israel's inheritance. The wealthy guest exposes the instability of rabbinic claims to expertise because the biblical text in fact supports the guest's interpretation that Torah can be claimed by every Jew and does not once mention the need for a rabbi. To be seen as an expert, rabbis had to claim and defend the boundaries of their expertise. The convivium table was its own battleground where rabbis performed as experts and asserted authority over wealthy householders, whose friendship they both desired and needed to put in its place.

Rewards for Hosting Torah Scholars

In Mishnah Avot chapter one householders are urged to "let your house be a meetinghouse (*beit va'ad*) for sages."[96] This statement, attributed to Yose ben Yoezer describes the ideal kind of householder who opens his home for the assembling of Torah scholars.[97] Yose was a priestly sage himself from the late second century BCE. The Mishnah invokes his statement as part of a lineage of oral teaching delivered from learned men of the past—going all the way back to Moses himself at Mount Sinai. The weight of this exhortation, therefore, goes beyond a mere suggestion. We are to consider it Torah.

What exactly is meant by a meeting house and the terms of this entreaty are not completely specified. Does this meeting obligate the householder to provide dinner and attendants? How long are these sages expected to reside? Would renting space suffice? The vagueness in part stems from the cultural understanding of hospitality operating as the force for the command. Mishnah Avot resembles the terms of formalized Roman guest-friendship (*hospititum*), where aristocratic families hosted banquets and extended hospitality in order

96. M. Avot 1:4. See *Avot de-Rabbi Natan* A 6:1, *Avot de-Rabbi Nathan* B 14:1 for its reception. On Avot and its cultural context, see Tropper, *Wisdom, Politics, and Historiography*.

97. Yose ben Yoezer and his colleague Yose ben Yochanan are said to have served as the first *zugot* or pair of Judean leaders in the Second Temple period. Yose ben Yoezer is also described as one of the "pious of the priesthood." M. Hagigah 2:7.

to display wealth and form beneficial contacts.[98] Guest-friendship was initiated through an official invitation to the guest that offered "to invite him into house and home" (*invitare eum tecto ac domo*).[99] The relationship was often recorded on an inscribed token called *tessera hospitalis*.

Guest-friendship could be hereditary across generations, linking entire families together, so these material tokens offered proof of their joint attachment.[100] Such invitations of hospitality created a network that could be called upon to offer services such as business contacts, donations, gifts, protection, favors, or recommendations for leadership positions.[101] As Katherine Dunbabin writes, the "complex system of mutual obligations" ordinarily enacted between Roman patrons and clients "was closely interwoven into the patterns of hospitality."[102]

The implications of patronal reciprocity within hospitality relationships might explain why the Mishnah continues with exhortative words describing the appropriate posture of the householder when in the presence of their rabbinic guest: "powder yourself (*mitabek*) in the dust of their feet, and thirstily drink of their words." To powder oneself in dust is a metaphor for sitting on the ground at someone's feet, a space ordinarily reserved for slaves or social inferiors. To sit on the floor signified that someone was not worthy to have a designated seat on the couches. This text encourages the householder to take up such a posture in order to drink not of wine but of the words flowing from the mouths of Torah experts.

Those who invited sages into their homes entered into an attachment of reciprocal hospitality. For the rabbis these benefits would involve both tangible and intangible resources that went beyond the one-time visit to a householder's home. One invitation could become future invitations to make use of their friend's estate or urban property or to attend banquets where more contacts with local notables could be made. But of even more significance to this passage, the invitation of the sage into a householder's home recognized the expertise of the Torah scholar. Wealthy friends validated their knowledge as worthy of support. However, once hospitality was exchanged and with it a

98. Nicols, "Hospitality Among the Romans."

99. See Nicols, "Practice of *Hospitium*," 325 for other similar formulae.

100. Plautus *Poen.* 1046–50. See Patterson, "Relationship of the Italian Ruling Classes," 140–41.

101. See 2 Macc. 6:8 for an example of protection extended from formal friendships. Nicols, "Practice of *Hospitium*," 329.

102. Dunbabin, *Roman Banquet*, 13.

kind of social debt, rabbis would be beholden to relationships that could lay claim to their expertise. This threat to scholarly autonomy—the projection of which went hand in hand with claims to exclusive knowledge—required careful negotiation. Writing of the broader Mediterranean landscape of expertise, Kendra Eshelman contends that to acknowledge the power of non-experts over experts "threatens to undermine academic autonomy and the ideal hierarchy of performer and consumer, and to blur the distinction between insider and outsider."[103] Rabbis could not become so friendly with the wealthy elite that the boundary between expert and non-expert collapsed.

The portrait of the guest-host relationship in this mishnah upends many social conventions of the period and inverts expected power dynamics. It imagines the host physically sitting on the floor as he listens to the words of Torah scholars. This kind of gathering does not elevate the status and wealth of the host through the exhibition of strategic entertainment but rather uplifts the expertise of the Torah scholar as the focal point of the gathering. The text does not outright reject such a sense of reciprocity but actively reframes it. The rabbinic guest is not obligated to the householder for the invitation; rather, the householder is obligated to the rabbi for gifting an opportunity to hear the precious words of Torah.

Given the close conceptual relationship to patronage, it is no surprise that rabbinic texts are suspicious of the implied reciprocity of hospitality. In one text Rabbi Yohanan stresses the mutual obligation of hospitality as a social force that lingers: "'Evil will not depart from the house of one who returns evil for good' (Prov. 17:13). Rabbi Yochanan said: If your neighbor entertained you with lentils and you entertained him with meat, you are still indebted to him. Why? Because he showed hospitality to you first."[104] The text draws attention to the role of food as a signifier of status at a banquet. The householder offered meat in exchange for an inferior meal of lentils, but Rabbi Yochanan warns that the expectation of reciprocity will not depart. Invoking a proverb describing clinging evil personifies hospitality as a malignant power that hovers over participants.

The particular tensions of host-guest relationships with rabbinic experts are best illustrated with the friendship of Rabban Gamaliel, the first Jewish patriarch, and Boethus ben Zenon of Lydda. Boethus ben Zenon was a wealthy merchant who owned property in Lydda, the center of wealthy Jewish life

103. Eshleman, *Social World of Intellectuals*, 78.

104. Gen. Rab. 38:3 (Albeck, ed., 352). For analysis of the association of reciprocity with gemilut hasadim, see Novick, "Charity and Reciprocity," 41.

following the destruction of the Jerusalem Temple.[105] Their two families seem to have had close ties. According to one Tosefta passage, Rabban Gamaliel and the sages were reclining in the house of Boethus, and "they were occupied with the laws of the Passover that entire night, until the rooster crowed."[106] This Passover convivium was likely not the first nor the last gathering of sages at Boethus's table. Comparable to the wealthy man of Laodicea who invited Rabbi Ḥiyya bar Abba to dine, here a rich merchant desires to host rabbis.

Yet this relationship imposed its own reciprocal expectations of access to Rabban Gamliel, as described in the Palestinian Talmud:

> Boethus b. Zenon asked Rabban Gamliel and the Sages at Yavneh: May one make *seriqin* with figures on Passover? They told him: no because a woman would spend time with it, and it would become leavened. They told him: One would say that all *seriqin* are forbidden. But the *seriqin* of Boethus b. Zenon are permitted. (Y. Pesaḥim 2:4 (5), 29b)
>
> שאל בייתוס בן זונין את רבן גמליאל וחכמים ביבנה. מהו לעשות סריקין המצויירין בפסח. אמרו לו. אסור. מפני שהאשה משתהא בהן והן באין לידי חמץ. אמר להן. אם כן יעשו אותן בטפוס. אמרו לו. יהו אומרים. כל־הסריקין אסורין וסריקי בייתוס בן זונין מותרין.[107]

Here Boethus ben Zenon raises the issue of using seriqin, a Syrian twisted flatbread, as a suitable dough for the Passover commandment of eating matzah, or unleavened bread. Interestingly, in the Tosefta, he joined Rabban Gamaliel in a Seder convivium conversation about the laws of Passover, and here in the Talmud he poses a question related to Passover yet again. His association with hosting Passover convivium meals, of which rabbis were in regular attendance, makes him a ready example to think with. His attention in the Talmudic passage is focused upon the food for the banquet table. He petitions to use an intricate flatbread. The halakhic issue is that due to its shaping, there is a risk that the extra time would leaven the dough and thus make it invalid for the mitzvah of eating unleavened bread. The rabbis conclude that seriqin should be forbidden but would make an exception for him.

105. Rosenfeld, "'Boundary of Gezer' Inscriptions," 239.

106. T. Pesaḥim 10:12. Y. Bava Metzi'a 5:3, 10b.

107. Sussmann, ed. col. 511. On this passage see Ilan, *Mine and Yours Are Hers*, 229. See B. Pesaḥim 37a for a case where Rabban Gamliel eats shaped matzah.

This anecdote between Rabban Gamaliel and Boethus ben Zenon provides a glimpse at the potential challenges of entering into hospitality friendships. These friendships imposed feelings of obligation. The rabbinic ruling in Boethus's favor demonstrate the pressure to modify rabbinic expertise toward the desires of their wealthy friends. It is not much of a stretch to say that while the Tosefta records one dinner party, Boethus likely invited these sages to his home on more than one occasion. Both passages suggest an interest in Torah knowledge—at least in the case of knowledge related to Passover feasts—and Boethus is on personal terms with the Jewish patriarch.[108]

In another passage Boethus ben Zenon asks a different question concerning one of his shipments of figs that had gone awry when a barrel of libation wine cracked and fell upon it.[109] He wonders whether he might still sell the now idolatrous goods to Jews. The rabbis rule that since the wine imparted no "beneficial flavor," it is still permitted for sale. While this passage does not outright say that the rabbis bend their ruling to Boethus, yet again they side in his favor, which is itself significant. Their logic is also suspect. The Romans used a fig wine, called *caricarum* because of the Carica figs of which it was made, for sauces and gravy to enhance savory dishes.[110] Soaking dates and figs in wine plumps them up and is intentionally used by cooks to impart flavor. While wine in antiquity was much stronger than conventional wines today, often requiring dilution with water, it would have had similar affect. The passage goes on to liken the scenario of Boethus's wine-soaked figs to vinegar spilled upon beans, the implication being that the vinegar has a similar ill-effect. But anyone who has cooked Alison Roman's vinegar-marinated butter beans knows how alluring that combination can actually be. Even if the rabbinic authors felt fully confident in their ruling, their legal interpretations show deference to the wealthy merchant. I think that they were compelled to find a reasonable solution that would salvage their friend's damaged goods because of the social expectations of their friendship. Their dining habit produced a larger relationship of complicated favors.

We know that hospitality friendships like that of Rabban Gamaliel and Boethus were common. Mishnah Avot's command to share a householder's home for the gathering of Torah scholars shares resonances with a broader cultural

108. And yet his Greek name suggests a measure of assimilation. While it is possible that Boethus is a non-Jew, I think his association with Lydda, which was a central Jewish town, makes it more likely that he is a Romanized Jew.

109. M. Avodah Zarah 5:2.

110. Apicius, *De Re Coquinaria,* recipes 55, 235, and 458.

habit of extending hospitality to intellectuals. Especially well-known scholars in the Roman world could be invited as honored houseguests, with the expectation that they would entertain guests after dinner by giving readings and lectures.[111] Greg Woolf states that patrons provided accommodations and hosted meals in support of scholastic work. These were not insignificant gestures; as Woolf writes, "the wealth and friendship of Roman patrons seems to have been essential for most intellectuals."[112] Not only did these invitations provide tangible provision but they introduced scholars to networks of personal connections, resources, and books to further scholarship. The scholar's expertise could in turn benefit the householder through the education of his sons, the social capital of knowing an expert, and making use of the scholar's knowledge to edify himself.

Mention is made of recurring locales, namely Akko, Achzib, Caesarea Philippi, Jericho, and Lydda, where rabbis gathered in the homes of Jews who were not themselves rabbinic specialists. Rabbis, portrayed in these texts as sets of two or three men, traveled to these locations and relied on their kin networks and social circles to supply lodging and meals. In some cases they stayed with the households of other rabbis or their kin.[113] Other times they stayed with householders named either as a non-rabbi or not named at all.[114] Some might have lived in the named city but convened in the home of another householder in order to do rabbinic work. In all of these occasions, rabbis assume the use of the building for the conduct of rabbinic discussion and debate.

A number of texts in the Tosefta describe rabbis holding a vote on a particular point of legal interpretation while meeting as guests in someone else's home. On one occasion Rabbi Yehudah ha-Nasi, Rabbi Ishmael, Rabbi Yose, and Rabbi Eliezer ha-Qappar spent Shabbat "in the shop of Pazzi in Lydda." Rabbi Pinchas ben Ya'ir was sitting before them, and they sought his opinion on whether to declare the city of Ashkelon free of the obligation of tithes before calling for a vote.[115] The setting for this riveting rabbinic debate is named but only subtly so. The location has no apparent baring on the question at hand

111. Fantham, *Roman Literary Culture*, 28.

112. Woolf, "Greek Archaeologists at Rome," 152.

113. T. Sukkah 1:9.

114. T. Pesaḥim 10:12.

115. T. Ohalot. 18:18. See A. Baumgarten, "Rabbi Judah I and His Opponents," for a survey on attempts to ease the burden of tithe observance and its controversy. On the development of Lydda as a Roman town, see J. Schwartz, "Morphology of Roman Lydda." Also, J. Schwartz, *Jewish Settlement in Judaea*, 259, 261, 264; See Safrai, "Unique Nature of the Settlement," 66.

and serves to simply pin this particular vote to a location. The Pazzi family offered their space as a meeting place for a rabbinic gathering in which a formal vote was held. However, probing the identity of the Pazzi family reveals a powerful social network.

Certain rabbinic scholars are associated with the Pazzi family through marriage and apprenticeship. As already noted in the prior section, formalized guest-friendship (*hospititum*) often linked families for generations. We see this in the case of the Pazzi family. The Palestinian Talmud states that sons of Pazzi became related to Rabbi Yehudah ha-Nasi, the first Jewish patriarch, through marriage.[116] It further names a later descendent, Rabbi Yehudah ben Pazzi, as a rabbinic scholar.[117] We can conjecture that this family was supportive of the Patriarch and his rabbinic associates, which led to marriage between their families and at least one son pursuing rabbinic apprenticeship. The provided gathering space for rabbinic discussion stemmed from the reciprocal obligation of their hospitality relationship. This text provides a glimpse of the kind of kin networks operative at the time of the early rabbis.

Lydda was a site of strong rabbinic activity. Rabbi Eliezer ben Hyrcanus, for example, is said to have lived there and owned a vineyard on the east side of the town near Kefar Tavi.[118] Both Rabbi Eliezer and Rabbi Tarfon established rabbinic academies in Lydda.[119] It was also conveniently the home of the wealthiest families in the district.[120] It would have put rabbis living in or traveling to Lydda in the path of local notables with whom to form friendships. While rabbinic study could take place within the local synagogue or academies, it is also described as happening in the homes of Jews in the area.

In another account, a vote was held "in the upper floor of the house of Arius in Lydda."[121] According to archaeologist Ann Killebrew, upper story dwellings are fairly common in Galilee, likely serving as a sleeping loft and primary residential space.[122] It was not unusual for the houses of the rich to have a second

116. Y. Shabbat 12, 13c; Y. Horayot 3, 48c.

117. R. Yehudah b. Pazzi in Y. Sanhedrin 1, 18c–d.

118. T. Ma'aser Sheni 5:16 and B. Beitzah 5a–b; B. Rosh Hashanah 31b.

119. Song of Songs Rab. 1:3; *Mekhilta D'Rabbi Ishmael*, Amalek, parasha 1 (ed. Horovitz-Rabin, 177). For R. Tarfon, see M. Beitzah 3:5; Cf. Y. Beitzah 3, 62a; Esther Rabbah 6:1. M. Eruvin 4:4; Cf. Y. Eruvin 4, 22a.

120. Rosenfeld, "'Boundary of Gezer' Inscriptions," 239.

121. Y. Pesachim 3:7, 30d; Sifre Deut. 41:3.

122. This upper level is designated as *'aliyah* in the Mishnah in juxtaposition with the lower level called *bayit*. For reference to the upper story in rabbinic literature, see M. Eruvin 9:4,

level.[123] References to the "upper floor" of a householder's estate serving as a private meeting space for rabbis appear elsewhere in the Tosefta. In one text, the heavenly voice (*bat kol*) spoke to a group of tannaitic sages "gathered together in the upper floor of the house of Guria in Jericho."[124] Rabbi Yehudah remarked about once staying in the "upper floor of Nitze's house in Lydda," where he learned that members of the household did creative things to extend the light of the Shabbat candles.[125] On another occasion, Rabbi Yehudah stayed not in an upper floor but in "the courtyard of the house of Geludah in Lydda," at home enough in the space to observe the cooking of lentils for the meal.[126]

The owners of these houses are not always specified by the texts, but we can presume that hospitality is being provided in some measure. Other texts that do name the owner of the home mirror this practice of lending space for the gathering of rabbis. Ḥananiah ben Hezekiah ben Garon, for example, provided an upper floor for a vote.[127] Hezser argues that householders were trying to win the favors of certain rabbis through hospitality.[128] We cannot know how widespread such invitations were or much of the historical realia behind the texts that we have, but if Hezser is correct, then certain Jewish householders thought it was worthwhile to extend invitations to well-known Torah scholars to make use of their space for a gathering.

In a slightly different vein, Joshua Schwartz has conjectured that these named houses functioned similarly to the *stationes municipiorum* (or *stationes civitatum exterarum*) in Rome. These were rooms in houses that were rented to organized translocal merchants from other cities who routinely did business in Rome. These voluntary associations (collegia) functioned to strengthen the relations between persons sharing the same or similar profession. They were ordinarily comprised of businessmen of middling rank but whose time and money were an integral part of the social life of their host cities.[129] They

M. Nedarim 7:4, M. Bava Metzi'a 10:1, M. Bava Batra 2:2. Killebrew, "Village and Countryside," 199. See also, Hirschfield and Birger-Calderon, "Early Roman and Byzantine Estates," 106.

123. For example, Early Christ followers in Acts 1:13 gathered in an upper room of the house they were staying at in Jerusalem following the death of Jesus. See, Beebe, "Domestic Architecture of the New Testament."

124. T. Sotah 13:3.

125. T. Shabbat 2:5.

126. T. Eruvin 6:2.

127. M. Shabbat 1:4.

128. Hezser, *Social Structure of the Rabbinic Movement*, 355–56.

129. On the class of voluntary associations, see Verboven, "Resident Aliens and Translocal Merchant Collegia."

funded processions and feasts, commissioned honorary inscriptions, and supported politicians and subsequent electoral propaganda. They also displayed their integration into their host city's social life by honoring important patrons and aristocrats through monumental inscriptions.[130] Members of a collegium could wield their collective power to form a contact with these local notables of higher rank. Some of the rabbis named in these passages possessed estates of their own, so perhaps their relationship with members of the voluntary association would stem from this patronage practice.

Inscriptional evidence attests to Roman *stationes* of such places as Ephesus, Heraclea, Tarsus, Tyre, Sardis, Tiberias, and Claudiopolis.[131] There is no evidence of such *stationes* existing outside of Rome, but if Schwartz's theory is correct, these locations in the Tosefta might have been associated with respective villages (e.g., Geludah from Galod, Arius from Arus) who routinely rented space. Schwartz proposes that these sorts of houses were often vacant and thus good venues for meeting with the approval of the non-resident owners.[132] Schwartz's theory offers an intriguing possibility of the kinds of contacts that these rabbis would have possessed. Collegia were always associated with particular cults. On this point Koenraad Verboven writes, "The question is never 'are we dealing with a religious association?', but rather what other purposes did the association serve and how did its religious dimensions contribute to this?"[133] An integral component of their very association was experiencing a shared community's cultural identity through the honoring of national gods and performing of cultic practices. It could be the case that the collective owners of the houses described in the Tosefta saw the beneficence of their homes to certain sages as an extension of their association's Jewish piety.

In either case, these texts suggest that the expertise of individual rabbis was recognized by Jews through hospitality. The examples surveyed above all depict the formation of rabbinic knowledge within the homes, courtyards, and shops of non-specialists. Some families, like the Pazzi family, had a vested interest in supporting rabbis because of kinship ties. Other individual notables appear to have struck up relationships with certain rabbis, perhaps because of their own status, wealth, and prestige. However, one element not always mentioned in descriptions of hosting rabbis is the meals or wine and work associated with

130. Verboven, 347.

131. Noy, *Foreigners at Rome*, 160–61; Ricci, *Orbis in Urbe*, 57–60.

132. J. Schwartz, "Morphology of Roman Lydda," 43.

133. Verboven, "Resident Aliens and Translocal Merchant Collegia," 343.

the gathering. Surely these rabbis ate food and that food had to be prepared by somebody. A lot of invisible hands were behind the scenes making the gathering of rabbinic experts possible. We are talking about the attachment between significant households with family members, students, attendants, cooks, house slaves, and so forth. Households joined to rabbis through hospitality relationships comprised a number of people whose identity is not explicitly named in the text but who would have played a significant role in the facilitation of these relationships and expansion of rabbinic circles. Rabbinic knowledge was formed through the tangible support of those in their social circles, and those social circles included entire households of people.

Just as rabbinic literature reframed the convivium table from emphasizing wealth to elevating Torah, rabbinic texts also reframed the hospitality extended to rabbis. One way they did that was by invoking the logic of investment. Redemptive giving, particularly with alms, was a widely understood incentive for the rich.[134] Richard Finn has demonstrated how by the fourth century CE a robust theological understanding of donor benefits animated Christian charitable giving.[135] An exchange of "material for spiritual goods" promised that the donor would be rewarded with spiritual capital—an assured return on investment. Palestinian rabbinic texts use similar redemptive rewards as an encouragement to give to Jewish charity collection.[136] Gregg Gardner has further noted that redemptive almsgiving belongs to a broader investment model that motivated Jewish giving in late antiquity.[137] Otherworldly returns that benefit the giver invoked the social understanding of euergetism inflected with Jewish piety.

This language of reward for pious deeds was extended to include hosting Torah scholars. Already we have seen in Mishnah Avot a promise that householders could "thirstily drink" of the words spoken by their Torah scholar guests. Whether that reward would be compelling to all householders or not, the text assumes a shared understanding of Jewish piety. If the householder wants access to Torah, and by extension access to the Jewish God, the rabbis imply that it can be accessed through their expertise. In this way, the

134. Gray, "Redemptive Almsgiving"; Garrison, *Redemptive Almsgiving*; Urbach, "Political and Social Tendencies," 17.

135. Finn, *Almsgiving in the late Roman Empire*, 179–82.

136. Gray, "Redemptive Almsgiving."

137. Gardner, *Wealth, Poverty, and Charity*.

householder needs the Torah scholar in order to generate merit, which upends the power dynamics of a traditional hospitality relationship.

This language of redemptive almsgiving for hosting Torah scholars also appears in Leviticus Rabbah, a midrashic compilation produced in fifth-century Galilee. In this passage the biblical prooftext "And bring the homeless (*merudim*) poor into your home" (Isa. 58:7) is invoked, but four new identities for the homeless poor are introduced through linguistic exercises. These identities include: (1) the chronically poor, (2) the formerly wealthy poor, (3) mourners, and (4) Torah scholars and their students. The chronically poor are those poor "from their youth" or מנעוריהם. The formerly wealthy poor are those householders who "descend" or שירדו from their honor. The mourners are those who "mourn and attend" the dead (אבלים ומרי נפש). What is striking is that in addition to the folk root associations justifying the categories, the first three identities all share "natural" relationships to poverty. Whether one is poor from birth or loses wealth, they are both reasonably understood within the category of those possessing little. Care for the dead is similarly classified in rabbinic literature as a paradigmatic charitable act under the category of *gemilut hasadim* because it cannot be reciprocated.[138]

But then the passage transitions to a less obvious category and suggests that the final potential identity for the merudim poor are Torah scholars and their students:

> "And bring the homeless (*merudim*) poor into your home" (Isa. 58:7)—these are the Torah scholars (*talmidei chachamim*)[139] who enter the homes of the common folk (*amei haaretz*) and quench [their thirst] with words of Torah. Therefore, it states, "And bring the homeless poor to your home."
>
> "And bring the homeless (*merudim*) poor into your home" (Isa. 58:7)—these are the Torah scholars (*talmidei chachamim*) and their students who teach Israel the difference between impurity and purity and the difference between what is forbidden and permitted and teach them to do the will of their Father in heaven. Therefore, it states, "And bring the homeless poor to your home" (Isa. 58:7).[140]

138. Gardner, "From the General to the Specific," 217. See relatedly *Avot de-Rabbi Nathan* A 4 and Gen. Rab. 96:5.

139. Munich, Bayerische Staatsbibliothek heb. 117 glosses: זה סנהדרי שהיא מרוה

140. Munich, Bayerische Staatsbibliothek heb. 117 glosses: ד"א ועניים מרודים תביא בית אל תהי קורא עניים מרודי' אלא עניים מרוין זה סנהדרי שהיא מרוה את ישראל בדברי תורה תביא.

R. Avin said:[141] It states here "bring" and it states there, "the choicest first fruit of your land you shall bring" (Exod. 23:19). Just as there first fruits, so too here (Lev. Rab. 34:13).

ועניים מרודים תביא בית, אילי תלמידי חכמים[142] שהן נכנסין בבתיהן שלעמי הארץ ומרווין אותן מדברי תורה. לכך נאמר ועניים מרודים תביא בית. ועניים מרודים תביא בית, אילו הן עניים מרודים, אילו חכמים ותלמידיהם שהן מורין את ישראל בין טומאה לטהרה בין אסור להתר ומלמדין אותן לעשות רצון אביהן שבשמים. לכך נאמר ועניים מרודים תביא בית.[143] ר' אבין אמר נאמר כאן תביא ונאמר להלן ראשית ביכורי אדמתך תביא מה תביא האמור להלן ביכורים אף תביא האמור כאן ביכורים.[144]

In these two cases the word for homeless poor, merudim, is isolated and combined with two consonant root associations. The first pairs מרודים (homeless) with the near-homophone מרווין (quenches). The second מרודים (homeless) with the near-homophone מורין (teaches).

The Torah scholars are deemed to be the homeless poor not because of an association with literal poverty but by virtue of their expertise to teach and metaphorically quench those who desire to hear Torah. Their exclusive knowledge is framed as a life-giving contribution that warrants an extension of charitable hospitality and a captive audience.

These folk linguistic connections generate their own logic. If the merudim poor deserve to be brought into a householder's home and the sages belong in that same category, then extending hospitality to Torah scholars is akin to charity. Further, if the poor and Torah scholars share the same conceptual logic under the category of merudim, then those who give to Torah scholars will share in the same or similar investment rewards for charitable giving. Rabbi Avin's grammarian exercise compounds this logic—not only is care for each of the four categorical identities, including Torah scholars, framed as support for the poor, it also functions to fulfill the agricultural redistributive laws of the Mosaic covenant.

This passage applies particularly Jewish notions to relationships of obligation in order to offer two incentives for the extension of hospitality to rabbis: the

141. A line of clarification to R. Avin's interpretation is found only in manuscript 1512 Constantinople: "Whoever hosts a Torah scholar in his home is regarded by Scripture as if he offered first fruits." כל המארח תלמיד חכם בביתו הקריב בכורים מעלה עליו הכתוב

142. Munich, Bayerische Staatsbibliothek heb. 117 adds instead: זה סנהדרי שהיא מרוה

143. Munich, Bayerische Staatsbibliothek heb. 117 glosses: ועניים מרודים תביא בית אל תהי קורא עניים מרודי' אלא עניים מרוין זה סנהדרי שהיא מרוה את ישראל בדברי תורה תביא. ד"א

144. Margulies, *Midrash Wayyikrah Rabbah*, 800.

potential for personal piety and the promise of reward. First, in exchange for hospitality the rabbis offer Torah expertise that will spiritually benefit the householder. As Alyssa Gray writes about the passage, "The implicit combined message is that by supporting Torah scholars who teach them how to do their heavenly Father's will, these householders will successfully perform that will and hence not be punished by a loss of wealth."[145] The text offers a fairly direct means to secure spiritual rewards through personal contacts with rabbinic experts.

Second, the theme of charity couches the whole ritualized social relationship in the rhetoric of Jewish piety, reframing the expectation of typical reciprocity in terms that deflect encroachment upon rabbinic autonomy. The rabbinic expert has already reciprocated the householder's hospitality by giving back something highly valuable: Torah that will quench their thirst. The rabbi is no longer in a social debt because they have offered their own reward and God will take care of the rest. By creating a grammarian connection in order to expand the category of merudim, not only are Torah scholars included in the conceptual category of the poor so that inviting them into one's home generates mitzvot, but the Roman culture of hospitality and debt is subsumed under the banner of charity. This provides a further example of what Schwartz describes as a theme of "rabbis exploiting the culture of euergetism to advance their own interest in the performance of the *mitzvah* of charity."[146] The reciprocal implications of the social relationship are effectively redirected by the framing of hospitality as charitable piety.

The same theme appears in Sifre Deuteronomy. Here the midrashic commentator expands upon the words "*di-zahav*" found in Deuteronomy 1:1, which in context refers to a place nearby where Moses gives his speech. In the Sifre, the commenters depart from the verse's contextual meaning and explore instead the conceptual meaning of *di-zahav*, the literal meaning of which is "abounding with gold". The citation of gold makes an easy connection with the iconic golden calf the Israelites erected for worship when Moses delayed his return from Mount Sinai in Exodus 32. The Sifre begins with the voice of God extrapolating upon the words *di-zahav*: "I can overlook all you have done, but the incident of the [golden] calf pains Me the most!" A series of analogies follow that explain the position. Rabbi Yehudah offers one analogy about a friend who continues to cause trouble for his companion until the companion is exasperated enough to cry, "Hey man, I can overlook all you have done, but

145. Gray, *Charity in Rabbinic Judaism*, 76.

146. S. Schwartz, *Were the Jews a Mediterranean Society?*, 131n.57.

this latest incident pains me the most." Another analogy, this time about hospitality for Torah scholars, follows:

> R: Shimon says: There is an analogy—a certain fellow received sages and their disciples, and everyone sang his praises. Then non-Jews came, and he received them. Then bandits came and he received them. People began to say: It must be So-and-so's way to receive anyone! Thus did Moses say to Israel: That's enough gold (*dia-zahav*) for the Tabernacle. That's enough gold for the calf.
>
> R: Banyah says: Since Israel served a foreign cult, they should have been worthy of annihilation! The gold [collected for] the Tabernacle offers absolution for the gold [collected for] the calf. R. Yose b. Ḥaninah says: "And you shall fashion a cover of pure gold" (Exod. 25:17)—the gold [collected for] the Ark-cover offers absolution for the gold [collected for] the calf. (Sifre Deut. 1 [ed. Finkelstein, 6]).

> ר׳ שמעון בן יוחאי אומר: משל למה הדבר דומה? לאחד שהיה מקבל חכמים ותלמידים, והיו הכל מאשרים אותו. באו גוים וקבלם. באו לסטים וקבלם. והיו הבריות אומרים כך היא ווסתן של פלונ לקבל את הכל! כך אמר משה לישראל: ודי זהב למשכן ודי זהב לעגל.
>
> ר׳ בניה אומר: עבדו ישראל לע״ז, הרי הם חייבים כלייה! יבוא זהב משכן ויכפר על זהב עגל.

The basic sense of Rabbi Shimon's analogy is explained through the parallel statements of Rabbi Banyah and Rabbi Yose bar Ḥaninah. A certain householder hosted Torah scholars as well as non-Jews and bandits. The public are confounded by his willingness to engage hospitality relationships with a range of characters, even from polar opposites of an ideal Jewish society. The midrashic commentators use grammarian skills to propose a new sense of *di-zahav,* this time *dia-zahav,* or "enough gold," which they insert into the mouth of Moses. Rabbi Banyah's statement helps explain why Moses is imagined as saying "enough gold" for the Tabernacle and "enough gold" for the calf. The gold collected for the Tabernacle provides "absolution" for the gold of the calf. Thus, the householder hosting Torah scholars merited "absolution" for also hosting less desirables.

The argument that a householder would merit rewards—either personal edification through words of Torah or absolution for other wrongs—from hosting Torah scholars is a tactic of rabbinic persuasion. Those who host Torah scholars are making the worthiest choice in their social networks that will benefit them in the end. Were householders persuaded? Some likely were. There is no reason to think that some Jews did not feel compelled by rabbinic attention to Torah and mitzvot. Even if they chose to live their lives with a patchwork of personal piety, anecdotal rabbinic advice, and the customs of their neighbors, someone who cared about Torah would likely respect sages who devoted their lives to its study.

However, I think that question is less important than the question of why rabbis felt inclined to try this line of reasoning. The reframing of hospitality in terms of divine investment, redemptive almsgiving, and atonement injected well-known attributes of Jewish piety into standard Roman relationships of reciprocal obligation. This did not erase all feelings of debt, but it reframed them in terms that asserted the authority of the rabbi's expertise over any competing status claims from their hosts. It supported the illusion of autonomy, so that rabbis could appear unentangled in the social webs of obligation that supported the life of their cities. The Torah and by extension its rabbinic experts were elevated in the eyes of the Jewish public.

Conclusion

It would make for a simpler end if I could conclude this chapter by choosing one of two possible interpretations, either that the rabbis desired and benefitted from the hospitality of the wealthy elite or that rabbis were uncomfortable with the proximity and demands of those relationships. As with many things in life, both were likely true. Hospitality proved to be a multisided die that invoked feelings of solidarity and competition, piety and power, expectation and benefit, joy and resentment, simultaneously and to varying degrees. Mireille Rosello, writing from the lens of postcolonial national hospitality toward immigrants, describes hospitality as a gift that transforms the host and the guest by the cultural laws that govern their relationship. They are brought into close proximity, and that intimacy inflames feelings, expectations, and perceptions between the two. In the process, the two enter into a relationship that may require, as Rosello writes, that "both the host and the guest accept, in different ways, the uncomfortable and sometimes painful possibility of being changed by the other."[147] It was this promise of being changed by the other that posed a particular challenge to rabbis, whose status as experts required the boundary between specialists and non-specialists, a boundary that hospitality exposed as constructed and porous.

147. Rosello, *Postcolonial Hospitality*, 176.

This chapter surveyed stories of feasting rabbis and their hospitality relationships. The social power of dinner parties lies in their ability to bring people together in an intimate setting, where they can share food, conversation, and experiences. Dinner parties can create a sense of community, foster new relationships, and strengthen existing ones. They can also serve as a platform for social and cultural exchange, where guests can learn about each other's backgrounds, interests, and perspectives. These settings provided rabbis the perfect space to impress others with their facility in Torah and to establish themselves within the hierarchy of their communities and within their specialist group. They made Torah and by extension their expertise the star of the Jewish table, and non-rabbinic specialists were initiated into the domain of rabbinic knowledge, acquiring a measure of interactional expertise that helped spread rabbinic teaching and ideas. The rabbinic reclined banquet had direct bearing on their sense of groupness and growing the perception of themselves as Torah experts among peers and friends.

Rabbis also negotiated the threat of hospitality, reframing their tables and hosts using the language of Jewish piety. They used the logic of redemptive almsgiving, already pervasive in their period, to offer rewards to their wealthy friends. In the process, their texts resisted the encroachment of reciprocity and imagined a space of expert autonomy. Much of this logic was likely aspirational. Rabban Gamliel's relationship with Boethus ben Zenon demonstrates just how much expectation creeped into friendships. But it also offered a promise to those who cared about Torah. If you would support rabbinic Torah scholars, you would gain access to God. It would be trite to say this was merely a tactic to gain rabbinic authority within the Jewish community. People cared about Torah and rabbis cared about Torah. What separated their care was the specialized knowledge of the rabbinic expert group. Rabbis did not seek to dismantle this boundary, it was essential to their status as experts, but they did seek to demonstrate that if you cared about Torah, it would make sense to support rabbis. Rabbi Yannai's exchange with the wealthy guest illuminates how rabbis sought to persuade other Jews to recognize their expertise. And there was no better way to gain recognition than sharing a meal together.

The next two chapters will examine the tangible results of such conviviality through the tithes, donations, employment, and gifts rabbis could receive from those with whom they became socially acquainted. Rabbinic literature does not expressly draw a connection between the two, but by situating rabbinic dining within a broader matrix of social relations, we can see how expectations of reciprocity and gifting went hand in hand with hospitality.

3

Tithes for Torah Expertise

ONLY A FEW places in rabbinic literature indicate that some Jews brought donations to rabbis and called them tithes. Scholars have been uncertain about the significance of these sources, acknowledging their existence while cautiously contending that it is "impossible to estimate the significance of tithes in providing financial support for the sages."[1] Yet despite the limited surviving evidence, the notion that Jews might give tithes to rabbis was significant for claims of rabbinic expertise. Tithes were one of several types of donations described in rabbinic literature that clients might offer rabbis in exchange for advice and instruction.[2] As individual rabbis gained a reputation as Torah experts, clients sought their advice on matters of ritual purity, agriculture, and family law.[3] The support of this client network provided tangible gifts and donations, and also served as a mechanism for affirming rabbinic expertise.[4] Since the Jerusalem Temple no longer stood and with it the priestly stewards who could shepherd such gifts to God, the Jewish tithing system was open to reinterpretation. Rabbinic authors

1. Levine, *Rabbinic Class*, 71. Cf. Satlow, "Markets and Tithes in Roman Palestine," which is more optimistic about the likelihood of the practice.

2. Levine, *Rabbinic Class*, 69–76, and on rabbinic fundraising from the third century on, 162–67.

3. For a survey, see Hezser, *Social Structure of the Rabbinic Movement*, 360–72. The matters with which rabbis were consulted were wide ranging and these anecdotes punctuate both tannaitic and amoraic literature. Issues of purity and family law comprise the bulk of tannaitic cases, while we find more amoraic texts discussing property and damages, particularly in tractates Bava Metzi'a and Bava Batra. See, for example, Y. Bava Metzi'a 5:1, 10a for a tenant dispute or Y. Bava Batra 9:8, 17a for the validity of a sale.

4. Note Miller's important point that such client networks were comprised of people quite close to these rabbis and did not require a large scale to be influential (*Sages and Commoners*, 456).

reconsidered the purpose of tithes, which were ordinarily reserved for priestly descendants, and developed textual rationale to explain why Torah scholars were worthy recipients. In the process, they made an argument for their own role as experts, inserting themselves into a biblical tradition that made no mention of them.

The previous chapter argued that one of the important avenues for developing rabbinic expertise was through the gift of hospitality. Rabbis mingled with peers, kin, and wealthy householders through invitations to home and table and in so doing were offered a domestic stage with which to perform their expertise in Torah. Invitations of hospitality served as a means of validating that a particular rabbi was a worthwhile social investment and paved the way for more tangible forms of gift exchange among friends. These relationships also imposed expectations of reciprocity, which prompted rabbinic authors to employ divine investment logic. They framed hospitality as a type of charity that would bring immediate rewards to the householder. This chapter turns to tithes as another type of donation that rabbis could receive as an extension of their expert/client relationship. Such donations closely resembled patronage, if not considered as such in the giver's mind.[5] While we cannot be certain how widespread such tithe gifts were, they are an important piece of a larger puzzle of ancient Jewish donations. Taking seriously the implications of tithing for Torah expertise enables us to theorize why some Jews might feel compelled by the practice and how rabbis would have navigated expert–client relationships.

The first half of this chapter traces the exegetical argument the Palestinian Talmud makes for giving tithes to rabbis of priestly descent. There was no office or tribe of rabbis in the Torah. While priests and Levites were owed communal support because the Mosaic covenant allotted them tithes as a tribal inheritance, the rabbis had no such claim.[6] Therefore, rabbinic interpreters sifted through the biblical text for proof that they belonged within the networks of Jewish giving. Grammarian piety focused upon the linguistic formulas of the biblical tradition in order to identify useful units for thinking with. Rabbinic interpreters found such a unit in a verse from 2 Chronicles

5. Saller emphasizes that the umbrella of patronage covered a range of relationships between Romans their clients (*Personal Patronage*). A similar umbrella emerges within rabbinic literature. See also Konstan, "Patrons and Friends."

6. On the post-70 CE priesthood, see P. Alexander, "What Happened to the Jewish Priesthood after 70?"; Grey, "Jewish Priests and the Social History of Post-70 Palestine."

that emphasized the Torah expertise of priests as part of a royal tithing campaign. Here rabbinic interpreters found proof that Torah expertise had always been part of the logic of the priestly tithe. This argument could rationalize a place for the priestly tithe in Jewish giving even after the destruction of the Temple because the rabbis were the new specialist group of Torah experts.

Not only could an interpretive proof integrate rabbinic expertise into existing hierarchies of expertise, but tithe donations were a tangible validation of the rabbinic specialist group. Donors communicated that rabbinic knowledge was worthwhile by choosing to support the study of sages using the logic of tithing as justification for their gifts. Calling the donation a tithe endowed the gift with a religious imperative, but I argue that in practice these tithes functioned as a form of private donations that were embroiled with reciprocal expectations. While rabbis might benefit both tangibly from tithes and socially from the respect and attentions of donors, their donor also presumed to benefit. Tithe donors could expect their funded rabbis to exercise judicial rulings in their favor, to provide personal instruction, or to act in accordance with their donor's demands. The tithe was a hook that latched onto a rabbi and held him close to his donor. This double-edged dynamic made tithe donations both desirable and dangerous.

The second half of the chapter turns to two textual cases describing rabbis operating under the constraints of tithed patronage. In the first case, there is suspicion that a rabbi may have manipulated the laws to satisfy his donor. In the second one, a wealthy woman anticipates that her tithes will secure her personalized rabbinic instruction. Because both texts describe tithe gifts, the aspects of patronage within the text have been largely ignored. I bring attention to the dynamics of patronage invoked when donations are given to experts and explore how the donors in these stories thought their tithes might buy them benefit. These sources suggest that texts describing rabbinic tithe relationships cannot be read simply as disinterested expressions of Jewish commitment to Torah and Temple. Certainly, there was some of that too, but the solidarity invoked by naming the donation a tithe did not insulate the gift from the reciprocal expectations of donor networks.

These tithe donations elicited strong reactions from the rabbis mentioned within the accounts because the expectations of the donors undermined the epistemic autonomy of the rabbinic guild, exposing the socially constructed nature of rabbinic expertise. These cases demonstrate the ways the expert/non-expert dichotomy breaks down through social proximity. Rabbinic texts often express caution toward non-rabbis encroaching upon the rabbinic domain.[7] This caution is justified, as Harry Collins and Robert Evans's concept of interactional expertise demonstrates. Interactional expertise is the ability to understand and communicate in the language of a discipline without the corresponding practical skills.[8] This concept exposes how social proximity can convey the qualities of a specialist group. It recognizes interactional expertise as a third space between the expert and non-expert, providing a way to include non-traditional experts within domains of expertise.[9] Those in close proximity to a specialist group can acquire its mannerisms, speech patterns, and knowledge that make them legible as expert.

Rabbinic literature is replete with accounts of interactional experts. These accounts depict non-rabbis and even non-Jews engaging in dialogue with rabbis, mimicking their interpretative logic and methods.[10] Regardless of whether these conversations actually occurred—scholars often regard these as rabbinic thought experiments—they illustrate what contemporary researchers identify as the real permeability of expert hierarchies.[11] Socialization produces the boundaries of a specialist group but hierarchies therein require work to maintain. The few stories of tithe donors preserved in the Palestinian Talmud offer a useful vantage into the way a religious gift denoting solidarity also imposes a social proximity that threatens the autonomy of expertise.

7. Kalmin in "Relationships between Rabbis and Non-Rabbis" draws the tensions between the two in sharp relief, while Labendz, *Socratic Torah,* and Wasserman, "Rabbis and Their Others" soften the division by advocating for the ways rabbis treated non-rabbinic persons as worthwhile interlocutors.

8. H. Collins, "Interactional Expertise as a Third Kind of Knowledge"; Collins and Evans, "Expertise Revisited"; Collins and Evans, *Rethinking Expertise.*

9. See the nuanced application of this concept in Plaisance and Kennedy, "Pluralistic Approach to Interactional Expertise."

10. See for example, Gen. Rab. 8:9, Theodor-Albeck 62–63; Y. Berakhot 9:1, 12d when a rabbi "rebuffs" the minim with a reed. On the trope of rebuffing with a reed, see Tropper, "Le-Mashma'ut ha-bituyim," and Labendz's nuancing of this position, Labendz, *Socratic Torah,* 118. Labendz argues that rabbis engaged in productive dialogue with non-rabbinic experts.

11. The notion that stories about rabbinic encounters with others is a textual foil rather than a historical event was an important development in rabbinic studies aimed to illuminate the rhetorical nature of the texts. Recent examples of this method include Ronis, "Imagining the Other"; Hidary, *Rhetoric of Rabbinic Authority*; Labendz, *Socratic Torah*; Grossberg, *Heresy and the Formation of the Rabbinic Community*; Kiel, *Sexuality in the Babylonian Talmud*; and Novick, "Tradition, Scripture, Law, and Authority."

From Priestly Tithes to Rabbinic Donors

When the Roman general Gaius Caesar sought to reward the Jews for supporting his campaigns in the Alexandrian war (47 BCE), he did so through the reorganization of their taxes.[12] He and the Roman Senate regulated the annual tribute from Jerusalem and gave administrative control of the city to the Hasmonean Hyrcanus II as the ethnarch and high priest of the Jewish state. Among the stipulations for tribute and taxes came the demand for the Jews to pay tithes to their priestly class "just as they paid to their forebearers."[13] These tithes were intended to support the Temple personnel and enable them to keep their services going. The fact that Caesar includes mention of these tithes speaks to the significance of tithe collection to the Jewish state. The Temple served as the area's primary economic center that not only collected taxes but drew in immense wealth from pilgrimage and diasporic donations.[14] Tithes were deemed essential to the continuity of that work.

The prominence of tithes in Jewish thought lingered even after the Temple's destruction. Rabbinic literature devotes entire tractates to the minutia of tithes and assumes that some Jews continued to set aside at least a small percent of their harvest for the priestly descendants in their midst.[15] This suggestion is itself remarkable since many priestly families had long acquired their own land

12. Kasher, "New Light on the Jewish Role in the Alexandrian War of Julius Caesar"; and *Jews in Hellenistic and Roman Egypt*, 13–18.

13. Josephus, *A.J.* 14.202–03. On the debates over this text, see Udoh, *To Caesar What Is Caesar's*, 36–40. For the relationship between Jews and their priests, see also, Josephus, *A.J.* 14.194–95, 199, 208.

14. Lapin, "Feeding the Jerusalem Temple," 426; Lapin, "Jerusalem the Consumer City."

15. For analysis of these tractates, see Brooks, *Support for the Poor in the Mishnaic Law of Agriculture*; Haas, *History of the Mishnaic Law of Agriculture*; Mandsager, "Making of Rabbinic Agricultural Spaces." Ramos argues that rabbinic knowledge of the Torah's agricultural laws must derive outside the bounds of rote exegesis of Torah ("Torah, Temple, and Transaction," 132). Josephus assumes the Sabbatical Year's existence, writing, "the Sabbatical Year . . . was still going on and forced the land to lie uncultivated" (*Ant.* 15.7) and states that Julius Caesar exempted the Jews from tribute payments in the Sabbatical Year, which "compelled them to leave the land uncultivated" (*Ant.* 14.202) and would bring a "large sum of money" for the priestly due (Josephus, *Vita* 63). The tithing obligations were directly linked to the religious statues of the Torah, which would have conditioned the social relationships of those claiming to adhere to ancestral law. Horsley calls this social structuring a "moral economy," whereby local customs and traditions guide the social-economic interaction of people (*Scribes, Visionaries and the Politics of Second Temple Judea*, 24–25).

and personal wealth and their cultic function was disrupted with the loss of the Temple.[16] It would be reasonable for Jews to forgo the priestly tithe as a bad investment. But the prominence of thinking about tithes attests to the widespread and ancient habit of supporting a priestly class through gifts for God. While these tithes were no longer an imperially recognized tax, some Jews felt compelled to tithe to their personal priestly descendant contacts as a way of expressing piety and ethnic affiliation.[17]

The obligation to support the tribe of Levi with a tithe (*ma'aser*, lit. "tenth") of one's harvest appears throughout the Pentateuch.[18] This tribe did not receive any land when the Israelites crossed into Canaan; instead, they were chosen to become the priests and cultic administrators of Israel. Because they lacked land with which to grow their own food, God compelled the Israelites to set aside a tithe of their harvest as a symbolic gift allotted to the Levitical tribe. This tribe included Aaronic priests and Levitical ministers, gatekeepers, scribes, and musicians. These tithes would support the livelihood of the priestly class and enable them to perform their cultic work.

The Israelites were not alone in tithing for their priests. The imposition of religious taxes and fees in order to finance the services of temple personnel was common throughout the ancient world.[19] The Israelites, like their neighbors, were supposed to set aside a religious tax necessary for the maintenance of cultic centers whose vitality ensured divine favor.[20] The collection of priestly tithes often coincided with the collection of other taxes, which Temple committees diverted toward imperial governing sectors. For example, the Persian Achaemenid Empire encouraged the collection of the priestly tithes upon the rebuilding of the Jerusalem Temple and empowered the priests as its stewards.[21]

16. Himmelfarb, *Kingdom of Priests*, 160–61.

17. Satlow, "Markets and Tithes in Roman Palestine," 320, 322–26.

18. Lev. 27:30–33; Num. 18; Deut. 14:22–66. Note that it does appear that these tithes were largely voluntary in practice, but the biblical narrative imposes a divine obligatory sanction. See Bedford, "Temple Funding and Priestly Authority" 336.

19. Weinfeld, "Tithe"; Kaufmann, *Toldot ha-emunah ha-yisre'elit*,148–54; Stevens, *Temples, Tithes, and Taxes*. Cf. Fawcett's work with religious taxes in classical Athens, "'When I Squeeze You with *Eisphorai*'"; and Sokolowski, "Fees and taxes in the Greek Cults." On inscriptional data, see Haensch, "Inscriptions as Sources of Knowledge."

20. On tithes as a tax, see Oppenheimer, The *'am Ha'aretz*, 25.

21. See Schaper, "Jerusalem Temple," 528–39; Horsley, *Scribes, Visionaries, and the Politics of Second Temple Judea*. For a more restrained view of the powers of the Jerusalem Temple, see Bedford, "Economic Role of the Jerusalem Temple."

Nehemiah's committee is said to have collected both the *ma'aser/terumah* (tithes for Levites and priests) and the imperial *midda* (tribute tax), *belo* (poll tax), and *halak* (land tax).[22] Each of these taxes were funneled from "temple to palace" under the oversight of the empire.[23] The centralized collection and management of tithes and taxes was a major part of the Jerusalem Temple's administrative role as an intermediary between imperial rulers and the general populace.[24]

What distinguished the tithe for Israel's priests from other ancient temple taxes and fees was the framing of this tithe as the Levite's hereditary right. They were chosen from among the Israelite tribes to serve as stewards of the Temple cult following the deliverance of the Israelites from slavery in Egypt. The other tribes were given portions of the land of Canaan as their inheritance, though this inheritance was more of a symbolic loan. God retained ultimate property rights, insisting, "The land shall not be sold in perpetuity, for the land is mine; with me you are but foreigners and tenants" (Lev. 25:23). Each householder was obligated to set aside tithes so as to acknowledge that their agricultural gains were produced under the auspice of a divine gift. In this sense the deliverance of the Israelites from Egypt generated a "primordial debt," or a gift from the gods that can receive no sufficient counter-gift.[25] In the case of the Israelites, God determined that the Israelites must set aside tithes, particularly tithes earmarked for the Levitical tribe, as part of the terms of this debt. The Levitical claim to tithes was therefore a hereditary right for perpetuity.

Despite this strong divine sanction to tithe, ancient Jewish texts suggest that priestly tithes were neglected on more than one occasion.[26] One of the recurring themes within the Hebrew Bible is the reconstitution of the Temple and its tithes following periods of decline.[27] Whether through the negligence

22. Neh. 13:13. See Eph'al, "Syria-Palestine under Achaemenid Rule," 158; and Schaper, "Jerusalem Temple as an Instrument," 528–39.

23. Fried, *The Priest and the Great King*, 35.

24. For analysis of tax collection in Judaea, see Honigman, *Tales of High Priests and Taxes.*

25. Primordial debts bound ancient people to their gods through the imposition of continuous economic obligations because no counter-gift could sufficiently repay the initial debt. Godelier insisted, "From the outset mankind is therefore indebted to the powers that fashioned man and bequeathed him the world he lives in, and this debt is ineffaceable" (Godelier, *Enigma of the Gift*, 185).

26. See 1 Macc. 3:49–50, for example, which states that it was impossible to bring the tithes to Jerusalem at that time. Also, Tob. 1 describes Tobit's pilgrimage to bring tithes to Jerusalem as exceptional rather than the norm and proof of his immense piety.

27. Barrera, "Economics and the Law," 68–69.

of idolatrous kings or through the disruption of siege and exile, seasons of neglect were followed by periods of persuading Israelites to again tithe for the support of the priesthood. One such episode during the reign of King Hezekiah as recounted in 2 Chronicles was particularly useful to later rabbinic exegetes. This biblical passage framed the need for supporting the priestly class as not just a tribal right but as a way to value Torah expertise in order to encourage the resumption of regular tithes.

The passage begins with the ascension of Hezekiah to the throne after the death of his father (Ahaz) who was the literal worst. He worshipped the foreign gods of the people he conquered, erecting altars to those false gods throughout Jerusalem.[28] After years of shuttered Temple doors and rampant idolatry, the ascension of his more righteous son Hezekiah promised a restoration of the cultic life of Judah. The chronicler states that Hezekiah's first act as king was to summon the priests and the Levites and order them to sweep clean the filth from the Temple grounds. In an impassioned speech, Hezekiah lamented that the lamps and incense had lain dormant and implored the priests and Levites to be diligent in their restoration. Rising early following the final day of sanctuary cleansing, Hezekiah led the officials of the city and their sacrificial flocks to the Temple grounds and ordered the priests to slaughter the animals upon the newly scrubbed altar of the Lord.[29]

Part of Hezekiah's restoration of the Temple complex involved commanding the residents of Jerusalem to "deliver the portions of the priests and the Levites, so that they might devote themselves to the *torah* of the Lord" (2 Chron. 31:4).[30] The biblical text recounts the abundance of tithes piled into heaps in the Temple—grain, wine, oil, honey, and all the produce of the field. Outside of Jerusalem, the cities of Judah sent tithes of "cattle, sheep, and sacred things."[31] Not only did these tithes support the priests and Levites of the Temple in Jerusalem, but the chronicler insists "Hezekiah did this throughout all Judah" (2 Chron. 31:20). Town administrators allocated tithe portions to the priests and the Levites who resided in "the fields of common land belonging to their

28. See 2 Chron. 29; and 2 Kings 16.

29. 2 Chron. 29. For a survey of the chronicler's priestly theme, see Knoppers, "Hierodules, Priests, or Janitors?"

30. This account might reflect the circumstances of the chronicler's own time when the people had neglected their tithe payments, as described in Mal. 3:8–10. For analysis of Hezekiah's cultic restoration and tithes, see T. Clark, "First Fruits and Tithe Offerings," 197–200.

31. See J. Baumgarten, "On the Non-Literal Use of Ma'ăśēr/Dekatē" for analysis of the different categories of tithe referenced here.

towns" (2 Chron. 31:19).[32] As a result of the restoration of the tithe, the chronicler insists that the people's agricultural yields increased, for upon inspection of the heaps of tithes, the chief priest Azariah remarked: "the Lord has blessed his people, so that we have this great supply left over" (2 Chron. 31:10).

The chronicler argues that tithing to priests and Levites was necessary for two reasons.[33] First, priests and Levites were owed tithes because their tribe functioned as the administrators of the Temple cult. The text indicates that the priests were enrolled in the distribution ledgers according to their ancestral houses and the Levites by their offices (2 Chron. 31:17). The entire tribe allocated their respective tithes based on division and genealogy. The chronicler maintains that the collection of these tithes was necessary for the reconstitution of the Temple and with it the vitality of Judah.[34] Second, in addition to supporting the Temple system, the chronicler insists that tithe collections should be allocated to the priests "so that they would make themselves strong in the *Torah* of the Lord." The verb *yehezku*, literally meaning to "make themselves strong" (with the Torah), cleverly plays on the shared root *hazak* in Hezekiah's name. More than just a pun, the phrase emphasizes the Torah expertise of priests that requires communal support. Tithes not only sustained the tribal institution of the priesthood and kept the Temple oil burning but they also preserved knowledge of Torah through the support of the priestly office.

This verse and the emphasis upon expertise in Torah was useful for rabbinic reinterpretation. The Temple priesthood and its Levitical administrators claimed hereditary rights that originated in the Torah. This meant that Jews who wished to observe biblical commandments could not easily overlook the obligation to tithe. Just as Hezekiah launched a tithing campaign with rhetorical appeal, rabbinic interpreters formed an exegetical argument to explain tithing for Torah expertise rather than for Levitical heritage. In tractate Ma'aser Sheni in the Palestinian Talmud, Hezekiah's prooftext provides support for the rabbinic Torah scholar as a new recipient of the priestly tithe:

32. Num. 35:1–8 proscribes that each Israelite tribe should give towns for the Levites to live in, as well as the surrounding pasture lands for their flocks. There were to be forty-eight cities in total, with the greater number of cities taken from the larger tribes.

33. On the presence of late Iron Age pottery suggesting designated vessels for the terumah tithe gifts, as depicted in 2 Chron. 31:10 and 31:12, see Maeir, "'And brought in the offerings and the tithes and the dedicated things faithfully' (2 Chron. 31:12)." This marking of vessels is attested in M. Ma'aser Sheni 4:11.

34. See Lev. 14:28–29. Whenever the people failed to bring their tithes, the priests and Levites would invariably leave their Temple positions, such as in Neh. 13:10.

> R. Yonah gave his tithes to R. Aḥa bar Ulla, not because he was a priest but because he studied Torah. What is the reason? (2 Chron. 31:4): "He [Hezekiah] said to the people, the inhabitants of Jerusalem, to give the part of the priests and the Levites, so that they would make themselves strong in the Torah of the Lord." (Y. Ma'aser Sheni 5:3 (5), 56b)

> ר׳ יונה (בעי) [יהב] מעשרוי לר׳ אחא בר עולה, לא משום דהוה כהן אלא משום דהוה לעי באוריתא. "ויאמר לעם ליושבי ירוש׳ לתת מנת הכהנים והלוים למען יחזקו בתורת יי׳."[35]

This text juxtaposes the claim of priestly descent against Torah expertise and uses the prooftext from 2 Chronicles to justify privileging expertise. While Rabbi Aḥa bar Ulla was entitled to the tithe by virtue of his priestly lineage, Rabbi Yonah's tithe is understood as a donation that serves to recognize the value of Rabbi Aḥa bar Ulla's Torah expertise.

On its surface this passage could look like a coup. The Talmudic argument establishes the potential precedent that tithes could be given to support Torah scholars even if they were not priestly descendants, effectively coopting the tithe from the priests. Such a reading would resonate with the overall fact that rabbinic sages elevated Torah learning rather than priestly descent as the main qualifier for status. This standard is expressed sharply in the following Mishnaic statement: "A bastard disciple of the sages takes precedence over an unlearned High Priest."[36] The rabbis privileged aptitude and clever thinking rather than priestly genealogical determinacy as the qualification for religious leadership.[37]

The contrast between these claims of expertise and genealogical descent have fueled a scholarly perception of a rivalry between rabbis and priests as distinct and opposing groups. Indeed, rabbinic literature preserves criticism of the priesthood that suggests a fierce competition.[38] Peter Schäfer argues

35. Sussmann, ed., col. 307.

36. M. Horayot 3:8. Found also in Y. Shabbat 12, 13c; and Y. Horayot 3, 48c.

37. Philip Alexander insists, "rabbi and priest constitute two fundamentally different types of religious authority, the one based on expertise in torah, and so, in principle open to anyone, the other based on descent" ("What Happened to the Jewish Priesthood after 70?," 29). Though this meritocracy was mainly in theory, since family and social connections appear to have played a large role in the rise of prominent rabbis.

38. Exemplified by Schürer: "The internal development of Israel after the exile was essentially determined by two equally influential groups: the priests and the scribes" (*History of the Jewish People*, 238). See Hidary, "Rhetoric of Rabbinic Authority," 16, which frames ancient

that the rabbis took measures to eliminate the memory of priestly supremacy in both the Jewish past and present.[39] Priests, of course, remained key players in the story of Israel, but the rabbis rewrote biblical and post-biblical history to feature themselves as the heroes of Israel's past—effectively "forgetting" the prominence of the priests in the Second Temple period.[40] Some of this rabbinic insecurity, Marjorie Lehman suggests, could be tied to apprehension about the imminent return of the priestly caste. If the Temple were rebuilt, priestly prominence could supplant rabbinic ambitions.[41] Lehman also suggests that the priestly caste's genealogical superiority troubled the rabbis, whose status as experts lacked similar claims to hereditary rank. While priestly lineage may have been a sought-after marker of a social elite, it also represented a claim to cultural prestige that the rabbinic office did not self-evidently have.[42] Burton Visotzky relatedly claims that Leviticus Rabbah replaces the priesthood by turning the priestly and ritual topics of Leviticus into a rabbinic text.[43] The rabbis "try on the priesthood for size" in their exegesis of a biblical text that understandably situates the priesthood at the center.[44] He perceives a "rabbinic ambivalence" toward the priesthood, acknowledging that in some places the rabbis seem critical while in others they assert the prestige of the priesthood. Visotzky writes, "They are wary of treading on the priests' sacred ground, but conversely they do not like the idea that the priests might yet claim authority over what was now construed as rabbinic turf."[45]

Despite rabbinic criticism of the priesthood and the tension between competing claims of expertise, Rabbi Yonah's tithes for Torah study should not be

---

Jewish history this way. Reuven Kimelman suggests that the priests after 70 CE retained their influence as a social group in Galilee. However, Kimelman relies primarily on a single source: Y. Shabbat 12:3, 13c =Y. Horayot 3:5, 48c. Kimelman, "Ha-Oligarkiyah ha-kohanit ve-talmidei hahamim be-tekufat ha-Talmud"; S. A. Cohen, *Three Crowns*, 167; Schäfer "Rabbis and Priests." Sanders, *Judaism*. See also Strack and Stemberger, *Introduction to the Talmud and Midrash*, 2.

39. "They rewrote biblical and post-biblical history, and in so doing they almost eradicated the priests from the collective memory of their people and replaced them with themselves, the new heroes of Judaism." Schäfer, "Rabbis and Priests," 157.

40. See the recent work of Balberg on the significance of forgetfulness to the establishment of rabbis as experts (*Fractured Tablets*, especially 182–83 and 193–94 in regard to priests).

41. Lehman, "Imagining the Priesthood in Tractate Yoma," 90.

42. See Schürer, *History of the Jewish People*, 2:240.

43. Visotzky, *Golden Bells and Pomegranates*, 60.

44. Visotzky, 60.

45. Visotzky, 64. See also p. 62: "The rabbis might wish to replace the priesthood, but the best they can do is hint at its replaceability."

interpreted as part of a larger polemic. Rather, this passage makes an altogether different argument that challenges the notion that priests and rabbis were categorically at odds. In fact, priests and rabbis were not so different from each other. About half of the named first generation tannaim were members of priestly families, which was not a coincidence. The priesthood wielded the authority to teach and transmit the Torah's laws and traditions. This authority was derived from the Torah itself, where priests were instructed to "teach the Israelites the statutes that the Lord has spoken to them through Moses" (Lev. 10:11). The priestly class was involved not only in Temple administration but also in scribal, judicial, and teaching roles and was associated with literacy and textual collection in the Hebrew Bible.[46] An entwined relationship between cultic performance and Torah expertise further runs throughout the tales of the Israelite monarchy. During King Jehoshaphat's reforms of Jerusalem, for example, the chief priest Amariah oversaw the central Jerusalem judicial court and established certain Levites as legal officers (2 Chron. 19:8–11). Likewise, the Levites serving under King Josiah's reforms undertook a variety of Temple-related trades as musicians, scribes, officials, and gatekeepers, as well as serving as "teachers of Israel" (2 Chron. 34:3).

When early rabbis collaborated in Galilee, they used their existing Torah knowledge to develop unique interpretive tools. This was not a new class opposing the priesthood but rather a new type of expertise. This new domain relied on an increasingly citational body of knowledge, derived from a grammarian piety that marked the rabbinic specialist group as a distinct kind of expert. Establishing this expertise required constructing a bounded hierarchy that implied a measure of authority over other competing claims. Mira Balberg has shown that tannaitic literature repeatedly subsumes Temple cultic practice under rabbinic textual mastery.[47] The classic example concerns the high priest's preparations on the Day of Atonement, in which the high priest must demonstrate extensive textual knowledge about the "order of the day" before he may be deemed fit to perform the service.[48] The rabbis serve as instructors and

46. Priests exercised juridical authority to settle land disputes, marital contracts, and inheritance. See Leuchter, "Priesthood in Ancient Israel," 100–110. Seth Schwartz emphasizes that priests, in particular lower-level priests, would have assumed the roles of teacher and judge (*Josephus and Judean Politics*, 69). See also Himmelfarb, "'Found Written in the Book of Moses.'"

47. Balberg, *Fractured Tablets*, 183.

48. M. Yoma 1:3. See Balberg, *Blood for Thought*, 211–16 for the rabbinic instruction of the high priest in preparation of his sacrificial duties.

evaluators of the high priest, which subordinates the priestly class to the rabbinic expert. Rather than read this example as a polemic against the priesthood, we might consider it through the lens of grammarian piety. It would be expected for the high priest to internalize Torah knowledge, and for the rabbis to be part of the religious service. If the Torah is all-encompassing and the rabbis offer a new professionalization in its service, a grammarian pietist might believe that rabbinic expertise and priestly service should indeed be integrated.

Since the study of Torah had always been associated with the priesthood, many rabbinic men came from priestly families. They did not denounce their priestly connections but used them to gain a reputation as a new kind of Torah expert, offering clients different access in a landscape that had fundamentally changed. Their own personal piety would likely have prevented rabbis from ever dismissing the priesthood out of hand. Instead, they honed their skills as grammarians and used the linguistic elements of the biblical text to carve out a unique place for themselves within the priestly tradition. They not only found a way to incorporate themselves into the Torah's tithing obligations but also justified how their specialist group fit into Jewish cultic history. The rabbinic reading of the biblical prooftext from 2 Chronicles challenges a simplistic dichotomy between priest and rabbi or genealogy and expertise. It presents the argument that proficiency in Torah has always been a vital part of the equation.

This point is further reinforced by closely examining where and how the argument stands within the tractate. The passage appears within an extended discussion about who the proper recipient of the priestly tithe should be. The ambiguity of the recipient stemmed from the vague and unsystematic description of tithes in the biblical text. Three primary passages make up the contours of the tithe. Numbers 18 insists that God gave every tithe of Israel to the Levites as their tribal inheritance. From this tithe portion, the Levites were instructed to separate their own tithe specifically for the priests descendant of Aaron. By comparison, Leviticus 27:30–33 stipulates that all tithes from the land and every tenth of the flock should be "holy to the Lord." While Leviticus directs the tithing of produce and animals, it keeps its recipient vaguely "to the Lord" rather than naming the priests or Levites explicitly. In Deuteronomy, farmers are instructed to tithe yearly from their agricultural produce and consume the food in a place designated by God (Deut. 14:22–26). This tithe was to be shared with the Levites and accompanied by a verbal recognition that the land's fertility was directly tied to God's beneficence (Deut. 26). Every third year—that is, every third and sixth year of the Sabbatical cycle—farmers were also to give a special tithe to the Levites, foreigners, and the poor (Deut. 14:29).

The rabbis took the disparate biblical tithing texts and systematized them. Other Jewish interpreters had trod this path before. In the books of Jubilees and Tobit, Deuteronomy's calendar cycle appears as three separate tithes given every year of the harvest-gleaning years (years one to six): (1) a tithe consumed by the householder, (2) a tithe apportioned to the Levites and priests, and (3) a tithe for the poor.[49] Josephus echoes these three distinct tithes, though limits the tithe for the poor to the third years (years three and six).[50] The early rabbis formalized these tripartite categories into the *ma'aser rishon*, or the "first tithe" for Levites; *ma'aser sheni*, or the "second tithe" to be consumed by the householder in Jerusalem; and the *ma'aser 'ani*, or the "poor tithe."[51] From the *ma'aser rishon*, "first tithe," Levites were instructed to set aside a tenth of the tithe (terumah) for the priests, who were also members of the tribe.

Even with the formulation of three distinct tithes, the proper recipient of the priestly "first tithe" remained a matter of question. Because priests received their own tithe from the non-priestly Levites, rabbinic interpreters were uncertain whether they should also take part in the first tithe, effectively double-dipping in the tithe pool. The book of Nehemiah regards the entire tribe of Levi (including the priests) as the legitimate recipients of the tithe.[52] This idea is mirrored in the Book of Tobit, which suggests the tithe was given both to the priests and Levites.[53] Other texts, like Jubilees (13:25–27, 32:1–15) and the Testament of Levi (9:3–4), speak only of tithes for priests and neglect

49. Scholars disagree about the exact number of tithes represented by these two systems. Sanders describes Tobit as reflecting a fourteen-tithe system, that is, three tithes every year but the seventh (*Judaism*, 149). However, Fabian Udoh suggests Tobit follows an eighteen-tithe system, giving a tithe to the Levites, expenditure in Jerusalem, and the poor in each of the six years of the Sabbatical cycle (*To Caesar What Is Ceasar's*, 247). By comparison, Jubilees designates a yearly tithe to the Levites or priests and a yearly tithe to be consumed in Jerusalem, representing a twelve-tithe system. Sanders suggests that the tithe for the poor is assumed in Jubilees, and thus would represent either a fourteen- or eighteen-tithe system.

50. Josephus, *A.J.* 4.226–27. See also Judith 11:13.

51. The *ma 'aser rishon* encompassed two related measures: first, a portion designated for the Levitical class, and, second, a fraction of the Levitical portion reserved for the priests, called terumah. See M. Berakhot 9:1, 9:7. See B. Yevamot 86b, B. Sotah 47b, and B. Ḥullin 131b for rabbinic explanations for the shift of the Levitical tithes to the priests. Rabbinic literature assumes the existence of the priestly tithe, though we do not know the extent of tithing practices in the rabbinic period. Levine, *Rabbinic Class*, 71.

52. Neh. 10:38, 13:10.

53. Though it is unclear whether the author of Tobit envisions a special portion for the priests specifically or a general tithe divided between the priests and Levites. On the one hand

the Levites altogether, which some scholars suggest represents a polemic within priestly groups at the time.[54] A later tradition in the Babylonian Talmud states that Ezra transferred the right to the tithe from the Levites to the priests for their failure to return to their Jerusalem Temple posts under the Persian empire, though we should be skeptical of the historicity of such a claim as none of the biblical books of Ezra, Nehemiah, nor Chronicles describe punitive action toward the Levites.[55]

Chapter 5 of tractate Ma'aser Sheni addresses this ambiguity and takes the opportunity to consider alternative qualifications for the first tithe recipient. A lengthy discussion about when and to whom the tithe should be given ensues:[56]

> A: R. Binyamin bar Gidul and R. Aha were sitting together and saying, is it not written (Neh. 10:38): "Will the priest, a descendent of Aaron, share with the Levites in the Levite's tithe"? To give him terumah of the tithe. But is it not written (Neh. 10:38): "The Levites shall bring [the terumah] of the tithe"?
>
> B: R. Huna was among his colleagues and one of them said "to the descendants of Levi." Why does the verse say (Num. 18:21): "And to the descendants of Levi"? From here we learn that one gives tithes to priests. The other said, even if it were only written "to the descendants" one would give tithes to priests. If somebody would say, my son X shall take property Y and the rest of my properties my sons shall inherit, does he not participate with them? (Y. Ma'aser Sheni 5:3 (5), 56b)

רבי בנימין בר גידול ורבי אחא הוון יתיבין אמרון והא כתיב והיה הכהן בן אהרון עם הלוים בעשר הלוים ליתן לו תרומת מעשר. והכתיב והלוים יעלו את המעשר.

רבי חונא וחברייא חד מינהון אמר לבני לוי מה תלמוד לומר ולבני אלא מכן שנותנין מעשר לכהונה. וחרנא אמר אפילו לית כתיב אלא לבני נותנין מעשר לכהונה. אילו מאן דאמר פלן ברי יסב מקמת פלן ושאר נכסיי ירשו בניי דילמא לא נסב עמהון.[57]

---

he describes his "first-fruits and tithes" given to priests, and then states he gave "the tithe" to the sons of Levi.

54. See Finkelstein, "Some Examples of the Maccabean Halaka," 34; Werman, "Levi and Levites in the Second Temple Period."

55. B. Ketubbot 26a. See also B. Bava Batra 81b and B. Ḥullin 131b.

56. Parts of this chapter also appear in Sifre Deut. 109.

57. Sussmann, ed., col. 307.

This debate tries to determine what share of the tithes allotted to the tribe of Levi should go to the priests. The priests get their own tithe from the Levites directly, 1 percent of the tithe, so the question is whether they will also share in the full tithe portion. In part A, the rabbis focus on the ambiguous wording of Nehemiah 10:38, which states in full: "And the priest, descendant of Aaron, shall be with the Levites when the Levites receive the *tithes*; and the Levites shall bring up *a tithe of the tithes* to the house of our God, to the chambers of the storehouse."[58] A suggestion is posed that the tithe mentioned in the first half of the verse actually refers to the "tithe of the tithe" (terumah); therefore, the priests would only be entitled to their small 1 percent of the tithe portion. However, this proposal is rejected because if that were the case then the verse would be redundant. In classic rabbinic hermeneutics, the presence of the same word twice signals that they represent two separate things. Thus, the first mention of "tithe" that the priests partake in must refer to the full priestly tithe and the second mention of "tithe of the tithes" refers to an additional tithe received from the Levites.

The passage continues in part B with another ambiguous verse, Nehemiah 18:21, which designates the tithes of Israel to the descendants of Levi with no mention of the priests at all. This time the inclusion of the priests is explained through an appeal to inheritance logic. Because the verse specifies "descendants of Levi," the rabbinic commentators argue that the priests are also of the tribe of Levi and so are entitled to the tithe inheritance alongside the rest of the Levites. The Talmudic argument states, "If somebody would say, my son X shall take property Y and the rest of my properties my sons shall inherit, does he not participate with them?" Thus, even if one were to specify a portion for a particular son, that son inherits the sum remainder alongside his brothers in addition to the specific portion. In the same vein, even though the priests are entitled to a special "tithe of tithe" portion (terumah), the priests are included in the full first tithe (*ma'aser rishon*).[59]

58. Emphasis added.

59. However, while this position is accepted in the Babylonian Talmud (Yevamot 86b), the resolution is far from settled in the Palestinian Talmud. In the next passage, we find a stark division among rabbinic opinion: "R. Yehoshua ben Hananiah said, 'One does not give *ma'aser* to Cohanim,' but R. Eleazar ben Azariah said, 'one gives *ma'aser* to Cohanim'" (Y. Ma'aser Sheni 5:5, 56d). Conveniently for both parties, R. Yehoshua is a Levite and R. Eleazar ben Azariah a priest. The two rabbis represent the two potential lineages in question who might be eligible for the acquisition of tithes.

Rabbi Yonah's passage about tithing for Torah expertise appears directly after this debate, which provides further context to how the argument for expertise is operating. Rabbi Yonah's actions initially validate the preceding position that priests are entitled to the general tithe portion, in addition to their special 1 percent portion, because he gives the tithe to a priestly descendent without reservation. But the text then argues that his actions are not actually support for the proceeding Talmudic debate because those tithes supported Rabbi Aḥa bar Ulla as a Torah expert. In a chapter focused upon descent and tribal claims, the passage brings Torah expertise into the conversation as new justification for the priestly tithe. The proof for this claim is found in the very verse from 2 Chronicles where King Hezekiah persuaded the Israelites to bring their tithes in order to support the mastery of Torah. While the preceding Talmudic passages focused upon the genealogical claim of the Levites and priestly descendants of Aaron, this prooftext provides grounds for expertise as part of the rationale of the tithe. The interpreters cleverly demonstrate how emphasizing Torah expertise is not a new rabbinic tactic. It was there in the biblical text the entire time.

Linguistic units from the biblical text were a gateway for the rabbis to formulate a rationale for tithes following the Temple's destruction and, in the process, establish a place for themselves in Jewish habits of giving. If tithes were dependent upon a tribe whose job no longer existed, it would be reasonable for some Jews to scoff at the idea of giving produce to a guy just because his last name was Cohen. But if tithes had always been given for the support and recognition of Torah expertise, that was something that could endure. Even if formal tithing could not be largely re-institutionalized, rabbinic experts could lean into the logic of the biblical text and persuade others that supporting Torah scholars was an enduring Jewish obligation.

In these examples, it becomes clear that the principle of tithing for Torah expertise is not solely a rabbinic invention. Rather, it can be traced back to the textual tradition used in advocating for priestly funding. By drawing a correlation between tithes and the Torah, I have demonstrated that the rabbinic claim to tithes extends beyond a mere power grab or institutional rivalry. The rabbis are aligning themselves with a tradition that acknowledges the cultural importance of supporting Torah expertise. In doing so, the rabbis were contesting other potential experts, not due to a direct conflict with the Temple, but because they championed a Torah supremacy that implicitly elevated their professional skills.

Constraints of Tithe Donations upon Rabbinic Epistemic Autonomy

The hermeneutic feat of finding a place for rabbis within the Torah's tithing system was remarkable in theory, but in practice it posed significant challenges to rabbinic expert autonomy.[60] Tithes given for Torah expertise functioned as personal donations to individual rabbis, which imposed upon both parties the expectations of a donor relationship. Not only might donor demands be annoying or disagreeable, but they shattered the projection of autonomy that is fundamental to expertise. The ideal of expert autonomy imagines that experts are free from lay supervision and interference, exchanging their competence for the trust of clients.[61] This autonomy is earned by their specialized training and intellectual achievements that separate the expert from society because of their epistemic superiority. Rabbinic literature tries to assert such an epistemic superiority by maintaining a barrier through credentialization, an increasingly citational body of knowledge, and eventual control of study spaces.[62] Not everyone could be a rabbinic scholar, nor were they encouraged to be. Torah expertise required a specialized set of grammarian methods that had to be learned through close apprenticeship. Rabbinic experts performed a "gatekeeping function" by amassing and introducing new knowledge about Torah within their epistemic community only accessible to those within their ranks.[63]

An expert's autonomy, however, does not mean avoidance of all social relationships. What some scholars might interpret as rabbinic insularity is rather the projection of an epistemic autonomy on which their claims of expertise rested.[64] Specialist groups are inherently insular because they claim professional

60. On the need for experts to have epistemic autonomy, see Dellsén, "Epistemic Value of Expert Autonomy."

61. On the problems of functionalist definitions, see Rueschemeyer, "Professional Autonomy and the Social Control of Expertise."

62. On fees for study, see Marks, "Who Studied at the Beit Midrash?," 298–307.

63. On the gatekeeping function, see Savolainen, "Manifestations of Expert Power in Gatekeeping."

64. S. J. Cohen, "Rabbi in Second-Century Jewish Society," 975; and more recently reframed by Miller, *Sages and Commoners*, 460; Kalmin, *Jewish Babylonia Between Persia and Roman Palestine*, particularly 9, 19, and 47. Other recent scholars have pushed back on the assumption of insularity: Mokhtarian, *Rabbis, Sorcerers, Kings, and Priests*, 19–21, 23, 42; Gross, *Babylonian Jews and Sasanian Imperialism*, 14–29.

independence and social control of their domain of knowledge. This insularity, however, should not be regarded as fact but as a social construction that helps maintain the distinction between expert and non-expert. Experts are always embroiled in social relationships, particularly client relationships that provide funding and/or a vested interest in the expert's domain.[65] As a relational view of expertise contends that expertise is dependent upon social recognition, clients are a particularly valuable means of validating expertise. But as we will see in the following two case studies, clients can disrupt the veil of expert autonomy in ways that made rabbinic authors apprehensive.

Case #1: Silanus and Rabbi Ḥiyya bar Abba

The first case involves Rabbi Ḥiyya bar Abba and his tithe donor Silanus. He is notably mentioned in the passage above that made the initial argument for tithing to Torah scholars. Following the declaration that Rabbi Yonah gave tithes because of Rabbi Aḥa bar Ulla's Torah study, we learn that a number of rabbis refused to take the tithe:

> R. Huna did not take a tithe, R. Aḥa did not take a tithe. R. Ḥiyya bar Abba instructed himself to go outside the Land of Israel, so as not to take a tithe. He asked R. Shmuel bar Nahman who asked R. Yonatan, "may one take?" He said to him, "Take! What fell to your tribe fell to you." (Y. Ma'aser Sheni 5:5 (3), 56b)

ר׳ הונא לא נסב מעשר. ר׳ אחא לא נסב מעשר. ר׳ חייה בר בא הורי על גרמיה לצאת לחוץ לארץ בגין דלא מיסב מעשר. שאל בר נש ר׳ שמואל בר נחמן שאל לרבי יונתן שאל לר׳ (יוחנן) [יונתן]. מהו דנסב. אמ׳ לו: סב ומה דנפל לשב(ת)[ט]ך נפל לך.[66]

The composition of this passage weaves a delicate thread between genealogy and expertise. The preceding passages argued that a priestly descendent was entitled to the full tithe because of their tribal heritage. Then Rabbi Yonah gave his tithes to Rabbi Aḥa bar Ulla because of his expertise in Torah. The passage ends with the third generation amora Rabbi Shmuel bar Nahman asking his teacher Rabbi Yonatan whether taking a tithe was halakhically valid. Rabbi Yonatan asserts that such tithes belong to the Levitical tribe. If Jews wanted to give tithes to priestly descendants, they were halachically entitled to accept.

65. Turner, *Politics of Expertise*, 1–10.
66. Sussmann, ed., col. 307.

The redactors end the passage with Rabbi Yonatan's teaching, returning the textual conversation to the tractate's larger issue of genealogical right but leaving unsettled the issue of tithing for expertise.

The obvious question to ask is why the named rabbis would refuse a tithe donation. The matter at hand has shifted from the exegetical question of whether priestly members of the Levitical tribe should accept the priestly tithe to a contemporary social question of whether rabbis should. Of the named rabbis who refused to take a tithe, Rabbi Ḥiyya bar Abba's case is preserved in more detail in tractate Shevi'it and illuminates the issues at hand. Shevi'it opens with a discussion regarding when a farmer may pile manure into dung heaps in order to fertilize the following year's harvest during the Sabbatical year. We learn that Rabbi Ḥiyya bar Abba feared the suspicion that he might use his Torah expertise to gain unjust profit from his tithe donor.

> "When may one bring out," etc. Is it permitted to assemble a dungheap at the door of one's courtyard before the agricultural workers stop? Silanus asked R. Ḥiyya bar Abba and he forbade it to him. R. Ḥanina said he actually permitted it, and they were gossiping about him that he was taking the tithe. He instructed himself to leave the Land of Israel, so that he could not take the tithe. (Y. Shevi'it 3:1 (34b))
>
> מאימתי מוציאין כול׳. עד שלא פסקו עובדי עבודה מהו שיהא מותר לעשות אשפה על פתח חצירו. סילני שאל לר׳ חייא בר בא ואסר ליה. ר׳ חנינא אמ׳ שרא ליה והוון אמרין דו נסב מעשר. והורי על גרמיה לצאת לחוץ לארץ דלא למיסב מעשר.[67]

Silanus, a rich landowner, asked Rabbi Ḥiyya bar Abba whether he could pile the dung earlier in the year.[68] The text insists that Rabbi Ḥiyya bar Abba forbade Silanus to do so. But then the text reveals that Rabbi Ḥanina thought that Rabbi Ḥiyya bar Abba did allow Silanus to get a head start on field fertilization. The people gossiped that Rabbi Ḥiyya favored Silanus because Silanus was giving him tithes. To avoid suspicion, the text insists Rabbi Ḥiyya bar Abba returned to Babylonia and thus avoided any potential profit from Silanus's yields.

The relationship between Rabbi Ḥiyya bar Abba and Silanus provides a case of when halakhic theory and practice meet. By all intents and purposes, Rabbi Ḥiyya bar Abba was entitled to take a tithe as a priestly descendant. However, the text presumes that by taking the tithe, it embroiled the rabbi in a relationship

67. Sussmann, ed., col. 186.

68. Silanus is a cognomen of the gens Junia and was associated with a noble Roman family who rose to prominence in the early first century CE.

that imposed unwanted constraints upon him.[69] The text goes to great lengths to reassure us that Rabbi Ḥiyya did not use his expertise in order to profit, but the truth mattered little when the gossip mills started flowing. To everyone else it looked like Rabbi Ḥiyya bar Abba had a habit of favoring his donor in such a way that would ultimately benefit him with a greater tithe yield. They assumed that a donor relationship enacted mutual obligation between the parties that would challenge Rabbi Ḥiyya bar Abba's claims of neutrality.

A number of theorists have analyzed the widely held social perception that experts should possess a moral virtue that renders them as disinterested parties.[70] An expert's epistemic superiority rests in part upon the perception of their moral character, demonstrated through the conduct of impartiality, intellectual honesty, and autonomy. Disinterestedness presumes that the expert will unhesitatingly choose honesty rather than dishonesty and use their knowledge toward its analytical ends without tampering with the outcome. For example, in the opening hearing remarks of Supreme Court nominee Ketanji Brown Jackson, she promised: "I evaluate the facts, and I interpret and apply the law to the facts of the case before me, without fear or favor."[71] This emphasis of impartiality "without fear or favor" is integral to the establishment of experts. A community of experts earn public trust because they are trained by credible institutions, and their profession adopts a commitment to disinterest. The public trusts that the training the expert has will lead them to evaluate data without feeling compelled to lie or distort them. Experts may possess technical knowledge, but their impartiality in the application of those skills makes their advice trustworthy.

Disinterestedness becomes even more important when clients are involved. Expertise, in this case, is not autonomous but rather something that can be packaged and delivered at the request of someone else. Personal relationships of trust form through the exchange of knowledge from an expert to client with the assumption that there is a system of ethical or institutional checks in

69. This is not to say that tithes given to priests in the Second Temple period did not have the capacity to generate reciprocal relationships, but tithes given to priestly descendent rabbis appear to have invoked the reciprocal expectations of late antique aristocratic patronage and triggered tactics for negotiating those tensions.

70. H. Collins, *Are We All Scientific Experts Now?*; Shapin, "Wisdom of 'Mom,'" and *Scientific Life*; Turner, "What Is the Problem with Experts?"; Croce, "Epistemic Paternalism"; Grundmann, "Problem of Expertise in Knowledge Societies"; Ziman, "Continuing Need for Disinterested Research."

71. David Leonhardt, "Why KBJ Is Different," *New York Times*, March 22, 2022, https://www.nytimes.com/2022/03/22/briefing/ketanji-brown-jackson-hearings-supreme-court.html.

place.[72] Clients fundamentally rely on trust and judge the legitimacy of experts accordingly. This dynamic imposes two constraints. One of the tensions is that clients are stakeholders who may articulate an interest or prefer one conclusion over another. Their special interest places an imaginary weight upon the expert and forces the expert to make decisions about how to deliver their expertise with their client in mind. The second tension comes in the public perception of the expert. If the expert were found to be deriving unjust benefit from the expertise shared with their clients, they would risk losing the perception of impartiality that is the basis of their status as expert. Trust could be suspended, culminating in the rejection of their expertise.

Public perception plays a substantial role in matters of law, where the relationship between donors and judges can quickly assume the form of bribery. For example, the Roman legal profession underwent a transition in the first century BCE as *homines novi* or "new men" began to dedicate themselves to law as a profession rather than as an aristocratic service.[73] Without the means to support themselves otherwise, they demanded fees for their services on behalf of clients. The notorious methods of extortion that accompanied some of these legal practitioners tarnished the reputation of the entire profession.[74] Several Roman imperial edicts asserted the stature of Roman lawyers, such as the *Codex of Justinian* (506 CE), which affirmed the financial value of their salaries: "The calling of advocate is one which is praiseworthy and necessary to human life, and it should, by all means, be remunerated with princely generosity."[75]

The Jewish God insists in Deuteronomy that he is "God of gods and Lord of lords, the great God, mighty and awesome, who is not partial and takes no bribe (*shochad*)."[76] The assertion of God's greatness as a divine judge is predicated on his pronouncement of impartiality and echoed throughout the Hebrew Bible. The eighth-century BCE Hebrew prophet Micah, for example, accused the judges, priests, and prophets of Israel of unjust gain:

> 9 Hear this, you rulers of the house of Jacob
> and chiefs of the house of Israel,

72. Turner, *Politics of Expertise*, 2.

73. Chroust, "Legal Profession in Ancient Imperial Rome," 559, though Chroust's disdain for the non-aristocratic professional should be set aside from the textual evidence. For a recent survey of fees and salaries for roman bureaucrats, see C. Kelly, *Ruling the Later Roman Empire*.

74. Chroust, "Legal Profession in Ancient Imperial Rome," 554.

75. *Codex of Justinian*, Book 2, title 8:5.

76. Deut. 10:17. On bribery in the Hebrew Bible, see Hamilton, "Bribery at the Boundaries of Gift-Giving."

who abhor justice
  and pervert all equity,

10 who build Zion with blood
  and Jerusalem with wrong!

11 Its rulers give judgment for a bribe
  its priests teach for a price;
  its prophets give oracles for money

yet they lean upon the Lord and say,
  "Surely the Lord is with us!
  No harm shall come upon us."

12 Therefore because of you
  Zion shall be plowed as a field;

Jerusalem shall become a heap of ruins,
  and the mountain of the temple a wooded height. (Micah 3:9–12)

The correlation between bribe, price, and money in Micah's thought is no accident. These terms all refer to funds for public-facing experts with direct access to Israel's God. The Torah explicitly forbids bribes influencing just judgments, and prophets regularly spoke against them. For instance, Isaiah 1:23 insists: "Your princes are rebels and companions of thieves. Everyone loves a bribe and runs after gifts."[77] The passage assumes that priests and prophets charged for their services, which could also be influenced by bribes, as John Goldingay explains, "the prophets' message is determined by who pays them."[78] Micah assumes that corruption abounds when payment is demanded, and this corruption must explain why the kingdoms of Israel were destroyed by invading empires.[79] The theme of exploitation runs throughout the prophetic material and seeks to chastise governing leaders and the wealthy elite for their hand in rampant exploitation.[80] Micah narrows this prophetic critique to the role of payment for expert access. By

77. See also Exod. 23:8; Deut. 10:17, 16:19, and 27:25. See 1 Kings 15:19; 2 Kings 16:8 for the influence of bribes upon politics.

78. Goldingay, *Hosea–Micah*, 503.

79. On the broader ethical implications of the book of Micah, See Coomber, "Importance of Biblical Economics."

80. See, for example, Mal. 2:6; Hosea 10:13; Amos 6; and Isa. 1:23.

demanding a price, access to God's justice, cult, or wisdom was limited to those who can pay.

The Tosefta similarly worries about the relationship of bribery and expert judgment:

> When those who displayed partiality in judgment multiplied, [the commandments] "You must not be partial in judging" and "You shall not be intimidated by anyone" were annulled (Deut. 1:17). And they removed the yoke of Heaven from themselves, and accepted the authority of the yoke of mortal man.
>
> When they compelled householders to be their business agents, bribes abounded, and justice was perverted. "And they went backward and not forward" (Jer. 7:24). And about them is said what is said about the sons of Samuel, "Yet his sons did not walk in his ways, but turned aside after gain; they took bribes and perverted justice" (1 Sam. 8:3). (T. Sotah 14:4–5)[81]

משרבו רואין לפנים, בטל (דברים א׳:י״ז) "לא תכירו פנים במשפט" [ופסק] "ולא תגורו מפני איש". ופרקו מהן עול שמים והמליכו עליהם עול בשר ודם.
משרבו מטילי מלאי על בעלי בתים, רבה שוחד והוטה משפט. "והיו לאחור ולא לפנים." ועליהם נאמר כעל בני שמואל (שמואל א ח׳:ג׳) "לא הלכו בניו בדרכיו [וגו׳] וכי לקחו שוחד ומשפט הטו."

The first case invalidates the authority of judges who think they rule as an extension of the Torah's authority but whose impartiality renders their charge worthless. This judge is one who rules favorably toward their friends or clients, or who bends under the pressure of other powerful people. In so doing, they have nullified the commandments and therefore forfeit the rewards of Heaven.

The second case concerns judges who abuse their position in order to generate profits for themselves. When wealthy judges, who were also estate owners, wanted to sell the crops of their land, they would task merchants and other estate owners to sell it on their behalf. If one refused, they would lose their status and good reputation in the eyes of an influential judge. The prooftext aligns such judges with the model of priest-judges who could demand tithes and other gifts with vengeance.[82] The sons of Samuel, the

81. Relying on Vienna MSS 142r&v and ed. Lieberman, 236. See Lieberman, *Tosefta Ki-Fshuta*, 751–52. See also B. Shabbat 56a. On the themes of Tosefta Sotah chapters 10–15, see Rosen-Zvi, "Between Wisdom and Apocalypse."

82. This idea is amplified in the later *Targum Pseudo-Jonathan*. See Mortensen, "Considerations of the Priest's Function," for analysis.

rabbinic interpreters cite, openly demanded their tithes in an aggressive and violent manner.[83] Their example paints a picture of judges who openly abuse their position to seek profit and power.

The passage continues by narrating the actions of the sons of Samuel (1 Sam. 8:3) who took bribes and demanded their tithe portions, eventually asserting that "the whole kingdom went rotten, declining more and more." The emphasis upon ruin is striking because it suggests a collective consequence for the actions of individual leaders. The corruption that follows their unjust profit makes it so that the very presence of God is repelled. These apocalyptic terms of crisis, which Ishay Rosen-Zvi suggests permeate the textual unit, tell the story of a "continuous deterioration of divine revelation."[84] The potential of payment to breed ill conduct stands out as a corrosive plot point in the Tosefta's version of narrative decline.

The suspicion of Rabbi Ḥiyya bar Abba illustrates a social scrutiny of rabbis who received tithes. The acceptance of tithe donations could serve as either a bribe or a more nefarious business partnership. Even if Rabbi Ḥiyya bar Abba did nothing wrong, the public perception still affected his social interactions. The constraints imposed by a landowner's tithes put all judicial rulings that he might offer under public scrutiny. Rabbi Ḥiyya bar Abba's flight was therefore not only necessary to avoid the appearance of unjust profit, as the text explicitly states but also to defend his status as a Torah expert. He was mindful of the suspicion that he might not be impartial in his legal rulings because of his donor relationship. The text directly links public suspicion to the fact that Silanus regularly gave tithes to him, demonstrating how well-known their donor relationship was in the community, and how much public perception affects the standing of experts. By fleeing, Rabbi Ḥiyya bar Abba avoided any potential benefit, which in turn reassured the public and his peers that he remained an impartial expert.

The case of Rabbi Ḥiyya bar Abba was significant as it could influence the overall trust in the rabbinic collective voice. Individual rabbinic authority stemmed from their role as Torah spokespeople. This collective authority was a relational phenomenon upheld by all representatives speaking on its behalf.[85] Therefore, expert rabbinic pronouncements had to gain public trust and align with public perception, formed by people's interactions with other rabbis. Individual rabbis leveraged this broader perception to assert their own value and the value of the Torah. Mere claims of autonomy and disinterest

83. 1 Sam. 8:3 in T. Sotah 14:6, and B. Ḥullin 133a.

84. Rosen-Zvi, "Between Wisdom and Apocalypse," 60.

85. Turner, *Politics of Expertise*, 23.

were insufficient; Rabbi Ḥiyya bar Abba even left the land of Israel to assure the public of his impartiality, thereby implying the impartiality of his peers who stayed. This highlights the importance of public attribution in establishing experts and the rabbis' keen awareness of this power. They needed to work hard to attain and maintain their expert status.[86]

Case #2: The Matrona and Rabbi Eliezer

I turn now to a second case that raises a different set of concerns with tithe donors. In addition to the constraints of public perception or risk of violating impartiality, donors could expect personal instruction and presume to dictate the scholar's focus. The idea of mandated expertise has been recently taken up by social scientists assessing the differences between donor mandated research and autonomous "pure" research.[87] While donor mandated research can channel expertise toward important social ends, it also imposes restrictions upon the expert, including asking experts to give up their own preferences or even comprise their personal convictions in order to follow the whims of the one who holds the money. This case is attentive to that dynamic and actively dissuades from such expectations forming between certain tithe donors and rabbis.

In the Palestinian Talmud tractate Sotah, a wealthy woman (lit. *matrona*) who possessed knowledge of Torah sought instruction from her tithe-funded rabbi. On the surface this passage looks like a stereotypical gendered exchange, but identifying the donor relations at play illuminates the rabbinic defense of expertise in the text.

> A matrona asked R. Eliezer: "How is it that, though only one sin was committed during the golden calf event, those who died, died by three kinds of punishments?" He said to her, "Woman has no wisdom except at the spindle, for it is written, 'And all the women that were wise-hearted spun with their hands'" [Exod. 35:25]. Hyrcanus, his son, said to him: "So as not to answer her with a single teaching from the Torah, you made me lose three hundred *kors* of tithe per year!" He said to him, "May they burn the words of Torah rather than deliver them to women." (Y. Sotah 3:4, 19a).

מטרונה שאלה את רבי לעזר: מפני מה חט אחת במעשה העגל והן מתים בה שלש מיתות. אמ׳ לה. אין חכמתה של אשה אלא בפילכה. דכת׳ וכל אשה חכמת לב בידיה טוו

86. Hilgartner, *Science On Stage.*

87. Salter, *Mandated Science*; Whyte, "Trust, Expertise, and the Philosophy of Science"; Scheman, *Shifting Ground.*

[שמות לה]. אמ׳ לו הורקנוס בנו. בשביל שלא להשיבה דבר אחת מן התורה איבדת ממני שלש מאות כור מעשר בכל שנה. אמ׳ ליה. ישרפו דברי תורה ואל ימסרו לנשים.[88]

The matrona asks Rabbi Eliezer a smart question regarding the punishments that the Israelites received following their construction of a gilded calf in Exodus 32. Why three punishments if there was a singular sin? Her question incisively probes the narrative multiplicity in the Exodus account, which describes the Israelite construction of an idol when Moses failed to return speedily from Mount Sinai. In the biblical text, the Israelites died from three different punishments for the singular sin of constructing a golden calf: the Levites killed three thousand men (Exod. 32:28), some people died of a plague (Exod. 32:35), and Moses ground the golden calf to dust and spread it over the water supply, forcing the people to drink in imitation of the *sotah* ritual (Exod. 32:20).[89] Not only does her question attend to the intricacies of the biblical narrative but it also reflects the rabbinic hermeneutical assumption of measure for measure punishments.[90] The matrona therefore asks a trenchant exegetical question of the Torah, animated by rabbinic hermeneutical concerns.

The fact that this exchange occurs in tractate Sotah is striking. The *sotah* ritual derives from Numbers 5:11–31, which describes the proper process for jealous husbands who wish to investigate wives they suspect of adultery. The husband is instructed to bring his wife before a priest to consume a prepared potion of "holy water" mixed with dust from the tabernacle floor. The priest writes the words of the *sotah* curse on parchment and stirs the ink into the water before prompting the woman to drink of the mixture. After the woman drinks, the potion manifests the bodily evidence of her guilt, her "belly swelling and thighs wasting away," if condemned (Num. 5:27). The rabbinic tractate

88. Sussmann, ed, col. 920. See the parallel in B. Yoma 66b where every aspect of the matrona's class and status is stripped from the text. No longer is she a matrona, but she is rather a "wise woman" (אשה חכמה). Hyrcanus's protest at the loss of tithes and R. Eliezer's harsh retort are absent. There is a slight variant in the Vatican MS Ebreo 133, and in the reconstruction from the Geniza fragments published by Ginzberg, *Yerushalmi Fragments from the Genizah*, 209, which render ממני as ממנו. This variant does not affect the sense of the story. See also Num. Rab. 9.

89. The grinding of the golden calf in imitation of *sotah* is also discussed in B. Avodah Zarah 44a in the context of turning idols to dust. See 2 Chron. 25:16 and 2 Kings 18:4 for other occasions of idol destruction.

90. As an example of this principle see Mishnah Avot 2:6: "Moreover he saw a skull floating on the face of the water. He said to it: because you drowned others, they drowned you. And in the end, they that drowned you will be drowned." Rosen-Zvi argues that the rabbis employ this principle as a hermeneutical tool especially in discussions about the *sotah* ritual ("Measure for Measure as a Hermeneutical Tool," 269. Rosen-Zvi, *Mishnaic Sotah Ritual*.

expanded upon the biblical sotah ritual in what Rosen-Zvi describes as a "fantasy of control" and used the ritual as a means for thinking about the nature of women broadly so as to transform the "sinful, proactive and dangerous wife into a passive, submissive and unthreatening subject."[91] The ritual served as the site for analyzing the "threats inherent to womankind," which the rabbis could control and neutralize in their conceptions of how women *ought* to behave.[92]

The sharp gendered boundary that Rabbi Eliezer draws around Torah study makes sense within a tractate devoted to controlling the threat of women. The matrona story appears among a series of passages responding to a mishnah concerning women's involvement in Torah study. Scholars have theorized whether the passage might represent the lives of real women or serves as a rhetorical construct. Satlow contends that the matrona in this anecdote functions literarily as a propeller for the rabbis' belief that women categorically do not learn Torah,[93] writing, "The only point of her question is to serve as a vehicle for the comments of R. Eleazar [*sic*] and his son."[94] Conversely, Daniel Boyarin and Tal Ilan read the mishnah and related matrona story as a historical possibility, though to different ends. Boyarin thinks there is a small opposition party within the rabbinic movement that supported the inclusion of women in Torah study; thus, the matrona is a literary foil for a broader historical platform.[95] Ilan, however, disagrees that these texts indicate "dissident voices of opposition within rabbinic culture" and believes that they rather represent "slips of the pen which reflect reality."[96] For Ilan, the debate over women and Torah reflects the real engagement of women with learning in the ancient world.

With such focus on the matrona's gender and its relationship to Torah, an overlooked statement in the passage has escaped analytical notice. Rabbi Eliezer's son, Hyrcanus, responds to his father's dismissal of the matrona in alarm, saying, "in order not to give her an answer you made me lose 300 *kors* of tithe every year!"[97] While this statement is either

91. Rosen-Zvi, *Mishnaic Sotah Ritual*, 229.

92. Rosen-Zvi, 225.

93. Satlow, "'Try to Be a Man,'" 35.

94. Satlow, 35.

95. Boyarin, *Carnal Israel*, 173.

96. Ilan, *Mine and Yours Are Hers*, 169.

97. Broshi uses the Babatha documents of sale from palm groves to approximate ancient Judean units of measurement, including the *kor*: "A *bet se'ah* (the area of sowing a *se'ah*), according to a Talmudic source, is 50 × 50 cubits (a *beraitha* quoted in BT Erub. 23b). In modern metric terms, *bet se'ah* is 625 m.2; *bet kor* 30 times bigger: 18,750 m.2; and *bet qab* a sixth of a *bet se'ah*: 104 m.2." ("Agriculture and Economy in Roman Palestine," 234).

ignored,[98] or treated as a rhetorical setup for Rabbi Eliezer's rejection of teaching women,[99] the exclamation nevertheless assumes that the woman is a donor who expects to engage with Torah study because she feels entitled to the rabbi's expertise. Whether the matrona is operating as a literary foil or not does not diminish the assumption of the authors that such a tithe donor might insert herself into the rabbinic domain. The author imagines that a wealthy woman (a) could have a combative exchange with a rabbi over Torah and, consequently, (b) could affect the tithe donations a rabbi's family receives. In this case, the anxiety within this story is less simplistically about "what do we do if a woman wants to engage in Torah?" than "what do we do when a donor who is also a woman both engages in Talmudic thinking and expects a rabbi to respond with his expertise as if she were a student?"

On the surface, the passage would seem to suggest that her vice lies solely in her gender—women categorically should not study Torah. This binary, however, is complicated by the fact that both the matrona and Hyrcanus expected Rabbi Eliezer to answer the question. They react as if Rabbi Eliezer is the one out of line: the matrona breaks off her donor relationship with his family and Hyrcanus scolds his own father. These reactions suggest that the severe gendered boundary is not a natural distinction but rather an operational tactic within this encounter. I argue that if we reframe this exchange between the matrona and Rabbi Eliezer as one where Torah expertise is at stake rather than just a misogynistic teaching, we can illuminate how social relationships with women donors might have impinged upon the epistemic autonomy of a rabbinic expert. What is ordinarily perceived as an obvious gendered rebuke of women's access to Torah is actually encoded with the tensions of a donor mandating instruction as reciprocal exchange for her tithe.

Within the encounter Rabbi Eliezer defends his epistemic autonomy by deflecting the encroachment of his family's tithe donor in two specific ways. First, Rabbi Eliezer cites a prooftext from later in the Exodus account when the Israelites began constructing the *mishkan*, or tabernacle, following the renewal of the covenant after their disastrous episode with the golden calf. Israelites brought free-will offerings of jewelry, animal skins, acacia wood, and precious metals to "be used for the tent of meeting, and for all its service,

98. Labendz, *Socratic Torah*, 108; Ilan, *Jewish Women in Greco-Roman Palestine*, 191.

99. "Matrona is used as a foil. Her question, which this text itself admits is a good one, is derisively dismissed." Satlow, "Try to Be a Man," 35.

and for the sacred vestments" (Exod. 35:20). Certain women with particular skill wove yarn and rich linen as a donation to this cause (Exod. 35:25–16). From this passage, Rabbi Eliezer brings the prooftext about women spinning with their hands, extrapolating that "woman has no wisdom except at the spindle." Rabbi Eliezer's choice of prooftext is particularly illuminated by the fact that the matrona is a donor. She withdraws her yearly tithe in response to his dismissal. Not only does his message suggest that she has no part in Torah study because of her gender, but the context of the prooftext reminds her that pious donations should be given with no expectation of reciprocity. All of the gifts brought for the *mishkan*, including the women's weaving, were given by those "whose hearts made them willing to bring anything for the work that the Lord had commanded by Moses to be done" (Exod. 35:29).

By contrast the matrona expects that the rabbi to whom she brings annual tithe will spend personal time on her instruction. This expectation would not have been so unheard of in the late ancient Mediterranean. Women donors played a particular role in the support of Christian scholars, for example, and received personal correspondence and instruction in exchange.[100] In reciprocation for their gifts, pious persons received attention from their religious experts, as Jerome, the fourth-century monastic scholar, remarked to a patron, "You send us gifts, we send you back letters of thanks,"[101] letters filled with religious instruction. Donors could delight in the personal satisfaction of the knowledge acquired through individual study. Jerome elsewhere writes of his donor Paula, who learned Hebrew with "zeal" so as to sing psalms in the original.[102] In this way, donations cultivated a posture of piety. Nor were the benefits of donor networks one-sided. Religious experts made use of their friends' gifts in a whole host of tangible ways, framed as part of their religious devotion. Funds contributed to the material production of texts, such as buying papyrus or parchment; to the building of personal libraries; and even to the hiring of stenographers to take dictation and assistants to read over drafts. Social networks assisted with the dissemination of materials and spread the word of an individual scholar's acumen, all to the glory of God. In this sense pious gifts, even if idyllically framed as free gifts, imposed an expectation of obligation upon the social relationship. Rabbi Eliezer resists any sense of

100. See E. Clark, "Patrons, Not Priests"; Bowes, *Private Worship, Public Values*; Kuefler, "The Merry Widows of Late Roman Antiquity."

101. Jerome, *Epist.* 44.1: "Vos dona transmittis, nos epistulas remittimus gratiarum."

102. Jerome, *Epist.* 39.1.

obligation to the matrona and in no uncertain terms tells her to stay in her lane and leave the Torah expertise to him.

The rigid boundary Rabbi Eliezer constructs between an expert and non-expert represents the porousness of interactional expertise. Collins and Evans explain that acquiring interactional expertise is accomplished by "engaging in conversation with the experts."[103] Interactional expertise, in his theory, does not require mastery of the life of the specialist group but rather "mastery of the language pertaining to the form of life."[104] Over time, those who interacted with rabbinic experts could acquire facility in their specialist discourse. Perhaps on prior occasions the matrona had lingered in the house of Rabbi Eliezer, overhearing heated debates from students in a nearby room. Perhaps the matrona and Rabbi Eliezer's families had dined together, reclined around the convivium table, and engaged in learned conversation.[105] Or, perhaps this was not the first time the matrona had called upon Rabbi Eliezer for Torah expertise—what started as small inquiries in passing that Rabbi Eliezer demurely evaded might have evolved to a more intrusive request for personal instruction. Whatever the imagined scenario in the mind of the rabbinic authors, the matrona displays both primary source knowledge and the linguistic register of the rabbinic specialist community. The passage is attentive to the danger of donors who cross the boundary between expert and non-expert through the acquisition of interactional expertise.

Next Rabbi Eliezer responds to his son's admonishment. The matrona withdrew her annual tithe commitment to the chagrin of Hyrcanus, who cannot understand his father's refusal to teach a single element of Torah to their wealthy donor. Rabbi Eliezer rebukes his son with insistence that one should burn the words of Torah rather than "deliver" (ימסרו) them to women. We have reason to suspect that Rabbi Eliezer is being hyperbolic. His wife, for example, is Imma Shalom, sister to the famed Patriarch Gamaliel II and remembered in later rabbinic traditions as a learned individual in her own right.[106] Elsewhere when Rabbi Eliezer rules against teaching Torah to daughters, he does so in the context of the *sotah* ritual for suspected adultery.[107] In this mishnah he instructs that

103. Collins and Evans, *Rethinking Expertise*, 32.

104. Collins and Evans, 77.

105. On women at Roman convivia, see Roller, "Horizontal Women: Posture and Sex in the Roman Convivium."

106. See B. Nedarim 20a; B. Eruvin 63a, B. Bava Metzi'a 59b; and B. Shabbat 116a.

107. M. Sotah 3:4.

teaching Torah to a daughter is akin to sexual immorality, presumably because he thinks that it provides her a way to generate mitzvot and create an adultery loophole—her Torah study could negate any adulterous sins and protect her from the ritual's curse. Here Rabbi Eliezer's concern is not so much that a woman might study Torah but in the contextually loaded possibility that daughters might use their study to deflect the consequences of sexual immorality. His fear is not that women might come into contact with Torah but rather that Torah in the hands of women is powerful.

Further, the use of the verb מסר ("to deliver") is notable. Rather than describe the request as instruction, he uses the language of possession. The verb denotes the sense of handing over or giving one the authority over something, such as in M. Sanhedrin 7:1 where four types of executions are given (נִמְסְרוּ) to the court or in Y. Shabbat 2:7 (5b) where the three commandments of *niddah, challah,* and shabbat candle lighting were handed over (נִמְסְרוּ) to women. The verb is also used to describe the transmission of the Oral Law, as the famous opening of *Mishnah Avot* describes: "Moses received the Torah at Sinai and transmitted it (וּמְסָרָהּ) to Joshua." Thus, Rabbi Eliezer understands the matrona's request not in terms of ordinary instruction but in a request to participate in a particular realm of Torah expertise that would provide her with a sense of ownership of Torah knowledge.

The text continues with Rabbi Eliezer's students pressing him to answer her good question once she leaves: "Rabbi, this one you pushed away with a stick, but what would you explain to us?"[108] Different rabbinic voices weigh in with explanations to this seeming textual problem, further validating the perceptive contours of the question. Yet however astute her question may be, it triggers a visceral dismissal from Rabbi Eliezer. When Rabbi Eliezer speaks in universalizing terms he draws a gendered distinction upon all women, but in context he is actually speaking to the particular situation with a woman donor. The matrona physically entered rabbinic study space, attested by the spectacle of their exchange witnessed by rabbinic students, and she modeled rabbinic interpretive principles. Her presence shattered the idyllic representation of rabbinic autonomy with the reality of donor demands. Rabbi Eliezer constructed a rhetorical boundary between himself and the matrona on the basis of her gender so as to mask her power as a donor. The literary trope deployed by his students ("this one you pushed away with a stick") ushers the matrona's

108. רבי לזר דחיתה בקנה לנו מה אתה משיב.
On the use of this phrase in rabbinic literature, see Labendz, *Socratic Torah*, 101–20.

question into the safety of their specialist domain. While R. Eliezer admonishes transmitting Torah to women writ large, he is reacting to a specific social relationship by defending his epistemic autonomy.

The textual case of the matrona's tithe reflects the complicated power differential between experts and clients. The expert has authority because of their skills, the authorizing credentials of their group, and their epistemic superiority. In short, experts know things that by definition non-experts do not, which requires them to package their knowledge into a deliverable to their donor. However, the donor can upset that balance in the assertion of their power as benefactor. What was an expert-client relationship becomes a donor-client relationship, where the expert becomes beholden to the donor. This power dynamic is never settled. It teeters back and forth as an undercurrent of mutual obligation within the relationship.

The cases of Rabbi Ḥiyya bar Abba with the tithe donor Silanus and Rabbi Eliezer and the tithe donor matrona illustrate the kinds of donor relationships rabbis might have had with their wealthy contacts in their social networks. These wealthy donors understood the broader culture of patronage that saturated the Roman world. Donating to the production of knowledge was an attractive investment for patrons in the late ancient Mediterranean.[109] By aligning themselves with individual scholars, as well as structures of expertise, their gifts created an avenue for influence that generated social and cultural capital. While the formal patronage of antiquity took different forms from that of contemporary support for scholarship, these tithing cases illuminate a trans-temporal element of expertise that draws the tension between receiving support and maintaining epistemic autonomy in sharp relief.

Conclusion: Considering the Realia

Rabbinic literature indicates that some Jews donated tithes to rabbis, which played a significant role in affirming rabbinic expertise. The Torah does not anticipate the finality of the Roman destruction of Jerusalem nor foresee the rise of rabbinic expertise built upon the need to adapt the Torah to new social constraints. Tithing was one habit of Jewish giving disrupted by the loss of the

109. Wallace-Hadrill, *Patronage in Ancient Society*, 65. See examples, such as the work of Too, *Rhetoric in Isocrates*, 161–64 for analysis of patronage support of scholars within the second sophistic; or Schironi, "Enlightened Kings or Pragmatic Rulers?" for analysis of Ptolemaic imperial patronage of scholarship.

Temple and was therefore ripe for hermeneutic scrutiny. Rabbinic interpreters sifted through the biblical text and found ways for tithing to make exegetical sense without the presence of a Temple. First fruits (*bikkurim*), for example, could no longer be brought, but other tithes of grain and animals could still be set aside for local use.[110] In the process of imagining a place for tithing in their present, the rabbis found an interpretive place for themselves within the networks of Jewish giving. Tithe donations given to local rabbis would have been reciprocated with advice and instruction as a form of patronage that validated the rabbi's expertise and created a system of support.

The idea of tithing for Torah expertise persisted. *Pesikta de-Rav Kahana,* a midrashic text dated to the fifth or early sixth century CE, states that merchants (*pragmateutes*) and seafarers (*mepharshei yama*) should "set aside one portion out of ten for those who labor in Torah."[111] Similarly, the seventh-century Aramaic Targum to Song of Songs relays that Ezra the priest and Nehemiah along with their advisors used "their storehouses full of the holy tithes, the vow offerings, and the free-will offerings" in order to "enable them to be occupied with Torah, day and night."[112] *Tanhuma Asser Te'asser* repeatedly insists that a person who does not tithe will lose his wealth.[113] Sacred accounting, whether through tithes, fees for cultic services, or temple maintenance, was ubiquitous in the ancient world.[114] The notion that piety might drive a Jew to allocate a portion of their resources according to covenantal obligations made a lot of sense in a landscape where Gods and men routinely interacted.

At the same time, the mixing of Torah expertise with tithe gifts produced a complex donor relationship, especially for rabbis who lacked the same kind of claim to tithes as the hereditary priesthood. Rabbinic interpreters may have found an exegetical basis for themselves as tithe recipients, but they were not

110. M. Sheqalim 8:8. The tithes of animals and grain derive from the description in Num. 18:12–19, which are given to God and then apportioned for the Levites as their inheritance, and thus are independent from the Temple.

111. *Pesikta de-Rav Kahana* 10:10. On dating issues, see Strack and Stemberger, *Introduction to the Talmud and Midrash,* 295. Rosenfeld and Menirav, *Markets and Marketing in Roman Palestine,* 127. On the different translation options for *pragmateutes* in tax receipts, see the discussion in Cromwell, *Recording Village Life,* 115–17.

112. Targum Song of Songs 7:3

113. On the reception of this passage, see Fleisher, "Parashat 'asar taaser' u'kri'atah b'yamot hag lephi minhagot 'eretz Israel"; Hollender, "Parashat 'Asser Te'asser.'"

114. See Pafford, "Priestly Portion vs. Cult Fees" for an overview of Greek sacred laws regarding temple finances.

immune to the socially understood pressures of patronage. The next chapter will take up this tension more closely and examine how rabbinic interpreters navigated the problems associated with funding Torah expertise. But the fact that rabbinic texts devote time to thinking about the tensions of funding Torah expertise suggests that it was a real concern.

It is important to see the rabbinic argument of tithing for expertise not as an attack on or in competition with the priesthood. It was first and foremost an interpretive sense that the rabbinic grammarian pulled from the Torah out of deep devotion. Rabbis participated in the giving practices of their day and made sense of them with their interpretive logic. It is also possible that ordinary Jews gave gifts to rabbis and called them tithes out of their own habits of practice. In both cases, ancient Jews made sense of themselves through the language of giving found in the Torah. Rabbis fashioned a place for themselves in the Jewish past that could make their claims of expertise legible and tap into a shared cultural object that other Jews valued.

4

Rabbinic Fundraising and the Double Bind of Persuasion and Profit

RABBI YOSE ben Kisma was once traveling abroad when he encountered a man with an enticing offer. From afar the man glimpsed the rabbi and rushed to greet him. He inquired, "Rabbi, where do you come from?" With pride Rabbi Yose described his urban home. "I come from a great city of sages and scribes," Rabbi Yose boasted.[1] The man pounced on the opportunity produced by this chance encounter. "Rabbi," he exclaimed, "would you wish to dwell with us in our place? I will give you a million golden dinars and precious stones and pearls." Such an offer would surely coax Rabbi Yose to leave his scholarly home for this remote region. Yet Rabbi Yose's expertise could not be bought. He insisted, "My son, if you gave me all the silver and gold and precious stones and pearls in the world, I would not dwell anywhere except in a place of Torah."[2]

This legendary story speaks to an idyllic motif of Torah study independent from profit. The rich man hoped to coax the rabbi to reside in his area with an

1. Shmuel Safrai suggests that this great city was Tiberias because it held a rabbinic academy. "Jewish Cultural Nature of Galilee," 160. While this association is a theory at best, R. Yose is said to have spent time in Tiberias according to a tradition in *Tanhuma*, wa-yishalah 8.

2. M. Avot 6:9. On the relatively late dating for this chapter, see Ilan, "Double Canonization of Tractate Avot"; and Lerner, "Tractate Avot." Lerner posits that the addition took place in the Geonic period when it was customary to study Avot on Shabbat. See Diamond, *Holy Men and Hunger Artists*, 32–33 for the point that sages should endure financial hardship for intensive study of Torah. Lehmhaus, "'Were Not Understanding Given to You from Heaven?'" for analysis of the parallel in *Seder Eliyahu Zuta*. Lehmhaus claims that the Mishnah's version seems more focused on spiritual gain in the world to come rather than this-world focused.

offer of immense wealth, but it could not compare to a city of sages. The contrast between the riches of Torah and worldly wealth gives the impression that rabbinic experts were unattached to material concerns. Rabbis would prefer to dwell with others in their specialist group rather than receive a grand salary. This aspiration is certainly not practical—even Torah scholars need to eat—and such assertions of financial independence did not reflect the everyday reality for rabbis. Instead, this idealized unattachment asserted an expert autonomy that elevated the sanctity of Torah. In the previous chapter, I illustrated how tithe donors could encroach upon rabbinic autonomy, which posed challenges to their credibility as Torah experts. This story constructs a similar boundary by valorizing the rabbinic expert as one unmoved by the glamour of profit. The ideal rabbinic expert is one who is sustained on the Torah of their specialist group alone.

At the same time, this assertion of rabbinic independence encodes a bold vision of the social value of Torah experts. While Rabbi Yose may not be swayed by material wealth, this passage envisions that Torah scholars are worth a huge investment. The text imagines that Rabbi Yose is so recognizable as a rabbinic expert that a rich man might spot him from afar and immediately offer a grand salary.[3] This hyperbole illustrates the sharp tension between expert autonomy and the recognition that funding provides. Some rabbis might protest the allure of profit for the sake of study, but rabbis collectively benefitted from reinforcing that the rabbinic specialist group was worth a donor's investment.[4] Indeed, protesting profit might have been a strategy itself intended to allure donors like the one plying Rabbi Yose.

This chapter examines how rabbis might negotiate the tension sustained when experts receive and solicit funding. Contrary to the image of financial independence painted by the story of Rabbi Yose, rabbis were supported through a range of external sources. Funding was, on the one hand, a reality for a specialist group comprised of judges and teachers, and whose ideal required men to occupy their full time with Torah study.[5] While there are

3. One could speculate that R. Yose was wearing a distinctive cloak that marked him as a Torah expert. See Sifre Deut. 343:11 for a description of the sages' particular dress. On the social markers of rabbinic appearance, see Hezser, *Rabbinic Body Language*, 24–68.

4. Gen. Rab. 92:1, ed. Albeck, 1136 asserts that Torah study should bring one to the point of suffering, presumably financial hardships.

5. Sifre Deut. 42; M. Qiddushin 4:14; and T. Qiddushin 5:15–16. For a survey of salaried school teachers in the Roman Empire, see Laes, "School-Teachers in the Roman Empire," 110–12. On the evolution of judicial fees, see Haensch, "From Free to Fee?"

accounts of rabbis engaged in side occupations, the rabbinic exemplar was a man who devoted himself fully to study, even to the extent of leaving his family for the study house for periods at a time.[6] On the other hand, sources of support, whether through fees, donations, paychecks, or patrons, were an essential part of scholastic work.[7] Expertise is made possible through direct and indirect payments whose sum impact is sometimes difficult to grasp in standard economic models, but nevertheless signify the complex social relationships that make legible the production of knowledge.

The rabbinic domain was not the only one to encounter the double bind associated with funding expertise. The work of Stephen Turner examines the role of patronage and employment in the enterprise of contemporary scientific knowledge production. He argues that there is a feedback loop where funding decisions both shape and limit the kind of science possible, while also providing the recognition that justifies these same funding decisions.[8] The acknowledgment of expertise through external support is vital but also carries with it the power to constrain expert autonomy, as external entities impose obligations and threat.[9] There is a universal balance that must be struck between experts and funding sources that negotiates expert decision-making with external interests. While the specifics of funding expertise vary in relation to institutional support, public involvement, and payment mechanisms—there were no NEH-funded rabbis in antiquity—theorists of expertise draw

6. For a lengthy list of examples, see Hezser, *Social Structure of the Rabbinic Movement*, 257–64. On the precedence of Torah over other labor, see Gen. Rab. 13:7, ed. Albeck, 117.. See Boyarin, *Carnal Israel*, 134–66; Diamond, *Holy Men and Hunger Artists*, 21–31; Satlow, "'And On the Earth You Shall Sleep.'" On the deprivation of a livelihood, see T. Qiddishun 5:15 and Y. Sanhedrin 2:6, 20c. Rabbi Simeon Ben Azzai famously asserts a kind of sexual asceticism by claiming that his heart "lusts for Torah," though his example is exceptional. T. Yevamot 8.7; and Gen. Rab. 34:14, ed. Albeck, 326–27. M. Ketubbot 5:6 sets a timeframe for husbands to be away from their wives in pursuit of Torah study, and Lev. Rab. 19:1 preserves a case of rabbis being away from home for thirteen years. On the Babylonian phenomenon of temporary marriages while away from home, see Gafni, "Institution of Marriage in Rabbinic Times," 24–25.

7. For a survey of Roman sources, see Mohler, "Roman Answer to the Salary Question," which demonstrates that there was a mix of salaries, fees, and personal gifts that supported educators and judges and lawyers.

8. Turner, "Normal Accidents of Expertise," 252. On the relationship between patronage and scientific expertise, see the collected essays in Turner, *Politics of Expertise.* On the tensions between democracy and scientific funding, see Pamuk, *Politics and Expertise.*

9. Turner, "Quasi-science and the State," 249.

attention to the persistent mediation of the constraints funding imposes that at the same time make the enactment of expertise possible.

The rabbinic specialist group shared in these broader dynamics of funding expertise, but their position was also inflected by a distinct system of piety. Their claims of ritual and legal expertise were rooted in the Torah. A number of recent scholars have examined the intertwined expertise of ritual, legal, and spiritual authority in late antiquity.[10] Heidi Marx, for instance, describes the work of Roman Platonists at the turn of the second century who fashioned themselves as "philosopher-priests" by laying claim to the broader religious landscape. She writes that in making these claims, "they were completely in earnest, being motivated by deep religious or spiritual experiences."[11] Her subjects range from Christian thinkers and Roman polytheists, but she demonstrates that they each felt a strong moral responsibility for their claims of ritual expertise. They sought to advise people who shared a common spiritual landscape, whether invited to serve in those roles or not.[12]

Rabbis similarly were moved by a strong pietistic inclination that framed their Torah expertise in moralizing terms. Profit struck at a core belief that the Torah was worth more than anything in the world.[13] Torah study by extension was the most precious occupation one could engage in. To hawk its wisdom would cheapen its value, muddying it in the grime of everyday work. At the same time, this ideology framed resistance to profit in particularly persuasive terms to potential donors. By elevating the Torah scholar above all else, it fashioned rabbinic expertise as the most lucrative investment.

This chapter begins by surveying the strain between financial support and rabbinic expertise. As the number and visibility of rabbinic scholars increased, more formal funding relationships are attested in amoraic sources. The Tosefta, as discussed in chapter two, underlines the hospitality that made such relationships possible. Friends and kin opened up their homes to rabbis, put food on the banquet table, and shared their largesse with rabbis. Such relationships were expected to lead to reciprocal exchange of gifts and favors. What started as small-scale relationships fostered by everyday social encounters

10. Marx-Wolf, *Spiritual Taxonomies and Ritual Authority*; Eshleman, *Social World of Intellectuals*; Wendt, *At the Temple Gates*; Balberg, "Rabbinic Authority, Medical Rhetoric, and Bodily Hermeneutics"; Frankfurter, "Dynamics of Ritual Expertise."

11. Marx-Wolf, *Spiritual Taxonomies and Ritual Authority*, 2.

12. Marx-Wolf, 6, 131.

13. T. Bava Metzi'a 3:24; Sifre Devarim 48:7; Y. Pe'ah 1:1, 1a.

gradually expanded to the point where certain rabbis could actively fundraise or seek employment based on the reputation they had gained.

The increase in funding sources came with its own difficulties. I survey fears of employer encroachment upon the autonomy of Torah teachers, of social suspicion that rabbis are grossly profiting off of the Torah, and accusations of corruption and bribery. We have seen these fears before in prior chapters when less formal donor relationships provoked the same set of concerns. Funding expertise exposes an inherent tension between the epistemic significance of expert knowledge and its social value.[14] These sources are attuned to the social scrutiny upon rabbinic work as Torah professionals and the many interested parties that rabbis encountered.

The second half of the chapter explores how this tension surfaced within Palestinian rabbinic literature when rabbis accepted various forms of financial support. Scholars have studied the rabbinic aversion to formal patronage, attributing it to rabbinic values rooted in Torah ideals that resisted social debt between Jews.[15] However, these ideals did not prevent rabbis from engaging in patronage or patronage-like relationships. I demonstrate how this dissonance was made to work in the text by framing fundraising under the umbrella of charity.[16]

The notion that one might receive divine reward for fulfilling religious commandments, in particular charity, was ubiquitous in Jewish and Christian sources in late antiquity.[17] The recent work of Gregg Gardner has shown that

14. See Pamuk, *Politics and Expertise*, 133–60 on funding justifications in contemporary science.

15. S. Schwartz, *Were the Jews a Mediterranean Society?*, 10–13 on Jewish antireciprocal cultural imperatives; and Wilfand, *Poverty, Charity, and the Image of the Poor*, 218–20, 233–35 on rabbinic aversion to presenting themselves as patrons. Sorek, *Remembered for Good*, relatedly claims that patronage "could not at this period or any other have been an important feature of any system of benefaction operated by the Jews in Palestine" (37). This claim acknowledges the distinct ethical and ideological imperatives for Jews at this time but overstates the point. Multiple motivations can be operative at the same time, as this chapter will demonstrate.

16. On redemptive almsgiving, see Gray, "Redemptive Almsgiving" and *Charity in Rabbinic Judaism*, 67. For "investment strategy" as an overarching category, see Gardner, *Wealth, Poverty, and Charity*, 117.

17. Garrison, *Redemptive Almsgiving*; Anderson, *Charity*, 67; Holman, *The Hungry Are Dying*, 54–63; Rhee, *Loving the Poor, Saving the Rich*; Finn, *Almsgiving in the Later Roman Empire*; Brown, *Ransom of the Soul*, 29, and *Treasure in Heaven*, 4–6. For differences in rabbinic literature, see Gray, *Charity in Rabbinic Judaism*, 93–94.

ancient Jews and Christians saw such giving as an "investment strategy."[18] As a type of employment relationship between the giver and God, Gardner argues that the ancients thought "giving charity to other humans would earn one pay or recompense from God, who is a trustworthy employer."[19] This social understanding of divine investment was useful for rabbis seeking financial support on two counts. First, it reframed the relationship between the donor and the recipient as one between the donor and God, with the rabbi acting as a conduit for the donor's divine investment. Second, by invoking the persuasive discourses of redemptive almsgiving and divine investment, they provided a pious incentive for supporting rabbis. This should not be read as spiritual manipulation but rather an extension of the rabbis' own personal piety. The Torah was worth communal support, and even if they were its human interpreters, their intellectual product was itself of divine and spiritual import. By framing such gifts as charity, they both provided an ideological motivation for rabbinic support, while at the same time masking the power asymmetry of both charity and patronage by positioning God as the ultimate employer or patron.

I close the chapter with a brief survey of the reception of these ideas into the medieval period. This temporal range is useful because most of the evidence for rabbinic funding comes from later sources. By looking at medieval commentary on the issue of funding rabbinic expertise, we can see how initial anxieties in Palestinian rabbinic literature played out under more formalized rabbinic academies. This does not imply that earlier rabbis were oblivious to the implications or tensions of financial support; rather, it offers a broader vantage with which to consider the theoretical issues that emerge when funding expertise.

The Fear of Profit

In Mishnah Avot we learn that Hillel, one of the earliest rabbinic sages and founder of a legendary dynasty of scholars, taught that the Torah should not be used as a means for income. "He who makes worldly use of the crown shall perish," he says, to which an editorial voice explains, "From this you learn: He who uses words of Torah for his own benefit removes his life from the

18. Gardner, *Wealth, Poverty, and Charity*, 117. Gardner makes the significant point that redemptive almsgiving, which often features alms in exchange for the expunging of sins, is part of a broader category of wealth investment.

19. Gardner, 116.

world."[20] Other aphorisms punctuate tractate Avot contrasting Torah study with common occupations. "Engage little in business, and busy yourself with the Torah," Rabbi Meir extolls.[21] "Whoever takes upon himself the yoke of the Torah, they remove from him the yoke of government and the yoke of worldly concerns," Rabbi Neḥuniah ben Hakkanah insists.[22] Here Rabbi Nehuniah elevates Torah study into an undertaking under divine rather than human jurisdiction. These distinctions aim to set rabbinic expertise apart as special. Torah scholars are not undertaking an ordinary profession, even if they work in recognizable trades as schoolteachers, judges, and grammarian textualists. It is a calling, not an income. Their work is undertaken for motives of heaven, not the worldly concerns for profit or prestige.

The ideal that rabbis should resist financial support was neither practical nor the only ideal they could uphold. Funding Torah study not only facilitated the work of Torah but also served as a means to honor it through compensating its experts. In fact, as discussed in the previous chapter, compensation for the priestly class was one of the foundational components of the Torah's laws of tithing. But three concerns emerged about funding Torah expertise: suspicion of gross profit, accusations of corruption, and encroachment upon rabbinic epistemic autonomy.

Talmudic texts take these tensions to heart and attempt to uphold ideals of *pro gratis* expertise with the expectations of fundraising and income. In the Mishnah, rabbis who served as judges could have their rulings voided if they took a salary, yet the Palestinian Talmud states that fees could be collected in exchange for the judge's time.[23] In the Mishnah, those who taught rabbinic teachings did not receive payment.[24] Moses is repeatedly upheld as a model Torah scholar who taught the Israelites *behinam*, or free of charge. But later rabbinic texts ease the expectations: "The verse says [Moses taught] 'laws and rules.' You have to teach 'laws and rules' for free; you do not have to teach Bible and translations for free."[25] The passage continues with a further extension of the policy from Rabbi

20. M. Avot 4:5, quoting Hillel from M. Avot 1:13.

21. M. Avot 4:10.

22. M. Avot 3:5.

23. M. Bekhorot 4:6; T. Bekhorot 3:8–9. See Y. Sanhedrin 1:1, 18b.

24. M. Nedarim 4:3. The text states that one may teach midrash, halakhah, and Aggadah to one who is under a vow not to receive benefit from an associate. The logic is that this is not a case of a "freebie" learning session since those topics never receive payment.

25. Deut. 4:5 is invoked as a proof text in Y. Nedarim 4:3, 38c. See also B. Nedarim 36–37b; B. Bekhorot 29a; B. Ketubbot 105a; Deut. Rab. 4:5.

Yudan, the son of Rabbi Ishmael, who explains that those who taught early rabbinic traditions could charge fees because "they take payment for lost time." By redirecting fees as an exchange for time rather than for the content of the expert's knowledge itself, the interpretation shifts the perception that payment is required for access to expertise and rather only serves to supplement the time of the expert. The distinction is fine, and perhaps unpersuasive, but the argument demonstrates the difficulty with resolving the tension.

However, in a different Talmudic tractate of Sheqalim, we learn that even Moses, who taught for free, did not escape suspicion of profiting from Torah. The passage states:

> R. Ḥamma bar Ḥaninah said: Moses got rich from the chips of the tablets. That is what is written, *carve for yourself two stone tablets* (Exod. 34:1). *Carve for yourself*: the leftovers (*pesolet*) shall be yours. R. Ḥaninah said, The Holy One blessed be He created[26] a quarry of precious stones and pearls in his tent, and from this Moses got rich.
>
> It is written, *they looked after Moses until he reached the tent* (Exod. 33:8). Two Amoraim [disputed the meaning of "looking"]: one said it was meant favorably [to find something to praise] and the other that it was meant unfavorably [to find fault in him]. He who thought unfavorably, says: "look at the thigh, look at the feet, look at his flesh. He eats from the Jews, drinks from the Jews, everything he has is from the Jews." He who thought favorably, says "to simply look upon the just is meritorious." (Y. Sheqalim 5:2, 49a and Lev. Rab. 32:2)

> אמ׳ ר׳ חמא ביר׳ חנינה: מפסולת הלוחות העשיר משה. הדא הוא דכת׳ ״פסל לך שני לוחות אבנים.״ ״פסל לך.״ שתהא הפסולת שלך. אמ׳ ר׳ חנין: מחצב שלאבנים טובית ומרגליות ברא לו הקב׳ה מתוך אהלו וממנו העשיר משה. כת׳ ״והביטו אחרי משה עד בואו האהלה.״ תרין אמורין. חד אמ׳. לגנאי. וחד אמ׳. לשבח. מאן דאמ׳ לגנאי. חמון שקין חמון כרעין חמון קופדן. אכיל מן דיהודאי ושתי מן דיהודאי. כל מדליה מן דיהודאי. ומאן דאמ׳ לשבח. מחמי ... [צדיקיא] ומזכי [טוביא דזכת למחמי יתיה].[27]

This passage begins with the assumption that Moses was quite wealthy and so the source of this wealth comes into question. Rabbi Ḥamma bar Ḥaninah explains that Moses derived benefit from his role in the production of the stone

26. British Library MS Or 2822 states that God uncovered the gems within the tent: ״מתוך אהל גלה לו הבה למשה״ (folio 350v).

27. Sussmann, ed, column 621. For analysis, see Beer, *Sages of the Mishnah and the Talmud*, 344–61.

tablets. In the biblical text God destroyed the first two tablets after the Israelites sinned with the golden calf. God then commanded Moses to cut two tablets from stone so as to copy the words again.[28] Rabbi Ḥamma bar Ḥaninah assumes that these tablets contained precious materials so that their physical *pesolet,* or "leftovers" from the chiseling generated his wealth. Moses did the work; it's only fair that he receives the reward. This interpretation conflates the value of the Torah itself with the physical materials that bear its words. Rabbi Ḥaninah offers a relatedly generous suggestion that God provided a gem-filled quarry in Moses's tent as his salary. Both explanations attribute Moses's wealth to divine providence, and are thus perfectly acceptable, as a sign of value for Moses's expertise.

The introduction of a proof text sparks a discussion about a relevant amoraic dispute.[29] One anonymous amora suggested that Moses was entirely sustained—in perhaps excessive amounts—by the Israelites. This interpretation assumes that Moses profited grossly from his position, and the passage recognizes the kinds of ill speech that might circulate in society when scholars sustain their livelihoods from donations or payment. The fact that both amoraim remain anonymous is striking. Elsewhere in rabbinic literature those who whisper or grumble against rabbinic experts are referenced in anonymous terms.[30] This anonymity helps to illustrate commonly held perceptions that might circulate about the rabbinic specialist group. Some might support Torah experts as a way to achieve pious merit, while others could criticize the communal expense. It is not so much the funding that is the problem but the appearance that Moses was a fat cat using Torah to get rich, thereby weakening his credibility as a Torah expert. However, the text mitigates potential negative views of Moses's financial support by specifying that only the *pesolet,* or leftovers, sustain him. As Alyssa Gray explains, "Moses's wealth is pure" because he was only enriched from the unused chips that fell as the second set of tablets were made.[31]

This image of Moses sustained from the hewn leftovers serves as an exemplar of one who earns a divine wage for work in Torah. The notion that employment deserves just compensation is one prized in rabbinic literature.[32]

28. Exod. 34:1.

29. This parallel appears in Y. Bikkurim 3:3, 65c in the context of determining when one rises before an elder. In this case, two Amoraim debate whether people arose in Moses's presence in order to acquire merit or in order to slander him. Cf. B. Qiddushin 33b; and *Tanḥuma Ki Tissa* 26.

30. See the discussion earlier in this chapter about T. Sotah 14:3 and the discussion in chapter 3 regarding Y. Shevi'it 3:1, 34b.

31. Gray, "Wealth and Rabbinic Self-Fashioning in Late Antiquity," 57.

32. M. Avot 1:1; M. Bava Qamma 1:1; M. Shabbat 16:3; Sifre Devarim 279:1–3; Y. Bava Metzi'a 5:3, 20b.

Gardner has recently shown that this idea extends even to actions taken in obedience to divine commandments, so that it is as if every mitzvah has a correlated wage.[33] The *Mekhilta*, for example, imagines that Moses was paid every time he went between the Israelite people and God.[34] Gardner argues that this midrash provides a model of "the legitimacy of pursuing personal payment for performing a commandment."[35] The labor that Moses performed as both divine intermediary and steward of Torah is inflected by a broader discourse of divine investment that offers a compelling incentive to motivate pious giving.[36] This midrash does not imagine that Moses is growing rich from these efforts, but rather maintaining a modest lifestyle sustained by his labor on behalf of God and community. Torah study is seen as fulfilling the greatest divine commandment, with reward for that expertise seen as just recompense.[37]

The tension with payment appears elsewhere in Sifre Deuteronomy. One passage likens the Torah to fresh water, which—prior to the manufacturing of plastic bottles—was another resource obscene to profit from: "Just as water is free for all, so, too, is Torah free for all, for it is said: 'Oh, all who thirst! Go to the water!' (Isa. 55:1)."[38] This analogy insists that Torah is as precious as other elements needed for people to survive. To treat its study as one would any other occupation would diminish its purity. A related teaching preserved in the minor tractate *Derekh Eretz Rabbah* similarly insists that Torah scholars should not take a salary from words of Torah because "the Holy One, blessed be He, gave it free of charge. If you take a salary for the words of Torah, it is as if you have destroyed the whole world."[39] Such a strong hyperbole warns rabbis that taking salaries risks cosmic consequences. The notion that one's action might destroy the world is elsewhere invoked in the context of murder.[40] Salaries are configured in this passage as a similarly disruptive social act for two reasons. First, because taking a salary diminishes the integrity of the Torah that

33. Gardner, *Wealth, Poverty, and Charity*, 102–3, citing *Mekhilta*, BaChodesh 8; T. Ḥullin 10:16; Sifre Num. 115. See also Hirschman, "On the Nature of Mitzva and Its Reward," 56.

34. *Mekhilta*, BaChodesh 2. See Schofer, *Making of a Sage*, 129–34 for this logic in *Avot de-Rabbi Natan*.

35. Gardner, *Wealth, Poverty, and Charity*, 103.

36. T. Pe'ah 4:17.

37. M. Avot 2:16.

38. Sifre Deut., 48.

39. *Derekh Eretz* tractate Yirat Het, chapter Talmidei Hakhamim. On the special relationship between M. Avot 6 and *Derekh Eretz Zuta* and this tractate, see Van Loopik, *Ways of the Sages*, 10. On the Derekh Eretz literature in the Geonic period, see Lerner, "External Tractates."

40. M. Sanhedrin 4:5; Y. Sanhedrin 4:9, 23a.

was freely given by God. Second, because taking a salary impinges God's reputation as a just employer, who promises to sustain Torah scholars without any need for them to take earthly payment for teaching.

At the same time, the effect of this rhetorical framing is to both render rabbinic expertise as a profession unlike ordinary professions and to assert the pious merits one could gain by contributing tangible support to those doing the work. A well-known example of this preference for Torah study over other trades is found in a later addition to the Mishnah's tractate Qiddushin, which presents rabbinic expertise as a superior profession:

> R. Nehorai says, "I would put aside all the crafts in the world, and I would not teach my son anything but Torah, for a man eats from its wages (*sakhar*) in this world, and the principal (*keren*) remains for him for the World-to-Come. And all other crafts are not like this, for when a man comes to illness, or old age, or sufferings, and is not able to occupy himself with his work, he dies of hunger. And Torah is not like this, but rather it protects him from all evil in his youth, and gives him a future and hope for his old age. Regarding his youth, what does it say? *But they who trust in the Lord shall renew their strength* (Isa. 40:31). Regarding his old age, what does it say? *They still produce fruit in old age* (Ps. 92:14)." (M. Qiddushin 4:14)[41]

Scholars have emphasized how Rabbi Nehorai's assertion, which comes amid a discussion about which trades one should or should not teach their sons, elevates the rabbinic profession as one whose divine rewards will provide in the present world.[42] This is not just aspirational thinking, or a foolhardy belief that "eternal life will suffice," but a claim that Torah study will in fact provide enough to sustain an earthly profession in addition to garnering otherworldly rewards.[43] Other trades may feed the family, but Torah study provides additional benefits felt in the material present and spiritual future. I suggest this late addition to the tractate reflects a genuine assumption that one could make Torah a profession and serves to exhort rabbinic students to pursue this work.

41. See the alternative ending as provided in the *Oxford Annotated Mishnah* (Cohen, Goldenberg, and Lapin, 329–31). For the gendered dynamics in this passage, see Labovitz, "The Scholarly Life—The Laboring Wife," 12–13. On textual redaction of this addition, see Epstein, *Introduction to the Mishnaic Text*.

42. Rubenstein, *Talmudic Stories*, 131; Labovitz, "The Scholarly Life—The Laboring Wife," 12. On the Roman assumption of the moral criteria and hierarchy of trades, see Freu, "Who's Afraid of Wage Labour?," 157.

43. Rubenstein, *Talmudic Stories*, 131.

Another compilation that makes explicit emphasis of the valid appointment of rabbinic judges and magistrates is Sifre Deuteronomy. Stephen Fraade has thoroughly examined this collection's persistent preoccupation with the biblical precedent for the "*centralized* appointment of *local* lay magistrates" who served at Moses's behest.[44] By situating rabbinic discipleship within a tradition of communal appointment, the text stresses the importance of public service as part and parcel with the rabbinic "intellectual vocation."[45] Even so, the text also wrestles with the tensions of funding expertise. Rabbinic labor is done "'to love the Lord your God' (Deut. 30:16), lest you say: I shall learn Torah to be rich, to be called Rabbi, to receive reward in the world to come. All that you do shall be out of love alone."[46] The warning against profiting too much from Torah hangs heavy in the air as rabbis are directed to focus on the elevated purpose of their calling.

Much of the tension between funding Torah expertise stems not just from the sanctity of the Torah but from the potential for corruption that follows compensating expertise. This worry was particularly salient for a specialist group whose status as experts was not yet normalized and for whom management of credibility directly impacted how the rabbinic specialist domain was perceived. In addition to suspicion that rabbis might grow rich, the introduction of funding raised the potential for corruption and bribery. This concern went beyond lamenting that a few corrupt people might use their expert authority for nefarious purposes to concerns that such bad actors would diminish the perception of rabbis as the corporate spokespeople of Torah.

In cases when rabbis served as judges, financial or food gifts were particularly fraught. Rabbinic courts were informal and voluntary in nature because they did not have official judicial authority within the Roman provincial system.[47] And yet, as Kimberly Czajkowski argues, the Roman jurisdictional sphere was slow to impose on the region while local practices persisted with remarkable resilience.[48] Rabbinic texts assume that at least some Jews wanted the legal

44. Fraade, *From Tradition to Commentary*, 105, emphasis original.

45. Sifre Deut. 13. See T. Berakhot 6:24, where Hillel recommends only teaching Torah when the community appreciates it.

46. Sifre Deut. 41:16.

47. For a survey of rabbinic legal cases, see Lapin, "Rabbinic Class Revisited."

48. S. Schwartz, *Imperialism and Jewish Society*, 111 claims that by failing to recognize their jurisdiction, the Romans made them "effectively powerless to compete," though Czajkowski explains that the slow spread of the Roman legal system in Judaea made the viability of informal courts likely. Czajkowski, "Law and Romanization in Judaea."

advice of rabbinic sages and some accounts record the gifts and honorifics that they received in return.[49] In one example, a man kissed Rabbi Yonatan's feet as a display of public honor in exchange for Rabbi Yonatan's help with a family matter.[50] In another account a woman "honored R. Yonatan with figs" when he was serving as judge for her case, but he refused her gift to avoid suspicion of taking bribes.[51] The passage notes that he was known for "judging properly," suggesting the importance of stressing his credibility. The Mishnah describes a certain non-Jew who brought a fish to Rabban Gamaliel only to have the gift refused not on halakhic grounds but because Rabban Gamaliel did not want to be obligated to the man.[52]

The fact that rabbinic judges lacked imperial institutional power made the matter of their credibility more significant while at the same time highlighting their very need for funding. They were not imperially salaried judges who could count on institutional support for their labor. The only authority rabbis wielded came from the trust of other Jews who sought their advice and offered gifts or payment in return. Accusations that rabbinic judgments could be influenced by gifts threatened this trust, particularly as there was no institutional enforcement of fairness.

In one account, Theudas of Rome led the Jews therein to celebrate Passover by roasting a young animal whole, arranging its hooves and entrails on its head in the manner of the sacrifices of the destroyed Jerusalem Temple. This practice enraged the sages in Galilee who wrote to him saying, "Were you not Theudas, we would excommunicate you!"[53] This threat lacked substance, however, for Theudas had sent financial assistance (*parnestehon*) to those very same rabbis. They were caught between their halakhic preference and the reality that they had to appease their donor. The acceptance of direct donations imposed the reciprocal expectations of gift exchange on rabbinic recipients, prompting some to be cautious about from whom they accepted patronage.

49. S. Schwartz, *Imperialism and Jewish Society*, 104.

50. Y. Pe'ah 1:1, 15d. R. Yonatan had authorized the man to publicly shame his son into providing support. Such a kiss served to publicly honor R. Yonatan, one of the three kinds of kisses that Genesis Rabbah states does not lead to immorality. Gen. Rab. 70, 45b.

51. Y. Pe'ah 7:4, 20a; and Y. Bava Batra 2:14, 13c. See Hezser, *Form, Function, and Historical Significance*, 157–63.

52. M. Beitzah 3:2.

53. Y. Pesaḥim 7:1, 34a; and Y. Mo'ed Qatan 3:1, 81d. Also found in B. Pesaḥim 53b, where Todos is described as someone who "places inventory in the pocket of Torah scholars." B. Berakhot 19a states that Simeon ben Shetah sent the warning.

Rabbinic pronouncements did not exist in isolation but were influenced and perceived by non-experts whose feelings could affect the ruling. Even if a rabbinic ruling was "correct," it faced public scrutiny when linked to a context of recurring exchange and expectation. In one passage we learn about a householder who was known for lending boards to serve as dining tables to folks in the community when needed for funerals and banquets.[54] When he saw the sages had need of them, he gave them the boards as a gift. However, the text reveals that while the rabbis had always declared these boards ritually clean when the householder used them for charitable ends, as soon as they became the property of the rabbis, they were deemed unclean. This ruling reversal suggests that rabbis could be influenced by social perceptions—in this case positively so as to avoid becoming the "bad guys" by disrupting a generous local habit. Relatedly, in a different Talmudic account, Rabbi Yehudah ha-Nasi received two radishes that were suspected of having been grown during the Sabbatical Year. In order to accept the gift without causing a scene, he ruled that one may buy vegetables immediately after the end of the Sabbatical Year.[55]

The final difficulty with funding expertise stemmed from the financial relationship in which rabbis found themselves. The donor, employer, or patron could exercise their personal interest because of their investment. This is a recurrent tension that stems from the different roles that experts are called to fill. Torbjørn Gundersen argues that in the contemporary context scientific experts fulfill two types of roles: (1) researchers, generating knowledge; and (2) contributors, sharing knowledge for the purposes of policymaking, education, or administrative oversight.[56] These two types of roles—the former internal to the specialist group and the latter external facing—work in tandem to support the advancement of "science," even as they perform different functions. The researcher represents the siloed expert in pursuit of "pure" knowledge. Their aims are framed as detached and disinterested in the affairs of the public in order to preserve their objectivity and focus upon data.[57] But scientists are also selected for a wide range of public-facing roles, such as advisor, lecturer, administrator, or public intellectual, that each carry a different set of normative expectations. These social roles plunge scientists into relationships that impose

54. T. Kelim Bava Metziah 5:3.

55. Y. Pe'ah 7:3, 20b; parallel in Y. Bava Batra 9:5, 17a.

56. See Gunderson, "Scientists as Experts," which offers a nuanced reframing of H. Douglas, *Science, Policy, and the Value-Free Ideal,* and the general "separability view."

57. On the difficulties of objectivity, see Latour, *Inquiry into Modes of Existence,* 8–11.

obligation and infuse other demands into their work. Where scientific researchers can presume epistemic significance because the production of knowledge is self-evidently valuable to them, scientific consultants must prove their societal significance and persuade others to value their opinions. Gundersen argues that the two roles are entangled in practice, requiring the scientific community to consider their collective contribution both in regard to individual research and in regard to how it will be understood by a non-specialist public.[58]

There was social precedent for funding scholastic work in late antiquity.[59] Grammarians served as paid advisors and teachers, renowned not just for their valued specialization amid a largely illiterate populace but for the resulting privileged clientele that they served.[60] As dramatized narrative accounts suggest, such as Suetonius's *De grammaticis et rhetoribus*, written in the second century CE, men could rise to great fame by teaching grammar and rhetoric. Some even sought imperial patronage as court orators.[61] Patrons often invested in knowledge production as aristocratic families associated themselves with intellectual talent for self-promotion.[62] As Andrew Wallace-Hadrill explains, patrons saw those they supported as extensions of themselves, so that "the Roman noble felt himself almost naked without an entourage of dependents, which he expanded to the best of his ability, and who acted as the visible symbol of his social standing."[63] They would share personal libraries, purchase books for scholars as a form of civic benefaction, or act as personal advocates when necessary.[64]

These relationships were built on reciprocal exchange, with the donor or employer providing financial support in exchange for the scholar's loyalty and services.[65] Such relationships were inherently asymmetrical because the

58. Gunderson, "Scientists as Experts," 58.

59. Dufault, *Early Greek Alchemy, Patronage and Innovation*, 15–25 argues in particular that client scholars were "unlikely to represent their ties with patrons as anything else but friendship" (25).

60. Kaster, *Guardians of Language*, x, 28, 230.

61. Omissi, "Rhetoric and Power."

62. On the inequality between literary and cultural patronage, see Saller, *Personal Patronage*, 7, 11–15. On intellectual civic contributions as their own form of benefaction, see Sausville, "Intellectual Euergetism."

63. Wallace-Hadrill, *Patronage in Ancient Society*, 65.

64. Williams, *The Monk and the Book*, 137–38.

65. Saller, *Personal Patronage*, 1–3. Saller contends that as a state administration expands, providing services and protections for citizens, the need for patrons declines. He defined a patronage relationship with three defining features: reciprocal exchange, long-term relationships, and asymmetrical status between the patron and client.

funder controlled the purse strings and so held a measure of power over the recipient. As Christel Freu writes of the scholars of the Second Sophistic, those intellectuals who entered employer relationships "gave up their independence to bind themselves to another through the obligations of the contractual relationship."[66] Plato notoriously resented the moneymaking success of the Second Sophistic.[67] For example, in the dialogue *Major*, Socrates states that Gorgias of Leontini spoke well in public and taught the young men of the city, receiving a great sum of money in return. Prodicus, too, Socrates says, arrived in an official capacity from Ceos and received great reputation (ηὐδοκίμησεν) speaking before the Council and earning a "marvelous sum of money" (χρήματα ἔλαβεν θαυμαστὰ ὅσα) from educating young men. Socrates then ironically suggests that the scholars of the past would never think to exact payment or display their knowledge in a public spectacle, who were "so unconscious of the fact that money is of the greatest value."[68]

Despite the ideological difficulties with funding, some rabbis actively sought communal appointments as teachers and lecturers that provided salaries as a more permanent form of financial support.[69] Rabbi Yehudai ben Nahman and Rabbi Levi, for example, are reported to have received two *sela* per week for lecturing on Shabbat.[70] Others taught children, an arena where Hayim Lapin contends that rabbis "competed to present themselves as ritual

66. Freu, "Who's Afraid of Wage Labour?," 160.

67. E. L. Harrison has shown that thirty-one references in Plato allude to the Sophists' acceptance of money for instruction ("Was Gorgias a Sophist?," 191n.44).

68. Plato, *Hipp. maj.* 282b–d. Xenophon, *Cyn.* 13.8–9 similarly insists that "the [S]ophists speak to deceive and write for their own profit (κέρδει), and they never benefit anyone in any way."

69. On amoraim as a *sofer*, which could denote children's instruction, see Y. Shabbat 9:2, 12a; Y. Sukkah 2:5, 53a; and Y. Megillah 3:8, 74b. According to Lev. Rab. 30:1, teachers received a minimum wage salary, but Y. Hagigah 1:7, 76c describes donor support. Y. Pe'ah 8:7, 21a describes a communal tax. See Y. Rosh Hashanah 4:1, 59b; Y. Beitzah 1:6, 60c; Y. Sotah 1:4, 16d; and Lev. Rab. 32:7 for examples of homilists. The later Song of Songs Rab. 1:1 and *Avot de-Rabbi Nathan* A 4 assumes that rabbis taught the public in communally appointed roles. See Y. Shabbat 12:3, 13c; Y. Horayot 3:4, 48b; Y. Hagigah 2:1, 77b for rabbis teaching in the study house. There appear to be very few officially appointed rabbinic judges, so most operated as unofficial legal advisors who would likely have been paid through gifts, as was the typical custom. On midrash as public instruction, see Mandel, *Origins of Midrash*, 261–71.

70. Y. Sheqalim 4:2, 48a; Gen Rab. 98:11. In another tradition, Torah scholars received a salary from the Temple for instructing priests in the laws regarding ritual slaughter.

experts and authorities."[71] Rabbis had to persuade local communities that they were the Torah experts to employ. One passage in the Palestinian Talmud tractate Hagigah develops an argument for their appointment:

> R. Simeon b. Yochai stated: When you see towns torn from their place in the Land of Israel, know that they did not contribute to the wages of Bible and Mishnah teachers. What is the reason? "Why is the land ruined, torn down like an uninhabited wilderness? The LORD said, because they abandoned My Torah" (Jer. 9:11–12). R. Yudan ha-Nasi sent R. Ḥiyya, R. Assi, and R. Immi to tour the towns of the Land of Israel in order to appoint teachers of Bible and tannaitic tradition. They came to one place where they found neither teachers of Bible nor tannaitic tradition. They said to them, "bring us the watchmen of the town." They brought them the watchmen of the town. They told them, "these are not the watchmen of the town, they are the destroyers of the town." They asked them, "who would be the watchmen of the town?" They told them, "The teachers of Bible and tannaitic tradition." That is what is written: "If the LORD did not build the house, etc" (Ps. 127:1). (Y. Hagigah 1:7, 76c)

תני ר׳ שמעון בן יוחי: אם ריאת עיירות שנתלשו ממקומן בארץ ישראל דע שלא החזיקו בשכר סופרים ומשנים. מה טע׳ "על מה אבדה הארץ נצתה כמדבר מבלי יושב. ויאמר יי על עזבם את תורתי." ר׳ יודן נשייא שלח לר׳ חייה ולר׳ אסי ולר׳ אמי למיעבור בקרייתא דארעא דישראל למתקנא לון ספרין ומתניינין. עלון לחד אתר ולא אשבחון לא ספר ולא מתניין. אמרין לון: אייתון לן נטורי קרתא. אייתון לון סנטורי קרתא. אמרון לון: אילין אינון נטורי קרתא. לית אילין אלא חרובי קרתא. אמרין לון: ומאן אינון נטורי קרתא. אמרין לון: ספרייא ומתנייניא. הדא היא דכתיב: "אם יי׳ לא יבנה בית."[72]

The text begins with an explicit warning that the failure to provide wages for Torah teachers will result in devastation for the town. Not only is this devastation assured but it is also divinely sanctioned through the invocation of a prooftext. In this verse God cautions that the ruined land is a direct result of the Israelites abandonment of Torah. The resulting story is not so much an illustration of Rabbi Simeon ben Yochai's warning but an extension of

71. Lapin, *Rabbis as Romans*, 84.

72. Sussmann, ed., col. 779–80. Hayim Lapin states that this passage reflects a strategy for gaining influence in rural settlements through the organization of personal visits. Lapin, *Economy, Geography, and Provincial History*, 187. See also *Pesikta de-Rav Kahana*, 120b.

it—three commissioned rabbis carry the warning with them from town to town as they appoint Torah teachers to communally funded positions.

Upon arrival to this particular place, they call for the סנטורי or watchmen. The root נטר is the Aramaic equivalent of the root שמר. This root, while associated with literal guarding, can also describe the "guarding" or observance of the Torah commandments. The psalm at the conclusion of the story mirrors this root's association with observance of God's commands as a final punchline. When read in full, the psalm states: "If the Lord did not build the house, *they labor in vain who build it; If the Lord did not guard (ישמר) the city, the watchmen (שומר) wake in vain*" (Ps. 127:1). When the visiting rabbis request the metaphorical watchmen, that is, the rabbis, the town's representatives bring the literal סנטורי or town watchmen, playing on the similar sounding Aramaic and Latin.[73] However, by relying on earthly guardsmen, these elders have threatened and endangered the town. The significance of this threat is profound. The text conjures memories of Roman imperial destruction when Rabbi Simeon ben Yochai remarks pointedly, "When you see towns torn from their place in the Land of Israel." This is not a hypothetical but a reality some Jews had lived. The rabbis use this literal interpretation of their request as an opportunity to introduce the significance of communally appointed rabbinic experts, whose very presence will ensure the security of the town because of their holy calling.

The story is exhortative, describing a scenario in which a group of rabbis travel from town to town, with the intention of appointing rabbis to expert positions within local communities. It presumes that some locales would be resistant to the expense and offers a promise of a divine sentry to encourage the allocation of resources for rabbinically appointed Torah teachers. It also envisions the power of rabbis to make communal appointments.[74] Such power was likely aspirational, though it went hand in hand with cultivating expertise. After all, who better to select the right Torah educator than a member of the rabbinic specialist group? Not only does this passage claim

73. Sokoloff defines ירוטנס as "watchmen" (*A Dictionary of Jewish Palestinian Aramaic*, 384), but Saul Lieberman argues that it represents the Latin *saltuarius*, or agricultural estate managers (*Tosefta Ki-Fshutah*, 365n.47. These village guard positions were poorly paid and communally appointed in rural areas of Roman provinces. On the role of city watchmen in Roman provinces, see Bagnall, "Army and Police."

74. See S. Schwartz, *Were the Jews a Mediterranean Society?*, 132 for related appointments of *archontes* in Y. Pe'ah 8.7, 21a.

the authority to make such appointments, but it assumes that rabbis have earned the right.

Yet, communal appointments introduced their own set of reciprocal expectations that invoked the tensions of payment for expertise. Employed rabbis had to listen to non-expert opinions, take advice from uninformed people, and even change their behavior to appease others. The Sifre Deuteronomy describes this development as becoming indentured (משועבדים) to the public, a term often used to describe land assets confiscated by a lender when the borrower fails to repay.[75] The association of mortgages and debt served to emphasize how the power dynamics were reversed when rabbinic experts lost their financial independence.

Palestinian Talmud tractate Megillah, for example, describes the kinds of problems that could emerge when Torah teachers were funded through communal funds, presumably provided by wealthy benefactors of the locale.

> The people of his town told R. Simeon, the teacher of Terbenth: "cut the sentences which our sons are reading." He [R. Simeon] went and asked R. Ḥaninah, who told him, "Do not listen to them even if they cut off your head." He did not listen to them and they dismissed him from his teaching position. (Y. Megillah 4:4, 75b)

> ר׳ שמעון ספרא דטרבנת אמרין ליה בני קרתיה: קטע בדיבירייא דיקרונון בנינן. אתא שאל לר׳ חנינה. אמר ליה אין קטעין רישך לא תשמע לון. ולא שמע לון ושרון ליה מן ספרותה.[76]

The elders of the town tried to control Rabbi Simeon's pedagogical methods, insisting that he split the verses of Torah into smaller parts so that they were easier for the students to memorize. The rabbis in turn maintain that these verses must be treated as complete sentences.[77] Here the pedagogical methods of rabbinic experts are directly challenged, and the offending rabbi is dismissed. The preference of people in charge won out over the presumed expert. Later in the passage Rabbi Zeira hears this story and praises the actions of Rabbi Simeon, but the potential problems from non-experts who might decide to interfere in rabbinic methods hangs uneasily in the air. The consolation

75. Sifre Deut. 16:1.

76. Sussmann, ed., col. 772.

77. Anxiety about separating Torah is also found in B. Gittin 60a, where the rabbis debate whether Torah can be divided into separate scrolls.

of this praise does not lessen the sting of potential dismissal when employers or benefactors wanted to interfere.

Furthermore, public judgment intensified the importance of rabbinic visibility, especially when employers had their own expectations or found their appointed rabbi inadequate. In one story, Rabbi Yehudah ha-Nasi was traveling through Simonia, a village a few hours from Sepphoris. The town's leaders asked him to appoint a rabbi who could teach them "Scripture and Mishnah and be our judge."[78] He appointed Rabbi Levi ben Sisi, and the town elders erected a giant platform for him to teach from. The narrative indicates that they asked him three questions, but he fled the town in embarrassment when he could not answer them. Upon his return, Rabbi Yehudah was surprised that Rabbi Levi could not respond to such simple halachic questions. Levi explained that he did in fact know the answers, but the grandiose platform made him arrogant, causing him to forget his teachings.

The passage invokes a biblical proverb as context for this anecdote: "If you have been foolish, exalting yourself . . ." (Prov. 30:32). Rabbi Levi's elevation on the platform symbolizes the downfall of his pride. Nevertheless, it also serves as a warning to rabbinic experts. Communal roles often blur the distinction between experts and the public. When experts are placed under public scrutiny, their resolve could falter. This spotlight could cause shame, anger, and frustration, especially for those who must share their specialized knowledge with the uninitiated. In a small village without connections to the broader network of Torah scholars, the appointed rabbi faced significant pressure.[79]

Financial support from other Jews was instrumental in the expansion of the rabbinic specialist group, but it came with drawbacks. First, it created a need to convince Jewish communities that rabbinic experts deserved their salaries or communal funds. Ideally, the Torah's sanctity should be self-evident, leading Jews to readily support its proclaimed experts. However, in reality, rabbis had to defend and promote the value of their specialized expertise. Second, financial influence over rabbis led to situations where rabbis could face criticism, reprimands, or demands. Any notion that rabbinic experts led insulated lives amid other specialists was shattered when, for instance, an employer dictated how a rabbi should teach Torah, or a donor criticized a rabbi's legal

78. Gen. Rab. 81:2.

79. Lapin, *Rabbis as Romans*, 69 and 224.

advice. The power that funding provided could, at best, be annoying and, at worst, disrupt rabbinic autonomy.

Such encroachment of scholastic autonomy was shared by other scholars in antiquity. Kendra Eshleman, writing about the power of patronage of the Second Sophistic, framed the tension as one of competing authority that blurred the distinction between the expert performer and client consumer.[80] The intimacy that comes with patronage and salaries can blur the lines between experts and non-experts, even though these funds often help establish these boundaries by enabling expert work. Eshleman argues that sophists managed this tension through a "cognitive dissonance" with their patrons, where they held in one hand their ideals and in the other hand the tangible support they required. They understood that their success relied on support and salaries and used mental gymnastics to assert their autonomy in the face of external intrusion.

Consequently, they created a discourse that projected a fundamental asymmetry to maintain their autonomy. Eshleman uses Aristides as an example of how this was achieved. He downplayed the influence of outsiders by pledging allegiance to his ultimate divine patron, Asclepius.[81] A divine patron's interests could overrule any mortal patron, allowing the scholar to assert power over their worldly patron and maintain their independence. An appeal to a divine patron or shared moral value disavowed the negative effects of human patronage. For instance, a series of homilies in the Palestinian Talmud tractate Berakhot 9:1 (13a) depict a patron as aloof; when his client is on the brink of death, the patron is nowhere to be found.[82] The Holy One, by contrast, stands by his client's side and rescues him from calamity.[83]

It need not only be a divine patron either. The Athenian Sophist Isocrates, famous for composing stirring speeches and molding skilled orators from his students, took pains to reframe the association of Sophistry with money. While Isocrates does not deny teaching for pay, he took pains to reframe his fees as gifts motivated by gratitude. Yun Lee Too argues that Isocrates

80. Eshleman, *Social World of Intellectuals*, 78.

81. Eshleman, 88.

82. Y. Berakhot 9:1, 13a.

83. The rabbis were also particularly critical of patronage support for the poor that placed insurmountable debt on those unable to repay. Wilfand, *Poverty, Charity, and the Image of the Poor*, 234, 265–66; Gardner, "Charity Wounds."

understood payment as client reciprocity for the superior gift he initially bestowed. Isocrates thereby frames the teacher-student relationship in the terms of friendship (*philia*) or a guest-host relationship (*xenia*), and resists commodification of his expertise.[84]

Rabbis lived in a social context that scrutinized the payment of scholars and at the same time compelled them to return reciprocal favors. Recognizing the balance between religious devotion, epistemic autonomy, and the constraints of social persuasion in rabbinic literature reframes rabbinic exhortations against profiting from Torah from strictly moral assertions to strategic rhetorical tactics. "Know before Whom you labor—the Master of your work is trustworthy to pay you the wage for your activity," a mishnah from Avot declares.[85] The proclamation of a heavenly direct deposit served to frame Torah labor as worthy of just compensation that God was sure to supply. It differentiated rabbinic experts and constructed a sense of their holy autonomy and cultural capital.[86] Such a boundary was prescriptive rather than descriptive, asserting the special quality of rabbinic experts even as rabbis became entangled in the public work through which they would earn payment.

Fundraising as Divine Investment Strategy

The financial support of sages introduced lay people as a meaningful entity in the enactment of their expertise. E. Summerson Carr explains that expertise is not just a relationship between an individual and an object of knowledge—in this case between the rabbi and Torah—but it is also a relationship between "experts and laities."[87] Fundraising for rabbinic interests provided a meaningful way for the rabbinic specialist group to gain visibility and cultivate trust with other Jews.[88] Recent studies on donor motivation and stewardship theory identify four strategies for effective fundraising: reciprocity, responsibility, reporting, and relationship nurturing.[89] Whoever is providing funds expects something in return, whether a measure of oversight, involvement, or even a simple thank you note. Responsibility refers to the trustworthiness of the

84. Too, *Rhetoric of Identity in Isocrates*, 161–64. Tell, *Plato's Counterfeit Sophists*, 50.
85. M. Avot 2:14.
86. Wimpfheimer, *Narrating the Law*, 122–46.
87. Carr, "Enactments of Expertise," 22.
88. See Sperber, "Patronage in Amoraic Palestine," 227–52.
89. K. Kelly, *Effective Fund-Raising Management*, and "Stewardship."

recipient who can assure the donor that their gift is helping them achieve worthy goals, as evidenced through routine reports on the investment. These all work together to nurture a relationship between donors and their recipients. Fundraising is therefore not just about the gift of money but about the way shared values are activated through those gifts. There may be specific needs motivating the solicitation of funds, but they serve a larger purpose of increasing buy-in to the ideals of a funded project. In this way, soliciting gifts for rabbinic interests cultivated investment in the larger enterprise of rabbinic expertise.

Effective fundraising requires generating broad appeal and enthusiasm for a cause among a non-specialist audience. This goal can be achieved by creating a bond between public-facing experts and donors that is rooted in shared values and objectives. This bond is enhanced not just by providing tangible reasons for donating but also by aligning with the donor's personal quest for purpose.[90] As Donald Ritzenhein suggests in an essay on donor motivation, fundraising should aim to "bring new joy to the lives of donors by helping them fulfill their innate needs for purpose, value, efficacy, and self-worth."[91] His assertion is based on data from a study of college alumni donors, where the main reason for their ongoing support was the connection and partnership they felt with the university.[92] The study revealed that donors derive a sense of self-worth from these feelings of partnership and impact.

A similar activation of a shared partnership fueled rabbinic fundraising for Torah study, first through the construction of physical spaces.[93] Rabbinic literature describes *batei midrash*, or study houses, where sages could gather.[94] Sometimes "houses of meeting" or "great halls" are described as serving a similar function.[95] The details about these spaces are scarce in the texts and even less in the archaeological record, but it is apparent that such spaces required benefactors.[96] Rabbi Ḥaninah, for example, constructed a study house

90. Herzberg, "How Do You Motivate Employees?"

91. Ritzenhein, "How Do You Motivate Donors?," 66.

92. Ritzenheim, 62.

93. For a survey of study houses, see Oppenheimer, "Batei Midrash in Eretz-Israel in the Early Amoraic Period," 80–89. Also, Marks, "Who Studied at the Beit Midrash?"

94. See the description in Y. Megillah 3:1, 74d.

95. Y. Bava Qamma 9:3, 6d; Y. Berakhot 2:8, 5c; Y. Bikkurim 3:3, 65c.

96. See Hezser, *Social Structure of the Rabbinic Movement*, 202–14. For an overview, see Marks, "Who Studied at the Beit Midrash?" According to Lev Rab. 34:16, R. Akiva donated a huge sum of money for rabbinic students. See also discussion in Lapin, "Jewish and Christian Academies," 511.

in Sepphoris from the profits of his honey sales.[97] Sometimes soliciting for such sites put rabbis in direct competition with other communal needs. In one passage, Rabbi Ḥamma bar Ḥaninah praised his father's generous donations to the synagogue of Lod, while Rabbi Hoshaiah countered that the gift would have been better spent on a place for Torah scholars.[98] This is not to suggest that rabbis considered themselves in competition with synagogues. Both synagogues and study houses are portrayed as the mainstays of Jewish life in rabbinic literature, as Rabbi Abbahu states: "'Seek out the Lord where He may be found' (Isa. 55:6). Where may He be found? In the synagogues and study houses."[99] However, the narrative does imply a hierarchy of ideal gifts.[100] The passage continues with Rabbi Abun boasting about the gates he installed on the great hall (*sidrah rabbah*). But Rabbi Mana exclaims, "Were there no people laboring in Torah?" This misguided donation of decorative doors for a study house, which, while aiding the infrastructure of Torah study, could have gone directly toward supporting scholars. This emphasis on direct support of Torah scholars reflects what Susan Marks identifies as the struggle to solicit donations for salaries and scholarships rather than buildings.[101]

The honorifics associated with the culture of roman euergetism made buildings an attractive investment. One source shifts potential donors away from a preoccupation with their name on the building, and instead promises direct access to Torah expertise, attempting to activate the share value of Torah as a cultural object. In this case, Rabbi Ḥiyya bar Abba organized a fundraiser for a study house in Tiberias.[102] A member of the Silani family, known for their generous donations and also a donor to Rabbi Ḥiyya himself, pledged a pound of gold.[103] To honor this act, Rabbi Ḥiyya offered him a seat among the sages and recited the proverb, "A man's gift eases his way and gives him access to great men" (Prov. 18:16). This practice of honoring donors is also evidenced in a Greek third-century inscription from Phocaea, which pays

---

The Tosefta describes Zonen who was in charge of the study house in Lydda (T. Pes. 3:11) and was likely a benefactor of the space.

97. Y. Pe'ah 7:4, 20b. See also discussion in Lapin, "Jewish and Christian Academies," 511.

98. Y. Sheqalim 5:4, 49b; parallel in Y. Pe'ah 8:8, 21b.

99. Y. Berakhot 5:1, 8d–9a. Lapin, "Jewish and Christian Academies," 508.

100. Marks, "Who Studied at the Beit Midrash?," 294. On the evidence of synagogue donors, see Brooten, *Women Leaders in the Ancient Synagogue*; Sorek, *Remembered for Good*.

101. Marks, "Who Studied at the Beit Midrash?," 294.

102. Y. Horayot 3:7, 48a.

103. See chapter 3. Y. Shevi'it 3:1, 34b.

tribute to Tation, daughter of Straton, son of Empedon. After she contributed to the construction of the assembly hall and courtyard, she was presented with a "golden crown and the privilege of sitting in the seat of honor."[104]

The chosen proverb carries a dual message. First, it promised a return on investment. The donor's "way" will be made smoother through divine rewards earned by their gift, illustrating that rabbis, like other scholars, justified the donations they sought within a value-laden framework through interpretive persuasion. Second, it served as a reminder to generous donors that their contributions to facilitate the work of Torah study were appreciated. Publicly acknowledging the honor of these "great men" garnered enthusiasm and interest for future donations in the service of fulfilling mitzvot. Galit Hasan-Rokem suggests that this passage offers an example of how rabbis could open "channels of communication" between their specialist group and the general public.[105] Not only would these donors receive honors but they would become physical partners in rabbinic work.

This insight can help illuminate how rabbinic fundraising was most effective when activating a shared value with their donors. One way this was achieved was through the category of charity.[106] In chapter 2 we saw how rabbis framed hospitality—an act akin to charity—as a gift for rabbis that would reward the host. Rabbinic fundraising shared this strategy of divine investment, explicitly using the category of charity to solicit funds for rabbis:

> It once happened that R. Eliezer, R. Yehoshua, and R. Akiva went to a suburb of Antioch in order to fundraise for the sages. There was there a certain Abba Yudan who gave alms (lit. *mitzvah*) generously. He became impoverished. He saw our teachers approaching his house and his face paled. His wife asked him, "why are you looking sickly?" He told her the problem, "Our teachers are here and I do not know what I will do for them." His wife, who was righteous, told him: "We have only one field left; go, sell half of it, and give [the proceeds] to them." He went and did so. Then gave [the proceeds] to them. They said to him, "May the Omniscient One replace your loss."
>
> Our teachers left. He went out to plough. While plowing his half of the field, the Holy One enlightened his eyes—the earth opened up before him

104. Ameling, *Inscriptiones*, 36 (see Lifshitz 13 and CIJ 738); translation in R. Kraemer, *Women's Religions in the Greco-Roman World*, 163, 661. For analysis of this inscription, see Marks, "Follow That Crown," 86.

105. Hasan-Rokem, "Gifts for God, Gifts for Rabbis," 233.

106. Gardner, *Wealth, Poverty, and Charity*.

and his cow fell and broke her (leg)—he went down to lift her up and found underneath her treasure. He said, "for my benefit my cow broke her leg." When our teachers returned, they inquired about him. "How is Abba Yudan doing?" They answered, "who can appear before Abba Yudan? Abba Yudan of his goats, Abba Yudan of his donkeys, Abba Yudan of his camels!"

He came to them and said to them, "Your prayer produced for me fruits and fruits and fruits." They told him, "Even though others have given more than you, we wrote you on top of the record." They took him, made him sit with them, and recited for him this verse: "*A man's gift eases his way*" (Prov. 18:16). (Lev. Rab. 5:4; parallel in Y. Horayot 3:4, 48a)[107]

מעשה בר׳ אליעזר ור׳ יהושע ורבי עקיבה שהלכו לחולת אנטוכיא לעסוק במגבית חכמים.[108] הוה תמן חד אבא יודן שהיה עושה מצוה בעין יפה וירד מנכסיו.[109] כיון שראה רבותינו עלה לביתו ופניו חולניות.[110] אמרה לו אשתו מה לך פניך חולניות. תני לה עובדה, רבותינו כן ואיני יודע מה אעשה להן. אשתו שהיתה צדקת[111] מה אמרה לו, לא נשתיירה לך שדה אחת, לך מכור חציה ותן להן. הלך ועשה כן. כשהוא נותן להן[112] אמרו לו המקום ימלא חסרונך. הלכו להם רבותינו. יצא לחרוש,[113] עם כשהוא חורש חצי שדהו האיר לו הקב״ה עיניו ונבקעה הארץ לפניו ונפלה פרתו ונשברה, ירד להעלותה[114] ומצא תחתיה סימא. אמר לטובתי נשברה רגל פרתי. כשחרו רבותינו שאלון עליה ההוא אבא יודן מה עביד, אמרי מן יכיל למיחמי אפוה דאבא יודן.[115] אבא יודן דעיזיא, אבא יודן דחמריא, אבא יודן דגמלויא.[116] בא אצלן ואמר להן נעשת תפילתכם עלי פירות ופירי פירות. אמרו לו אפעלפי שנתנן אדם אחר יותר ממך לך כתבנו בראש טימוס. נטלוהו והושיבוהו אצלם וקראו עליו מתן אדם ירחיב לו.[117]

107. Margulies, ed., 110–13. See also Deut. Rab. 4:8.

108. Oxford, Bodleian Opp. Add. fol. 5; and Toronto, Friedberg, Sasson 920 states צדקה instead of חכמים, and 1512 Constantinople states צדקה לחכים.

109. 1512 Constantinople reads in light of Y. Horayot, with the exception of הסנרפ for הוצמ.

110. 1512 Constantinople includes שם ונכמרו רחמיו הלך לו אצל.

111. Oxford, Bodleian Opp. Add. fol. 3; Oxford, Bodleian Opp. Add. fol. 51; Jerusalem, JNUL Heb 24° 5977; and Toronto, Friedberg, Sasson 920 all lack אשתו שהיתה צדקת.

112. 1512 Constantinople and Cambridge T-S C2.66 add נתפללו עליו.

113. 1512 Constantinople לאח׳ ימים הלך לחרוש בחצי שדהו.

114. 1512 Constantinople adds after והאיר הקב״ה עיניו.

115. Only London, British Library Add. 27,169, Munich, Bayerische Staatsbibliothek heb. 117, and Cambridge T-S C2.66 have this statement in full.

116. 1512 Constantinople adds the following line: אבא יודן דתורי יכל למחמי סבר אפוי דאבא יודן כיון ששמע

117. Vatican, Ebr. 32; Paris, Bibliothèque Nationale héb. 149; Jerusalem, JNUL Heb 24° 5977; Oxford, Bodleian Opp. Add. fol. 51; and Toronto, Friedberg, Sasson 920 add the following line: ולפני גדולים ינחינו

This account begins with the travel of three tannaitic rabbis to the outskirts of Antioch, one of the largest cities in the later Roman empire whose harbor sat along the eastern side of the Orontes River.[118] The Jewish community of Antioch had a tumultuous status following the Judean rebellion from Rome in 66 CE.[119] Josephus states that the populous, riled up out of racial anger, attacked the Jews of the city with brutal force on two separate occasions. When the Roman governor Titus arrived in the city, the Antiochenes petitioned for the expulsion of the Jews.[120] Titus refused, but thereafter the relations between Jews and other residents of the city were reportedly tense.

A certain man known for giving alms generously lived in Antioch. The term used here for alms is *mitzvah*, which is usually translated as "commandment" but became a term for "charity" in Palestinian rabbinic literature.[121] This man, Abba Yudan (Aramaic for Yehudah), became impoverished, but the text does not mention the circumstances of his property loss.[122] Though some scholars believe that Abba Yudan's generosity caused him to give away most of his property, therefore leaving him penniless, it is more plausible that his generosity reflects the social status he once held as a wealthy almsgiver prior to facing hardship, as Alyssa Gray argues.[123] Gray suggests that such a focus on formerly wealthy poor might have been motivated by the "hope that the latter might display generosity to the rabbis if and when their fortunes improved."[124] Abba

118. Downey, *History of Antioch in Syria*. Rabbinic literature usesאיכוטנא תלוח "a harbor of Antioch" rather than simply "Antioch" most likely in reference to a Jewish settlement near Daphne, potentially the area associated with the synagogue John Chrysostom references. Jastrow, *Dictionary of the Targumim*, 435. Visotzky thinks the reference is to the hot springs of Daphne, a suburb of Antioch (*Golden Bells and Pomegranates*, 124). The Palestinian Talmud associates Daphne with the location of King Nebuchadnezzar's camp when he arrived to destroy the first Temple. Y. Sheqalim 6:3, 50a. See Kraeling, "Jewish Community at Antioch," 141. John Chrysostom references the Jewish community at Antioch, describing them as a πολιτεία and referencing Jewish patriarchs. 1 Adv. Jud. Orat., I:3, PG, vol. XL; Op.Cit 6:5. Rice grows in the sands of the harbor, as noted in Y. Demai 2:1, 22d.

119. Brooten, "Jews of Ancient Antioch."

120. Josephus, *A.J.* 12.122–24.

121. See also Lev. Rab. 34:4. For *mitzvah* as charitable giving, see Lieberman, "Two Lexicographical Notes," 69–72.

122. His name translates to "Father of the Jews," a possible honorific title for his charitable actions. See Visotzky, *Golden Bells and Pomegranates*, 125.

123. Cf. Satlow, "'Fruit and the Fruit of Fruit,'" 246–47 with Gray, "Formerly Wealthy Poor," 111.

124. Gray, "Formerly Wealthy Poor," 112. Also, Kalmin, *Sage in Jewish Society*, 29–33.

Yudan's case represents a situation of a generous donor who has slipped into poverty and thus merits divine attention.

Whatever the reason for Abba Yudan's property loss, it seems he was quite familiar with the rabbis' fundraising habits. Upon spotting them from afar, he pales at the thought of not being able to fulfill their expected request. His wife suggests selling half of their remaining field. He promptly does so and gives the proceeds to the rabbis. In return, they offer a blessing asking God to replace his losses. This blessing is no ordinary farewell benediction; it is understood to invoke a transmission of divine power in exchange for Abba Yudan's donation. A blessing, or *berakah* in Hebrew, εὐλογέω in Greek, could have miraculous results.[125] For example, in the synoptic Gospels, Jesus blessed (εὐλογέω) five loaves and two fishes, and they multiplied enough to feed thousands (Matt. 14:19; Luke 9:16). Indeed, when Abba Yudan goes to plow the remaining half of his field, the earth splits open to reveal a treasure. His cow's broken leg becomes a side note to this miraculous reward. If there were any doubt about the source of Abba Yudan's newfound wealth, he tells the rabbis, "Your prayer produced for me fruits and fruits and fruits."[126]

The logic of divine investment is obvious, but scholars have struggled to categorize the recipients of such fundraising because the gift is framed as charity. For example, Burt Visotzky insists that the collection does not represent charity because it is not explicitly directed toward poor individuals,[127] while Gardner convincingly argues that the rabbis at least "*present* the collection of the sages as an exercise in organized charity."[128] Either these rabbis were poor or they were, as Gardner notes, redirecting funds "from the needy to the rabbinic movement."[129]

It is likely that these rabbis were not destitute. The majority of scholars assume that by the amoraic period the rabbinic specialist group was comprised of a mix of primarily wealthy individuals and some men of lesser means.[130] While

125. For this phenomenon in Christian literature and its association with material gifts, see Caner, "Towards a Miraculous Economy," and *The Rich and the Pure*.

126. For more analysis of this story, see Satlow, "'Fruit and the Fruit of Fruit,'" 246–47; Gray, *Charity in Rabbinic Judaism*, 103.

127. Visotzky, *Golden Bells and Pomegranates*, 125.

128. Gardner, *Origins of Organized Charity*, 189, emphasis original.

129. Gardner, 189.

130. However, a minority of scholars maintain few were wealthy. Urbach asserts that the sages came "from all classes and walks of life" and did not seek power or leadership ("Talmudic Sage," 123, and "Class-Status and Leadership"); and Wilfand argues for greater socio-economic

stories about rabbis and charity are assumed to be donations directed toward rabbis with self-evident "financial need,"[131] Hayim Lapin pushes back on the assumption that these stories constitute actual cases of poverty.[132] He argues that the themes of wealth and economic security are doing a number of things in the texts, including valorizing mythic sacrifice of wealth for Torah, critiquing the patriarch's insufficient patronage, and theorizing the tensions within a growing rabbinic collective.[133] Thinking practically about rabbinic recruitment, Lapin contends that their pool of candidates would have been relatively narrow and restricted to a provincial sub-elite with access to formal education of some kind. Likewise, Michael Satlow suggests that stories about individual rabbis rising from humble backgrounds were "clearly seen as exceptional."[134]

For instance, Leviticus Rabbah 34:16 recounts a related story about Rabbi Tarfon and Rabbi Akiva. Rabbi Tarfon gave to Rabbi Akiva six silver *centarii* to purchase property so that they might "earn a living from it and [be free to] labor in Torah." Despite Rabbi Tarfon hailing from a wealthy priestly family and Rabbi Akiva's Torah studies being supported by his affluent wife, they express a desire to "earn a living" in this tale.[135] However, the narrative reveals that Rabbi Akiva distributed the money to other Mishnah teachers and Torah students. He defends his actions by quoting Psalm 112:9, which says, "He who gives freely to the poor, his righteousness lasts forever." Visotzky uses this verse to argue that the money's recipients are "the most poorly paid members of the rabbinic educational establishment, the elementary teachers."[136] But it is more likely that the prooftext was not a literal description of the status of the students but the

---

diversity among the earliest rabbis ("Was There Really 'an Arrogance of Wealth'?"). See Beer, "Torah and Derekh Eretz"; Levine, *Rabbinic Class*; Hezser, *Social Structure of the Rabbinic Movement*, 36, 266; and Gardner, "Who Is Rich?" for different takes on this question.

131. Wilfand, *Poverty, Charity and the Image of the Poor*, 105; Gardner, "Who Is Rich?"

132. Lapin, *Rabbis as Romans*, 71.

133. Lapin, 73. Lapin frames the tension as "the internal struggle of a non-homogenous but largely propertied group to define itself in the context of a world in which true poverty was ubiquitous, in which Torah ought in principle to belong to all of Israel, but in which, in practice, Torah was accessible only through some combination of wealth, patronage, and sacrifice" (73). On the relationship between rabbis and the patriarch, see Levine, "Jewish Patriarch (Nasi) in Third Century Palestine."

134. Satlow, "'Fruit and the Fruit of Fruit,'" 245.

135. Some later traditions do depict R. Akiva as one who is initially poor and only attains wealth through Torah study. *Avot de-Rabbi Nathan* A 6. See Yadin-Israel, *Scripture and Tradition*.

136. Visotzky, *Golden Bells and Pomegranates*, 126.

recurring divine investment logic of almsgiving that perceived rabbis as valid recipients within the conceptual framework of Jewish charitable giving.

This is a textual argument rather than a social argument. As discussed in chapter 2, rabbinic interpreters read into the biblical text and reimagined themselves as a new category of "homeless poor." Because there was no office of rabbi in the biblical text itself, rabbis had to make the case that they were potential recipients of charitable giving. Primarily the priests and the poor were accounted for in the Torah's vision of agricultural redistribution because of their lack of access to land.[137] This conceptual relationship is illustrated in the Mishnah, where the category "gifts for the poor" (מתנות עניים) are paralleled with "gifts for the priesthood" (מתנות לכהן), suggesting a persistent analogy in the rabbinic perception of these groups.[138] But the rabbis were not priests because the rabbinic office lacked a genealogical claim, nor were they chronically poor because the rabbis were literate men with some measure of capital. Instead, rabbinic interpreters conceived of themselves as a hybrid category—able to receive tithes because of their Torah study and able to receive charity because of their noble calling.

Even as rabbis were inserting themselves into charitable giving and asserting control over its distribution, they were not doing so to intentionally compete with the poor.[139] Rabbinic interpreters knew there was a connection between Torah experts and the poor in the biblical tradition. The prior chapter showed how rabbinic interpreters found a way to insert rabbis into the logic of the priestly tithe; therefore, it is not surprising that a similar connection between the poor and rabbis might be found. As grammarian textualists who undoubtedly saw themselves as the appropriate leaders of Jewish piety in a post-temple era, the rabbis read themselves into the biblical text.[140]

Gifts for Torah experts, whether hospitality, tithes, or charity, could activate the same range of divine rewards. It is a persuasive interpretive move to make. Seth Schwartz has argued that rabbis exploited the culture of benefaction in

137. As Brooks explains, "God supports both the priests and the poor because they neither own land nor attain the economic prosperity promised to all Israelites who live in the Land" (*Support for the Poor*, 17–18).

138. Wilfand, *Poverty, Charity, and the Image of the Poor*, 149–50.

139. On rabbinic involvement in the collection and distribution of charity, see Hezser, *Social Structure of the Rabbinic Movement*, 272; Levine, *Rabbinic Class*, 165; Urbach, "Political and Social Tendencies."

140. An idea famously illustrated in B. Bava Metzi'a 59a–b. See Schofer, *Making of a Sage*, for the piety of the rabbis.

order to promote Jewish investment in mitzvot.[141] This means that rabbis knew the cultural expectations of their donors and channeled them toward the Torah's commandments, not resisting the relationships of mutual obligation but using them to advance the work of Torah. This also means that those who offered financial contributions to rabbinic scholars did so for a variety of reasons. Not only did they benefit from the cultural value of associating with experts but they could gain religious merit from supporting the work of Torah.

I claim that the framing of fundraising as charitable investment with divine rewards was a useful donor management strategy because it deflected from the need for rabbis to perform reciprocity because God would provide the reward. Elsewhere in Leviticus Rabbah we learn that God himself promises to pay wages (*sakhar*) and provide male heirs to a bachelor who donated toward Bible and Mishnah teachers.[142] The case of Abba Yudan employs a similar logic. The proverb offered to honor him is the same prooftext used to honor a study house benefactor described above, connecting both acts—benefaction for a study house and charity for rabbis—as related actions that will bring rewards.

The rabbis did not just solicit donations for their members outright; their grammarian fixation upon biblical ambiguity expanded the meaningful applicability of the Torah into an indisputable web of associations. As part of this process rabbis carved out an interpretive place for themselves in the Torah's vision of God's relationship with Israel. Where the Torah did not specify an office of a rabbi, their interpretive work could reveal that a place for rabbinic expertise was present all along. Hasan-Rokem relatedly posits that the Abba Yudan case belongs to a larger rabbinic interpretive trend to transform the biblical institution of sacrifice to support of the rabbis.[143] Charity represented a tangible act that anyone could perform while there was no Temple complex. Rabbinic literature draws attention to the plight of the poor and encourages

141. For example, Seth Schwartz notes the striking overlap with Greco-Roman norms—R. Ḥiyya bar Ba appoints *archontes,* or municipal euergetists, as *parnasim,* or Jewish charity collectors (*Were the Jews a Mediterranean Society?,* 168); R. Yosi promises his interlocutors that their memory would be preserved by their charitable deeds. Y. Pe'ah 8.7, 21a.

142. Lev. Rab. 27:4. Marks, "Who Studied at the Beit Midrash," 292; Lapin, *Rabbis as Romans,* 70.

143. Hasan-Rokem, "Gifts for God, Gifts for Rabbis," 234. This idea is amplified in the Babylonian Talmud with a statement attributed to Rabbi Elazar: "One who performs charity is greater than one [who sacrifices] all [types] of offerings."

Jews to perform charity as a mitzvah.[144] Charity was therefore not just a meaningful form of Jewish giving; it was one that rabbis could rightfully claim access to because of their profession.

The rewards for charitable investment applied even when rabbis themselves were the benefactors. In one story, charity provides miraculous salvation through the hands of rabbinic *parnasim*, or charity collectors. On the night of Rosh Hashanah, Rabbi Simeon ben Yochai dreams that in the coming year his nephews will be fined six hundred denarii—more than a yearly wage. Faced with this disastrous vision, Rabbi Simeon devises a plan. He appoints his nephews, against their will, to the communal administrative position of parnas, or charity distributor.[145] Parnasim, according to Y. Ta'anit 1:4, 64b "are particular people, those who were appointed overseers over the public." Their office is often depicted as the overseers of public spending, including charitable collection or distribution and building projects.[146] What precisely this office encompassed is a matter of some speculation. Gedaliah Alon defined the position as a "spiritual leader, judge and decisor,"[147] while Lee Levine suggests that the term changes over time but involves some oversight over charitable contributions.[148] Steven Fraade demonstrated that there is a "positive relation" between rabbinic learning and appointment as parnas that suggests rabbinic interpreters wanted rabbinic expertise to be a necessary prerequisite for those appointed.[149] In all of these accounts, parnasim collect funds to serve the public good, and in particular the poor.

At first the nephews protest the appointment, asking, "מן דמא מפתקא / Who will finance the expense?" Rabbi Simeon, withholding his dream knowledge, assures them that at the end of the year he will settle their losses (אנא משופי לכון), presumably because he believes that his plan will succeed in outwitting the

144. For a survey of these ideas in tannaitic literature, see Gardner, *Origins of Organized Charity*.

145. By appointing his nephews, R. Simeon actually contradicts a halakhic ruling that two brothers could not both be appointed parnasim.

146. T. Megillah 2:12, 2:15 and T. Gittin 2:13. For an overview of the parnas in rabbinic and epigraphic sources, see Fraade, "Local Jewish Leadership in Roman Palestine." In addition to a position of communal administration, parnasim are depicted as administrators of private estates (M. Ketubbot 7:1) and as national leaders (T. Sotah 11:8; Sifre Deut. 334, 357).

147. Alon, *Jews, Judaism, and the Classical World*, 444.

148. Levine, *Rabbinic Class*, 162–67.

149. Fraade, "Local Jewish Leadership in Roman Palestine," 163, commenting on Sifre Deut. 306 (ed. Finkelstein, 339).

Roman fine. Here Rabbi Simeon both appoints his nephews as parnasim and expects them to fund the position themselves. The nephews go so far as to protest the added expense of the position, a not too atypical response to communal appointments. Rabbi Yosi's appointments in the village of Kifra were met with resistance as well.[150] The parnas position here is presented as a classical benefaction position funded by wealthy elites.[151]

Shortly after Rabbi Simeon's nephews become parnasim they run into trouble. Presumably they are seen distributing communal funds, and as a result, anonymous slanderers spread rumors that Rabbi Simeon's nephews must be merchants in silk. After the rumors spread, a Roman official appears and demands that Rabbi Simeon's nephews either make a *purpura,* or costly purple cloth, garment for the emperor or suffer a fine of six hundred denarii.[152] Because these parnasim are not actually merchants of purpura cloth, they are unable to fulfill the demand. Nor does it seem that they are able to pay the fine because the text assumes that their funds have been spent serving as public benefactors of communal charity. As a result, Rabbi Simeon's nephews are thrown in prison. Up until this point, the characters are subject to the customary demands of a Roman world. But then the narrative flips the script. Rabbi Simeon arrives, he takes the six denarii left from his nephews' initial six hundred, and like any good hero he uses the money to bribe the guard and free his nephews.

The subtext of the nephew's redemption story is its larger midrashic context, which is a chapter devoted to charity's power for redemption. The chapter begins with the biblical verse, "If your brother becomes poor, let his kinsman redeem him" (Lev. 25:25). Throughout the chapter, various prooftexts are brought to make sense of the scope of the verse:

> "Happy is the person who considers the poor, the Lord will deliver him on the Day of Evil." (Ps. 41:1)
> "He that is gracious to the poor, lends to the Lord." (Prov. 19:17)
> "The merciful man does good to his own soul." (Prov. 11:17)

Redemptive almsgiving themes encode this story—because Rabbi Simeon's nephews gave charity from their own funds as parnasim, they generated enough mitzvot to bring about physical redemption from imprisonment through the hands of Rabbi Simeon.

150. Y. Peah 8:7, 21a.
151. Revell, *Roman Imperialism and Local Identities,* 49.
152. Elliott, "Purple Pasts."

The efficacy of the story's plot lies in the power of rabbinic expertise that both engineered the appointment of the parnasim and brought about their miraculous redemption; Rabbi Simeon knows how to activate the divine rewards of charitable giving. It also provides a case of how closely interrelated charity, benefaction, and rabbinic expertise could be. Rabbinic fundraising capitalized upon already pervasive notions of how wealth could facilitate spiritual good that activated rewards from God. In the case of Rabbi Simeon, his own nephews provided the funds, but the same promise of reward could apply to anyone. This passage offers a strong argument for other wealthy benefactors to invest funds for holy endeavors and receive similar benefit.

Employing the logic of redemptive almsgiving and divine investment strategies, rabbis brought God into Jewish financial relationships. God was portrayed as rewarding the donor, thus relieving the rabbi of reciprocal responsibility. As Jennifer Quigley has shown in relation to Paul's financial language in his letter to the Philippians, people in antiquity—whether Christian, Jewish, or some other Roman sect—expected to encounter gods in economic transactions. She insists, "Imperial and divine eyes watched over transactions that occurred within commercial spaces."[153] Rabbinic texts attest to the ways rabbis were situated within a broader context that understood the logics of pious giving.

It is tempting to see this interpretive argument as a bid for rabbinic control over communal charity funds. It is likely that support for rabbinic expertise drew from a finite pool of donors, creating competition for funds. However, the argument also stemmed from a grammarian piety that thought rabbinic expertise could fit within the Torah's logic for communal redistribution of goods and money. If those who labor in Torah have always been supported, and the priests, like the poor, warranted communal support, why shouldn't rabbis also benefit? By funding rabbinic expertise, donors were fulfilling the divine commands of the Torah, and therefore partnering in the work of elevating its status to that which has immeasurable value.

Conclusion: Anxiety Persists

The tension between remuneration and expertise is constant. In today's world, experts are still bound to intricate funding systems. Financial support, whether from restricted or unrestricted funds, employment terms, or fellowships and grants, imposes expectations and obligations on experts, even as it enables

153. Quigley, *Divine Accounting*, 32.

their work and reinforces their expert status. Expertise is a multifaceted machine requiring external maintenance. This means that the rabbis were not unique in feeling the sting of patronal oversight; such dynamics are inherent in the relationship between experts and their clients.

I opened this chapter with a maxim from Mishnah tractate Avot: "From this you learn: He who uses words of Torah for his own benefit removes his life from the world."[154] When Maimonides, the famed twelfth-century rabbinic commentator, analyzed this passage, he took the words at face value. He insisted that nowhere in rabbinic literature do we find rabbis requesting money from people or collecting on behalf of rabbinic academies. To request money was "a desecration of [God's] name in the eyes of the masses because they would think that Torah is a profession from the professions through which a person lives and it will become disgraced in their eyes."[155] Maimonides was certainly wrong in his traditionalist estimation that sages never fundraised, but what is important about his commentary is how he illustrates the fear of profiting from Torah expertise at a much later point in the institutionalization of the rabbis. In a period when rabbinic academies have long established patronal support, he worries that Torah study would be debased if it were likened to an ordinary trade.[156]

However, other medieval commenters disagreed with Maimonides and welcomed tangible support from benefactors. Simeon ben Zemah Duran (or the Rashbaz, late fourtheenth to early fifteenth centuries) insisted that communal funds had always supported Torah scholars, and Solomon Luria (or the Maharshal, sixteenth century) argued that not taking money could cause *bitul Torah*, or the cessation of Torah.[157] Supporting Torah scholars, in their view, was the tangible way that Jewish communities could preserve not only the text of the Torah but its languages and centuries of interpretation. Rabbi Ovadiah ben Abraham of Bartenura (c. 1445 to 1515) asserted that a communally

154. M. Avot 4:5, quoting Hillel from M. Avot 1:13.

155. M. Avot 4:7. Maimonides suggests that those rabbis who were poor were occupied in supplemental labor, such as Yoḥanan ben Zakkai, who chopped wood in order to sustain his livelihood. On Maimonides's rejection of yeshiva fundraising campaigns, see Halbertal, *Maimonides*, 44.

156. For analysis of Maimonides's position, see Frank, "Teaching for a Fee"; Kanarfogel, "Compensation for the Study of Torah"; and Leibowitz, "Pursuit of Scholarship and Economic Self-Sufficiency."

157. Simeon ben Zemah Duran, *Shut Tashbetz* 1:142; Solomon Luria, *Yam Shel Shlomo Chullin* 3:9. See Kanarfogel, "Compensation for the Study of Torah," for a survey of positions.

appointed rabbi should take payment and rewards so that "his food may be healthy" and so that he would be perceived to be "great like the high priest of old."[158] Supporting Torah scholars, in his estimation, was a way of honoring the Torah itself, just as they honored the high priest in ancient Israel because he served as the human representative of God. Similarly, other commentators suggest that rabbis should be exempt from taxes, using the textual proof of Ezra 7:24 that exempts priests and Levites from tribute and taxes under the Persian Empire.[159] Just as the priests were the stewards of Torah in days long ago, so now were rabbis the appropriate beneficiaries of communal support.

Rabbi Shimon ben Tzemach Duran (or the Tashbaz, late fourteenth to early fifteenth centuries) wrote that someone important to a community may accept money from it without violating the prohibition against benefiting from the Torah "for he is honoring the Torah, not using it."[160] For ordinary Jews who could not devote themselves to full-time Torah study, financial support offered a meaningful way to partner in such holy labor. Hence, while some rabbinic criticism of funding was certainly informed by pious notions of the Torah's sanctity, there were additional factors influencing an ideological reluctance to accept financial support.

Maimonides, however, is attuned to the double bind of funding rabbinic expertise. He predicts that rabbis who take a salary for teaching will find themselves ensnared by meddlesome oversight. In a letter to his student Yosef ibn Aknin upon hearing of his plan to open a house of study in Baghdad, Maimonides states the problem bluntly:

> I fear, however, that you will be constantly involved in disputes with those people and fail to achieve your proper objectives. Moreover, if you assume the practice of teaching, your business affairs will be neglected, and you dare not accept any financial reward from them. It is far better for you to earn a single drachma as a weaver, tailor or carpenter than be dependent on the license of the Exilarch. If you dispute with any of them, you will lose your earning. And if you accept from them favors, you will be humiliated. (Stitskin, "From the Pages of Tradition," 157)

158. He cites B. Yoma 18a as a proof.

159. *Ikar Tosafot Yom Tov*; *Tosafot to Bekhorot* 29a. On this exception, see Ta-Shma, "On the Exemption of Torah Scholars from Taxes."

160. *Magen Avot*, Avot 4:5.

With perhaps the bitterness of personal experience, Maimonides scorns the professionalization of the rabbinate.[161] He sees the life of a funded rabbi as one at the beck and call of those who finance his position. The rabbi who takes payment becomes dependent upon the good will of his employer or donor and constrained by their demands. These demands can put rabbis in difficult positions. He warns Yosef that "should one bow to public pressures in order to please one's constituents, he will be guilty of bias and hypocrisy which is forbidden in the Torah."[162]

Another concern echoed in this later context was worry about the public perception of rabbinic expertise if rabbis were to accept payment. Maimonides is especially concerned about the perception of Torah's special quality in "the eyes of the masses" more than extolling the intrinsic difference of labor in Torah. In his commentary on Avot, he mentions twice that the eyes of others may no longer value Torah expertise if it were associated with ordinary work. This fixation reveals how significant it was for rabbis to persuade the public of their worth. Expertise is not just constituted by the possession of specialized knowledge but by the recognition the public gives when they accept someone as an expert. Maimonides is aware of this dynamic when he suggests that rabbinic credibility and trustworthiness would be threatened by the collection of money. It was not just a rabbi's personal piety at stake, but the public perception of rabbinic expertise as a collective entity.

This brief excursus into the rich medieval debates about funding expertise demonstrates how longstanding the issue was for rabbinic experts. Though experts generate knowledge they deem significant—and in the eyes of the rabbis, performing the most holy of labors—they are also attentive to external interests.[163] This common tug-of-war between epistemic value and social worth is compounded by the rabbinic belief that their expertise derived from a priceless treasure, the Torah, which they wanted others to care about. Some rabbis might claim autonomy as experts and assert the insularity of a life of Torah study, but the collective status of the rabbinic specialist group required persuading other Jews of their social value and soliciting investment. One argument that emerged was to use the logic of redemptive almsgiving and divine investment for their cause. If a donor can be assured rewards for hospitality

161. Halbertal, *Maimonides*, 43–44.

162. Stitskin, "From the Pages of Tradition," 158.

163. See Pamuk, *Politics and Expertise*, 133–60 on funding justifications in contemporary science.

and charity, how much more return on investment could one expect for supporting Torah scholars?

The social production of expertise is a complex phenomenon that involves various factors, one of which is the financial support that experts receive. Experts depend on the public recognition and validation of their expertise, no better legitimated than through financial support. The funding that an individual rabbi received not only enabled that specific rabbi to teach, study, and judge but it also emphasized the credibility of the domain of rabbinic knowledge. This validation by others played a crucial role in the social construction of rabbinic expertise. Experts gain legitimacy and authority in their field when their expertise is recognized as valuable and essential. For this reason, rabbis could not hope to claim expert status and ignore the social dynamics of financial support. Whatever their aversion to patronage might be, rabbis engaged in patronage and salaried financial relationships and developed hermeneutic rationales to detract from donor encroachment into their domain, even as the inherent tension between resisting profit and the social persuasion of intellectual worth could never be fully resolved.

CONCLUSION

Becoming Experts

THE RABBI of Roman Palestine was the singular expert of Torah and Jewish traditions, or so rabbinic literature would have its readers believe. These texts take for granted that rabbis could uncover the meanings of Torah through their precise hermeneutical methods and apply them to the concerns of their day. Yet those same texts provide glimpses of a reality where rabbis did not exist in social isolation. Their livelihoods were supported by family and close friends. They dined with neighbors and mingled with merchants and householders alike. For all their sense of themselves as the exclusive experts of Torah, their fundamental engagement with other non-rabbis was dependent on their ability to persuade.

This book has examined the social aspects of enacting rabbinic expertise, pointing to the embedded landscape of Jewish piety that informed interactions between rabbis, rabbinic households, and their neighbors. Rabbinic expertise was not merely dependent on their intellectual prowess but also on their social standing—their relationships with others, their reputations, and their perceived value within their locales. Their emergence coincided during a period when Torah expertise was at a critical juncture. The loss of Jewish autonomy brought about by the Romans resulted in not just a theological problem but also one that caused tangible institutional destabilization. The traditional priesthood was unmoored from their institutional base. At the same time, Judaea had seen a flourishing of Jewish holiness projects that facilitated an interest in Torah. This shared interest drove the earliest rabbis to mingle, and through that socialization a new kind of expertise emerged.

In establishing themselves as a new kind of Torah expert, rabbis faced the challenges of any expert: the need to persuade others of their value, competition from other sources of expertise, and even resistance from non-rabbinic Jews. These challenges are not a product of ancient Jews either accepting or rejecting their natural experts but are in fact integral dynamics to the production of expertise. Classic narrations of the rise of the rabbis assumed that expertise was something the rabbis possessed that self-evidently authorized their power within the Jewish community. Take for example Urbach's characterization:

> The force of [the rabbi's] authority derived first and foremost from his knowledge of the Torah. Thus, also was his attitude to the powers that be or to the rich, at all times determined solely by their morals. He neither sought nor shunned their company but was intent upon retaining his position of independence, gaining a livelihood by means of manual occupation. ("Talmudic Sage," 121)

Urbach depicts rabbinic expertise as a kind of authority guaranteed by knowledge of Torah. He draws a distinction between rabbis and the rich and imagines that rabbis remained unburdened with relationships of financial obligation. This portrait asserts both an epistemic and financial independence that envisions a kind of authoritative purity for those who possess Torah. The problems with this narrative notwithstanding, it does point to an important component of rabbinic expertise. Rabbis derived their authority from the Torah not because they possessed knowledge but because they drew upon the corporate phenomenon of Torah. As Martin Jaffee describes eloquently, "For Torah to be present the Sage must be present as its unmediated source and embodiment in word and deed."[1] Any authority and influence that came with developing rabbinic expertise were intertwined in a genuine assumption that such interpretive work was meaningful to at least some other people. Urbach's characterization assumes that rabbis and their friends shared a common sense of the Torah's value. This did not give rabbis automatic status as Jewish experts, but it did give them a framework with which to situate their new expertise.

The rabbinic period was rife with contenders for expert status who competed within the late ancient Mediterranean knowledge marketplace for social trust. Not only had the dismantling of the Jewish priesthood made it less obvious where Jewish ritual and legal expertise could be found, but the very basis for those claims had shifted with the constraints of imperialism. Rabbinic expertise emerged in this period through the socialization of like-minded men

1. Jaffee, "Oral-Cultural Context of the Talmud Yerushalmi," 55. Jaffee extends his point to argue that the amoraic insistence upon the oral nature of rabbinic tradition refers to a rhetorical performance of Torah rather than a reliance on only oral transmission.

who advocated a grammarian piety. They viewed the Torah as a shared cultural object that rabbinic experts could use to unlock new layers of meaning through the anchoring of grammatical structures and biblical verses. The way of knowing that emerged drew a boundary between those who knew Torah in a rabbinic way and those who did not.

The rabbinic orbit was therefore both insular, as is the nature of a specialist group, and enmeshed in a wide array of social circles. Expertise is forged through the dynamic encounter between people and objects of knowledge. The dissemination of awareness about a specific knowledge domain through socialization is integral, even if access to that knowledge is not equally distributed. This point is crucial as studies of the rabbis often emphasize either the exclusive nature of rabbinic circles or the transgressive potential for ordinary people to penetrate their insularity. Both socialization within and outside their specialist group was a necessary dynamic. Rabbinic specialists comprised a select group of people who underwent apprenticeships, training, and socialization into a unique way of knowing. However, this same group of people also had to interact with non-experts in order to enact their expertise. Everyday social interactions were vital sites where others could learn rabbinic habits, disseminating an interactional expertise that produced the sense of what it meant to belong to the rabbinic orbit.

The social connections between rabbis and their clients provided an important mechanism for the development of rabbinic expertise, even as they brought risk. The very thing that enables expertise also poses a threat to it, creating a paradox at the heart of its enactment. To establish their authority, experts must project a certain level of autonomy over their domain and assert their knowledge of the "truth." Meanwhile, they must also maintain sufficient disinterest in their research outcomes to defend their credibility and objectivity. Personal sentiments expressed by an expert, for instance, can threaten the aura of objectivity they are meant to present. Clients introduce interests and influences that disrupt this autonomy, creating a precarious balance for expertise. The relationship between experts and their funders is one of epistemic asymmetry, with the expert's status affording them a measure of autonomy and authority, but it is also one of donor asymmetry because donors or employers may use the fact of their funding as justification for their own demands or interests. The stories that rabbis narrated about their funding highlight the tension of these competing power claims. Such proximity provoked rabbinic apprehension, not because rabbis viewed themselves as essentially separate from other Jews in their communities, but because of the potential blurring of the power hierarchies between expert and non-expert.

At this point, I hope that the reader has realized that this book will not live up to its title. I cannot in fact explain how rabbis became experts, as if expertise marks a transition from point A to point B. Such a claim supposes that expertise is a possession that one acquires with enough diligence and study. Expertise certainly requires a level of facility and technical skill, but what we mean when we name rabbis as experts is actually the confluence of many social arrangements that made the enactment of expertise possible. Rabbis never became experts but were always in the process of becoming.[2] This formulation, like other social constructions, can be troubling to swallow. Indeed, much of contemporary expertise studies is concerned with precisely this problem. If we cannot ensure that expertise is a real thing, how can we compel others to listen to expert advice?[3]

The value of recognizing the social enactment of rabbinic expertise is that we realize that the rabbinic domain was not in fact the elite possession of a small group of literate men but instead required meaningful contributions from a variety of people. Expertise is not just about knowledge but also about how that knowledge is perceived, accepted, and valued by others. Gil Eyal argues that a full explication of expertise must explore the "social, material, spatial, organizational, and conceptual arrangements that serve as its conditions of possibility."[4] This means that expertise is not a fixed or stable ontology but rather a complex configuration. Any expert statement or performance is linked to a range of social conditions that make such an event possible.[5] In short, many hands made possible the sense of rabbinic "naturalness" as experts, especially relationships with wealthy friends and acquaintances, who provided rabbis with resources, public validation, and social capital.

In some ways this project calls the "bluff" of rabbinic literature, which demarcates a strong expert boundary between rabbinic knowledge and skill and

2. Here I borrow from Simone de Beauvoir's iconic formulation that "one is not born, but rather becomes, a woman," which pushes us from attributing social values or functions as natural gendered behavior. For analysis in light of gender studies, see Butler, "Sex and Gender in Simone de Beauvoir's *Second Sex*.

3. Collins and Evans, *Rethinking Expertise*.

4. Eyal, "Expertise," 8.

5. Eyal, "For a Sociology of Expertise."

the ordinary people the texts at times disdain. Expertise studies compel us to ask: How do rabbis gain public recognition and trust that they were legitimate spokespeople? How did rabbis maintain credibility? How did rabbis resist intrusion upon their epistemic autonomy? Recognizing how expertise is a social relation does not solve the problem of who possesses objective truth, but it does highlight how experts and ordinary people are engaged in an ongoing process of trust that is continually mediated through each moment of enactment.

BIBLIOGRAPHY

Editions of Rabbinic Literature

Albeck, Chanoch. *Mishnah: Six Orders*. Jerusalem: Bialik, 1955–59.

Finkelstein, Eliezer Aryeh, ed. *Sifre ʿal sefer Devarim*. New York: Jewish Theological Seminary, 1969.

Lieberman, Saul, ed. *The Tosefta*. 5 vols. New York: Jewish Theological Seminary of America, 1955–1988.

Margulies, Mordecai, ed. *Midrash Wayyikra Rabbah*. Critical ed. Jerusalem: Warhmann Books, 1982.

Mendelbaum, Dov, ed. *Pesikta de-Rav Kahana According to an Oxford Manuscript*. 2 vols. 2nd ed. New York, Jewish Theological Seminary, 1962.

Schechter, Solomon, ed. *Avot de-Rabbi Nathan*. Critical ed. New York: Jewish Theological Seminary, 1997.

Sussmann, Yaacov, ed. *Talmud Yerushalmi: According to Ms. Or. 4720 (Scal.3) of the Leiden University Library, with Restorations and Corrections*. Jerusalem: The Academy of the Hebrew Language, 2001.

Theodor, J., and Albeck, C., eds. *Midrash Bereshit Rabbah*. Critical ed. Jerusalem: Wahrmann Books, 1965.

Zuckermandel, Moses Samuel, ed. *Tosefta*. Pasewalk: M. S. Zuckermandel, 1880.

General Bibliography

Adler, Rachel Anne. "The Archaeology of Purity: Heterodoxy in Ritual Bathing in Early Judaism." PhD diss., University of Pennsylvania, 2007.

Adler, Yonatan. *The Origins of Judaism: An Archaeological-Historical Reappraisal*. New Haven, CT: Yale University Press, 2022.

Agier, Michel. *The Stranger as My Guest: A Critical Anthropology of Hospitality*. Hoboken, NJ: John Wiley & Sons, 2021.

Agnew, Neil M., Kenneth M. Ford, and Patrick J. Hayes. "Expertise in Context: Personally Constructed, Socially Selected and Reality-Relevant?" *International Journal of Expert Systems* 7, no. 1 (1997): 65–88.

Ahuvia, Mika. "Jewish Towns and Neighborhoods in Roman Palestine and Persian Babylonia." In *A Companion to Late Ancient Jews and Judaism: Third Century BCE to Seventh Century CE*, edited by Naomi Koltun-Fromm and Gwynn Kessler. Hoboken, NJ: John Wiley & Sons, 2020.

Alexander, Elizabeth Shanks. *Transmitting Mishnah: The Shaping Influence of Oral Tradition*. Cambridge: Cambridge University Press, 2006.

Alexander, Philip S. "The Rabbis and Their Rivals in the Second Century CE." In *Christianity in the Second Century: Themes and Developments*, edited by James Carleton Paget and Judith Lieu. Cambridge: Cambridge University Press, 2017.

———. "What Happened to the Jewish Priesthood after 70?" In *A Wandering Galilean: Essays in Honour of Seán Freyne*, edited by Zuleika Rodgers with Margaret Daly-Denton and Anne Fitzpatrick McKinley. Leiden: Brill, 2009.

Allison, Penelope M. "Naming Tablewares: Using the Artefactual Evidence to Investigate Eating and Drinking Practices Across the Roman World." *Text and the Material World: Essays in Honour of Graeme Clarke*, edited by Elizabeth Minchin and Heather Jackson. Uppsala: Paul Forlag Astroms, 2017.

Alon, Gedaliah. *Jews, Judaism, and the Classical World*. Jerusalem: Magnes Press, 1977.

———. *The Jews in Their Land in the Talmudic Age: 70–640 CE*. Cambridge, MA: Harvard University Press, 1989.

———. "Those Appointed for Money: On the History of the Various Juridical Authorities in Eretz-Israel in the Talmudic Period." In *Classic Essays in Early Rabbinic Culture and History*, edited by Christine Hayes. Abingdon, UK: Routledge, 2018.

Altmann, Peter. "The Significance of the Divine Torah in Ptolemaic Egypt in Documentary and Literary Sources from the Third and Second Centuries BCE." *Journal for the Study of Judaism* 53, no. 1 (2021): 1–31.

Apicius. *De Re Coquinaria*, edited by M. E. Milham. Leipzig, DE: BSB B. G. Teubner Verlagsgesellschaft, 1969.

Ameling, Walter. *Inscriptiones Judaicae Orientis*. Tübingen: Mohr Siebeck, 2004.

Anderson, Gary A. *Charity: The Place of the Poor in the Biblical Tradition*. New Haven, CT: Yale University Press, 2013.

Applebaum, Shimon. *Jews and Greeks in Ancient Cyrene*. Leiden: Brill, 1979.

Atkinson, Kenneth, and Jodi Magness. "Josephus's Essenes and the Qumran Community." *Journal of Biblical Literature* 129, no. 2 (2010): 317–42.

Aviam, Mordechai. "Yodefat/Jotapata. A Jewish Galilean Town at the End of the Second Temple Period: The Results of an Archaeological Project." In *The Archaeological Record from Cities, Towns, and Villages*, edited by David A. Fiensy and James Riley Strange. Vol. 2 of *Galilee in the Late Second Temple and Mishnaic Periods*. Minneapolis: Fortress Press, 2015.

Avi-Yonah, Michael. "Scythopolis." *Israel Exploration Journal* 12, no. 2 (1962): 123–34.

———. "When Did Judea Become a Consular Province?" *Israel Exploration Journal* 23 (1973): 209–13.

Avshalom-Gorni, Dina, and Nimrod Getzov. "Phoenicians and Jews: A Ceramic Case-Study." In *The First Jewish Revolt*, edited by Andrea Berlin and J. Andrew Overman. Abingdon, UK: Routledge, 2003.

Azzan-Yadin, "The Halakhic Midrashim and the Mishnah." In *What Is the Mishnah?: The State of the Question*, edited by Shaye Cohen. Cambridge, MA: Harvard University Press, 2023.

Bagnall, Roger S. "Army and Police in Roman Upper Egypt." *Journal of the American Research Center in Egypt* 14 (1977): 67–86.

Balberg, Mira. *Blood for Thought: The Reinvention of Sacrifice in Early Rabbinic Literature*. Berkeley: University of California Press, 2017.

———. *Fractured Tablets: Forgetfulness and Fallibility in Late Ancient Rabbinic Culture*. Berkeley: University of California Press, 2023.

———. *Purity, Body, and Self in Early Rabbinic Literature*. Berkeley: University of California Press, 2014.

———. "Rabbinic Authority, Medical Rhetoric, and Body Hermeneutics in Mishnah Nega'im." *Association for Jewish Studies Review* 35, no. 2 (2011): 323–46.

Barrera, Albino. "Economics and the Law." In *The Cambridge Companion to the Hebrew Bible and Ethics*, edited by Carly Crouch. Cambridge: Cambridge University Press, 2021.

Barton, Carlin A., and Daniel Boyarin. *Imagine No Religion: How Modern Abstractions Hide Ancient Realities*. New York: Fordham University Press, 2016.

Baruch, Eyal. "Adapted Roman Rituals in Second Century CE Jewish Houses." In *Jews and Christians in the First and Second Centuries: The Interbellum 70-132 CE*, edited by Joshua Schwartz and Peter J. Tomson. Leiden: Brill, 2017.

Baumgarten, Albert I. "Rabbi Judah I and His Opponents." *Journal for the Study of Judaism in the Persian, Hellenistic, and Roman Period* 12, no. 2 (1981): 135–72.

Baumgarten, Joseph M. "On the Non-Literal Use of Ma'ăśēr/Dekatē." *Journal of Biblical Literature* 103, no. 2 (1984): 245–51.

———. "Tannaitic Halakhah and Qumran—A Re-Evaluation." In *Studies in Qumran Law and Thought*, edited by Ruth Clements and Daniel Schwartz. Leiden: Brill, 2022.

Becker, Adam H. "2 Baruch." In *Outside the Bible: Ancient Jewish Writings Related to Scripture*, edited by Louis H. Feldman, James L. Kugel, and Lawrence H. Schiffman. 3 vols. Philadelphia: Jewish Publication Society, 2013.

Bedford, Peter R. "The Economic Role of the Jerusalem Temple in Achaemenid Judah: Comparative Perspectives." In *Shai le-Sara Japhet: Studies in the Bible, Its Exegesis and Its Language*, edited by Moshe Bar-Asher. Jerusalem: The Bialik Institute, 2007.

———. "Temple Funding and Priestly Authority in Achaemenid Judah." In *Exile and Return: The Babylonian Context*, edited by Jonathan Stökl and Caroline Waerzeggers. Berlin: De Gruyter, 2015.

Beebe, Keith. "Domestic Architecture of the New Testament." *The Biblical Archaeologist* 38 (1975): 101–4.

Beer, Moshe. *The Sages of the Mishnah and the Talmud: Teaching, Activities and Leadership*. Ramat-Gan: Bar-Ilan University Press, 2011. [Hebrew]

———. "Torah and Derekh Eretz." *Bar-Ilan: Annual of Bar-Ilan University Studies in Judaica and the Humanities* 2 (1964): 134–62.

Bergquist, Birgitta, "Sympotic Space: A Functional Aspect of Greek Dining-Rooms." In *Sympotica: A Symposium on the Symposion*, edited by Oswyn Murray. Oxford: Oxford University Press, 1990.

Berkowitz, Beth A. *Execution and Invention: Death Penalty Discourse in Early Rabbinic and Christian Cultures*. Oxford: Oxford University Press, 2006.

Berlin, Andrea M., and J. Andrew Overman. *The First Jewish Revolt: Archaeology, History and Ideology*. Abingdon, UK: Routledge, 2003.

Berthelot, Katell. *Jews and Their Roman Rivals: Pagan Rome's Challenge to Israel*. Princeton: Princeton University Press, 2021.

Bhikha, Rashid, and John Glynn. "The Theory of Humours Revisited." *International Journal of Development Research* 7, no. 9 (2017): 15029–34.

Bilalić, Merim, and Guillermo Campitelli. "Studies of the Activation and Structural Changes of the Brain Associated with Expertise." In *The Cambridge Handbook of Expertise and Expert Performance*, edited by K. Anders Ericsson, Robert R. Hoffman, Aaron Kozbelt, and A. Mark Williams. Cambridge: Cambridge University Press, 2018.

Bohak, Gideon. "Jewish Amulets, Magic Bowls, and Manuals in Aramaic and Hebrew." In *Guide to the Study of Ancient Magic*, edited by David Frankfurter. Leiden: Brill, 2019.

Bokser, Baruch M. "Ma'al and Blessings Over Food: Rabbinic Transformation of Cultic Terminology and Alternative Modes of Piety." *Journal of Biblical Literature* 100, no. 4 (1981): 557–74.

———. *The Origins of the Seder: The Passover Rite and Early Rabbinic Judaism*. Berkeley: University of California Press, 2020.

Boulanger, Andre. *Aelius Aristide et la Sophistique dans la Province d'Asie au IIe Siècle de Notre ère*. Paris: E. de Boccard, 1923.

Bourdieu, Pierre. *Language and Symbolic Power*. Cambridge, MA: Harvard University Press, 1991.

———. *The Logic of Practice*. Redwood City, CA: Stanford University Press, 1990.

Boustan, Ra'anan, and Karen Britt. "Historical Scenes in Mosaics from Late Roman Syria and Palestine: Building on the Seleucid Past in Late Antiquity." *Journal of Late Antiquity* 14, no. 2 (2021): 335–74.

Bowes, Kimberly Diane. *Private Worship, Public Values, and Religious Change in Late Antiquity*. Cambridge: Cambridge University Press, 2008.

Boyarin, Daniel. *Carnal Israel: Reading Sex in Talmudic Culture*. Berkeley: University of California Press, 1993.

Brooks, Roger. *Support for the Poor in the Mishnaic Law of Agriculture: Tractate Peah*. Chico, CA: Scholars Press, 1983.

Brooten, Bernadette J. "The Jews of Ancient Antioch." In *Antioch: The Lost Ancient City*, edited by Christine Kondoleon. Princeton, NJ: Princeton University Press, 2000.

———. *Women Leaders in the Ancient Synagogue: Inscriptional Evidence and Background Issues*. No. 36. Chico: Scholars Press, 1982.

Broshi, Magen. "Agriculture and Economy in Roman Palestine: Seven Notes on the Babatha Archive." *Israel Exploration Journal* 42, no. 3/4 (1992): 230–40.

Brown, Peter. *The Ransom of the Soul: Afterlife and Wealth in Early Western Christianity*. Cambridge: Harvard University Press, 2015.

———. *Treasure in Heaven: The Holy Poor in Early Christianity*. Charlottesville: University of Virginia Press, 2016.

Büchler, Adolf. *The Political and Social Leaders of the Jewish Community of Sepphoris in the Second and Third Centuries*. Oxford: Oxford University Press, 1910.

Butler, Judith. "Sex and Gender in Simone de Beauvoir's *Second Sex*." *Yale French Studies* 72 (1986): 35–49.

Caner, Daniel. *The Rich and the Pure: Philanthropy and the Making of Christian Society in Early Byzantium*. Berkeley: University of California Press, 2021.

———. "Towards a Miraculous Economy: Christian Gifts and Material 'Blessings' in Late Antiquity." *Journal of Early Christian Studies* 14, no. 3 (2006): 329–77.

Carr, E. Summerson. "Enactments of Expertise." *Annual Review of Anthropology* 39 (2010): 17–32.

Carrier, James G. *Gifts and Commodities: Exchange and Western Capitalism Since 1700*. Abingdon, UK: Routledge, 2005.

Cetina, Karin Knorr. *Epistemic Cultures: How the Sciences Make Knowledge*. Cambridge, MA: Harvard University Press, 1999.

Chalmers, Matthew. "Samaritans, Biblical Studies, and Ancient Judaism: Recent Trends." *Currents in Biblical Research* 20, no. 1 (2021): 28–64.

Chamorro, Paloma Balbín. "Ius Hospitii y Ius Civitatis." *Gerión* 24, no. 1 (2006): 207.

Chin, Catherine M. *Grammar and Christianity in the Late Roman World*. Philadelphia: University of Pennsylvania Press, 2008.

Chou, Cynthia, Susanne Kerner, and Morten Warmind, eds. *Commensality: From Everyday Food to Feast*. London: Bloomsbury, 2015.

Chroust, Anton-Hermann. "Legal Profession in Ancient Imperial Rome." *Notre Dame Law* 30 (1954): 521–616.

Clark, Elizabeth A. "Patrons, Not Priests: Gender and Power in Late Ancient Christianity." *Gender and History* 2, no. 3 (1990): 253–74.

Clark, Timothy Scott. "First Fruits and Tithe Offerings in the Construction and Narratives of the Hebrew Bible." PhD diss., Emory University, 2014.

Coady, David. *What to Believe Now: Applying Epistemology to Contemporary Issues*. Hoboken, NJ: John Wiley & Sons, 2012.

Coffee, Neil. *Gift and Gain: How Money Transformed Ancient Rome*. Oxford: Oxford University Press, 2017.

Cohen, Naomi G. "'Al Taseg Gevul 'Olim' (Pe'ah 5:6, 7:3)." *Hebrew Union College Annual* 56 (1985), 145–66.

Cohen, Shaye J. D. "The Conversion of Antoninus." In *The Talmud Yerushalmi and Graeco-Roman Culture*, edited by Peter Schäfer and Catherine Hezser. Tübingen: Mohr Siebeck, 2001.

———. "Patriarchs and Scholarchs." *Proceedings of the American Academy for Jewish Research* 48 (1981): 57–85.

———. "The Place of the Rabbi in the Jewish Society of the Second Century." In *The Significance of Yavneh and Other Essays in Jewish Hellenism*, edited by Shaye Cohen. Tübingen: Mohr Siebeck, 2010.

———. "The Rabbi in Second-Century Jewish Society." In *The Cambridge History of Judaism*, edited by William Horbury and John Sturdy. Cambridge: Cambridge University Press, 1999.

———. "The Significance of Yavneh: Pharisees, Rabbis, and the End of Jewish Sectarianism." *Hebrew Union College Annual* 55 (1984): 27–53.

Cohen, Shaye J. D., Robert Goldenberg, and Hayim Lapin, eds. *The Oxford Annotated Mishnah*. Oxford: Oxford University Press, 2022.

Cohen, Stuart A. *The Three Crowns: Structures of Communal Politics in Early Rabbinic Jewry*. Cambridge: Cambridge University Press, 1990.

Cohn, Naftali S. "Affect and Ritual in the Mishnah." In *Beloved David—Advisor, Man of Understanding, and Writer: A Festschrift in Honor of David Stern*, edited by Naftali S. Cohn and Katrin Kogman-Appel . Providence, RI: Brown University Press, 2024.

———. *The Memory of the Temple and the Making of the Rabbis*. Philadelphia: University of Pennsylvania Press, 2013.

Collins, Harry. *Are We All Scientific Experts Now?* Hoboken, NJ: John Wiley & Sons, 2014.

———. "Interactional Expertise as a Third Kind of Knowledge." *Phenomenology and the Cognitive Sciences* 3 (2004): 125–43.

———. "Studies of Expertise and Experience." *Topoi* 37, no. 1 (2018): 67–77.

Collins, Harry, and Robert Evans. "Expertise Revisited, Part I—Interactional Expertise." *Studies in History and Philosophy of Science Part A* 54 (2015): 113–23.

———. *Rethinking Expertise.* Chicago: University of Chicago Press, 2019.

———. "A Sociological/Philosophical Perspective on Expertise: The Acquisition of Expertise through Socialization." In *The Cambridge Handbook of Expertise and Expert Performance,* edited by K. Anders Ericsson, Robert R. Hoffman, Aaron Kozbelt, and A. Mark Williams. Cambridge: Cambridge University Press, 2018.

Collins, John J. *The Invention of Judaism: Torah and Jewish Identity from Deuteronomy to Paul.* Berkeley: University of California Press, 2017.

———. "The Law in the Late Second Temple Period." In *The Oxford Handbook of Biblical Law,* edited by Pamela Barmash. Oxford: Oxford University Press, 2019.

Coomber, Matthew J. M. "The Importance of Biblical Economics to the Field of Biblical Studies." In *Economics and Empire in the Ancient Near East,* edited by Matthew J. M. Coomber. Eugene, OR: Wipf & Stock, 2023.

Cotton, Hannah M. "The Impact of the Roman Army in the Province of Judaea/Syria Palaestina." In *Roman Rule and Jewish Life: Collected Papers,* edited by Hannah M. Cotton. Berlin: De Gruyter, 2022.

———. "The Rabbis and the Documents." In *Jews in a Graeco-Roman World,* edited by Martin Goodman. Oxford: Oxford University Press, 1998.

———. "Some Aspects of the Roman Administration of Judaea/Syria-Palaestina." In *Roman Rule and Jewish Life: Collected Papers,* edited by Hannah M. Cotton. Berlin: De Gruyter, 2022.

Croce, Michel. "Epistemic Paternalism and the Service Conception of Epistemic Authority." In *Connecting Virtues: Advances in Ethics, Epistemology, and Political Philosophy,* edited by Michel Croce and Maria Silvia Vaccarezza. Hoboken, NJ: John Wiley & Sons, 2018.

Cromwell, Jennifer. *Recording Village Life: A Coptic Scribe in Early Islamic Egypt.* Ann Arbor: University of Michigan Press, 2017.

Czajkowski, Kimberley. "Law and Romanization in Judaea." In *Law in the Roman Provinces,* edited by Kimberley Czajkowski and Benedikt Eckhard, in collaboration with Meret Strothmann. Oxford: Oxford University Press, 2020.

———. *Localized Law: The Babatha and Salome Komaise Archives.* Oxford: Oxford University Press, 2017.

———. "The Need for Rabbinic Nomikoi: A Response to Yair Furstenberg." *Journal for the Study of Judaism* 55, no. 1 (2023): 65–75.

Czajkowski, Kimberley, and Benedikt Eckhardt. "Law, Status and Agency in the Roman Provinces." *Past and Present* 241, no. 1 (2018): 3–31.

Dalton, Krista N. "Rabbis as Recipients of Charity and the Logic of Grammarian Piety." *Journal for the Study of Judaism* 53, no. 1 (2021): 94–130.

———. "The Testimony of Ancient Books." In *Field Notes: Revisiting the Classics in the Study of Religion,* edited by Richard Newton and Vaia Touna. London: Bloomsbury Press, 2023.

Dannell, Geoffrey B. "Samian Cups and Their Uses." In *Romanitas: Essays on Roman Archaeology in Honour of Sheppard Frere on the Occasion of His Ninetieth Birthday*, edited by Roger Wilson. Oxford: Oxford University Press, 2006.

D'Arms, John. "Control, Companionship, and Clientela: Some Social Functions of the Roman Communal Meal." *Echos du Monde Classique: Classical News and Views* 28, no. 3 (1984): 327–48.

———. "Performing Culture: Roman Spectacle and the Banquets of the Powerful." *Studies in the History of Art* 56 (1999): 300–319.

———. "The Roman Convivium and the Idea of Equality." In *Sympotica: A Symposium on the Symposion*, edited by Oswyn Murray. Oxford: Oxford University Press, 1990.

Dellsén, Finnur. "The Epistemic Value of Expert Autonomy." *Philosophy and Phenomenological Research* 100, no. 2 (2020): 344–61.

Dentzer, Jean-Marie. "Aux Origines de L'Iconographie du Banquet Couché." *Revue Archéologique*, no. 2 (1971): 215–58.

Derrida, Jacques. *Given Time: I. Counterfeit Money*. Chicago: University of Chicago Press, 1992.

Diamond, Eliezer. *Holy Men and Hunger Artists: Fasting and Asceticism in Rabbinic Culture*. Oxford: Oxford University Press, 2004.

Dietler, Michael. "Theorizing the Feast: Rituals of Consumption, Commensal Politics, and Power in African Contexts." In *Feasts: Archaeological and Ethnographic Perspectives on Food, Politics, and Power*, edited by Michael Dietler and Brian Hayden. Washington, DC: Smithsonian Institution Scholarly Press, 2001.

Dinur, B. S. *Yisra'el ba-Golah* [*Israel in the Diaspora*]. Philadelphia: Jewish Publication Society of America, 1969.

Dohrmann, Natalie B. "Ad Similitudinem Arbitrorum." In *Legal Engagement*, edited by Katell Berthelot, Natalie B. Dohrmann, and Capucine Nemo-Pekelman. Rome: Publications de l'École française de Rome, 2021.

———. "The Boundaries of the Law and the Problem of Jurisdiction in an Early Palestinian Midrash." In *Rabbinic Law in Its Roman and Near Eastern Context*, edited by Catherine Hezser. Tübingen: Mohr Siebeck, 2003.

———. "Manumission and Transformation in Jewish and Roman Law." In *Jewish Biblical Interpretation and Cultural Exchange: Comparative Exegesis in Context*, edited by Natalie B. Dohrmann and David Stern. Philadelphia: University of Pennsylvania Press, 2008.

———. "Roman Civil Jurisdiction, Nezikin, and Rabbinic Professionalization in the Second Century: A Response to Yair Furstenberg." *Journal for the Study of Judaism* 55, no. 1 (2023): 57–64.

Donahue, John F. *Food and Drink in Antiquity: A Sourcebook*. London: Bloomsbury, 2014.

———. *The Roman Community at Table During the Principate*. Ann Arbor: University of Michigan Press, 2017.

———. "Roman Dining." *A Companion to Food in the Ancient World*, edited by John Wilkins and Robin Nadeau. Hoboken, NJ: John Wiley & Sons, 2015.

Douglas, Heather E. *Science, Policy, and the Value-Free Ideal*. Pittsburgh: University of Pittsburgh Press, 2009.

Douglas, Mary. "Fundamental Issues in Food Problems." *Current Anthropology* 25, no. 4 (1984): 498–99.

Downey, Glanville. *A History of Antioch in Syria: From Seleucus to the Arab Conquest*. Princeton, NJ: Princeton University Press, 2015.

Dufault, Olivier. *Early Greek Alchemy, Patronage and Innovation in Late Antiquity*. California Classical Studies, 2019. https://escholarship.org/uc/ucbclassics_ccs.

Dumit, Joseph. *Picturing Personhood: Brain Scans and Biomedical Identity*. Princeton, NJ: Princeton University Press, 2004.

Dunbabin, Katherine M. D. "Convivial Spaces: Dining and Entertainment in the Roman Villa." *Journal of Roman Archaeology* 9 (1996): 66–80.

———. *The Roman Banquet; Images of Conviviality*. Cambridge: Cambridge University Press, 2003.

———. "Triclinium and Stibadium." In *Dining in a Classical Context*, edited by William Slater. Ann Arbor: University of Michigan Press, 1991.

Dunbabin, Katherine M. D., and William J. Slater. "Roman Dining." In *The Oxford Handbook of Social Relations in the Roman World*, edited by Michael Peachin. Oxford: Oxford University Press, 2011.

Eck, Werner. "Die Colonia Aelia Capitolina: Überlegungen zur Anfangsphase der zweiten römischen Kolonie in der Provinz Iudaea-Syria Palaestina." *Electrum: Studia Z Historii Starożytnej* 26 (2019): 129–39.

Eck, Werner, and Aharon Oppenhaimer. *Rom und die Provinz Iudaea/Syria Palaestina: Der Beitrag der Epigraphik*. Berlin: De Gruyter, 1999.

Eidevall, Göran. *Amos: A New Translation with Introduction and Commentary*. New Haven, CT: Yale University Press, 2017.

Elias, Norbert. *The Civilizing Process*. New York: Urizen Books, 1978.

Elizur, J. "Ha-Kutim be-divrei ha-Tannaim, (Samaritans in Tannaitic Literature)." In *Israel ve-hamikra: mehkarim ge'ographiyim, historiyim ve-hagutiyim* (Israel and Scripture: Geographic, Historical and Ideological Studies), edited by J. Elizur, Y. Elizur, and A. Frisch. Ramat Gan: Bar-Ilan University Press, 1999. [Hebrew].

Elliott, Charlene. "Purple Pasts: Color Codification in the Ancient World." *Law and Social Inquiry* 33, no. 1 (2008): 173–94.

Emanuel, Sarah. *Humor, Resistance, and Jewish Cultural Persistence in the Book of Revelation: Roasting Rome*. Cambridge: Cambridge University Press, 2020.

Eph'al, Israel. "Syria-Palestine under Achaemenid Rule." In *The Cambridge Ancient History*, edited by John Boardman, N.G.L. Hammond, D.M. Lewis, and M. Ostwald. Vol. 4. Cambridge: Cambridge University Press, 1988.

Epstein, J. N. *Introduction to the Mishnaic Text*. Jerusalem: Hebrew University Magnes Press, 2000. [Hebrew]

Ericsson, K. Anders. "The Differential Influence of Experience, Practice, and Deliberate Practice on the Development of Superior Individual Performance of Experts." In *The Cambridge Handbook of Expertise and Expert Performance*, edited by K. Anders Ericsson, Neil Charness, Paul J. Feltovich, and Robert R. Hoffman. Cambridge: Cambridge University Press, 2018.

———. "Superior Working Memory in Experts." In *The Cambridge Handbook of Expertise and Expert Performance*, edited by K. Anders Ericsson, Neil Charness, Paul J. Feltovich, and Robert R. Hoffman. Cambridge: Cambridge University Press, 2018.

Ericsson, K. Anders, and Tyler J. Towne. "Expertise." *Wiley Interdisciplinary Reviews: Cognitive Science* 1, no. 3 (2010): 404–16.

Eshleman, Kendra. *The Social World of Intellectuals in the Roman Empire: Sophists, Philosophers, and Christians*. Cambridge: Cambridge University Press, 2012.

Esler, Philip F. *Babatha's Orchard: The Yadin Papyri and an Ancient Jewish Family Tale Retold*. Oxford: Oxford University Press, 2017.

Eyal, Gil. *The Crisis of Expertise*. Hoboken, NJ: John Wiley & Sons, 2019.

———. "Expertise," In *Emerging Trends in the Social and Behavioral Sciences*, edited by Robert A. Scott and Marlis C. Buchmann. Hoboken, NJ: John Wiley & Sons, 2015.

———. "For a Sociology of Expertise: The Social Origins of the Autism Epidemic." *American Journal of Sociology* 118, no. 4 (2013): 863–907.

———. "Response to Riccardo Emilio Chesta's 'What Is Critical about the Crisis of Expertise? A Review of Gil Eyal's The Crisis of Expertise.'" *International Journal of Politics, Culture, and Society* 35 (2022): 119–27.

Faas, Patrick. *Around the Roman Table: Food and Feasting in Ancient Rome*. Chicago: University of Chicago Press, 2005.

Fabry, Heinz-Josef. "Priests at Qumran—A Reassessment." In *The Dead Sea Scrolls*, edited by Charlotte Hempel. Leiden: Brill, 2010.

Fantham, Elaine. *Roman Literary Culture: From Cicero to Apuleius*. Baltimore: Johns Hopkins University Press, 1999.

Fawcett, Peter. "'When I Squeeze You with Eisphorai': Taxes and Tax Policy in Classical Athens." *Hesperia: The Journal of the American School of Classical Studies at Athens* 85, no. 1 (2016): 153–99.

Feldman, Louis H. *Jew and Gentile in the Ancient World: Attitudes and Interactions from Alexander to Justinian*. Princeton, NJ: Princeton University Press, 2021.

Fine, Steven. "'Epigraphical' Study Houses in Late Antique Palestine: A Second Look" In *Art, History, and the Historiography of Judaism in Roman Antiquity*, edited by Steven Fine. Boston, Brill: 2013.

———. "'Their Faces Shine with the Brightness of the Firmament': Study Houses and Synagogues in the Targumim to the Pentateuch." In *Biblical Translation in Context*, edited by Frederick W. Knobloch. Bethesda: University Press of Maryland, 2002.

———. *This Holy Place: On the Sanctity of the Synagogue During the Greco-Roman Period*. Eugene, OR: Wipf and Stock Publishers, 2016.

Finkelstein, Louis. "The Birkat Ha-Mazon." *Jewish Quarterly Review* 19 (1929): 211–62.

———. "Some Examples of the Maccabean Halaka." *Journal of Biblical Literature* 49, no. 1 (1930): 20–42.

———. "The Transmission of the Early Rabbinic Traditions." *Hebrew Union College Annual* 16 (1941): 115–35.

Finn, Richard. *Almsgiving in the Later Roman Empire: Christian Promotion and Practice 313–450*. Oxford: Oxford University Press, 2006.

Firth, Raymond. *Symbols: Public and Private*. Abingdon, UK: Routledge, 2013.

Fleisher, Ezra, "Parashat 'asar ta'aser u'kri'atah b'yamot hag lephi minhagot 'eretz Israel." *Tarbiz* 36 (1967): 116–55.

Fogel, Shimon. "The Orders of Discourse in the House of Study (Beit Midrash) in Palestinian Rabbinic Literature: Organizing Space, Ritual and Discipline." PhD diss., Ben-Gurion University, 2014. [Hebrew].

Fonrobert, Charlotte Elisheva. *Menstrual Purity: Rabbinic and Christian Reconstructions of Biblical Gender*. Redwood City, CA: Stanford University Press, 2002.

Foucault, Michel. *Archaeology of Knowledge*. Abingdon, UK: Routledge, 2013.

———. *Discipline and Punish: The Birth of the Prison*. New York: Pantheon Books, 1977.

Fraade, Steven. *From Tradition to Commentary: Torah and Its Interpretation in the Midrash Sifre to Deuteronomy*. Albany, NY: SUNY Press, 1991.

———. "Local Jewish Leadership in Roman Palestine: The Case of the Parnas in Early Rabbinic Sources in Light of Extra-Rabbinic Evidence." In *Halakhah in Light of Epigraphy*, edited by Albert I. Baumgarten, Hanan Eshel, Ranon Katzoff, and Shani Tzoref. Göttingen: Vandenhoek & Ruprecht, 2011.

———. "They Shall Teach Your Statues to Jacob': Priests, Scribes, and Sages in Second Temple Times." *Ancient Jew Review*, June 5, 2023 (1988). https://www.ancientjewreview.com/read/2023/6/5/they-shall-teach-your-statues-to-jacob-priests-scribes-and-sages-in-second-temple-times.

Franco, Cristiana. *Shameless: The Canine and the Feminine in Ancient Greece*. Berkeley: University of California Press, 2014.

Frank, Daniel H. "Teaching for a Fee: Pedagogy and Friendship in Socrates and Maimonides." In *Friendship East and West: Philosophical Perspectives*, edited by Oliver Leaman. London: Curzon 1996.

Frankfurter, David. "Dynamics of Ritual Expertise in Antiquity and Beyond: Towards a New Taxonomy of 'Magicians.'" In *Magic and Ritual in the Ancient World*. Boston: Brill, 2015.

———. "The Great, the Little, and the Authoritative Tradition in Magic of the Ancient World." *Archiv für Religionsgeschichte* 16, no. 1 (2015): 11–30.

Frazer, James George. *The Golden Bough*. London: Palgrave Macmillan, 1922.

Freu, Christel. "Who's Afraid of Wage Labour? Analysing Some Texts of the Second Sophistic." In *Valuing Labor in Greco-Roman Antiquity*, edited by Kim Bowes and Miko Flohr. Leiden: Brill, 2024.

Fricker, Elizabeth. "Testimony and Epistemic Autonomy." In *The Epistemology of Testimony*, edited by Jennifer Lackey. Oxford: Oxford University Press, 2006.

Fried, Lisbeth S. *The Priest and the Great King: Temple-Palace Relations in the Persian Empire*. University Park: The Pennsylvania State University Press, 2004.

Friedheim, Emmanuel. "Some Notes about the Samaritans and the Rabbinic Class at the Crossroads." In *Samaritans: Past and Present*, edited by Menachem Mor and Friedrich V. Reiterer. Berlin: De Gruyter, 2010.

Friedman, Shamma. "Mishnah and Tosefta." In *What Is the Mishnah?*, edited by Shaye J. D. Cohen. Harvard University Press, 2022.

———. *Tosefta Atiqta: Pesaḥ Rishon*. Jerusalem: Bar-Ilan University Press, 2002.

Furstenberg, Yair. "Am Ha-Aretz in Tannaitic Literature and Its Social Contexts." *Zion* 78 (2013): 287–319.

———. "Defilement Penetrating the Body: A New Understanding of Contamination in Mark 7.15." *New Testament Studies* 54, no. 2 (2008): 176–200.

———. "Jesus Against the Laws of the Pharisees: The Legal Woe Sayings and Second Temple Intersectarian Discourse." *Journal of Biblical Literature* 139, no. 4 (2020): 769–88.

———. *Purity and Identity in Ancient Judaism: From the Temple to the Mishnah*. Indiana University Press, 2023.

———. "The Rabbinic Movement from Pharisees to Provincial Jurists." *Journal for the Study of Judaism* 55, no. 1 (2023): 1–43.

———. "'We Rail Against You, Pharisees': The Creation of the Pharisaic Worldview in the Mishnah." In *Halakhah: Explicit and Implied Theoretical and Ideological Aspects*, edited by Dafna Schreiber and Avinoam Rosenak. Jerusalem: Van Leer, 2012. [Hebrew]

Gafni, Isaiah. "The Institution of Marriage in Rabbinic Times." In *The Jewish Family Metaphor and Memory*, edited by D. Kraemer. New York: Oxford University Press, 1989.

———. *Jews and Judaism in the Rabbinic Era: Image and Reality-History and Historiography*. Tübingen: Mohr Siebeck, 2019.

Gage, Ṣtephen. "The Boat/Helmsman." *Technoetic Arts* 5, no. 1 (2007): 15–24.

Galor, Katherine. "Domestic Architecture in Roman and Byzantine Galilee and Golan." *Near Eastern Archaeology* 66 (2003): 44–57.

Gambash, Gil. *Rome and Provincial Resistance*. Abingdon, UK: Routledge, 2015.

Gardner, Gregg E. "Charity Wounds: Gifts to the Poor in Early Rabbinic Judaism." *The Gift in Antiquity* (2013): 173–88.

———. "From the General to the Specific: A Genealogy of 'Acts of Reciprocal Kindness' (Gemilut Hasadim) in Rabbinic Literature." In *Religious Studies and Rabbinics: A Conversation*, edited by Elizabeth Shanks Alexander and Beth Berkowitz. London: Routledge, 2018.

———. "Let Them Eat Fish: Food for the Poor in Early Rabbinic Judaism." *Journal for the Study of Judaism* 45, no. 2 (2014): 250–70.

———. *The Origins of Organized Charity in Rabbinic Judaism*. Cambridge: Cambridge University Press, 2015.

———. "Pursuing Justice: Support for the Poor in Early Rabbinic Judaism." *Hebrew Union College Annual* 86 (2015): 37–62.

———. *Wealth, Poverty, and Charity in Jewish Antiquity*. Berkeley: University of California Press, 2022.

———. "Who Is Rich?: The Poor in Early Rabbinic Judaism." *Jewish Quarterly Review* 104, no. 4 (2014): 515–36.

Garnsey, Peter. *Food and Society in Classical Antiquity*. Cambridge: Cambridge University Press, 1999.

Garrison, Roman. *Redemptive Almsgiving in Early Christianity*. Sheffield, UK: JSOT Press, 1993.

Geiger, Joseph. "The Bar-Kokhba Revolt: The Greek Point of View." *Historia: Zeitschrift Für Alte Geschichte* 65, no. 4 (2016): 497–519.

Ginzberg, Louis. *Yerushalmi Fragments from the Genizah*. Hildesheim and New York: G. Olms, Texts and Studies of the Jewish Theological Seminary of America, 1909.

Gobot, F., and Charness, N. "Expertise in Chess." In *The Cambridge Handbook of Expertise and Expert Performance*, edited by K. Anders, Neil Charness, Paul J. Feltovich, and Robert R. Hoffman. Cambridge: Cambridge University Press, 2006.

Godbout, Jacques T., and Alain C. Caillé. *The World of the Gift*. Montreal: McGill-Queen's University Press, 1998.

Godelier, Maurice. *The Enigma of the Gift*. Chicago: University of Chicago Press, 1999.

Goldin, Judah. *Studies in Midrash and Related Literature*. Philadelphia: Jewish Publication Society of America, 1988.

Goldingay, John. *Hosea–Micah*. Baker Commentary on the Old Testament: Prophetic Books. Ada, MI: Baker Academic, 2021.

Goldman, Alvin I. "Expertise." *Topoi* 37, no. 1 (2018): 3–10.

———. "Experts: Which Ones Should You Trust?" *Philosophy and Phenomenological Research* 63, no. 1 (2001): 85–110.

———. *Social Epistemology: Essential Readings*. Oxford: Oxford University Press, 2011.

Goodblatt, David. *The Monarchic Principle: Studies in Jewish Self-Government in Antiquity*. Tübingen: Mohr Sieback, 1994.

Goodenough, Erwin Ramsdell. *Jewish Symbols in the Greco-Roman Period*. Abridged ed. Princeton, NJ: Princeton University Press, 2014.

Goodman, Martin. "Coinage and Identity: The Jewish Evidence." In *Coinage and Identity in the Roman Provinces*, edited by C. J. Howgego, Volker Heuchert, Andrew M. Burnett. Oxford: Oxford University Press, 2005.

———. *Judaism in the Roman World: Collected Essays*. Leiden: Brill, 2007.

———. "The Qumran Sectarians and the Temple in Jerusalem." In *The Dead Sea Scrolls*, edited by Charlotte Hempel. Leiden: Brill, 2010.

———. *State and Society in Roman Galilee, AD 132–212*. Elstree, UK: Vallentine Mitchell, 2000.

Goodman, Martin, and P. S. Alexander. *Rabbinic Texts and the History of Late-Roman Palestine*. Oxford: Oxford University Press, 2010.

Gouldner, Alvin W. "The Norm of Reciprocity: A Preliminary Statement." *American Sociological Review* 25, no. 2 (1960): 161–78.

Graetz, Heinrich. *Geschichte der Juden von den ältesten Zeiten bis auf die Gegenwart*. Leipzig, DE: Hansebooks, 1900.

Gray, Alyssa M. *Charity in Rabbinic Judaism: Atonement, Rewards, and Righteousness*. Abingdon, UK: Routledge, 2019.

———. "The Formerly Wealthy Poor: From Empathy to Ambivalence in Rabbinic Literature of Late Antiquity." *AJS Review* 33, no. 1 (2009): 101–33.

———. "Redemptive Almsgiving and the Rabbis of Late Antiquity." *Jewish Studies Quarterly* 18, no. 2 (2011): 144–84.

———. "Wealth and Rabbinic Self-Fashioning in Late Antiquity." In *Wealth and Poverty in Jewish Tradition*, edited by Leonard J. Greenspoon. West Lafayette, IN: Purdue University Press, 2015.

Green, William Scott. "What's in a Name? The Problematic of Rabbinic 'Biography.'" In *Approaches to Ancient Judaism*, edited by Jacob Neusner. Missoula, MT: Scholars Press, 1978.

Greenfield, Jonas C., and Hannah Cotton. "Babatha's Property and the Law of Succession in the Babatha Archive." *Zeitschrift für Papyrologie und Epigraphik* 104 (1994): 211–24.

Grey, Matthew J. "Jewish Priests and the Social History of Post-70 Palestine." PhD diss., The University of North Carolina at Chapel Hill, 2011.

Gribetz, Sarit Kattan. "Between Narrative and Polemic: The Sabbath in Genesis Rabbah and the Babylonian Talmud." In *Genesis Rabbah in Text and Context*, edited by Sarit Kattan Gribetz, David M. Grossberg, Martha Himmelfarb, and Peter Schäfer. Tübingen: Mohr Siebeck, 2016.

———. *Time and Difference in Rabbinic Judaism*. Princeton, NJ: Princeton University Press, 2020.

Gross, Simcha. *Babylonian Jews and Sasanian Imperialism in Late Antiquity*. Cambridge: Cambridge University Press, 2024.

———. "Hopeful Rebels and Anxious Romans." *Historia* 72, no. 4 (2023): 479–513.

Gross, Simcha, and Avigail Manekin-Bamberger. "Babylonian Jewish Society: The Evidence of the Incantation Bowls." *Jewish Quarterly Review* 112, no. 1 (2022): 1–30.

Grossberg, David M. *Heresy and the Formation of the Rabbinic Community*. Tübingen: Mohr Siebeck, 2017.

Gruen, Erich S. *Diaspora: Jews amidst Greeks and Romans*. Cambridge, MA: Harvard University Press, 2002.

———. *Heritage and Hellenism: The Reinvention of Jewish Tradition*. Vol. 30. University of California Press, 2023.

Grundmann, Reiner. "The Problem of Expertise in Knowledge Societies." *Minerva* 55, no. 1 (2017): 25–48.

Gundersen, Torbjørn. "Scientists as Experts: A Distinct Role?" *Studies in History and Philosophy of Science Part A* 69 (2018): 52–59.

Haas, Peter J. *A History of the Mishnaic Law of Agriculture: Tractate Maaser Sheni*. Chico, CA: Scholars Press, 1980.

Haensch, Rudolf. "From Free to Fee?." In *Law and Transaction Costs in the Ancient Economy*, edited by David Ratzan, Dennis P. Kehoe, and Uri Yiftach. Ann Arbor: University of Michigan Press, 2015.

———. "Inscriptions as Sources of Knowledge for Religions and Cults in the Roman World of Imperial Times." In *A Companion to Roman Religion*, edited by Jörg Rüpke. Hoboken, NJ: John Wiley & Sons, 2007.

Halbertal, Moshe. "The History of Halakhah, Views from Within: Three Medieval Approaches to Tradition and Controversy." Occasional Paper 5/94, Harvard Law School, Cambridge, MA, 1997. https://www.academia.edu/38287534/Moshe_Halbertal_The_History_of_Halakhah_Views_from_Within_Three_Medieval_Approaches_to_Tradition_and_Controversy_in_Harvard_Law_School_Gruss_Lectures_Cambridge_MA_Harvard_Law_School_1994_1_19.

———. *Maimonides*. Princeton, NJ: Princeton University Press, 2014.

———. "Mishnah and Halakhah." In *What Is the Mishnah? The State of the Question*, edited by Shaye J. D. Cohen. Cambridge, MA: Harvard University Press, 2023.

Halivni, David. "The Early Period of Halakhic Midrash." *Tradition: A Journal of Orthodox Jewish Thought* 22, no. 1 (1986): 37–58.

Halivni, David Weiss. *The Formation of the Babylonian Talmud*. Translated by Jeffrey L. Rubenstein. Oxford: Oxford University Press, 2013.

Hamilton, Mark W. "Bribery at the Boundaries of Gift Giving in the Hebrew Bible." *Biblische Notizen* 187 (2020): 39–58.

Harrison, E. L. "Was Gorgias a Sophist?" *Phoenix* 18, no. 3 (1964): 183–92.

Hasan-Rokem, Galit. "Gifts for God, Gifts for Rabbis: From Sacrifice to Donation in Rabbinic Tales of Late Antiquity and Their Dialogue with Early Christian Texts." In *The Gift in Antiquity*, edited by Michael Satlow. Oxford: John Wiley & Sons, 2013.

———. *Tales of the Neighborhood: Jewish Narrative Dialogues in Late Antiquity*. Berkeley: University of California Press, 2003.

Hauptman, Judith. *Rereading the Mishnah: A New Approach to Ancient Jewish Texts*. Tübingen: Mohr Siebeck, 2005.

———. "The Tosefta as a Commentary on an Early Mishnah." *Jewish Studies, an Internet Journal* 3 (2004): 1–24.

Hayes, Christine. *Between the Babylonian and Palestinian Talmuds: Accounting for Halakhic Difference in Selected Sugyot from Tractate Avodah Zarah*. Oxford: Oxford University Press, 1997.

Hayles, Katherine. *How We Became Posthuman: Virtual Bodies in Cybernetics, Literature, and Informatics*. Chicago: University of Chicago Press, 1999.

Heinemann, Joseph. "Birkath Ha-Zimmun and Havurah-Meals." *Journal of Jewish Studies* 13 (1962): 23–29.

Hempel, Charlotte. "Interpretative Authority in the Community Rule tradition." *Dead Sea Discoveries* 10, no. 1 (2003): 59–80.

Hendin, David. "Current Viewpoints on Ancient Jewish Coinage: A Bibliographic Essay." *Currents in Biblical Research* 11, no. 2 (2013): 246–301.

Herzberg, Frederick. *One More Time: How Do You Motivate Employees?* Cambridge, MA: Harvard Business Review Press, 2008.

Hezser, Catherine. *Form, Function, and Historical Significance of the Rabbinic Story in Yerushalmi Neziqin*. Tübingen: Mohr Siebeck, 1993.

———. "Interaction between Rabbis and Non-Rabbinic Jews in Palestinian Rabbinic Literature of Late Antiquity." In *The Use and Dissemination of Religious Knowledge in Antiquity*, edited by Catherine Hezser and Diana V. Edelman. Sheffield, UK: Equinox Publishers, 2021.

———. *Rabbinic Body Language: Non-Verbal Communication in Palestinian Rabbinic Literature of Late Antiquity*. Leiden: Brill, 2017.

———. "Rabbis and the Image of the Intellectual." In *The Routledge Handbook of Jews and Judaism in Late Antiquity*, edited by Catherine Hezser. Abingdon, UK: Routledge, 2024.

———. *The Social Structure of the Rabbinic Movement in Roman Palestine*. Tübingen: Mohr Siebeck, 1997.

———. "Uncertain Symbol: The Representation of Yavne in the Talmud Yerushalmi." In *Jews and Christians in the First and Second Centuries: The Interbellum 70-132 CE*, edited by Joshua Schwartz and Peter J. Tomson. Leiden: Brill, 2017.

Hidary, Richard. "Rhetoric of Rabbinic Authority: Making the Transition from Priest to Sage." In *Jewish Rhetorics: History, Theory, Practice*, edited by Michael Bernard-Donals and Janice W. Fernheimer. Waltham, MA: Brandeis University Press, 2014.

Hilgartner, Stephen. *Science on Stage: Expert Advice as Public Drama*. Redwood City, CA: Stanford University Press, 2000.

Himmelfarb, Martha. *Between Temple and Torah: Essays on Priests, Scribes, and Visionaries in the Second Temple Period and Beyond*. Tübingen: Mohr Siebeck, 2013.

———. "'Found Written in the Book of Moses': Priests in the Era of Torah." In *Was 70 CE a Watershed in Jewish History?*, edited by Daniel R. Schwartz and Zeev Weiss. Leiden: Brill, 2012.

———. "'A Kingdom of Priests': The Democratization of the Priesthood in the Literature of Second Temple Judaism." *The Journal of Jewish Thought and Philosophy* 6, no. 1 (1997): 89–104.

———. "The Torah Between Athens and Jerusalem: Jewish Difference in Antiquity." In *Ancient Judaism in Its Hellenistic Context*, edited by Carol Bakhos. Leiden: Brill, 2005.

Hippocrates, Heracleitus. *Hippocrates, Volume IV: Nature of Man*, translated by W. H. S. Jones. Cambridge, MA: Harvard University Press, 1931.

Hirschfeld, Yizhar. *The Palestinian Dwelling in the Roman-Byzantine Period*. Jerusalem: Franciscan Printing Press and Israel Exploration Society, 1995.

Hirschfeld, Yizhar, and Rivka Birger-Calderon. "Early Roman and Byzantine Estates Near Caesarea." *Israel Exploration Journal* 41 (1991): 81–111.

Hirschman, Marc, "On the Nature of Mitzva and Its Reward in the Mishnah and Tosefta." *Proceedings of the Tenth World Congress of Jewish Studies. Division C* 1 (1990): 54–60.

Hollender, Elisabeth, "Parashat 'Asser Te'asser' in Piyyut and Piyyut Commentary." In *Jewish and Christian Liturgy and Worship: New Insights into Its History and Interaction* edited by Albert Gerhards and Clemens Leonhard. Leiden: Brill, 2007.

Holman, Susan R. *The Hungry Are Dying: Beggars and Bishops in Roman Cappadocia.* Oxford University Press, 2001.

Honigman, Sylvie. *Tales of High Priests and Taxes: The Books of the Maccabees and the Judean Rebellion Against Antiochos IV.* Berkeley: University of California Press, 2021.

Horsley, Richard A. *Scribes, Visionaries, and the Politics of Second Temple Judea.* Louisville, KY: Presbyterian Publishing Corporation, 2007.

Hudson, Nicholas F. "Changing Places: The Archaeology of the Roman Convivium." *American Journal of Archaeology* 114, no. 4 (2010): 663–95.

Ilan, N. "The Double Canonization of Tractate *Avot*: Text, Commentary, and Polemic." *Netuim* 17 (2011): 57–72. [Hebrew]

Ilan, Tal. *Jewish Women in Greco-Roman Palestine: An Inquiry into Image and Status.* Tübingen: Mohr Siebeck, 2006.

———. *Mine and Yours Are Hers: Retrieving Women's History From Rabbinic Literature.* Leiden: Brill, 1997.

———. "The Torah of the Jews of Ancient Rome." *Jewish Studies Quarterly* 16, no. 4 (2009): 363–95.

———. "Witnesses in the Judaean Desert Documents: Prosopographical Observations." *Scripta Classica Israelica* 20 (2001): 169–78.

Isaac, Benjamin. *The Limits of Empire: The Roman Army in the East.* Oxford: Oxford University Press, 1992.

Isaac, Benjamin, and Israel Roll. "Legio II Traiana in Judaea: A Reply." *Zeitschrift für Papyrologie und Epigraphik* 47 (1982): 131–32.

Jaffee, Martin S. "The Oral-Cultural Context of the Talmud Yerushalmi: Greco-Roman Rhetorical Paideia, Discipleship, and the Concept of Oral Torah." In *Transmitting Jewish Traditions*, edited by Yaakov Elman and Israel Gershoni. New Haven, CT: Yale University Press, 2000.

———. "Oral Tradition in the Writings of Rabbinic Oral Torah: On Theorizing Rabbinic Orality." *Hebrew Oral Traditions* 14, no. 1 (1999): 3–32.

———. *Torah in the Mouth: Writing and Oral Tradition in Palestinian Judaism 200 BCE–400 CE.* Oxford: Oxford University Press, 2001.

Jastrow, Marcus. *A Dictionary of the Targumim, the Talmud Babli, and Yerushalmi, and the Midrashic Literature.* Vol. 2. New York: Luzac, 1903.

Kalmin, Richard. *Jewish Babylonia between Persia and Roman Palestine.* Oxford: Oxford University Press, 2006.

———. "Relationships Between Rabbis and Non-Rabbis in Rabbinic Literature of Late Antiquity." *Jewish Studies Quarterly* 5, no. 2 (1998): 156–70.

———. *The Sage in Jewish Society of Late Antiquity.* New York: Routledge, 2002.

———. *Sages, Stories, Authors, and Editors in Rabbinic Babylonia.* Providence, RI: Brown Judaic Studies, 1994.

Kaminka, Aharon. "R' Yohanan Ben Zakkai and His Disciples." *Zion* 9 (1944): 70–83. [Hebrew]

Kanarfogel, Ephraim. "Compensation for the Study of Torah in Medieval Rabbinic Thought." In *Of Scholars, Savants, and Their Texts: Studies in Philosophy and Religious Thought*, edited by Ruth Link-Salinger. New York: Peter Lang, 1989.

Kanter, Shamai. *Rabban Gamaliel II, the Legal Traditions*. Providence, RI: Brown Judaic Studies, 1980.

Kasher, Aryeh. *The Jews in Hellenistic and Roman Egypt: The Struggle for Equal Rights*. Tübingen: Mohr Siebeck, 1985.

———. "New Light on the Jewish Part in the Alexandrian War of Julius Caesar." *World Union of Jewish Studies* 14/15 (1959): 15–23. [Hebrew]

———. "Synagogues as 'Houses of Prayer' and 'Holy Places' in the Jewish Communities of Hellenistic and Roman Egypt." In *Ancient Synagogues: Historical Analysis and Archaeological Discovery*, edited by Dan Urman and Paul V.M. Flesher. Vol. 1. Leiden: Brill, 1998.

Kaster, Robert A. *Guardians of Language: The Grammarian and Society in Laṭe Antiquity*. Berkeley: University of California Press, 2023.

Kaufmann, Yeḥezkel. *Toldot ha-emunah ha-yisre'elit*. Jerusalem: Mosad Beya'lik, 1968.

Keddie, Anthony. "Triclinium Trialectics: The Triclinium as Contested Space in Early Roman Palestine." *Harvard Theological Review* 113, no. 1 (2020): 63–88.

Kelly, Christopher. *Ruling the Later Roman Empire*. Cambridge: Harvard University Press, 2006.

Kelly, Kathleen S. *Effective Fund-Raising Management*. New York: Routledge, 2012.

———. "Stewardship: The Fifth Step in the Public Relations Process." In *Handbook of Public Relations*, edited by Robert L. Heath with Gabriel Vasquez. Thousand Oaks, CA: Sage, 2001.

Kiel, Yishai. *Sexuality in the Babylonian Talmud*. Cambridge: Cambridge University Press, 2016.

Killebrew, Anne E. "Village and Countryside." In *The Oxford Handbook of Jewish Daily Life in Roman Palestine*, edited by Catherine Hezser. Oxford: Oxford University Press, 2010.

Kimelman, Reuven. "Ha-Oligarkiyah ha-kohanit ve-talmidei ḥaḥamim be-tekufat ha-Talmud." *Ẓion* 48 (1983): 135–47.

King, Philip J. *Amos, Hosea, Micah: An Archaeological Commentary*. Louisville, KY: Westminster John Knox Press, 1988.

Kiperwasser, Reuven. "From Oral Discourse to Written Documents." In *The Routledge Handbook of Jews and Judaism in Late Antiquity*, edited by Catherine Hezser. Abingdon, UK: Routledge, 2024.

Klawans, Jonathan. "Imagining Judaism after 70 CE." In *A Companion to Late Ancient Jews and Judaism: Third Century BCE to Seventh Century CE*, edited by Naomi Koltun-Fromm. Hoboken, NJ: John Wiley & Sons, 2020.

———. *Josephus and the Theologies of Ancient Judaism*. Oxford: Oxford University Press, 2012.

———. *Purity, Sacrifice, and the Temple: Symbolism and Supersessionism in the Study of Ancient Judaism*. Oxford: Oxford University Press, 2005.

Klein, Gil P. "Torah in Triclinia: The Rabbinic Banquet and the Significance of Architecture." *Jewish Quarterly Review* 102, no. 3 (2012): 325–70.

Klotz, Frieda, and Katerina Oikonomopoulou, eds. *The Philosopher's Banquet: Plutarch's Table Talk in the Intellectual Culture of the Roman Empire*. Oxford: Oxford University Press, 2011.

Knoppers, Gary N. "Hierodules, Priests, or Janitors? The Levites in Chronicles and the History of the Israelite Priesthood." *Journal of Biblical Literature* 118, no. 1 (1999): 49–72.

Kolm, Serge-Christophe. "Reciprocity: Its Scope, Rationales, and Consequences." In *Handbook of the Economics of Giving, Altruism and Reciprocity*, edited by Serge-Christophe Kolm and Jean Mercier Ythier. Amsterdam: Elsevier, 2006.

Komter, Aafke. "Gifts and Social Relations: The Mechanisms of Reciprocity." *International Sociology* 22, no. 1 (2007): 93–107.

Konstan, David. *Friendship in the Classical World*. Cambridge: Cambridge University Press, 1997.

———. "Patrons and Friends." *Classical Philology* 90, no. 4 (1995): 328–42.

Kraeling, Carl H. "The Jewish Community at Antioch." *Journal of Biblical Literature* 51, no. 2 (1932): 130–60.

Kraemer, David. *Jewish Eating and Identity through the Ages*. Abingdon, UK: Routledge, 2020.

———. "On the Reliability of Attributions in the Babylonian Talmud." *Hebrew Union College Annual* 60 (1989): 175–90.

Kraemer, Ross Shepard. *The Mediterranean Diaspora in Late Antiquity: What Christianity Cost the Jews*. Oxford: Oxford University Press, 2020.

———, ed. *Women's Religions in the Greco-Roman World: A Sourcebook*. Oxford: Oxford University Press, 2004.

Krauss, Shmuel. "Die Römischen Besatzungen in Palästina." *Magazin für die Wissenschaft des Judenthums* 20 (1893): 105–33.

Kuefler, Mathew. "The Merry Widows of Late Roman Antiquity: The Evidence of the Theodosian Code." *Gender and History* 27, no. 1 (2015): 28–52.

Kugel, James. "Thinking about Scripture in Second Temple Times." In *Early Judaism and Its Modern Interpreters*, edited by Matthias Henze and Rodney A. Werline. Atlanta: The Society of Biblical Literature, 2020.

Labendz, Jenny R. *Socratic Torah: Non-Jews in Rabbinic Intellectual Culture*. Oxford: Oxford University Press, 2013.

Labovitz, Gail. "The Scholarly Life—The Laboring Wife: Gender, Torah, and the Family Economy in Rabbinic Culture." *Nashim: A Journal of Jewish Women's Studies and Gender Issues* 13 (2007): 8–48.

Laes, Christian. "School-Teachers in the Roman Empire: A Survey of the Epigraphical Evidence." In *Acta Classica: Proceedings of the Classical Association of South Africa*, vol. 50, no. 1 (2007): 109–27.

Langer, Ruth. "Rabbis, Nonrabbis, and Synagogues in Roman Palestine: Theory and Reality." In *Synagogues in the Hellenistic and Roman Periods: Archaeological Finds, New Methods, New Theories*, edited by Lutz Doering and Andrew R. Krause. Göttingen: Vandenhoeck and Ruprecht, 2020.

Lapin, Hayim. *Early Rabbinic Civil Law*. Providence, RI: Brown Judaic Studies, 2020.

———. *Economy, Geography, and Provincial History in later Roman Palestine*. Tübingen: Mohr Siebeck, 2001.

———. "Feeding the Jerusalem Temple: Cult, Hinterland, and Economy in First-Century Palestine." *Journal of Ancient Judaism* 8, no. 3 (2017): 410–53.

———. "Jerusalem the Consumer City: Temple, Cult, and Consumption in the Second Temple Period." In *Expressions of Cult in the Southern Levant in the Greco-Roman Period:*

Manifestations in Text and Material Culture, edited by Oren Tal and Zeev Weiss. Turnhout, BE: Brepols Publishers, 2017.

———. "Jewish and Christian Academies in Roman Palestine: Some Preliminary Observations." In *Caesarea Maritima: A Retrospective after Two Millenia*, edited by Avner Raban and Kenneth G. Holum. Leiden: Brill, 1996.

———. "The Rabbinic Class Revisited: Rabbis as Judges in Later Roman Palestine." In *"Follow the Wise": Studies in Jewish History and Culture in Honor of Lee I. Levine*, edited by Zeev Weiss, Oded Irshai, Jodi Magness, and Seth Schwartz. Winona Lake, IN: Eisenbrauns, 2010.

———. "Rabbis and Cities: Some Aspects of the Rabbinic Movement in Its Graeco-Roman Environment." In *The Talmud Yerushalmi and Graeco-Roman Culture*, edited by Peter Schäfer and Catherine Hezser. Tübingen: Mohr Siebeck, 2000.

———. *Rabbis as Romans: The Rabbinic Movement in Palestine, 100–400 CE*. Oxford: Oxford University Press, 2012.

———. "The Rabbis of History and Historiography." In *The Literature of the Sages*, edited by Shmuel Safrai. Leiden: Brill, 2022.

Latour, Bruno. *An Inquiry into Modes of Existence*. Cambridge, MA: Harvard University Press, 2013.

———. *Science in Action: How to Follow Scientists and Engineers through Society*. Cambridge, MA: Harvard University Press, 1987.

———. *We Have Never Been Modern*. Cambridge, MA: Harvard University Press, 1993.

Lehman, Marjorie. "Imagining the Priesthood in Tractate Yoma: Mishnah Yoma 2:1–2 and BT Yoma 23a." *Nashim: A Journal of Jewish Women's Studies and Gender Issues* 28 (2015): 88–105.

———. "Who Gets a Voice at the Table?: Eating and Blessing with Rav Naḥman." In *Hakol Kol Yaakov*, edited by Robert A. Harris and Jonathan S. Milgram. Leiden: Brill, 2021.

Lehmhaus, Lennart. "'Were Not Understanding and Knowledge Given to You from Heaven?' Minimal Judaism and the Unlearned 'Other' in Seder Eliyahu Zuta." *Jewish Studies Quarterly* 19, no. 3 (2012): 230–58.

Leibowitz, Aryeh. "The Pursuit of Scholarship and Economic Self-Sufficiency: Revisiting Maimonides' Commentary to Pirkei Avot." *Tradition* 40, no. 3 (fall 2007): 31–41.

Lerner, M. B. "The External Tractates." In *The Literature of the Sages, First Part: Oral Tora, Halakha, Mishna, Tosefta, Talmud, External Tractates*, edited by Shmuel Safrai. Leiden: Brill, 1987.

———. "The Tractate Avot." In *The Literature of the Sages, First Part: Oral Tora, Halakha, Mishna, Tosefta, Talmud, External Tractates*, edited by Shmuel Safrai. Leiden: Brill, 1987.

Leuchter, Mark A. "The Priesthood in Ancient Israel." *Biblical Theology Bulletin* 40, no. 2 (2010): 100–110.

Levine, Lee I. *The Ancient Synagogue: The First Thousand Years*. New Haven, CT: Yale University Press, 2000.

———. "The Jewish Patriarch (Nasi) in Third Century Palestine." In *Religion (Judentum: Allegemeines; Paiastinisches Judentum* 19, no 2. (1979): 649–88.

———. *The Rabbinic Class of Roman Palestine in Late Antiquity*. New York: JTS Press, 2012.

———. "Synagogue Art and the Rabbis in Late Antiquity." *Journal of Ancient Judaism* 2, no. 1 (2011): 79–114.

Levinson, Joshua. "Enchanting Rabbis: Contest Narratives between Rabbis and Magicians in Late Antiquity." *Jewish Quarterly Review* 100, no. 1 (2010): 54–94.

Lévi-Strauss, Claude. *Introduction to the Work of Marcel Mauss*. Abingdon, UK: Routledge, 2013.

Lewis, Nicola Denzey. "Ordinary Religion in the Late Roman Empire: Principles of a New Approach." *Studies in Late Antiquity* 5, no. 1 (2021): 104–18.

Lieber, Laura S. "Jewish Prayer, Liturgy, and Ritual." In *A Companion to Late Ancient Jews and Judaism*, edited by Naomi Koltun-Fromm and Swynn Kessler. Hoboken, NJ: John Wiley & Sons, 2020.

Lieberman, Saul. *Hellenism in Jewish Palestine: Studies in the Literary Transmission Beliefs and Manners of Palestine in the I century BCE–IV Century CE*. New York: Jewish Theological Seminary of America, 1950.

———. *Tosefta Ki-Fshutah: A Comprehensive Commentary on the Tosefta*. 8 vols. 1955–88. Reprint, New York: Jewish Theological Seminary of America, 1995–2002. [Hebrew]

———. "Two Lexicographical Notes." *Journal of Biblical Literature* 65 (1946): 67–72.

Luley, Benjamin P. "Colonialism, Dining, and Changing Strategies of Power: The Example of Iron Age and Roman Mediterranean France at Lattara (ca 150 BC–AD 50)." *Journal of Archaeological Method and Theory* 21, no. 4 (2014): 750–80.

Lynch, Paul, Jennie Germann Molz, Alison Mcintosh, Peter Lugosi, and Conrad Lashley. "Theorizing Hospitality." *Hospitality and Society* 1, no. 1 (2011): 3–24.

MacRae, Duncan. *Legible Religion: Books, Gods, and Rituals in Roman Culture*. Cambridge, MA: Harvard University Press, 2016.

Maeir, Aren M. "'And Brought in the Offerings and the Tithes and the Dedicated Things Faithfully' (2 Chron. 31:12): On the Meaning and Function of the Late Iron Age Judahite 'Incised Handle Cooking Pots.'" *Journal of the American Oriental Society* 130, no. 1 (2010): 43–62.

Magness, Jodi. "'The Foundation Deposit' from the Dura Europos Synagogue Reconsidered." In *Architecture of the Sacred: Space, Ritual, and Experience from Classical Greece to Byzantium* edited by Bonna D. Wescoat and Robert G. Ousterhout. Cambridge: Cambridge University Press, 2012.

———. "Helios and the Zodiac Cycle in Ancient Palestinian Synagogues." In *Symbiosis, Symbolism, and the Power of the Past: Canaan, Ancient Israel, and Their Neighbors from the Late Bronze Age through Roman Palaestina*, edited by W. G. Dever and S. Gitin. University Park, PA: Penn State University Press, 2023.

———. "Sectarianism Before and After 70 CE." In *Was 70 CE a Watershed in Jewish History?: On Jews and Judaism Before and After the Destruction of the Second Temple*, edited by Daniel R. Schwartz and Zeev Weiss. Leiden: Brill, 2012.

Malinowski, Bronislaw. *Argonauts of the Western Pacific: An Account of Native Enterprise and Adventure in the Archipelagoes of Melanesian New Guinea*. Abingdon, UK: Routledge, 1978.

Mandel, Paul. "Concerning the Public Role of the Early Beit Midrash." *Zion* 3 (2014): 327–43. [Hebrew]

———. *The Origins of Midrash: From Teaching to Text*. Leiden: Brill, 2017.

Mandsager, John Robert. "To Stake a Claim: The Making of Rabbinic Agricultural Spaces in the Roman Countryside." PhD diss., Stanford University, 2014.

Manekin-Bamberger, Avigail. *Seder Mazikin: Law and Magic in Late Antique Jewish Society*. (Jerusalem: Yad Izhak Ben Zvi, 2024). [Hebrew]

Marks, Susan. "Follow That Crown: Or, Rhetoric, Rabbis, and Women Patrons." *Journal of Feminist Studies in Religion* 24, no. 2 (2008): 77–96.

———. "In the Place of Libation: Birkat Hamazon Navigates New Ground." In *Meals in Early Judaism: Social Formation at the Table,* edited by Susan Marks and Hal Taussig. New York: Palgrave Macmillan, 2014.

———. "Who Studied at the Beit Midrash?: Funding Palestinian Amoraic Education." *Journal of Ancient Judaism* 12, no. 2 (2021): 281–312.

Marks, Susan, and Hal Taussig, eds. *Meals in Early Judaism: Social Formation at the Table.* Berlin: Springer, 2014.

Martin, Ben L. "Experts in Policy Processes: A Contemporary Perspective." *Polity* 6, no. 2 (1973): 149–73.

Marx-Wolf, Heidi. *Spiritual Taxonomies and Ritual Authority: Platonists, Priests, and Gnostics in the Third Century C.E.* Philadelphia: University of Pennsylvania Press, 2016.

Matoesian, Greg. "Role Conflict as an Interactional Resource in the Multimodal Emergence of Expert Identity." *Semiotica,* no. 171 (2008): 15–49.

Mauss, Marcel. *The Gift: Forms and Functions of Exchange in Archaic Societies.* New York: W. W. Norton, 2000.

Mayer, Yakov Z. *Editio Princeps: The 1523 Venice Edition of the Palestinian Talmud and the Beginning of Hebrew Printing.* Jerusalem: Magnes Press, 2022. [Hebrew]

Mazor, Gabriel. "Imperial Cult in the Decapolis." In *Viewing Ancient Jewish Art and Archaeology: VeHinnei Rachel—Essays in Honor of Rachel Hachlili.* Leiden: Brill, 2015.

McKnight, D. Harrison, and Norman L. Chervany. "What Is Trust? A Conceptual Analysis and an Interdisciplinary Model." Americas Conference on Information Systems Proceedings, 2000, pp. 827–33. https://aisel.aisnet.org/amcis2000/382.

Meir, Ofrah. "The Historical Contribution of the Legends of the Sages." *Mahanaim* 7 (1994): 8–25. [Hebrew]

Mertz, Elizabeth. *The Language of Law School: Learning to "Think Like a Lawyer."* Oxford: Oxford University Press, 2007.

———. "Recontextualization as Socialization: Text and Pragmatics in the Law School Classroom." In *Natural Histories of Discourse.* Chicago: University of Chicago Press, 1996.

Meyers, Eric M. "Aspects of Everyday Life in Roman Palestine with Special Reference to Private Domiciles and Ritual Baths." In *Jews in the Hellenistic and Roman Cities,* edited by John R. Bartlett. Abingdon, UK: Routledge, 2003.

———. "Sepphoris." In *The First Jewish Revolt: Archaeology, History, and Ideology,* edited by Andrea M. Berlin and J. Andrew Overman. Abingdon, UK: Routledge, 2002.

Meyers, Eric M., and Steven Fine. "Ancient Synagogues: An Archaeological Introduction." In *Sacred Realm: The Emergence of the Synagogue in the Ancient World,* edited by Steven Fine. Oxford: Oxford University Press, 1996.

Mieg, Harald A., and Julia Evetts. "Professionalism, Science, and Expert Roles: A Social Perspective." In *The Cambridge Handbook of Expertise and Expert Performance,* edited by K. Anders Ericsson, Robert R. Hoffman, Aaron Kozbelt, and A. Mark Williams. Cambridge: Cambridge University Press, 2018.

Milikowsky, Chaim. "On the Formation and Transmission of Bereshit Rabba and the Yerushalmi: Questions of Redaction, Text-Criticism and Literary Relationships." *Jewish Quarterly Review* 92, no. 3 (2002): 521–67.

Millar, Fergus. "Inscriptions, Synagogues and Rabbis in Late Antique Palestine." *Journal for the Study of Judaism* 42, no. 2 (2011): 253–77.

———. *Rome, the Greek World, and the East.* Chapel Hill: University of North Carolina Press, 2002.

———. "Transformations of Judaism under Graeco-Roman Rule: Responses to Seth Schwartz's 'Imperialism and Jewish Society.'" *Journal of Jewish Studies* 57, no. 1 (2006): 140–58.

Miller, Stuart S. "'Epigraphical' Rabbis, Helios, and Psalm 19: Were the Synagogues of Archaeology and the Synagogues of the Sages One and the Same?" *Jewish Quarterly Review* 94, no. 1 (2004): 27–76.

———. "Intercity Relations in Roman Palestine: The Case of Sepphoris and Tiberias." *AJS Review* 12, no. 1 (1987): 1–24.

———. *Sages and Commoners in Late Antique 'Erez Israel: A Philological Inquiry into Local Traditions in Talmud Yerushalmi.* Tübingen: Mohr Siebeck, 2006.

———. "This Is the Beit Midrash of Rabbi Eliexer ha-Qappar." In *Talmuda de-Eretz Israel: Archaeology and the Rabbis in Late Antique Palestine* 73 (2014): 239–74.

Mohler, S. L. "A Roman Answer to the Salary Question." *The Classical Weekly* (1928): 105–7.

Mokhtarian, Jason Sion. *Rabbis, Sorcerers, Kings, and Priests: The Culture of the Talmud in Ancient Iran.* Oakland: University of California Press, 2021.

Mor, Menahem. *The Second Jewish Revolt: The Bar Kokhba War, 132–136 CE.* Leiden: Brill, 2016.

Moravec, Hans. *Mind Children: The Future of Robot and Human Intelligence.* Cambridge, MA: Harvard University Press, 1988.

Mortensen, Beverly P. "Considerations of the Priest's Function Where No Temple Exists." In *The Priesthood in Targum Pseudo-Jonathan*, edited by Beverly Moretensen. Leiden: Brill, 2006.

Murray, Oswyn. "Convivium." In *The Oxford Classical Dictionary*, 3rd ed. revised, edited by Simon Hornblower and Antony Spawforth, 387. Oxford: Oxford University Press, 2003.

———, ed., *Sympotica: A Symposium on the Symposion.* Oxford: Oxford University Press, 1990.

Nadeau, Robin. "Table Manners." In *A Companion to Food in the Ancient World*, edited by John Wilkins and Robin Nadeau. Hoboken, NJ: John Wiley & Sons, 2015.

Naiweld, Ron. "There Is Only One Other: The Fabrication of Antoninus in a Multilayered Talmudic Dialogue." *Jewish Quarterly Review* 104, no. 1 (2014): 81–104.

Najman, Hindy. *Losing the Temple and Recovering the Future: An Analysis of 4 Ezra.* Cambridge: Cambridge University Press, 2014.

Neusner, Jacob. *Development of a Legend: Studies on the Traditions Concerning Yohanan Ben-Zakkai.* Leiden: Brill, 1970.

———. *The Economics of the Mishnah.* Chicago: University of Chicago Press, 1990.

———. *Eliezer Ben Hyrcanus: The Tradition and the Man.* Eugene, OR: Wipf and Stock, 2003.

———. "Evaluating the Attributions of Sayings to Named Sages in the Rabbinic Literature." *Journal for the Study of Judaism* 26, no. 1 (1995): 93–111.

———. *First Century Judaism in Crisis.* Eugene, OR: Wipf and Stock, 2006.

———. *Judaism: The Evidence of the Mishnah.* Eugene, OR: Wipf and Stock, 2003.

———. "The Phenomenon of the Rabbi in Late Antiquity." *Numen* 16, no. 1 (1969): 1–20.

———. *The Rabbinic Traditions about the Pharisees Before 70.* Eugene, OR: Wipf and Stock, 2005.

———. "Rabbis and Community in Third Century Babylonia." In *Religions in Antiquity.* Leiden: Brill, 1968.

———. "Why We Cannot Assume the Reliability of Attributions: The Case of the Houses in Mishna-Tosefta Makhshirin." In *The Mishnah in Contemporary Perspectives*, edited by Alan J. Avery-Peck and J. Neusner. Boston: Brill, 2006.

Newmyer, Stephen T. "Antoninus and Rabbi on the Soul: Stoic Elements of a Puzzling Encounter." *Koroth* 9 (1988): 108–23.

Nicols, John. *Civic Patronage in the Roman Empire*. Leiden: Brill, 2014.

———. "Hospitality Among the Romans." In *The Oxford Handbook of Social Relations in the Roman World*, edited by Michael Peachin. Oxford: Oxford University Press, 2011.

———. "The Practice of *Hospitium* on the Roman Frontier." In *Frontiers in the Roman World*, edited by Ted Kaizer and Olivier Hekster. Leiden: Brill, 2011.

Niehoff, Maren R. *Jewish Exegesis and Homeric Scholarship in Alexandria*. Cambridge: Cambridge University Press, 2011.

Nielsen, Inge, and Hanne Nielsen. *Meals in a Social Context: Aspects of the Communal Meal in the Hellenistic and Roman World*. Aarhus, DK: Aarhus University Press, 1998.

Noam, Vered. "The Emergence of Rabbinic Culture from the Perspective of Qumran." *Journal of Ancient Judaism* 6, no. 2 (2015): 253–74.

———. *From Qumran to the Rabbinic Revolution: Conceptions of Impurity*. Jerusalem: Yad Izhak Ben-Zvi, 2010. [Hebrew]

Nongbri, Brent. *Before Religion: A History of a Modern Concept*. New Haven, CT: Yale University Press, 2013.

Novick, Tzvi. "Charity and Reciprocity: Structures of Benevolence in Rabbinic Literature." *Harvard Theological Review* 105, no. 1 (2011): 33–52.

———. "Covenant and Community in Early Rabbinic Literature." *Harvard Theological Review* (2024): 1–22.

———. "Tradition, Scripture, Law, and Authority." In *The Literature of the Sages: A Re-Visioning*, edited by Christine Hayes. Leiden: Brill, 2022.

———. *What Is Good, and What God Demands: Normative Structures in Tannaitic Literature*. Leiden: Brill, 2010.

Noy, David. *Foreigners at Rome: Citizens and Strangers*. Swansea, UK: The Classical Press of Wales, 2000.

Omissi, A. "Rhetoric and Power: How Imperial Panegyric Allowed Civilian Elites to Access Power in the Fourth Century." In *Leadership, Ideology, and Crowds in the Roman Empire of the Fourth Century AD*, edited by E. Manders and D. Slootjes. Leuven: Franz Steiner Verlag, 2020.

Oppenheimer, Aharon. *The 'Am Ha-Aretz: A Study in the Social History of the Jewish People in the Hellenistic-Roman Period*. Leiden, Brill: 1977.

———. "Batei Midrash in Eretz-Israel in the Early Amoraic Period." *Cathedra for the History of Eretz Israel and Its Yishuv Jérusalem* 8 (1978): 80–89. [Hebrew]

———. "The Jewish Community in Galilee during the Period of Yavneh and the Bar Kokhba Revolt." *Cathedra for the History of Eretz Israel and Its Yishuv Jérusalem* 4 (1977): 53–66.

Osteen, Mark, ed. *The Question of the Gift: Essays Across Disciplines*. New York: Routledge, 2013.

Overman, J. Andrew, and Robert MacLennan. *Diaspora Jews and Judaism: Essays in Honor of, and in Dialogue with, A. Thomas Kraabel*. Tampa: University of South Florida, 1992.

Padilla Peralta, Dan-el. *Divine Institutions: Religions and Community in the Middle Roman Republic*. Princeton, NJ: Princeton University Press, 2020.

Pafford, Isabelle. “Priestly Portion vs. Cult Fees—The Finances of Greek Sanctuaries.” In *Cities and Priests: Cult Personnel in Asia Minor and the Aegean Islands from the Hellenistic to the Imperial Period*, edited by Marietta Horster and Anja Klöckner. Vol. 64. Berlin: De Gruyter, 2013.

Pamuk, Zeyn,*Politics and Expertise: How to Use Science in a Democratic Society*. Princeton, NJ: Princeton University Press, 2021.

Parry, Jonathan. “The Gift, the Indian Gift and the ‘Indian Gift.’” *Man* 21, no. 3 (1986): 453–73.

Patterson, John R. “The Relationship of the Italian Ruling Classes with Rome: Friendship, Family Relations and their Consequences.” In *Herrschaft ohne Integration? Rom und Italien in republikanishcer Zeit. Studien zur Alten Geschichte* 4, edited by M. Jehne and R. Pfeilschifter. Frankfurt: Verlag Alte Geschichte, 2006.

Picus, Daniel. “The Words of the Righteous: The Death of Text and the Eternity of Stone.” *Hebrew Studies* 64, no. 1 (2023): 31–55.

Plaisance, Kathryn S., and Eric B. Kennedy. “A Pluralistic Approach to Interactional Expertise.” *Studies in History and Philosophy of Science* 47 (2014): 60–68.

Polanyi, Michael. *Personal Knowledge*. Abingdon, UK: Routledge, 2012.

Polci, Barbara. “Some Aspects of the Transformation of the Roman *Domus* Between Late Antiquity and the Early Middle Ages.” In *Theory and Practice in Late Antique Archaeology*, edited by Luke Lavan and William Bowden. Leiden: Brill, 2003.

Porton, Gary G. “Rabbinic Midrash: Public or Private.” *Review of Rabbinic Judaism* 5, no. 2 (2002): 141–69.

———. *Understanding Rabbinic Midrash: Texts and Commentary*. New York: Ktav Publishing House, 1984.

Price, Simon. *Rituals and Power: The Roman Imperial Cult in Asia Minor*. Cambridge, MA: Cambridge University Press, 1984.

Pucci Ben Zeev, Miriam. *Diaspora Judaism in Turmoil, 116/117 CE: Ancient Sources and Modern Insights*. Leuven, BE: Peeters Publishers, 2005.

———. “New Insights into Roman Policy in Judea on the Eve of the Bar Kokhba Revolt.” *Journal for the Study of Judaism* 49, no. 1 (2018): 84–107.

Quast, Christian. “Expertise: A Practical Explication.” *Topoi* 37 (2018): 11–27.

Quigley, Jennifer A. *Divine Accounting: Theo-Economics in Early Christianity*. New Haven, CT: Yale University Press, 2021.

Rajak, Tessa, “Jews and Christians as Groups in a Pagan World.” In *To See Ourselves as Others See Us: Christians, Jews, ‘Others’ in Late Antiquity*, edited by Jacob Neusner. Chico, CA: Scholars Press, 1985.

———. *Translation and Survival: The Greek Bible of the Ancient Jewish Diaspora*. Oxford: Oxford University Press, 2009.

Ramos, Alexander Jenaro. “Torah, Temple, and Transaction: Jewish Religious Institutions and Economic Behavior in Early Roman Galilee.” PhD diss., University of Pennsylvania, 2017.

Reade, Julian E. “The *Symposion* in Ancient Mesopotamia: Archaeological Evidence.” In *In Vino Veritas*, edited by Oswyn Murray and Manuela Tecuşan. Cambridge: Cambridge University Press, 1995.

Reed, Annette Yoshiko. “When Did Rabbis Become Pharisees?: Reflections on Christian Evidence for Post-70 Judaism.” In *Envisioning Judaism: Essays in Honor of Peter Schäfer on the Occasion of His Seventieth Birthday*, edited by Ra’anan S. Boustan, Klaus Herrmann,

Reimund Leicht, Annette Yoshiko Reed, and Giuseppe Veltri. Tübingen: Mohr Siebeck, 2013.

Regev, Eyal. "Flourishing before the Crisis: Mapping Judaean Society in the First Century CE," In *Jews and Christians in the First and Second Centuries: How to Write Their History*, edited by Peter J. Tomson and Joshua Schwartz. Leiden: Brill, 2014.

———. "The Hasmoneans' Self Image as Religious Leaders." *Siyywn* 77, no. 1 (2012): 5–30.

———. "The Sadducees, the Pharisees, and the Sacred: Meaning and Ideology in the Halakhic Controversies between the Sadducees and Pharisees." *Review of Rabbinic Judaism* 9, no. 1–2 (2006): 126–40.

Revell, Louise. *Roman Imperialism and Local Identities*. Cambridge: Cambridge University Press, 2009.

Rhee, Helen. *Loving the Poor, Saving the Rich: Wealth, Poverty, and Early Christian Formation*. Grand Rapids: Baker Books, 2012.

Ricci, Cecilia. *Orbis in Urbe: Fenomeni Migratori nella Roma Imperiale*. Rome: Quasar, 2005.

Ritzenhein, Donald N. "One More Time: How Do You Motivate Donors?." *New Directions for Philanthropic Fundraising*, no. 29 (2000): 51–68.

Roller, Matthew B. "Horizontal Women: Posture and Sex in the Roman Convivium." *American Journal of Philology* 124, no. 3 (2003): 377–422.

Ronis, Sara. "Imagining the Other: The Magical Arab in Rabbinic Literature." *Prooftexts* 39, no. 1 (2021): 1–28.

Rosello, Mireille. *Postcolonial Hospitality: The Immigrant as Guest*. Redwood City, CA: Stanford University Press, 2001.

Rosenblum, Jordan D. *Food and Identity in Early Rabbinic Judaism*. Cambridge: Cambridge University Press, 2010.

———. "Jewish Meals in Antiquity." In *A Companion to Food in the Ancient World*, edited by John Wilkins and Robin Nadeau. Hoboken, NJ: John Wiley & Sons, 2015.

———. *Rabbinic Drinking: What Beverages Teach Us about Rabbinic Literature*. Berkeley: University of California Press, 2020.

Rosenfeld, Ben-Zion. "The 'Boundary of Gezer' Inscriptions and the History of Gezer at the End of the Second Temple Period." *Israel Exploration Journal* 38, no. 4 (1988): 235–45.

Rosenfeld, Ben-Zion, and Joseph Menirav. *Markets and Marketing in Roman Palestine*. Leiden: Brill, 2022.

Rosen-Zvi, Ishay. *Between Mishnah and Midrash: The Birth of Rabbinic Literature*. Jerusalem: Gefen Publishing House, 2019. [Hebrew]

———. "Between Wisdom and Apocalypse: Reading Tosefta Soṭah Chapters 10–15." *Harvard Theological Review* 115, no. 1 (2022): 46–68.

———. "Introduction to the Mishnah." In *The Classical Rabbinic Literature of Eretz Israel: Introductions and Studies*, edited by Menahem Kahana, Vered Noam, Menahem Kister, and David Rosenthal. Jerusalem: Yad Ben-Zvi Press, 2018. [Hebrew]

———. "Is the Mishnah a Roman Composition?" In *The Faces of Torah*, edited by Michal Bar-asher Siegal, Christine Hayes, and Tzvi Novick. Göttingen, DE: Vandenhoeck & Ruprecht, 2017.

———. "Measure for Measure as a Hermeneutical Tool in Early Rabbinic Literature: The Case of Tosefta Sotah." *Journal of Jewish Studies* 57, no. 2 (2006): 269–86.

———. *The Mishnaic Sotah Ritual: Temple, Gender and Midrash*. Leiden: Brill, 2012.

———. "Rabbis and Romanization: A Review Essay." In *Jewish Cultural Encounters in the Ancient Mediterranean and Near Eastern World,* edited by Mladen Popovic, Myles Schoonover, and Marijn Vandenberghe. Leiden: Brill, 2017.

———. "Rabbis as Nomikoi? Questioning a New Paradigm: A Response to Yair Furstenberg." *Journal for the Study of Judaism* 55, no. 1 (2023): 1–13.

———. "The Rhetorical Self in Tannaitic Halakha." *Dead Sea Discoveries* 28, no. 3 (2021): 341–66.

———. "To See the Voices: Midrash and/as Revelation." *Maarav* 24, no. 1–2 (2020): 193–206.

Rossiter, Jeremy. "Convivium and Villa in Late Antiquity." In *Dining in a Classical Context,* edited by William J. Slater. Ann Arbor: University of Michigan Press, 1991.

Rozenfeld, Ben Tsiyon, and Chava Cassel. *Torah Centers and Rabbinic Activity in Palestine, 70–400 CE: History and Geographic Distribution*. Leiden: Brill, 2010.

Rubenstein, Jeffrey L. "Social and Institutional Settings of Rabbinic Literature." *The Cambridge Companion to the Talmud and Rabbinic Literature* (2007): 58–74.

———. *Talmudic Stories: Narrative Art, Composition, and Culture*. Johns Hopkins University Press, 1999.

Rueschemeyer, Dietrich. "Professional Autonomy and the Social Control of Expertise." In *The Sociology of the Professions: Lawyers, Doctors and Others,* edited by Robert Dingwall and Philip Lewis. New Orleans: Quid Pro, 1983.

Runesson, Anders. *The Origins of the Synagogue: A Socio-Historical Study*. Uppsala, SE: Almqvist & Wiksell, 2001.

Rüpke, Jörg. *From Jupiter to Christ: On the History of Religion in the Roman Imperial Period*. Oxford: Oxford University Press, 2014.

———. "Lived Ancient Religion: Questioning 'Cults' and 'Polis Religion.'" *Mythos* 5 (2011): 191–204.

Ryle, Gilbert. "Knowing How and Knowing That: The Presidential Address." *Proceedings of the Aristotelian Society* 46 (1945): 1–16.

———. *The Concept of Mind*. Abingdon, UK: Routledge, 2009.

Safrai, Shmuel, "The Jewish Cultural Nature of Galilee in the First Century." *Immanuel* 24 (1990): 147–86. [Hebrew]

Safrai, Ze'ev. *The Economy of Roman Palestine*. Abingdon, UK: Routledge, 2003.

———. "The Unique Nature of the Settlement in the Lod–Jaffa Region in the Mishnah and Talmud Periods." In *Between Yarkon and Ayalon: Studies on the Tel Aviv Metropolitan Area and the Lod Valley*. Jerusalem: Ramat Gan, 1983. [Hebrew]

Sahlins, Marshall. *Stone Age Economics*. Abingdon, UK: Routledge, 2013.

Saller, Richard P. *Personal Patronage Under the Early Empire*. Cambridge: Cambridge University Press, 2002.

Salter, Liora. *Mandated Science: Science and Scientists in the Making of Standards*. Dordrecht, NL: Springer, 1988.

Sanders, E. P. *Judaism: Practice and Belief, 63 BCE–66 CE*. Minneapolis: Fortress Press, 2016.

Satlow, Michael L. "'And On the Earth You Shall Sleep': Talmud Torah and Rabbinic Asceticism." *Journal of Religion* 83, no. 2 (2003): 204–22.

———. "'Fruit and the Fruit of Fruit': Charity and Piety among Jews in Late Antique Palestine." *The Jewish Quarterly Review* 100, no. 2 (2010): 244–77.

———, ed. *The Gift in Antiquity*. Hoboken, NJ: John Wiley & Sons, 2013.

———. "Markets and Tithes in Roman Palestine." In *Gift Giving and the "Embedded" Economy in the Ancient World*. Heidelberg, DE: Universitätsverlag Winter, 2014.

———. "'Try to Be a Man': The Rabbinic Construction of Masculinity." *Harvard Theological Review* 89, no. 1 (1996): 19–40.

Sausville, Rebecca C. "Intellectual Euergetism in Cities of the Roman East." PhD diss., New York University, 2023.

Savolainen, Reijo. "Manifestations of Expert Power in Gatekeeping: A conceptual study." *Journal of Documentation* 76, no. 6 (2020): 1215–32.

Schäfer, Peter. *The History of the Jews in Antiquity*. Abingdon, UK: Routledge, 2013.

———. "Rabbis and Priests, or: How to Do Away with the Glorious Past of the Sons of Aaron." In *Antiquity in Antiquity: Jewish and Christian Pasts in the Greco-Roman World*, edited by Gregg Gardner and Kevin Osterloh. Tübingen: Mohr Siebeck, 2008.

Schaper, Joachim. "The Jerusalem Temple as an Instrument of the Achaemenid Fiscal Administration." *Vetus Testamentum* 45, no. 4 (1995): 528–39.

Scheman, Naomi. *Shifting Ground: Knowledge and Reality, Transgression and Trustworthiness*. Oxford: Oxford University Press, 2011.

Schiffman, Lawrence H. "A Forty-Two Letter Divine Name in the Aramaic Magic Bowls." *Bulletin of the Institute of Jewish Studies* 1 (1973): 97–102.

Schironi, Francesca. "Enlightened Kings or Pragmatic Rulers? Ptolemaic Patronage of Scholarship and Sciences in Context." In *Intellectual and Empire in Greco-Roman Antiquity*, edited by Philip Bosman. Abingdon, UK: Routledge, 2018.

Schofer, Jonathan. *The Making of a Sage: A Study in Rabbinic Ethics*. Madison: University of Wisconsin Press, 2005.

Schremer, Adiel. "Avot Reconsidered: Rethinking Rabbinic Judaism." *Jewish Quarterly Review* 105, no. 3 (2015): 287–311.

———. *Brothers Estranged: Heresy, Christianity and Jewish Identity in Late Antiquity*. Oxford: Oxford University Press, 2010.

———. "The Religious Orientation of Non-Rabbis in Second-Century Palestine." In *Follow the Wise: Studies in Jewish History and Culture in Honor of Lee I. Levine*, edited by Zeev Weiss, Oded Irshai, Jodi Magness, and Seth Schwartz. University Park, PA: Penn State University Press, 2010.

———. "The Sages in Palestinian Jewish Society of the Mishnah Period: Torah, Prestige, and Social Standing." In *The Classic Rabbinic Literature of Eretz Israel: Introductions and Studies* 2 (2018): 553–81. [Hebrew]

Schumer, Nathan Still. "The Memory of the Temple in Palestinian Rabbinic Literature." PhD diss., Columbia University, 2017.

Schürer, Emil. *A History of the Jewish People in the Time of Jesus Christ*. New York: Simon & Schuster, 1891.

Schwartz, Daniel R., and Zeev Weiss, eds. *Was 70 CE a Watershed in Jewish History?: On Jews and Judaism Before and After the Destruction of the Second Temple*. Leiden: Brill, 2011.

Schwartz, Joshua. "Dogs in Jewish Society in the Second Temple Period and in the Time of the Mishnah and Talmud." *Journal of Jewish Studies* 55, no. 2 (2004): 246–77.

———. *Jewish Settlement in Judaea after the Bar-Kochba War and until the Arab Conquest.* Jerusalem: Magnes Press, 1986. [Hebrew]

———. "The Morphology of Roman Lydda." *Jewish History* 2, no. 1 (1987): 33–66.

Schwartz, Seth. *The Ancient Jews from Alexander to Muhammad.* Cambridge: Cambridge University Press, 2014.

———. "The Impact of the Jewish Rebellions, 66–135 CE: Destruction or Provincialization?" In *Revolt and Resistance in the Ancient Classical World and the Near East*, edited by John J. Collins and J.G. Manning. Leiden: Brill, 2016.

———. *Imperialism and Jewish Society: 200 BCE to 640 CE.* Princeton, NJ: Princeton University Press, 2009.

———. *Josephus and Judaean Politics.* Leiden: Brill, 2022.

———. "No Dialogue at the Symposium? Conviviality in Ben Sira and the Palestinian Talmud." In *The End of Dialogue in Antiquity*, edited by Simon Goldhill. Cambridge: Cambridge University Press, 2009.

———. *Were the Jews a Mediterranean Society?: Reciprocity and Solidarity in Ancient Judaism.* Princeton: Princeton University Press, 2012.

Shapin, Steven. *The Scientific Life: A Moral History of a Late Modern Vocation.* Chicago: University of Chicago Press, 2008.

———. "The Wisdom of 'Mom.'" *American Scientist* 96, no. 3 (2008): 243–46.

Shemesh, Aharon. *Halakhah in the Making: The Development of Jewish Law from Qumran to the Rabbis.* Berkeley: University of California Press, 2009.

Sivertsev, Alexei. *Households, Sects, and the Origins of Rabbinic Judaism.* Leiden: Brill, 2022.

———. *Private Households and Public Politics in 3rd–5th Century Jewish Palestine.* Tübingen: Mohr Siebeck, 2002.

Smith, Dennis E. *From Symposium to Eucharist: The Banquet in the Early Christian World.* Minneapolis: Fortress Press, 2003.

———. "The Greco-Roman Banquet as a Social Institution." In *Meals in the Early Christian World: Social Formation, Experimentation, and Conflict at the Table*, edited by Dennis E. Smith and Hal Taussig. New York: Palgrave Macmillan, 2012.

Smith, Morton. "Goodenough's Jewish Symbols in Retrospect." *Journal of Biblical Literature* 86, no. 1 (1967): 53–68.

Sokoloff, Michael. *A Dictionary of Jewish Palestinian Aramaic of the Byzantine Period.* Baltimore, MD: Johns Hopkins University Press, 2002.

Sokolowski, Franciszek. "Fees and Taxes in the Greek Cults." *Harvard Theological Review* 47, no. 3 (1954): 153–64.

Sorek, Susan. *Remembered for Good: A Jewish Benefaction System in Ancient Palestine.* Sheffield, UK: Sheffield Phoenix Press, 2010.

Sperber, Daniel. "Patronage in Amoraic Palestine (c. 220–400): Causes and Effects." *Journal of the Economic and Social History of the Orient* 14, no. 1 (1971): 227–52.

Stein-Hölkeskamp, Elke. "Class and Power." In *A Companion to Food in the Ancient World*, edited by John Wilkins and Robin Nadeau. Hoboken, NJ: John Wiley & Sons, 2015.

Stein, Siegfried. "The Influence of Symposia Literature on the Literary Form of the Pesah Haggadah." *Journal of Jewish Studies* 8, no. 1 (1957): 13–44.

Stemberger, Günter. "Dating Rabbinic Traditions." In *The New Testament and Rabbinic Literature*, edited by David Daube. Leiden: Brill, 2009.

Stephenson, John. "Dining as Spectacle in Late Roman Houses." *Bulletin of the Institute of Classical Studies* 59, no. 1 (2016): 54–71.

Stern, Karen B. *Writing on the Wall: Graffiti and the Forgotten Jews of Antiquity*. Princeton, NJ: Princeton University Press, 2018.

Stern, Sacha. "Attribution and Authorship in the Babylonian Talmud." *Journal of Jewish Studies* 45, no. 1 (1994): 28–51.

Stevens, Marty E. *Temples, Tithes, and Taxes: The Temple and the Economic Life of Ancient Israel*. Ada, MI: Baker Academic, 2006.

Stitskin, Leon. "From the Pages of Tradition: Religion and Philosophy Lead to the Same Truth: Letter from Maimonides to His Disciple Joseph Ben Judah ibn Aknin," *Tradition* vol. 13, no. 3 (1973): 154–60.

Stowers, Stanley. "The Religion of Plant and Animal Offerings Versus the Religion of Meanings, Essences, and Textual Mysteries." *Ancient Mediterranean Sacrifice*, edited by Jennifer Wright Knust and Zsuzsanna Várhekyi. Oxford: Oxford University Press, 2011.

Strack, Hermann Leberecht, and Günter Stemberger. *Introduction to the Talmud and Midrash*. Minneapolis: Fortress Press, 1931.

Strassfeld, Max K. *Trans Talmud: Androgynes and Eunuchs in Rabbinic Literature*. Oakland: University of California Press, 2022.

Sussman, Ya'akov. "The History of Halakha and the Dead Sea Scrolls." In *Miqsat Ma'ase ha-Torah, Discoveries of the Judean Desert*, edited by Elisha Qimron and John Strugnell. Vol. 10. Oxford: Clarendon Press, 1994.

Ta-Shma, Israel. "On the Exemption of Torah Scholars from Taxes in the Medieval Period." In *Iyunim beSifrut Chazal beMikra u-veToldot Yisrael Mukdash LeProfessor Ezra Zion Melamed*. Ramat Gan, Israel: Bar Ilan University Press, 1982.

Taves, Ann. *Religious Experience Reconsidered: A Building-Block Approach to the Study of Religion and Other Special Things*. Princeton, NJ: Princeton University Press, 2009.

Telfer, Elizabeth. "Friendship." *Proceedings of the Aristotelian Society*, vol. 71 (1970): 223–41.

Tell, Håkan. *Plato's Counterfeit Sophists*. Cambridge, MA: Harvard University Press, 2011.

Tiemeyer, Lena-Sofia. *Priestly Rites and Prophetic Rage: Post-Exilic Prophetic Critique of the Priesthood*. Tübingen: Mohr Siebeck, 2006.

Too, Yun Lee. *The Rhetoric in Isocrates: Text, Power, Pedagogy*. Cambridge: Cambridge University Press, 1995.

———. *The Rhetoric of Identity in Isocrates: Text, Power, Pedagogy*. Cambridge: Cambridge University Press, 1995.

Trebilco, Paul R. *Jewish Communities in Asia Minor*. Cambridge: Cambridge University Press, 1991.

Tropper, Amram. "Le-Mashma'ut ha-bituyim 'dahita be-kaneh' 'le-hotzi-akha halak i ephshar' she-bi-sifrut hazal." *Netuim* 16 (2010): 9–31.

———. "The State of Mishnah Studies." In *Rabbinic Texts and the History of Late-Roman Palestine*, edited by Martin Goodman and Philip Alexander. Oxford: Oxford University Press, 2010.

———. *Wisdom, Politics, and Historiography: Tractate Avot in the Context of the Graeco-Roman Near East*. Oxford: Oxford University Press, 2004.

Turner, Stephen. "Balancing Expert Power: Two Models for the Future of Politics." In *Knowledge and Democracy*. Abingdon, UK: Routledge, 2017.

———. "Circles or Regresses? The Problem of Genuine Expertise." *Social Epistemology Review and Reply Collective* 8, no. 4 (2019): 24–27.

———. "Normal Accidents of Expertise." *Minerva* 48 (2010): 239–58.

———. *The Politics of Expertise*. Abingdon, UK: Routledge, 2013.

———. "Quasi-science and the State: 'Governing Science' in Comparative Perspective." In *The Governance of Knowledge*, edited by Nico Stehr. Abingdon, UK: Routledge, 2017.

———. "Scientists as Agents." In *Science Bought and Sold*, edited by Philip Mirowski and Esther-Mirjam Sent. Chicago: University of Chicago Press, 2002.

———. "What Is the Problem with Experts?" *Social Studies of Science* 31, no. 1 (2001): 123–49.

Udoh, Fabian E. *To Caesar What Is Caesar's: Tribute, Taxes, and Imperial Administration in Early Roman Palestine*. Providence, RI: Brown Judaic Studies, 2020.

Upson-Saia, Kristi, Carly Daniel-Hughes, and Alicia J. Batten, eds. *Dressing Judeans and Christians in Antiquity*. Abingdon, UK: Routledge, 2016.

Urbach, Ephraim E. "Class-Status and Leadership in the World of the Palestinian Sages." *Proceedings of the Israel Academy of Sciences and Humanities* 2, no. 4 (1966): 1–37.

———. "Political and Social Tendencies in Talmudic Concepts of Charity." *Zion* 16 (1951): 1–27.

———. *The Sages: Their Concepts and Beliefs*. Jerusalem: Magnes Press, 1969.

———. "The Talmudic Sage: Character and Authority." *Journal of World History* 11, no. 1 (1968): 116–47.

Van Berkel, Tazuko. *The Economics of Friendship*. Leiden: Brill, 2019.

Van Loopik, Marcus. *The Ways of the Sages and the Way of the World: The Minor Tractates of the Babylonian Talmud: Derekh'eretz Rabbah, Derekh'eretz Zuta, Pereq Ha-shalom: Translated on the Basis of the Manuscripts and Provided with a Commentary*. Tübingen: Mohr Siebeck, 1991.

Verboven, Koenraad. "Friendship among the Romans." In *The Oxford Handbook of Social Relations in the Roman World*, edited by Michael Peachin. Oxford: Oxford University Press, 2011.

———. "Resident Aliens and Translocal Merchant Collegia in the Roman Empire." In *Frontiers in the Roman World*, edited by Ted Kaizer and Olivier Hekster. Leiden: Brill, 2011.

Verboven, Koenraad, and Christian Laes. *Work, Labour, and Professions in the Roman World*. Leiden: Brill, 2016.

Vermes, Geza, and Martin D. Goodman. *The Essenes According to the Classical Sources*. Sheffield, UK: Sheffield Academic Press, 1989.

Veyne, Paul. *Bread and Circuses: Historical Sociology and Political Pluralism*. Translated by Brian Pearce. London: Penguin Press, 1990.

Vidas, Moulie. *Tradition and the Formation of the Talmud*. Princeton, NJ: Princeton University Press, 2014.

———. *"What Is a Tannay?" Oqimta* 7 (2021): 21–96.

Visotzky, Burton L. *Golden Bells and Pomegranates: Studies in Midrash Leviticus Rabbah*. Tübingen: Mohr Siebeck, 2003.

Walfish, Miriam-Simma Reinhartz. "Parents and Sages as Agents of Culture in the Babylonian Talmud." PhD diss., Harvard University, 2022.

Wallace-Hadrill, Andrew. *Patronage in Ancient Society*. Abingdon, UK: Routledge, 1990.

Warde, Alan, Jessica Paddock, and Jennifer Whillans. "Domestic Hospitality: As a Practice and an Alternative Economic Arrangement." *Cultural Sociology* 14, no. 4 (2020): 379–98.

Wasserman, Mira Beth. "Rabbis and Their Others." In *A Companion to Late Ancient Jews and Judaism: Third Century BCE To Seventh Century CE*, edited by Naomi Koltun-Fromm and Gwynn Kessler. Hoboken, NJ: John Wiley & Sons, 2020.

Watson, Jamie Carlin. *Expertise: A Philosophical Introduction*. London: Bloomsbury, 2020.

Weiner, Annette B. *Inalienable Possessions: The Paradox of Keeping-While-Giving*. Berkeley: University of California Press, 1992.

Weinfeld, Moshe. "Grace after Meals in Qumran." *Journal of Biblical Literature* 111 (1992): 427–40.

———. "Tithe." *Encyclopedia Judaica*, 2nd ed., edited by Michael Skolnik. Vol. 15. Detroit: Macmillan, 2007: 736–39.

Weiss, Ruhama. *Meal Tests: The Meal in the World of the Sages*. Tel-Aviv: Hakibbutz Hameuchad, 2010. [Hebrew]

Weiss, Zeev. "Actors and Theaters, Rabbis and Synagogues: The Role of Public Performances in Shaping Communal Behavior in Late Antique Palestine." *Journal of Ancient Judaism* 8, no. 2 (2017): 271–79.

———. "Houses of the Wealthy in Roman Galilee." In *The Roman Villa in the Mediterranean Basin: Late Republic to Late Antiquity*. Cambridge: Cambridge University Press, 2018.

———. "Were Priests Communal Leaders in Late Antique Palestine? The Archaeological Evidence." In *Was 70 CE a Watershed in Jewish History?: On Jews and Judaism Before and After the Destruction of the Second Temple*, edited by Daniel R. Schwartz and Zeev Weiss. Leiden: Brill, 2012.

Wendt, Heidi. *At The Temple Gates: The Religion of Freelance Experts in the Roman Empire*. Oxford: Oxford University Press, 2016.

Werman, Cana. "Levi and Levites in the Second Temple Period." *Dead Sea Discoveries* 4, no. 2 (1997): 211–25.

Whyte, Kyle Powys, and Robert P. Crease. "Trust, Expertise, and the Philosophy of Science." *Synthese* 177, no. 3 (2010): 411–25.

Wiener, Norbert. *Cybernetics or Control and Communication in the Animal and the Machine*. Cambridge, MA: MIT Press, 1948.

Wilfand, Yael. *Poverty, Charity, and the Image of the Poor in Rabbinic Texts from the Land of Israel*. Sheffield, UK: Sheffield Phoenix Press, 2014.

———. "Was There Really 'an Arrogance of Wealth'?: Re-evaluating a Scholarly Description of Second-Century Rabbis." In *Rabbinic Study Circles: Aspects of Jewish Learning in Its Late Antique Context*, edited by Marc Hirshman and David Satran. Tübingen: Mohr Siebeck, 2020.

Williams, Megan Hale. *The Monk and the Book: Jerome and the Making of Christian Scholarship*. Chicago: University of Chicago Press, 2019.

Wimpfheimer, Barry Scott. "The Mishnah's Reader: Reconsidering Literary Meaning." *Jewish Quarterly Review* 113, no. 3 (2023): 335–67.

———. *Narrating the Law: A Poetics of Talmudic Legal Stories*. Philadelphia: University of Pennsylvania Press, 2011.

Winegard, Bo, Benjamin Winegard, and David C. Geary. "The Evolution of Expertise." In *The Cambridge Handbook of Expertise and Expert Performance*, edited by K. Anders Ericsson, Robert R. Hoffman, and Aaron Kozbelt. Cambridge: Cambridge University Press, 2018.

Wolf, Eric R. "Kinship, Friendship, and Patron-Client Relations in Complex Societies." In *The Social Anthropology of Complex Societies*, edited by Michael Banton. Abingdon, UK: Routledge, 2013.

Wollenberg, Rebecca Scharbach. *The Closed Book: How the Rabbis Taught the Jews (Not) to Read the Bible*. Princeton, NJ: Princeton University Press, 2023.

Woolf, Greg. "Greek Archaeologists at Rome." In *Ruling the Greek World: Approaches to the Roman Empire in the East*, edited by Juan Manuel Cortés Copete, Elena Munez Grijalvo, and Fernando Lozano Gómez. Stuttgart, DE: Franz Steiner Verlag, 2015.

———. "Provincial Revolts in the Early Roman Empire." In *The Jewish Revolt Against Rome*, edited by Mladen Popovíc. Leiden: Brill, 2011.

Wright, F. A. *Select Letters of St. Jerome*. Cambridge, MA: Harvard University Press, 1975.

Yadin, Azzan. "Rabbi Akiva's Youth." *The Jewish Quarterly Review* 100, no. 4 (2010): 573–97.

Yadin-Israel, Azzan. *Scripture and Tradition: Rabbi Akiva and the Triumph of Midrash*. Philadelphia: University of Pennsylvania Press, 2015.

———. *Scripture as Logos: Rabbi Ishmael and the Origins of Midrash*. Philadelphia: University of Pennsylvania Press, 2004.

Yadin, P. "Legal Interactions in the Archive of Babatha." In *Law in the Roman Provinces*, edited by Kimberley Czajkowski. Oxford: Oxford University Press, 2020.

Ziman, John. "The Continuing Need for Disinterested Research." *Science and Engineering Ethics* 8 (2002): 397–99.

Zissu, Boaz. "Rural Settlement in the Judaean Hills and Foothills from the Late Second Temple Period to the Bar Kohkba Revolt," PhD Diss., Hebrew University, 2002.

INDEX

A NOTE ON THE TYPE

This book has been composed in Arno, an Old-style serif typeface in the classic Venetian tradition, designed by Robert Slimbach at Adobe.